American Geographics

American Geographics

U.S. National Narratives and the Representation

of the Non-European World, 1830–1865

Bruce A. Harvey

STANFORD UNIVERSITY PRESS, CALIFORNIA   2001

Stanford University Press
Stanford, California
© 2001 by the Board of Trustees of the
Leland Stanford Junior University
Printed in the United States of America

Library of Congress Cataloging-in-Publication Data

Harvey, Bruce A.
  American geographics : U.S. national narratives and the representation of the non-European world, 1830–1865 / Bruce A. Harvey.
    p. cm.
  Includes bibliographical references (p.) and index.
  ISBN 0-8047-4045-3 (alk. paper) — ISBN 0-8047-4046-1 (pbk. : alk. paper)
    1. American prose literature—19th century—History and criticism. 2. Travelers' writings, American—History and criticism. 3. Americans—Travel—Foreign countries—History—19th century. 4. Latin America—Foreign public opinion, American—History. 5. Middle East—Foreign public opinion, American—History. 6. Oceania—Foreign public opinion, American—History. 7. Africa—Foreign public opinion, American—History. I. Title.

PS366.T73.H37   2001
910.4'07'2073—dc21   2001020607

This book is printed on acid-free, archival-quality paper.

Original printing 2001

Last figure below indicates year of this printing:
10   09   08   07   06   05   04   03   02   01

Typeset in 10/12.5 Minion by John Feneron

To my parents, Len and Shirl

Acknowledgments

This study began as a dissertation, and I wish to thank my Stanford University mentor, Jay Fliegelman, for his advice and encouragement, early and late, as it evolved into its present form. His counsel in this and other matters has been invaluable. Stanford University Press's readers provided extremely useful suggestions for revision, which not only brought to my attention important primary texts but also helped me to clarify a number of methodological cruxes. One of those readers, Robert Levine, is especially to be singled out for his exemplary assistance. A number of other friends and colleagues—Loren Rusk, Lowell Gallagher, Carolyn Karcher, Meri-Jane Rochelson, Jeffrey Knapp, Cindy Chinelly, Mary Free, Jamie Sutton, Lisa Blansett, Eric Leed, and John Ernest—merit my thanks for intellectual or emotional support as this book was being completed. I am fortunate in being at Florida International University, an institution of unusually warm collegiality; the English Department at large, its secretarial staff, and its chair (who, at several times, managed to arrange for some course relief) helped incalculably in reducing many of the stresses of a new faculty member. I would also like to thank the interlibrary loan departments of Temple University and Florida International University for facilitating the arrival of materials from archives elsewhere. Florida International University's Institution for Research provided a Summer Grant that enabled me to make progress on this project at a crucial juncture; and the College of Arts and Sciences helped to defray some production costs. The Index was prepared by Beth McNeer. An early version of Chapter 2 was published as "Precepts Graven on Every Breast: Melville's *Typee* and the Forms of the Law," *American Quarterly* 45, no. 3 (1993): 394–424, copyright the American Studies Association. It is reprinted by permission of the Johns Hopkins University Press. Finally, to my wife and sons—Liz, Aaron, and Jason—I give thanks (and hugs) for immeasurable sweetness and light, and patience as well, during the years of this book's composition.

Contents

Figures

American Geographics

Beyond Manifest Destiny

American Studies, National Identity,
and Other Worlds

B AYARD TAYLOR, feted in his own time as the "Great American Traveler," had from his youth an itch to visit exotic lands. The only book of
his still in print is *Eldorado, or, Adventures in the Path of Empire* (1850), a vivid
report of his trip to the Californian goldfields; before the Civil War, however,
the public it seems could not get enough of his ramblings through areas remote from the United States: the Levant, India, Central Africa (along the
White Nile), Spain, Greece, Sweden, and Russia. In his *At Home and Abroad*
(1859), a collection of travel vignettes, Taylor mused upon the origin of his
wanderlust. He recalled no childhood "instinct of perambulation; but on the
contrary, the intensest desire to climb upward—so that without shifting the
circle of my horizon, I could yet extend it, and take in a far wider sweep of vision."[1] It would be implausible to ascribe to the young Taylor what Mary
Louise Pratt refers to as a "monarch-of-all-I-survey" syndrome, the urge of
imperialistic-minded travelers to station themselves panoptically vis-à-vis the
lands they traversed; yet when we hear how the appeal of the panoramic vista
continued into his maturity, Pratt's rubric indeed will seem apt for him, albeit
in a variant form that even more so emphasizes the motif of lordly spectatorship.[2] In *At Home and Abroad* he tells us that among the most gratifying sights
of his worldwide travels was not some ancient monument, but rather the
European of the day who, as he puts it, had viewed nearly everything: "I
looked into [Alexander von Humboldt's] eyes which had not only seen this
living history of the world pass by, scene after scene . . . but had beheld the
cataract of Atures and the forests of the Cassiquiare, Chimborazo, the Amazon, and Popocatepetl, the Altaian Alps of Siberia, the Tartar steppes, and the
Caspian Sea." Humboldt has a body—his "nose, mouth, and chin had the
heavy Teutonic character"—yet this Saxon physiognomy for Taylor simply

denotes a massive *white* intellect, which has scopically mastered distant lands.³ He quests less after what Herman Melville in an 1859 lyceum lecture called the "sight of novel objects" that might lead to an "enlargement of heart and mind" than after a fellow Caucasian who has seen all and, in the process, almost transcended time and place.⁴

In *A Visit to India, China, and Japan, in the Year 1853* (1855), however, Taylor's own body becomes immersed in too much foreignness: on the occasion, for instance, of his "first sight of a large Chinese community" when, just before he joined Commodore Matthew C. Perry's U.S. naval expedition to Japan, he walked through a Singapore ghetto: "Their dull faces, without expression, unless a coarse glimmering of sensuality may be called such, and their half-naked, unsymmetrical bodies, more like figures of yellow clay than warm flesh and blood, filled me with an unconquerable aversion."⁵ This is not the most racist that Taylor gets. Subsequent passages speak of sundry Chinese iniquities, pollutions, and so forth with a note of near panic, suggesting weighty ideological pressure bearing down when the "Great American Traveler," to use his contemporary sobriquet, strolled through Singapore's streets.

Taylor turns to aesthetics to explain his reaction. Reflecting upon how Chinese florists habitually work to "produce something as much unlike nature as possible," he concludes that the "only taste which the Chinese exhibit to any degree, is a love of the monstrous. That sentiment of harmony, which throbbed like a musical rhythm through the life of the Greeks, never looked out of their oblique eyes. . . . [They] admire whatever is distorted or unnatural" (352–53). What finally in fact most disturbs him about the Chinese is their culture being *too* civilized, too artificial, too cloaked in strange protocols of state. The Chinese masses' "secrecy," he writes, "through the continual teachings of their government has become almost a second nature to them" (434). If the United States was Nature's Nation, then China was the land of bizarre artifice and cunning, a culture lacking, for instance, in those "simple" and "straightforward" (440) qualities that Taylor later says he admired in Perry. The Commodore, however, was hardly himself a frank emissary of U.S. intent. He used humiliating stratagems, such as staying below deck, obliging Japanese officials to parley with his lieutenants. In the story of the expedition, *Narrative of the Expedition of an American Squadron to the China Seas and Japan, Performed in the Years 1852, 1853, and 1854*, published by Francis L. Hawks in 1856, we learn how Perry, when some Lew Chew dignitaries came aboard, "from considerations of policy, thought it best to be invisible."⁶ Conversely, Perry's statecraft included a good deal of self- (or state-) fashioning. "It was a matter of policy to make a show [of the Commodore's visits ashore]," we are told, "and hence some extra pains were taken to offer an imposing spectacle."⁷ Taylor's account, though, served to confirm that when the United States courted the non-European world, notwithstanding facts to the contrary, it did so in a forthright, New World manner.

It is out of such cultural clashes that U.S. national narratives get told (here, implicitly, about the U.S. body politic being one of muscular, democratic ligaments with, to adopt Taylor's words, more symmetrical relations between rulers and masses). Taylor's *Visit to India, China, and Japan* does not just mimetically report on what he saw. Instead, his travel text stages the Orient, his own re-created identity, and indeed the United States itself in a way calculated to reconcile incompatible images of his homeland as being at once beyond and given to devious political intrigue. Works such as Hawks's or Taylor's today molder in the archives, and yet to those interested in how nations construe themselves they offer invaluable evidence: thick not with literary complexity (although that, too, at times) but the theatrics of nationhood and national subjects.

Oddly, though, Americanist scholars—including those who deplore national solipsism and devote themselves to cross-cultural issues—have for the most part yet to venture into the sizable corpus of pre–Civil War texts depicting noncontinental, non-European peoples and regions. The allure of charting or critiquing U.S. expansionism has been, it seems, too strong, overshadowing the rich array of antebellum texts about the various non-European domains not finally absorbed into the present-day United States.[8] We have many studies of the diplomatic and political exchanges with those domains (Peter Booth Wiley's superlative *Yankees in the Lands of the Gods: Commodore Perry and the Opening of Japan* is an example), but virtually no recovery and analysis of the texts that would better help us see the *cultural* dimensions of Americans abroad in the non-European world. This partiality has been unfortunate. Either we assume that few mid-nineteenth-century U.S. authors thought or had much to say about that world, or we simply bypass the pertinence of geographical, travel, and travel-related texts about those lands—Central America, Polynesia, the Orient or Middle East, and Africa—that lay beyond the immediate juggernaut of Manifest Destiny.

Such texts, however, often situate "America"—the national symbolic order—within a more global, and thereby more complex, sociocomparative context. In the works I examine, U.S. national ideologies, as embodied in the U.S. traveler-citizen, are literally put into circulation. They are thereby reconfirmed, interrogated, or at times contested in ways that encompass yet also extend beyond the two paradigms that traditionally have inflected how we understand the era: of the nation as an anxiously postcolonial one (in the older sense of the term), fretting over its claim of cultural independence from the Old World; or of the nation as an imperialist entity, consumed by the task of New World expansion. These paradigms will continue to be useful, but not if their explanatory power comes at the cost of disregarding alternative, mediating routes by which mid-nineteenth-century U.S. subjects thought of themselves, their land, and the non-European realms distant from the nation's boundaries.

Across the spectrum of field specialties—literature, political science, history, ethnography, and so on—we need to become more aware of the vast body of antebellum U.S. texts about non-European peoples and spaces. We cannot know what to make of the cultural archive if we do not know what it contains in the first place. Of late, important initiatives toward redressing this problem have been made through the publication of new volumes on American-authored travel literature in the *Dictionary of Literary Biography* and through studies covering American responses to particular geographical or cultural regions, especially the Middle East.[9] Indeed, going by the cross-cultural and global orientation of talks delivered at the last several annual meetings of the American Studies Association and other kindred organizations, we might well think that the field is witnessing a paradigm shift, a shift that will propel us all to more polygeographic terrains of study. But we are not there yet, and I would hazard to guess that, among the authors appearing herein, only Herman Melville and Martin R. Delany are familiar to most Americanists. Although not my primary intent, I wish to bring to light a largely forgotten host of U.S. authors germane to the dialectic of foreign encounter. Samuel Goodrich, Arnold Guyot, William F. Lynch, John Lloyd Stephens, Maria Susanna Cummins, Ephraim G. Squier, to name the remaining figures prominent in this study, were all in their own day renowned or highly regarded by their professional peers, and scholarship needs to begin to re-weave such authors or their neglected texts into the fabric of our understanding of antebellum culture. I will feel rewarded if the labor that I have spent resurrecting these authors and associated ones lessens the archival labor of subsequent scholars.

Taking stock of new antebellum voices would not be of much value, however, if they did not have something significant to tell us. The demonstration of importance will be the burden of my following chapters, but here at the outset I would like to confront head-on a looming question that must preoccupy any scholar focusing on cross-cultural journeys: what, exactly, do we learn? In the context of this project, a low-level answer would be that we find out that more mid-nineteenth-century U.S. citizens and authors were concerned about noncontinental, non-European realms than we usually acknowledge (because, as I cited earlier, westward expansion has dominated discussion, particularly in cultural criticism). Obviously, though, such still begs the question of what we are to glean from an archive that begins to take on a more global reach. We certainly do not learn very much that could be judged as accurate ethnography. Melville, for all his catholicity, is not a good guide to Polynesian culture; nor is Delany, for all of his keen Afrocentricism, of Yoruba culture. We could, of course, adopt the metacritical stance that these two authors' ultimate failure to pass over the cross-cultural divide tells us something about the resilience of American ideology or the embeddedness of American citizens within it: Melville and Delany remain American even as they critique the American way. That is a higher-level answer to my query, but so generalized as to be nearly useless.

We are on equally nebulous ground when we try to measure the weight of the foreign on U.S. culture at large. To say, for instance, that Melville deeply pondered Polynesian-U.S. relations when a young author, or that Delany throughout his career often had Africa on his mind, does not mean that either geographical region entered, in a sustained fashion, into the thoughts or ideologies of the average man or woman in the street, senators in Washington, or other, now famous authors such as Nathaniel Hawthorne or Walt Whitman. The nation as a whole, as we will come to see in my first chapter on geography textbooks, defined itself through hierarchical, racial taxonomies of foreign regions (the Orient, Latin America, Polynesia, and Africa). Comparative geography helped to shape national self-consciousness, and its stereotypical vocabularies and ideologies, absorbed in the schoolroom or family reading circle, perpetuated racial injustice. To assume just the mantle of critique, however, would be to indulge self-righteousness or to repeat what most of us already know: that the majority of citizens living in the nineteenth century *were* racist. The era's racism bled from genre to genre—whether textbook, political speech, medical treatise, travelogue, or exoticizing novel—and so geographical discourse should hardly be singled out as peculiar on that score.

I have suggested paths of inquiry, in respect to American geographics, that this study will *not* pursue in the main: I do not intend—at least not as my primary rationale—to conduct us to a more pluralistic ethnography, divulge hitherto undisclosed discourses or practices of racism or imperial depredation, or make vast claims about collective U.S. national identity. My goals are somewhat more modest. One task of the cultural historian is to negotiate reciprocal patterns of meaning that emerge between the specific and the national; and here the subject at hand—the antebellum representation of non-European locales—indeed provides, I think, an acute means of tracing ideological currents on both micro and macro levels. Geographical discursive nexuses or topoi, to be reviewed in the chapter summary below, feed into the amorphous entity that we label as U.S. national culture: the authors of geographically oriented works make their appeals or critiques by addressing "Americans." Yet if directed to a national audience, the messages thereby con-

veyed are invested with concerns animating discrete communities (missionaries, archaeologists, black separatists, and so forth); and they are shaped by the
specific non-European region under attention, insofar as some ideological issues registered more strongly, for instance, in the context of Africa than that of
Polynesia. The methodological trajectory from nation to discursive community obliges a final step: to the individual author, where matters may become
somewhat less unwieldy or abstract, yet more problematic as well. Throughout much of this study, I have also been interested in showing how the crossing of borders affects U.S. subjects on a more intimate, psychological level. In
the writers I have selected, idiosyncrasies of identity—the otherness within, as
it were—often becomes projected onto a foreign topography and its inhabitants. One result, to put it bluntly, is that the dialectic of encounter will sometimes seem to lose one of its dialectical sides: when the non-European world is
textually re-created in terms of authorial anxieties, the former may be deemed
in fact as being nonexistent. Still, in such cases I do not believe that mere self-
reflexivity prevails or that foreign peoples or places become weightless. The
cultural or psychological service that the non-European renders the U.S. subject by being a projective screen depends upon "native" particularities, upon
the U.S. subject cathecting with (which is not to say desiring) the *other*, a term
that I broadly conceive as encompassing foreign topographies, cultural relics
or monuments, social practices, as well as persons or bodies per se. It is,
moreover, the imperfect coincidence between citizenship and self, between
national and authorial identities, that permits a more than stereotypical or
propagandistic response to non-European lands in the first place.

My study traces the interplay between U.S. national self-thinking, what I
previously alluded to as discursive communities or nexuses, and authorial
(sometimes singular) concerns in respect to the crossing into non-European
domains. It seeks to fill in a large lacuna in Americanist scholarship by examining a spectrum of generically diverse texts representing the non-European
world. The topoi, repertoire of images, and rhetorics of those texts exceed being merely supplemental or subordinate to the country's agenda of expanding
its boundaries. Still, we cannot discount the fact that New World imperialism
often affected how antebellum Americans regarded foreign—especially unlettered or aboriginal—peoples living outside of the continent. Bigotry, bred at
home, led to a wholesale disdain for nonwhite, nonbourgeois cultures wher-
ever they might be found. Manifest Destiny is one of the few ideologies, in the
history of nations, that in its own time became so reified as to garner initial
capitals in its name. Its pervasiveness can hardly be ignored, and so obliges me
to take a detour from my subject proper of geographical writings pertaining to
noncontinental domains.

The term's tenets had become commonplaces at least four decades before it came into prominence in the late 1840s (it was coined in 1845 by John Louis O'Sullivan, editor of the *United States Magazine and Democratic Review*). They were trumpeted by clergy, politicians, literary writers, and scientists alike, and accepted as givens, with dissent being voiced, for the most part, only by the politically disenfranchised (blacks, in particular) or the intellectually alienated (Herman Melville, for example, who in his post-*Typee* career was not among the ranks of the popular literati). The average man or woman—reading newspaper articles about, say, Oregon or Mexico—could hardly not feel enthused about the nation spreading its wings. Assumptions about the superiority of the Anglo-Saxon race and republican government, about the legal right of advanced nations to appropriate undeveloped land, about the Protestant duty to spread the Gospel to heathen realms: all helped to justify the acquiring of new continental dominions. These ideas, although not suasive to all citizens, mystified the boundaries of the republic so that extending them through contiguous territories appeared to be both naturally and providentially ordained. The space within national boundaries was likewise mystified. The republic, rather than being victim to history's vagaries, seemed to be its apotheosis. It had surmounted the instabilities of all past empires. So spoke the New England transcendentalist Bronson Alcott: "[D]espite the foreign associations of our ancestral education, Nature has assumed her rightful influence and has shaped us in her molds. Living on the accumulated treasures of the past in a new theatre of action, we have monopolized the best of time and space, and stand on a vantage ground to which no people have ever ascended before."[10] And so spoke Bayard Taylor in his poem "The Continents" (1848), in which personifications of Asia, Africa, and Europe parade by, to conclude with the "radiant-browed, the latest born of Time!":

> "I bear no weight," so rang thy jubilant tones,
>   "Of memories weird and vast—
> No crushing heritage of iron thrones,
>   Bequeathed by some dead Past;
> But mighty hopes that learned to tower and soar
>   From my own peaks of snow—
>
> .   .   .   .
>
> Crowned with my constellated stars, I stand
>   Beside the foaming sea,
> And from the Future, with a victor's hand
>   Claim empire for the Free!"[11]

Intellectual histories, especially Ernest Tuveson's *Redeemer Nation: The Idea of America's Millennial Role,* can usefully answer the question of why Alcott and Taylor regarded the republic with such uncritical euphoria when they contemplated either the Old World or so-called savage and barbarian nations. Their paeans to what Amy Kaplan aptly labels the "cartography of American uniqueness" are part and parcel of a remarkably resilient utopianism that still has currency today.[12] Its longevity, from the Early Nationalist period up to our own era, largely derives from the perceived capacity of the country to remedy, in "the Future," contemporary national misdeeds. The belief in national progress allows the U.S. citizen to bracket the sins of the present, to read through them and behold the corrective and consolatory utopic horizon.

Such abstract utopianism should be weighed against the density of fact, against what we learn from the historical record in respect to U.S. diplomatic, commercial, military, or religious involvement in the areas covered by the term Manifest Destiny. Among many other treatises, Albert Weinberg's *Manifest Destiny: A Study of Nationalist Expansionism in American History*, Frederick Merk's *Manifest Destiny and Mission in American History*, and Richard Drinnon's *Facing West: The Metaphysics of Indian-Hating and Empire-Building* valuably chart the conjunctions and disparities between the abstractions of ideology and the particularities of U.S. imperialism. Another set of studies, most notably those of Henry Nash Smith, Richard Slotkin, and Annette Kolodny, diversely analyze the literary documents that reflected and helped create the mythology of the Western frontier itself. All of these works are, and will continue to be, influential ones, testifying not only to the quality of their scholarship but also to the sustained appeal of expansionism as an organizing theme for American studies at large.[13] No doubt if we could quantify such matters in a cliometric analysis of nineteenth-century speeches, magazine articles, and books, the historiographic soundness of that theme would be borne out. The history, myths, and prospects of the frontier's extension would prove to have echoed more loudly in the collective antebellum mentality than did representations of tropical America, Polynesia, Africa, or the Holy Land. Surely, though, the mere primacy of expansionist or frontier discourse should not cause us to ignore that many authors and their readers were also intrigued by, and had much at stake in pondering, the foreign lands that lay beyond the path of Manifest Destiny.

The archive of travel literature about non-European locales, not to speak of histories and geographical guides and textbooks, is staggeringly immense. The accounts written by Captain Cook, Mungo Park, Alexander von Humboldt, and other famed British or European travelers or explorers appeared in American editions shortly after their initial publication, or they could be read in redacted form in anthologies such as the Harper Family Library's *Historical Account of the Circumnavigation of the Globe, and of the Progress of Discovery in the Pacific Ocean* (1837), Charles Goodrich's *Universal Traveller* (1838), or Bayard Taylor's *Cyclopaedia of Modern Travel: A Record of Adventure, Explo-*

ration and Discovery (1856). A number of American travelers themselves wrote bestsellers. John L. Stephens followed the success of *Incidents of Travel in Egypt, Arabia Petræa, and the Holy Land* (1837) with the equally acclaimed *Incidents of Travel in Central America, Chiapas, and Yucatan* (1841) and its sequel, *Incidents of Travel in Yucatan* (1843). Bayard Taylor, after *Eldorado*, issued a stream of volumes—*A Journey to Central Africa; or, Life and Landscapes from Egypt to the Negro Kingdoms of the White Nile* (1854) and *The Lands of the Saracen; or, Pictures of Palestine, Asia Minor, Sicily and Spain* (1854) among others—in addition to his account of his travels in the Far East. The monthly journals of the day, from the *Knickerbocker Magazine* to the *Ladies' Repository*, carried excerpts and reviews of notable travel volumes, as well as articles and tales on a variety of non-European subjects; and, of course, missionaries—for example, Hiram Bingham in his *Residence of Twenty-One Years in the Sandwich Islands* (1847)—dutifully reported upon the progress of delivering the Gospel to benighted souls. All of the latter were directed toward a broadly educated audience, and a range of such volumes could typically be found in the cabinet libraries or drawing rooms of the middle class. For those involved directly or indirectly in the seafaring trade (which is to say, the bulk of business people in New England), a host of journals, books, and documents—whether *The Merchants' Magazine* or multivolumed accounts of naval expeditions—covered all that seemed to be needed for profitable commercial exchanges with foreign countries and regions.[14]

Addressed to an audience confident of the nation's seemingly privileged and glorious stature, few of these sources of fact or lore about non-Europeans avoid being culturally chauvinistic. *The Universal Traveller*, compiled by Charles Goodrich in 1838, includes an "extensive account of the world, in the manners, customs, rites, laws, governments, and other particulars respecting its inhabitants." Its special pleasure, though, apparently lies more in preserving cultural distance than shortening it. U.S. armchair travelers, in the "comfort and security of [their] homes," obtain the chance to "visit the most savage tribes, in perfect safety—Indians, Algerines, New Zealanders, barbarians, cannibals" and learn to be "more contented with the goodly land in which their lot is cast" and "those circumstances that contribute to national happiness." Goodrich does more than just proffer an embracing moral from the travel tales told. The "goodly land" becomes a moralized macro-space because, in part, the multiple domestic micro-spaces of "perfect safety" that compose it are the disciplinary sites of instruction about heathen, nongoodly lands.[15] Emerson, in his essay "Wealth" (from *The Conduct of Life* [1860]), draws a parallel lesson about the merits of travel and exploration literature. "It is the interest of all," he writes, "that there should be Exploring Expeditions; Captain Cooks to voyage round the world, Rosses, Franklins, Richardsons, and Kanes, to find the magnetic and geographic poles. We are all the richer for the measurement of a degree of latitude on the earth's surface."[16] The desire to be informed about faraway lands and cultures is laudable, and at least better than assuming Bronson Alcott's stance of lofty insularity; but what excites Emerson, in fact, is how those explorers tap into a global economy of virility, as is evident from his companion essay, "Power." When Western readers go "gypsying with Borrow in Spain and Algiers; riding alligators in South America with Waterton; utilizing Bedouin, Sheik, and Pacha, with Layard," a "surcharge of arterial blood" reinvigorates their moral-bodily economy. This surrogate influx of power depends upon "natural forces, which are best in the savage, who, like the beasts around him, is still in reception of the milk from the teats of Nature." Yet if Emerson deems the "aboriginal source" necessary, "savage" communities may be dismissed; for the "energy . . . in the civil and moral man" outweighs the "worth [of] all the cannibals in the Pacific."[17]

The travelers that Emerson cites intended other or additional effects than the restoration of Anglo-Saxon virility. Nonetheless, in the recirculation of these texts, even if only when Emerson briefly alludes to them, they and the foreign lands they represent become part of what Emerson elsewhere in "Wealth" calls the "stock" of Western knowledge.[18] The utility of travel texts, to provide Western mastery of the non-Western, is often profiled in editorial comments that preface travel anthologies. Consider the rationale one compiler offers for his compendium, _The Travels and Adventures of Celebrated Travellers in the Principal Countries of the Globe_ (1855):

To contribute to [knowledge about the world] is the design of this volume: to satisfy it completely, so as to know perfectly all people, is somewhat further than we can go. It would, for instance, be a pleasant task could we, for the reader's benefit, by some process spiritually uncap the cranium of a Chinaman or of an Arab, take a peep into his mental workshop, and watch its operations for a single day: but this being one of the curious undertakings not permitted us with even our own townspeople . . . it cannot be expected we should "take such liberties with strangers."

The invisible essence of the Chinaman or the Arab cannot be laid bare to observation. What can be told are the conditions that produce national mentalities, and in so doing, he continues, "we obtain that which liberalizes"; we learn "the important truth—that it is circumstance which creates national, alike with individual, characteristics; and out of this grows charity for peculiar national ideas and for heterodox personal opinions." He speculates that "had we been transported in babyhood to China and reared in a Chinese family, we should have . . . thought angular eyes and deformed feet the acme of beauty; the world square, like a table; [and] Confucius the most pre-eminent of mortals." The editor's self-professed liberalism is not so much undercut by his patronizing bonhomie or "charity" as by the fact, as it turns out, that the respect for difference or an enlargement of one's own cultural sensibility is beside the point. He goes on to celebrate how the advent of the Gospel transforms pagan islands: "[A] stranger, with a benign countenance and a book in his hand, lands upon their island. . . . Through the power of his words the islanders cast down their idols, they no longer sacrifice to false gods."[19] Here, the absolute weight of the invisible sign—the condition of the islanders' souls—out-balances the tolerance otherwise directed toward exterior, heterodox ethno-cultural signs.

The editor conflates the Gospel's puissance with those who transmit it, and he foregrounds, as do many other compilers of such travel collections, the mixed piety and patriotism that made the notion of the Redeemer Nation so compelling. Another way to conjoin individual to country, especially that country's claim to progress, was for the armchair traveler to follow the ex-plorer, who, with a will-to-knowledge about a foreign domain, annexed all that could be known about it to himself. Bayard Taylor, in the preface to his 1856 *Cyclopaedia of Modern Travel*, for example, declares the technology of exploration to be superior to military conquest. "One by one the outposts of barbarism are stormed and carried," he asserts:

[A]dvanced parallels are thrown up, and the besieging lines of knowledge, which, when once established, can never be retaken, are gradually closing round the yet uncon-quered mysteries of the globe. Modern exploration is intelligent, and its results are therefore positive and permanent. . . . The pencil, the compass, the barometer, and the sextant accompany [the modern explorer]; geology, botany, and ethnology are his aids; and by these helps and appliances, his single brain now achieves results which it would once have required an armed force to win.[20]

By Taylor's lights, the travel writings he compiles are exemplary both be-cause they supply valuable data about the globe and its inhabitants and because they illustrate the might of the "single brain" of the American or European to produce or survey that knowledge. We can easily mock such presumption or underestimate the relative purity of at least some readers' scientific curiosity; the quest to fill in the unknown or geographic vacancy need not be an aggres-sive pursuit (even when, as in the above passage, it is conceived via an aggres-sive analogy).

Yet the information obtained, regardless of its intent or immediate effect, served U.S. international interests in the long term. It became the handmaiden of commerce and was crucial in guaranteeing that the country would eventu-ally become a world power. Before the Civil War, New England merchants competed to secure trading rights in Central and South America, in Polynesia, and in Asia, laying the foundation for the spread of U.S. capital and industry in non-European regions in the later nineteenth and twentieth centuries.[21] The reports from mid-century U.S. naval expeditions—Charles Wilkes's *Narrative of the United States Exploring Expedition* (1845), William Lewis Herndon's *Exploration of the Valley of the Amazon* (1854), and Francis L. Hawks's *Narrative of the Expedition of an American Squadron to the China Seas and Japan*—amassed an encyclopedic array of geographical, geological, botanical, and ethnographical fact vital to America's ever-burgeoning reliance upon a global economy of trade.[22] The interests of commercialism or scientific curiosity, however, will not fully explain the public's satisfaction in reading these accounts. They included statistical tables, maps, engravings and lithographs, and extensive quotations from ambassadorial letters and related state documents. Their authors aspired toward a complete mimetic reprise of the voyage; and while the public might have found such minutiae tedious (obliging Wilkes to publish in 1849 a one-volume version of his expedition, containing "all the most interesting results as well as the exciting scenes of the cruise"), they at the same time immersed the reader in the militaristic process or state technology of exploration.[23]

The travel works and travel anthologies I have thus far cited fostered national conceit, what Dean MacCannell not too hyperbolically identifies as "the old arrogant Western Ego that wants to see it all, know it all, and take it all in, an Ego that is isolated by its belief in its own superiority."[24] Such texts may be construed, as well, as being implicated in imperialism or protoimperialism. They are the ones to which we would turn, besides those pertaining to the westward advance through Indian territory, to learn how knowledge about natives and their lands augmented expansionist fervor both within and beyond continental borders. The strategies used closely resemble those deployed in a long line of post-Renaissance European travel narratives and other documents of empire-building. Homogenizing indigenes into a collective "they"; predicting how much the latter would benefit from systematic law, Christianity, and modern commerce; or envisioning sites for future enterprise, with a concordant marginalization of the inhabitants' own claim to their land: these tactics seem universal in the long arc of imperialism, not peculiar to the United States.[25]

But cultural work less cognate with the designs of empire could also transpire when describing non-Europeans for several reasons that should give us pause. The idea of expansionism's legitimacy, first of all, was not a given. For all its force, the call of Manifest Destiny in the 1840s and 1850s was not hegemonically seductive. Some feared that the republic's affectional bonds would be sundered if the country grew too large. Others found empire and republicanism simply incompatible terms, and the lexicon of phrases used to justify the former mere mystifying cant. A Whig writer in *The National Intelligencer* (January 15, 1848) impatiently proclaimed that the "whole land" appeared "completely spellbound as if the lies of magic were realities, and a sylla-ble or two of gibberish could reverse all the laws of Nature and turn human intelligence into brutishness":

[S]ome . . . respectable confidant of the Divine decrees has bellowed to the prudent populace that to conquer all this continent is *"our Manifest Destiny"*; and, behold! that shallow and impious phrase passes for a received decree of Fate! . . . [W]ho shall assure us that it is not of the devil's fetching[?] . . . [Another] word-snare for national vanity and presumption is . . . *"Anglo-Saxonism."* . . . We are, it appears, of the "Anglo-Saxon race"—of a lineage of "land-stealers," a progeny of plunderers! Oh, pious genealogy![26]

Second, in the context of adjacent or near-adjacent territory—the tracts of the West and Southwest where the agenda of Manifest Destiny most directly applied—it was assumed that the lands to be prospectively conquered already belonged to the United States. As settlers gradually appropriated those lands, moreover, the indigenous Indians did not become colonial subalterns, but rather were forcibly relocated farther and farther west. This put the United States in the anomalous position of being, at least before the 1890s, with the invasion of the Philippines, imperialistic without being colonialist. Foreign land was to be assimilated, not subordinated and administered at a distance, as in the case of the British Empire, in which isle and colony were always geo-graphically distinct, and new lands did not become more England.[27] This as-pect of U.S. nineteenth-century imperialism, especially in its nascent years, had a crucial consequence: a reluctance to absorb regions, even if part of the continent, that would entail mixing the mostly Anglo-Saxon or Caucasian body politic with racially different populations who, unlike the Indians, could not be resettled so readily. John Calhoun, for one, disliked expansion into Mexico because he loathed the idea of "incorporating into our Union any but the Caucasian race." "Ours, sirs, is the Government of a white race," he told Congress; not one of a "mixed blood equally ignorant and unfit for liberty, [comprising] impure races, not as good as the Cherokees or Choctaws."[28] Senator John Clayton more stridently voiced nativist anxiety: "Yes! Aztecs, Creoles, Halfbreeds, Quadroons, Samboes, and I know not what else—'ring-streaked and speckled'—all will come in, and instead of our governing them, they, by their votes, will govern *us*."[29] Before Admiral George Dewey con-quered Manila in 1898, only those territories, such as Texas or California, were annexed in which vast land tracts were already held by white U.S. settlers or shortly would, with the sequestering of Indian groups. To enfold within na-tional boundaries what Calhoun refers to as "impure races" seemed to pose, as historian Bradford Perkins summarizes, "two equally unpalatable alternatives: Either they would, like other citizens, join in the political process, thereby de-basing it, or the United States would have to convert itself into an empire, ruling colonials, thereby abandoning" the "fundamental principle" of democratic suffrage.[30] The notion that distinct races were suited for specific geographies also discouraged expansion or colonialism beyond the Mexican territories. "Permanent, self-supporting colonization in another climate is impossible," Bayard Taylor warned in a lyceum lecture; this "knowledge should restrain our national ambition."[31] The path to empire (to borrow the subtitle from Taylor's *Eldorado*) might be westward, with some excursions to the immediate south or into the Caribbean, but for all of the nation's ever-increasing vastness even zealots of expansion were wary of linking it to radically foreign topographies and their populations.

The naval expeditions of Wilkes in 1838–42 and Perry in 1852–54 sought to safeguard New England trading interests in the Southern Hemisphere and the Far East, logged what natural resources might be exploited, and displayed the might of the nation—belligerently so, in the instance of Perry's gunboat diplomacy in Japan. Nonetheless, neither expedition resulted in colonialist settlements or immediate commercial inroads. Perry's venture was seen as an obligatory reaction against those nations deviating from the presumed natural order of free trade (England especially, being as Perry charged, an "unconscionable government"; but also Japan, for its self-imposed insularity).[32] Although the United States sought to protect its worldwide commercial interests and played a complicated game of geopolitics with the major imperial powers, the government did not wish to establish, strictly speaking, colonies in third-world countries. With the country led by a succession of jingoistic presidents (Polk, Taylor, Fillmore, Pierce, and Buchanan), fervid expansionists or filibusters entertained the possibility of appropriating Cuba and portions of Central America, the latter with greater urgency after 1848, when it became paramount to control an interoceanic rail or canal route to California and its goldfields. William Walker, the most famed (or notorious) of the filibusters, saw the "true field for the exertion of slavery" to be "in tropical America; there it finds the natural seat of its empire."[33] His charismatic leadership seduced his followers into a series of campaigns to take over Nicaragua, all of which failed (his domination of the country only lasted for ten months in 1856–57). Walker's delusions of racist grandeur were not unique to himself. Some Southern politicians and plantations owners—seeing the secessionist writing on the wall—dreamed of preserving the peculiar institution by way of its extension southward, through Mexico and the Caribbean. Matthew Maury, the famous oceanographer, could even envision the South's empire stretching as far as Brazil. But such prospects remained only fantasies, not an accomplished reality. The Whigs, habitually more diffident than the Democrats, feared in particular that too rapid an expansion would jeopardize the precarious balance of power between slave and nonslave states. Because no region within the Americas (much less Polynesia, Africa, or Asia) was subjected to a policy of full-scale colonialism, even the U.S. traveler-official whose mission was to gather information that might prove valuable for later territorial acquisitions cannot, without ample qualification, be said to be a state agent implementing or helping to maintain colonial dominion.

The lack of a concerted, state-authorized imperial agenda beyond the West and Southwest does not mean that U.S. texts about tropical America, Polynesia, Africa, or the Orient are free of ethnocentricism. Even when a text based upon a cross-cultural encounter deprecates aspects of the homeland, there is no guarantee that it will not hit, whatever the good intentions of its author, a mimetic barrier when it comes to giving an "inside" view of a non-European world. To the extent that the ideological itinerary of the U.S. traveler remains on American soil, the act of depicting non-European lands and their inhabitants becomes an asymmetrical one. In this situation, we are left with an awkward choice. Either we impugn *what* is represented, proffering some supposedly more authentic version of foreign peoples as they see themselves, and thus likely lose the focus on the *why* of the representing in the first place; or we attend seriously to that *why*, and leave ourselves open, potentially, to the charge of being complicity silent about the cultures behind the representations. Take, for example, how two of its better critics approach Herman Melville's *Typee: A Peep at Polynesian Life* (1846). Milton Stern argues that the text's *"raison d'être* is not 'A Peep at Polynesian Life.' Polynesia could have been the Arctic Circle or the Belgian Congo."[34] According to him, the Typees *themselves* do not matter. Imagining any so-called primitive society would suffice for Melville to posit the almost allegorical dichotomies (mind/body, culture/nature, and so on) that Stern deems to be thematically important, and thus he feels no need to challenge the book's *use* of the Typees. For Stern, *Typee*'s ethnography is virtual only, a means to highlight thematic contrasts. In a revisionary interpretation, Mitchell Breitwieser insists, however, that Melville implicitly censures Tommo for "celebrat[ing]" the Typees, for "exploiting their life rhetorically because he is only interested in them as a negation of what he detests rather than as a culture that is comprehensively alien to *all* aspects of his own."[35] Breitwieser does not imply that Tommo should have reported upon the Typees in their own terms but, rather, that he should have recognized that his own "peep" is mostly pretense, not genuinely cross-cultural. Tommo's blindness pertains not to what he does or does not see, but to the fact that he is not self-aware of the limitations of his own anthropological optic. Breitwieser, no less than Stern, regards *Typee* as a work of fiction, but for him the gap between actual Polynesian encounter and authorial re-creation afforded Melville the chance to critique the ethnographical inquiry, or noninquiry, of his fictional protagonist. The implicit conflict between Stern's and Breitwieser's exemplary readings arises not from their necessarily partial takes on some ultimate truth that Melville's text holds about either U.S. or Polynesian cultures. Their analyses of *Typee* reflect, rather, opposed attitudes about the ethics of depicting a foreign people and the ethics of interpreting those depictions.[36]

The ethical question extends beyond how we carry out any one interpretation. It involves how we, as Americanists, define the parameters of our field. Consider, for instance, what motivates us when we study how James Fenimore Cooper and other canonical writers portray Native Americans. We do so in part because their stories influenced how the dominant white culture would manage genocidal guilt or lay claim to being Nature's Nation, with the indigenous presence serving to disaffiliate white Americans from the corrupt artificiality of the Old World. Or we critique Cooper's fictional stereotypes because it is simply responsible to do so, one aspect of a valid effort to recover the past of Indian cultures that the country, in its inexorable push westward, nearly came to destroy. Yet we also study his novels because the native groups described are seen, retrospectively, as having lived within the ocean-to-ocean national geographical entity that we now designate as the United States. Indian territory, although obviously foreign land before U.S. citizens settled upon it, was seen proleptically as part of the United States; and it is seen (if we are white) by "us" as the space where "our" history took place, however much we may be inclined to denounce that history as largely the process of invading land that was not "ours." Accordingly, the ethical impulse to speak for Native Americans when we talk about Cooper and other white authors illustrates another, if oppositional, version of nationalism. The same may be said even when we bring into the fold—into the "canon"—otherwise marginalized native voices, past or present.[37] In both cases, previously neutral or laudatory accounts of U.S. policy and culture usually become replaced by anticelebratory ones that, although promoting a more open, egalitarian politics, nonetheless draw upon the inflated aura of America even as they expose its dark and violent underbelly. The intellectual frisson of debunking America partially depends, in short, upon its residual glory.

Thinking too nationally potentially leads to overly grandiose or facile critique; the logical alternative, it would seem, is to pry apart the national edifice. We have rightly learned to distrust mystifying narratives of a geographical teleology radiating out from New England or of a genealogical unity premised upon ethnicity or race.[38] The increased visibility or availability of materials about immigrant or diasporic groups, the recognition of the polyglossia of the frontier zone, and, in the twentieth century, the decentralization of media and capital: all have made dubious the likelihood that we can continue our labors within the field of American studies without questioning its boundaries. Here, though, an opposite problem arises: that of making a fetish of disjunction. Any reader of recent New Americanist literary scholarship will be struck by the many terms used—*contradictory, heterogeneous, multivalent, hybridity, rupture, deformation*—that, even as they justly testify to the complicated exchanges between dominant and resistant discourses and sites, also seem to confess the nonnarrativity of the field itself. The conscientious Americanist, worried about being a dupe of nationalist ideology, and yet also knowing the trap of infinite regress into the discrete, into the local, almost necessarily draws upon a vocabulary that seems less to relate things than to be stuck in the twilight zone of the relational as such. Deflating loose, baggy paradigms, to be sure, is healthy; the muse of literary or cultural history is not moribund. The danger, however, is that what might in an old-fashioned way be deemed positive knowledge ends up getting usurped by critical rubrics masking their own fuzziness.

My latter remark is not a jab against theory so much as a sign of my unease with practices that keep us in the shadowy realm of the in-between, or with what might be called postcolonial chiasmatics (the critic's hall-of-mirror inversions/transpositions of agency between subalterns and rulers), and do little else. There has been, over the last decade or two, no end of debate over the issue of how representations (of anything, not just the other) affectively inhabit cultural ideologies or the mind of the individual citizen. I would not want us to become Luddites against theory: I do, though, believe that theory works best when it emerges from—indeed, is earned by—an initial grounding in cases and circumstances.

Consequently, in the subsequent chapters I try to strike a balance among three critical concerns: elucidating national narratives, attending to the specific cultural lexicon of specific discursive communities (for instance, that of both black and white authors preoccupied with African-American repatriation), and coordinating the latter two with the idiosyncrasies of authorial identity. I also strive for theoretical cogency without burdening the reader with too abstruse discussion of the colonial or imperial agon. Most important, I assume that the cultures of societies do not exist in and of themselves. As the anthropologist James A. Boon remarks, "A 'culture' can materialize only in counterdistinction to another culture."[39] This is not, to my mind, a maxim that entangles us in an abyss of deferral or Gordian-knot hybridity, but rather one that posits, without undue fuss, that group structures and sentiments (tribal or nationalist) are inevitably comparativist. We could, following recent studies in Polynesian ethnohistory, try to surmise what the "real" Typees were in fact like, but even the Typees, at least according to how Tommo presents them, primarily define themselves in opposition to the Happars, the enemy tribe residing in a nearby valley. The last point does not mean that the actual Polynesian society that Melville described becomes immaterial to how we analyze his travel novel, but rather that Tommo should not be condemned *tout court* for his lack of ethnographical rigor. By attending to how non-European terrains and populations are represented as acts of U.S. national self-referencing, I do not wish to downplay the hazards of monologism. But, conversely, the urge to prove that all representations of third-world countries and peoples, written by those living in first-world countries, serve only the interests of domination will lead us to miss other culturally complex thematics. I also believe that the ethical imperative to show how human rights have been violated and how the oppressed fight oppression can better be obtained by traditional modes of inquiry. As Robert Young observes when assessing Homi K. Bhabha's practice of uncovering buried textual ambivalences or hybrid spaces within colonialist discourse, "[It] has to be said that documentary evidence of resistance by colonized peoples is not at all hard to come by, and is only belittled by the implication that you have to read between the lines to find it."[40] Even if the way the foreign was represented in antebellum travelogues and associated texts reinforced, indeed in part enabled, imperialistic rapacity (rather than being imperialism's epiphenomenon), ethical critique of those texts, however adroitly elaborated, will typically yield the same story: the powerful victimizing the less powerful. That story is always relevant, especially when it has continuities with present efforts to overcome oppression; but it is not the only story to be told about the past or the cultural texts of the past.

Concentrating too much on the calculus of control and resistance may also obscure the informing nuances of locale. When all issues axiomatically revolve about the tools, material or rhetorical, of imperial power, we will likely end up with an impoverished grasp of how specific ideological formations were shaped by or mediated encounters with specific foreign regions. Different zones of cross-cultural contact solicited, I would argue, different ideological responses—different, to refer to my title, American geographics. Would *Typee* have been the same if it had portrayed Africans or Eskimos rather than Polynesians? Maybe; but presumably however much Tommo (or Melville) may project a fantasy image upon the Typees, which tells us more about himself than the actual Typees, what he thereby reveals about himself and his culture to some degree depends upon the specificity of the people he met. The concern about the possibility and merits of natural legalism came into focus by thinking about Polynesians and Polynesia, not by thinking about the inhabitants and lands of tropical America. Obversely, representations of tropical America raised anxieties about racial admixture and declension, whereas representations of Polynesia typically did not. In short, what the imaginary of a foreign realm comprises, and what that imaginary does in ideological terms, will vary according to what non-European domain is being depicted.

If first-world travel texts filter third-world countries through a fairly stable set of rhetorical practices, as Edward Said among others maintain, I would suggest as well that the representations of particular regions or countries refract, construct, or help negotiate particular ideological complexes. In the antebellum period, those complexes, or the texts behind them, did not inevitably coalesce or fold into what we loosely call national consciousness. Travelistic works, then as now, cannot be said to collectively form a singular mirror reflecting the nation to itself in perfect coherence. They stage varied dramas, with the "nation" playing diverse roles, contingent upon authorial psychology or profession and the non-European land depicted. Here, I propose, we can see one avenue out of the quandary of one-way or asymmetrical representation. Imperialist thought relies upon stereotypes, and all subjects, whether governed or governing, find themselves inscribed within various subtle and not-so-subtle power structures. This need not mean, however, that they become incapable of questioning or rendering ambivalent the national script itself. Dissent, disenfranchisement, regional tensions, or simply the multitudinous elements that compose identity—all might compel a citizen to avoid monolithic othering, even when upholding imperialistic aims. Moreover, the sheer palpability of foreign topographies and peoples may quite likely, if not exactly pull the national subject out of the orbit of his or her own nationality, at least highlight tensions within the national order. Conversely, authors the most disinclined to yoke themselves unthinkingly to the nation—Herman Melville or Martin R. Delany, for example—also at times assume troubling postures of superiority in respect to the indigenous cultures they portray. The linkage between subject and nation is variable; and national citizens do not by default carry their citizenship as their only or heaviest psychological or ideological baggage. The belief in Manifest Destiny, I mentioned earlier, mystified the U.S. geobody; and no doubt many citizens' self-identity rested securely on a quasi-religious sense of national election. Not inevitably so, however: the residue, that which does not overlap with national subjecthood, is oftentimes what enables a traveler—or a reader of a travel volume—to negotiate or triangulate the facticity of a non-European land or people, the popular imaginary of the region, and different U.S. ideologies. (Our suspicion that no "self" exists transcendentally free of nurture, ideology, or what nineteenth-century savants would call the spirit of the people—national ardor, race, or creed—should not blind us to the fact that the "self," even if only an effect rather than an essence, will always supersede the categories—class, gender, race, ethnicity, religion, locale, and so on—of analysis.) The itinerary taken, both literally and ideologically, may always conclude with a return to the home country; but the intervening route also interrupts national narratives—revealing latent, contestatory, or at least equivocal contents.[41]

The interchanges between the traveler and the other culture's resisting materiality engender ambivalent narratives. I do not wish to assert, however, that the stories told enduringly deform or destabilize U.S. national identity. Divulging fissures within the imperialist mentality at key textual moments holds a faddish appeal, but such moments are usually local rather than paradigmatic, and more often than not, depend upon the interventionist, deconstructionist stance of the critic.[42] Although I believe the writers I discuss engage the other's materiality, this study itself does not ultimately evade the problem of repeating, even if warily, a version of nationalist practice. That it remains in the camp of American studies rather than embracing a more globally dialogic methodology is a limitation imposed, for the most part, by my sense of the odds against recovering the diverse perspectives of inhabitants of the countries represented in nineteenth-century geographical and travelistic writing, and by the amount of labor that can be devoted to any one scholarly project. My work, although sympathetic to, does not follow the lead of those who would ask us to dwell in the borderlands or to look at the United States from without.[43]

There is no canon of travel writers that might at first glance recommend certain ones as being more significant than others. The case-study approach I usually favor in the later chapters, however, is not merely arbitrary. I have selected authors that I believe best illuminate how different non-European regions resonated with a range of national narratives. It would be disingenuous, though, not to concede a degree of circular reasoning here, especially when the political elides with the personal. For example, Delany's wish to found an African-American state in the Caribbean or Africa involved career ambitions as much as a righteous fight on behalf of his people; and so to rely heavily upon Delany's texts when I discuss the relations between the United States and Africa is to tell a very partial story, one perhaps more biographical than national. Delany becomes representative of the antebellum United States–Africa link, but such representativeness—the conflation of the psychological and political—works only because many other African-Americans are not heard within the confines of this project. My inclusion of Melville begs a somewhat different question of evidence and argument. His voice is the most predominant one in this study, naturally enough because his texts blend the authority of actual encounter with that of authorial responsiveness. Bayard Taylor may have traveled more, but Melville *saw* more, or at least was capable of inscribing in his texts richer, more nuanced reflections about the foreign lands he visited or imagined. Whether the latter bespeaks Melville's largesse of mind, discomforts with his own culture, or his refined typicality (his capacity to mirror his age, but subtly so) I do not think is readily answerable. Much cultural scholarship hinges, I suspect, on assessing typicality, but typicality is notoriously difficult to pin down. Although Taylor quite likely comes the closest to being the most unexceptional travel author of his period, his works are also laden with psychological motifs (the desire to bond with great men is one) that extend beyond, even as they reflect, some nebulous discursive norm. Part of my argument, moreover, is that those practicing cross-cultural studies should not discount the biographical idiosyncrasies of any text or the discursive peculiarities of the professional or group affiliation of the author in question.

That said, I have tried in the following chapters to do justice to both typicality (the way authors and their texts address national issues) and the biographically specific (the way national issues and journeys to foreign lands *affectively* intersect within an author), without sacrificing one to the other. Exegesis will often gain impetus by way of the psychological, but I also provide fairly ample contextualization, about the broader historical-political relations between the United States and the non-European realm under consideration as well as what I take to be the most salient aspects of the popular imaginary of that realm.

Chapter 1 covers antebellum geographies—the means by which the average U.S. citizen or juvenile citizen-to-be would have first textually met non-European terrains and peoples. Samuel Goodrich and Arnold Guyot, authors of the period's best-selling volumes, sought to comprehend the world's diverse locales and communities in a morally interpretable pattern. Their works, and a host of kindred schoolroom geography textbooks, used rhetorical strategies that marked all non-European groups as being heteroclite to various degrees. These textbooks tell stories of the ark of civilization passing from the old Old World (Asia) to the Old World (Europe) and on to the United States, a land whose liberties were avowed to derive from a national teleos founded on both race (supposed Caucasian energy) and the ever-progressing frontier. The ideology embraced or what it palliated, slavery or class tension for instance, is hardly surprising, yet antebellum geographical writing deserves our attention because it also enabled the nation, although always mutating in its transit into futurity, to take shape, to be embodied. The geographical gaze when directed at non-European nations and races contrastively produced the body of the nation itself, which otherwise could not quite "see" itself, or only rhetorically so in, for example, July 4th speeches and other self-laudatory occasions.

Geographical textbooks confirmed U.S. exceptionality in global terms and instructed children in the disciplinary skills deemed requisite to maintaining that elevated position. Their pervasive use as a tool to train future citizens argues for their cultural heft; they did not just reflect normative white culture— they produced that culture, every day, at the sites of middle-class instruction. They merit study because of the cultural work they accomplished, but their techniques of representation also provide a new, and I think necessary, context for understanding the often more conflicted sociocomparative dynamics and self-fashioning of mid-nineteenth-century U.S. travel writers. The second, third, and fourth chapters look at authors who engaged corporeally rather than abstractly different non-European realms and wrote texts that variously reveal the fault lines of, or interrogate, national identity and ideologies. In their travel novels or travelogues (and associated missionary, archaeological, and ethnographical works), third-world terrains, relics, monuments, and peoples typically become tensely mediatory. Chapter 2 shows that although *Typee* reprises a stay with real Polynesians, it also re-presents them in order to explore conflicts pertaining to antebellum theorizing about social governance. When Tommo, Melville's persona, resorts to explaining that the Typees' harmonious social fabric is based upon an interior heart-law, he does so both because he cannot grasp their laws and because he desires, as did his contemporaries, a foundational law transcending temporal exigencies. Their idyllic polity, seemingly free of overt state authority, provides the means of critique. But, finally, insofar as Typeean law can only be construed in ethnocentric, Anglo-American terms, it also becomes at once a mirror or projection of aspects of antebellum law itself and, to the extent that Western tropes turn out to be inadequate in representing it, an opaquely alien system of regulation that forces Tommo to envision in *Typee*'s appendix legally unsanctioned authority—the charismatic rule of the British naval commander, Lord Paulet.

Chapter 3 turns to the Holy Land, which was at once intimately familiar to antebellum readers as the locus of their faith and distanced by the exoticizing discourses of nineteenth-century Orientalism. I trace the transcodings of desire and transgression in a sequence of texts—John L. Stephens's *Incidents of Travel in Egypt, Arabia Petræa, and the Holy Land*, William F. Lynch's *Narrative of the United States' Expedition to the River Jordan and the Dead Sea* (1849), Maria Susanna Cummins's *El Fureidîs* (1860), and Melville's *Clarel: A Poem and Pilgrimage in the Holy Land* (1876). These works have much to tell us about the era's religious anxieties, but my main interest lies less in their theology than in their more visceral, hermeneutical inquiries. Stephens, Lynch, Cummins, and Melville—or their narrative personae—pursue destinations both libidinally charged and scripturally luminous. To traverse the Holy Land, for them, was not only to travel back to the originary scenes of Christian faith in search of godly signs but also to work through homebred perplexities of desire via the mediating sensorium of the Near East: harems, reliquaries, architectural ruins, and a landscape at once wondrous and, as in the case of the Dead Sea, eerily desolate.

Stephens, discovering his métier with his popular 1837 Holy Land volume, embarked four years later for travels both archaeological and diplomatic in Central America. Chapter 4 looks at Stephens's *Incidents of Travel in Central*

America, Chiapas, and Yucatan and its sequel, *Incidents of Travel in Yucatan*, in their own right, but also as prefatory to an analysis of the career and writings of the now lesser known, yet no less intriguing, archaeologist-explorer Ephraim G. Squier. Both Squier and Stephens sought to unearth New World antiquities, what I refer to as a quest, at base masculinist, for the archaeological sublime. Stephens obsessively sought to become the first white discoverer of long-buried Mayan relics and monuments; and Squier, frustrated by being a belated, postheroic explorer, saw Central America as the locale in which he could fulfill his intense ambitions for professional glory. Squier's half-fantasy, half-factual travel novel, *Waikna; or, Adventures on the Mosquito Shore* (published under the pseudonym of Samuel Bard in 1855), unlike his archaeological and ethnographical treatises, provided him the means to insert himself within, as it were, the very mise en scène of original New World discovery, before the time of what he took to be Latin America's declension into hybridized history.

The previous writers, all white, in the main reflect majoritarian concerns. Chapter 5 focuses on Martin R. Delany, often hailed as a key forerunner of the back-to-Africa movement. His separatist politics led him to envision emancipatory spaces in a number of important texts: *The Condition, Elevation, Emigration, and Destiny of the Colored People of the United States* (1852), *Official Report of the Niger Valley Exploring Party* (1861), and the novel *Blake; or the Huts of America* (1861–62). These works acutely respond to the issue of African-American agency, the problem of being, as Delany put it, an abject "nation within a nation."[44] I argue that Delany's distinctive understanding of the internal and external aspects of political power at once enabled and mystified his role as a revolutionary black pedagogue. Throughout his career, he faced the challenge of conceptualizing black nationality—in the United States, in the Caribbean, or in Africa—in terms that did not merely revolve back upon his own inward sense of sovereignty. Ultimately, however, the terrain of black liberation was to be found only within rather than without—a sign at once of his arrogance and of his strong resilience in the face of an intransigently bigoted nation.

Most of the authors I examine wrote for a broad audience or used popular genres. But I think that we should be suspicious about popularity as a measure of a document's importance, and therefore I have not been worried about what might testify to popularity itself. Sales figures valuably index how any one text imagined, for the public, salient cultural anxieties and resolved or engendered cultural debate, and when a text was popular in the sense of having been widely distributed, I acknowledge it as such. We lack, though, a sure methodology by which we can attribute a work's contemporary fame to the cultural fantasies or fears that we, over a century later, see operating in it. And we cannot confidently surmise that a work did not sell well (Squier's *Waikna* is a case in point) because it failed to refract the preoccupations of the popular mind, a term suspect itself insofar as it collapses class, gender, and ethnic or racial distinctions. These matters invite theorizing, but the claim that any text resonates beyond itself in the way that we, today, regard it as so doing rests finally on the act, in part rhetorical, of persuasively situating it within its historical context. I have selected, I should add, authors whose motives for travel were especially complex. Writers such as Bayard Taylor—whose itineraries speedily took him through a host of countries and regions—have been reserved for contextual example and counterexample. Other travel authors (Richard Henry Dana, Jr., Nathaniel Parker Willis, and George William Curtis, to name a few) praised in their own time receive only passing mention. What I have found to be marginal, other scholars when surveying a different cluster of issues might very well conceive as being more central. The U.S. cultural topoi that I foreground in each chapter—over the law (Polynesia), religion and desire (the Holy Land), history (tropical America), race and nation (Africa)— could also be connected to genealogies and trajectories having little to do with foreign locales per se. The works might thereby become more symptomatic, more *nationally* weighty. Stephens's and Squier's pursuit of archaeological sublimity, for instance, could be linked to a theory about the male Romantic Sublime in a strictly U.S. context, in which the ascension into an unspoken but nonetheless present "white" meaning almost invariably requires the contrasts of racial or ethnic difference: for example, Henry David Thoreau's opposition of his own ascetic, virile economy to that of the debilitated Irish bog-farmer John Field; or James Fenimore Cooper's emphatic reminders of the whiteness of Natty Bumppo, who stalks with pure lethality through Indian-haunted woods. To follow up on such analogies, however, would also be to take a detour from the sociocomparative dynamics that I wish to make visible.

My analyses frequently pivot upon key scenes in which the body of the U.S. traveler stands as the mediating contact zone between non-European terrains or peoples and the traveler's U.S. affiliations. Consequently, except for the first chapter on antebellum geographies and later sections on Cummins's *El Fureidîs* and Delany's *Blake*, my study covers only those texts that represent actual flesh-and-blood journeys to non-European realms. I have excluded conspicuously fantasizing narratives such as Edgar Allan Poe's *The Narrative of Arthur Gordon Pym of Nantucket* (1838), William S. Mayo's *Kaloolah, or, Journeyings to the Djébel Kumri: an Autobiography of Jonathan Romer* (1849), or Marturin Murray Ballou's *The Turkish Slave; or, The Mahometan and His Harem: A Story of the East* (1850). In these fabular texts both the traveler's body and the other's body hold only a distant, spectral relation to the various American geographic topics I explore. Such novels catered to the taste for exoticism, and traded on the chiaroscuro effect of racial contrast, but in them geographical locale typically is not especially relevant. Margaret Fuller's comment on the novel trade is appropriate here: when novelists "set to work with geography in hand to find unexplored nooks of wild scenery" rather than "using their materials spontaneously," the result "is a sad affair indeed and 'gluts the market' to the sorrow of both buyers and lookers-on."[45] The potboilers of Mayo, Ballou, and other hack writers, to be sure, helped to reinforce dominant stereotypes: for instance, about supposed Oriental decadence or African savagery. Extensive discussion of their writings in this book, however, would pull my project back into the internal, as opposed to cross-culturally derived, ideologies of the nation at mid-century.

Portions of my chapters are indebted to feminist critiques of imperialism and travel literature; but I do not attempt to frame all of the selected texts, or more broadly the genres of geographical or travelistic writing per se, within the teachings of feminist theory. Major work on European travel literature and imperialistic discourse—that by Mary Louise Pratt, Anne McClintock, and others—emphasizes that empire-building invariably required that subaltern or native groups be viewed as less masculine than the invading colonizers; and some scholars have critiqued the traditionally male-dominated fields of travel and geography writing as being almost intrinsically phallocentric, part of a discursive or scopic regime that always reinforces Western, patriarchal power. Such arguments are theoretically compelling, and in one sense obviously valid—most U.S. travelers to non-European regions were male. In another sense, though, the lack of a countertradition of woman-authored texts also means that we cannot readily chart—as an *historically* available alternative—a feminist travelistic or geographical practice in respect to how the non-European world was perceived or textually re-created.[46] The journals or reports of missionary wives, not unexpectedly, typically focus on the domestic trials and delights of arranging new households, but such texts, besides being relatively few, for the most part reprise the rhetoric of the Redeemer Nation. Antebellum women who wrote schoolroom geographies seldom, if ever, use militaristic metaphors of appropriation, yet they also privilege disciplinary, bourgeois spaces over non-European ones perhaps more so than their male counterparts. I do not look at the travel texts of well-known women such as Lydia Sigourney or Harriet Beecher Stowe because their works, while of tremendous interest, are primarily touristic accounts of England, France, and Italy. Their volumes—and, more inclusively, of later nineteenth-century women travel writers or native American authors such as Black Elk (who went with Buffalo Bill to London and met Queen Victoria)—are appropriate texts to consider as Americanists continue to enlarge their frames of reference. But given their European locales or postbellum publication, they necessarily are not included here.[47]

With a few exceptions, such as Melville's Holy Land poem *Clarel* (published in 1879, but composed during the previous decade and drawing upon his 1856–57 trip to the Levant), I discuss only works appearing before the end of the Civil War. This is not just a matter of convention or tidiness. Historians, despite their discomfort with sharply splitting U.S. global relations before and after the war, regard the "new" imperialism that emerged in the last third of the century as more classically colonialist, in the sense of foreign land, people, and resources being controlled without being assimilated. After the Civil War, national identity became increasingly solidified as the United States began rampant industrialization and settlement of the West. The war heightened attention to the need for foreign naval and military bases, and although expansionist policy continued to be westward centered, the shift overseas was inevitable as the frontier began to close. As the balance shifted from an agrarian to industrial economy, importing from and exporting to the far-flung world began to supersede the energies spent on developing Western farming or grazing lands.⁴⁸ U.S. citizens, by and large, felt considerably less anxious about the nation's destiny or about national self-definition, except for the perceived threat of ethnic or racial dilution caused by the influx of non–Northern European immigrants. The latter worry was managed by a widespread trumpeting of masculinist tropes of nationhood and empire-building. Once the nation became more vehemently imperialistic, perspectives tended to be reduced to either crude yea or naysaying (or an equivocating mix of the two, most notably evident in Mark Twain's satiric *Following the Equator: A Journey around the World* [1897]). Postbellum literary and cultural documents have important continuities with the materials this study encompasses, but the profile of national identity (to white, Protestant Americans, at least) by the end of the nineteenth century had become sufficiently resilient to require only, it would seem, routine booster shots of jingoism and national self-praise.

CHAPTER ONE

The World as Pedagogical Spectacle

Antebellum Geography Textbooks

> [We] should aim at a higher object in the study of geography, viz.,
> the improvement of man's moral culture, by a more extended
> knowledge of the productions of different climes, and by bringing
> before him, on a large tabular scale, the moral and physical condi-
> tions of his race.
>
> —First issue of the *Bulletin of the American*
> *Geographical and Statistical Society*

O LD GEOGRAPHICAL TEXTS are the dross of the cultural past, offering at first glance perhaps only the odd allure of archaic knowledge: of
tables of facts, maps, descriptions, and so on that quaintly do not match our
more modern, comprehensive, or precise renderings of the world. They are
ephemera, and an argument to resurrect them from the archive cannot be
based on the notion that any one text might hold a singular interest. If they are
to speak to us, they do so largely through their *generic* attributes and their expression, taken together, of the cultural mentalities that they once reflected and
shaped. This applies, I believe, even to the genre's most capable and ingenious
practitioners. The works of Jedidiah Morse, Samuel Goodrich, and Arnold
Guyot bear the stamp of individual authorship, were innovative in their own
time, and outmatched competing texts in terms of popularity. Even with these
authors, however, geographical rhetoric comes close to being sheer propaganda; we in a sense know their ideas (their bigotry and assumption of U.S.
superiority) almost without having to open their volumes. In another sense,
though, that is why early geographical texts invite inquiry: they show us the
saturation of culture, its rudiment values, and the discursive, pedagogic
mechanism behind nation-making. The geographer-pedagogues deeply influenced how antebellum citizens, or citizens-to-be, thought of themselves and
the world beyond their own town, state, and nation. Their works—more so, I
think, than July 4th speeches, newspaper editorials, or other print or oratorical
means—were a way for the nation (a nebulous entity, to be sure) to articulate

itself to itself: to read the texts of Morse, Goodrich, Guyot, or their lesser-known peers was to read about the destiny of nations and, more particularly, about the central role that the United States had in helping the world progress into futurity.

Geographical writing was a patriotic genre. It affirmed the American way, the ideology of the country harboring the forces of liberty, and therefore tended to skip over the countervailing facts of slavery, the plight of Native Americans, or the resentments of the working class. Consequently, we will find little to admire as we trace these texts' effects. But they should not be dismissed: they were the primary means by which U.S. subjects defined themselves, not just within a global context but also by virtue of that context. That is, national self-definition—the feeling of nationhood itself—required the illumination of geographical comparison. The republic lacked a shaping sense of a dense anterior history, and this formlessness was intensified by the belief in Manifest Destiny, which compelled citizens to see the nation in terms of futurity, of the country's ever dissolving and reconstituting of its borders as it advanced westward. Such flux, the nation's seeming impermanence, distressed Morse as we will see, and he succumbed in his later years to anxieties about the fate of his homeland. The second generation of geographers, however, showed more confidence about the republic's permanence as well as the science of geography itself. Goodrich and Guyot complacently located the republic vis-à-vis all other countries and regions, placing it at the apex of a geographic hierarchy that lent form to the boundlessness that so strongly haunted their predecessor.

Authoring an American Geography

In 1809, the nineteen-year-old Samuel Morse (most renowned, later, as the inventor of the telegraph) painted the *Morse Family Group* (Figure 1). In it, Samuel, his two younger brothers, and his father, Jedidiah, the most eminent early-American geographer, stand around an elegant Chippendale parlor table upon which rests a globe, with Mrs. Morse seated to the side and in front of Samuel. Jedidiah, the dominant figure, points to a spot on the globe's surface, which he elucidates in terms of the geography textbook (presumably an edition of his *American Geography*, first published in 1789) that his youngest son, Richard, has opened. Extreme symmetry structures this scene of disciplined instruction: the globe is positioned nearly in the center; two family members flank Jedidiah; and two matched, shadowy alcoves recede behind the archways. The inner circuit of congruence—the stretched-out map held by Richard; the solidity of the globe and the tactile act of Jedidiah's measuring it; Mrs. Morse's sewing scissors (a visual pun on editing)—seems intended to under-

FIG. 1. Samuel F. B. Morse, *Morse Family Group* (1809). Watercolor on paper, 12 x 15 inches. (Courtesy of the National Museum of American History, Smithsonian Institution.)

score the accurate mimesis of the geographer's practice. At the same time, the patriarch's almost self-absorbed gaze, directed neither at the globe nor the viewer, registers the inward, ratiocinative, perhaps even moral aspect of geographical science. To comprehend the world involves more than charting its lines of longitude and latitude: to envision its diversity of terrain, inhabitants, and political contours as a cohesive assemblage is to interpret the globe as another book that reveals God's providential intent.

The painting pays homage to accurate representation. It also highlights the act of pedagogic instruction, particularly conveyed by the dignified, sacerdotal posture of Jedidiah (his first calling was as a minister) and by the other family members' focus upon the globe. The absence of mementos or ornamental pieces on the mantel and the rigor of the painting's formal design, all circles and rectangles, emphasize that this is no mere family portrait. Mrs. Morse, the only family member sitting, gazes on in mute respect as the patriarch delivers a geographic sermon with his sons' assistance. With sewing basket, pin-cu-

shion, and scissors, she remains in her proper place. She does not usurp the
pedagogue-minister's role, as did Hannah Adams, an early author of American
history textbooks who accused Jedidiah of plagiarism. Jedidiah's wife is relegated to the stitching of garments, not the editing of texts about history or geography.[1] The carefully arranged ensemble (Mrs. Morse attends to the lesson,
but does not participate; the sons assist, but are subordinate to their father)
adds an important qualification to the circuit of pious intellection and accurate representation. The family encircles the table and globe and thereby links
hierarchical, domestic harmony, the mainstay of republican virtue, to the
harmony of representation. Or more, the harmony of the family protects and
isolates mimetic-moral pedagogy, for beyond the cozy circle, beyond what
Samuel Morse chooses to depict, lies the darkened, nebulous spaces of the alcoves. Here, where the geometric pattern of the carpet—echoing the globe's
lines of longitude and latitude—precipitously ends, the painting offers us only
an unfathomable negative space, uncharted and vaguely ominous.

The world beyond family, congregation, or New England indeed troubled
Samuel's father.[2] In a letter to the German geographer Christoph Ebeling,
Jedidiah confided that "to keep pace with the progress of things, in this age of
discoveries, improvements, Changes, & revolutions" becomes a "[task] from
which I shrink, when I think of [its] difficulty and magnitude."[3] The mutability of the geographer's subject matter was one problem. Another was simply
the late-Enlightenment desire for total mimesis. Morse's and Elijah Parish's
New Gazetteer of the Eastern Continent (1802), which carried entries from Aa-
benraa to Zagazig, as Parish wrote to Morse, depended on travel accounts, the
many texts of which were at once not numerous enough and too numerous for
any one compiler to collate and digest: "I have procured, read & abstracted
from about 40 volumes besides those you sent me. I have nearly exhausted my
resources. Can you obtain Moore's collection of voyages and travels?"[4] For
Morse, the world's sheer plentitude of locales, regions, and countries would
always overtax the geographer's ability to render them textually; for Ebeling,
his longtime correspondent, the very incapacity to inscribe the world was, in a
sense, what excited the geographer's desire.[5] Rebuking the critics of Morse's
geographies, Ebeling told him: "Candid judges and true connoisseurs of geographical works will allow that no geography can be equally perfect and complete in all its parts, even if it was at the moment of writing it; the continual
fluctuation of its object will antiquate it before time exercises its power."[6] A
deluge of complaints heightened Morse's insecurities. Southerners condemned his New England bias; others detected miscellaneous errors of description; and still others commented that the maps, left unmodified through
successive editions, had become almost useless.[7] One detractor, William Bentley, smugly noted that he had read some "published remarks upon Morse's

Universal Geography which expose that Geographer so fully to the World, as to lay his geographizing abilities under suspicion."⁸ The geography text, rather than exposing the world to our view, here exposes its author.

The confounding of self-identity, of the labor of production, with the world-mimetic text is a liability of any writer with encyclopedic ambitions.⁹ Morse, in a fashion typical of his contemporary republicans, placed the motive for labor upon the public, rather than as arising from himself. In a letter to Ebeling, he observed that it "was my good fortune to hit upon a popular subject, & that, rather than the merit of the Author, has brought the American Geography into public notice. My subject has insensibly and unexpectedly led me into a situation which subjects me to a burdensome responsibility. I owe my assiduous and unrelenting labours to a generous public."¹⁰ Ambivalently, Morse at once defers to his appreciative audience and chafes at being indentured to it. Morse's vexation resulted from more, however, than just the impossible chore of making his works correspond mimetically to regions in continual flux—whether in the republic itself, with its changing frontier; in European countries, where war and revolution yearly rewrote national boundaries; or in the Pacific, where new islands, it seemed, were routinely being discovered. Most immediately, his congregation complained that his geographies distracted him from his pastoral duties. The dilemma of yoking his roles as minister and geographer could be solved only occasionally, as when he gave a Thanksgiving oration, *The Present Situation of Other Nations in the World, Contrasted with Our Own* (February 19, 1795), in which he expanded upon Deuteronomy: "What a nation is there so great, that hath statutes and judgements so righteous as all this law I set before you this day." This country, so "healthful, extensive, and fruitful," he said, is "equal to the support of the largest Empire that ever existed on Earth."¹¹ When he came to composing works informed by his piety, however, Morse knew that from a strictly geographical point of view they would be deemed unorthodox. The last section ("Prospective Geography") of his primer *Elements of Geography* (1825) admits that "it has not been the custom to write geography in this form," as it goes on simply by way of quotation and summary to recap the story of the Apocalypse.¹²

No one would likely dispute the Scriptural account of the final worldwide convulsion, but it did not exactly apply to contemporary political turmoil. What made Morse's job most challenging was his wish to impose political unity upon the country and to seal it off from the encompassing world. He employed the antiquated techniques of British geographers, who relied mainly upon political lineaments; yet that method, while suited to a compact island whose boundaries were stable, was hardly capable of mapping the continually changing political contours of the republic or of the wider world be-

yond it.[13] The newer German methods emphasized natural boundaries, but
even Ebeling recognized that the techniques of the geographical avant-garde
would not satisfy everyone, which he explained in a letter written to Morse in
1811: "[The new methods] divide the world into natural divisions . . . [but
such] will not be sufficient for men of business, travellers, etc., who want also
some statistical knowledge of governments . . . their military force, laws, trade
and other political matters. . . . The daily changes in Geography destroy almost
all former maps, and there should be published maps as have no boundaries
and not names of states on them."[14] Ebeling complacently accepted what
Morse could not—either geography would encompass political and civil information, and thus be imperfect; or it would be perfect by restricting itself to
charting natural contours, and thus lose its pragmatic utility.

The ambiguity in the titles of his major works reflects the final problem
facing Morse: how to relate American to worldwide geography. The *American
Geography* signifies by its title a text devoted to describing America alone
(though even the first editions offered synopses of world geography), but it
also suggests that the world will be envisioned in a distinctively American way,
one endowed with nationalist sentiment. When four years later, in 1793, Morse
issued the *American Universal Geography*, the title equivocates even more,
highlighting his predicament: how to assert his text's unique American status
and yet also claim it to be globally mimetic, how to subtend the world to the
meaning of America when, as Washington was to say in his Farewell Address,
"[it] is our true policy to steer clear of permanent alliances with any portion of
the foreign world, so far, I mean, as we are now at liberty to do it."[15] Martin
Brückner proposes that we should see Morse's geographies, together with
other early texts such as Noah Webster's grammars, as founding documents in
the political-ideological effort to inscribe U.S. subjects within a material, national narrative: "[F]or the first time in western print history, Morse imposes a
new world order by starting with the description of the United States and the
Americas *before* delineating Europe, Africa, and Asia. . . . [He] thus invariably
asks his readers to couple the imaginary acts of self-location to the acts of geopolitical identification that have undergirded the construction of nationalism
until today."[16] Brückner rightly notes Morse's seminality, his effort to *map* the
country's revolutionary separation from the Old World. His works promoted
a feeling of national belonging, and Washington in fact praised them, believ-
ing that they would foster "a better understanding between the remote citizens
of our States."[17] Yet I would also add that Morse could not confidently relate
national self-conception to the vast and myriad world, so threateningly vola-
tile, beyond the nation's borders. His texts are U.S.-centric insofar as the
United States is the nation that descriptively comes first; but paratactic pri-

macy does not guarantee safety from ethnonational or ideological contagion from abroad.

In his later years, Morse became increasingly isolationist and xenophobic, fearful that foreign conspiracies might be mounted against the young, unstable republic. He held the mantle of being the father of American geography uneasily, perhaps mostly because he expected so much of representation, ambitiously thought that to get an American geographics right would also be to lend guiding definition to his country's future. His correspondence and his son's *Morse Family Group* reveal, if glossed in a psychopolitical manner, an anxiety often implied in early representations of the country's political or cultural Founding Fathers: to authorize the nation, here in the sense of being the first author of an American geographical text, dangerously yoked together self, authorial role, and national identity. In Samuel Morse's painting, Jedidiah stands above globe and text; he is the patriarch who, almost ritualistically, sits his family down to learn lessons about the nation's privileges and responsibilities. The world, though, could become too much; and, rather than lording himself over it or its representation, Jedidiah also found himself "shrink[ing]" (as he wrote Ebeling) when he pondered the "difficulty and magnitude" of relating to what lay beyond the nation's boundaries. The role of more assuredly negotiating the geographical meaning of the United States in global terms was left to the next generation of geographer-pedagogues. The most innovative, Samuel Goodrich and Arnold Guyot, developed geographical works whose confirmation of the republic's values depended less on the *authority* of the geographic writer or compiler than on the careful positioning of the student's scopic gaze toward racialized body types and the world's major geoforms. These textbook writers surmounted Morse's insecurities about both the status of the nation and the capacity of geographical science to instruct citizens about, as the inaugural *Bulletin of the American Geographical and Statistical Society* phrased it in 1852, "the moral and physical conditions" of the world's inhabitants.[18]

Disciplined Looking

Being the first notable American geographer made Morse keenly sensitive about his texts' deficiencies, and he became embroiled in various controversies over their originality and accuracy. When Sidney E. Morse continued the labors of his father in the 1820s, however, the flaws that had provoked Jedidiah's critics no longer seemed so objectionable. A reviewer of Sidney's *New System of Modern Geography, or a View of the Present State of the World* (1823), for instance, after pointing out that Turkey's unified status as a political entity was not reconciled to its territorial division among Europe, Asia, and Africa, blandly concluded nonetheless that "it has perhaps as few defects as ought to be expected in any production, the subject of which is perpetually changing."[19] The geographies written from the 1830s to the late 1840s were preoccupied, no less than Morse's, with patriotic national self-confirmation. Yet they were also composed by nonspecialists, usually New England pedagogues, who, unlike Morse, did not set themselves the arduous task of advancing the geographer's practice per se. They sought, rather, to develop practical techniques of class-room instruction, and collated and refashioned material without qualm from Morse's or British and European works (especially Conrad Malte-Brun's mul-tivolumed *Précis de la Géographie Universelle*, available by 1826 in a translated, American edition).[20] Historians of geographical science and American educa-tion have found these early texts to be crude in method, a hodgepodge of natu-ral history, topography, customs-and-manners description, geology and as-tronomy, and overtly moralistic political and social commentary.[21] One sum-marizes that the subject declined from "valuable abstractions and models" to "disorganized minutiae and descriptive detail," and thereby lost its appeal as an intellectual discipline in the nation's colleges.[22] Not until 1849, with the ap-pearance of Arnold Guyot's *The Earth and Man*, was an American geography authored by an academic professional; and not until 1851 was the first U.S. geographical organization, the American Geographic Society, established.

Geography may have lapsed as a coherent academic science, yet it gained a new legitimacy at the primary sites of instruction—the schoolroom, the fam-ily circle—where its capacity to instruct the juvenile citizen-to-be about America's sociohistorical relations to the world at large was all the more effica-cious. These geographies' muddledness in terms of theory does not mean that they were muddled as a cultural practice. Typically, what concerned antebel-lum geographer-pedagogues was not the puzzle that exercised Morse—how to match geographical description accurately to the world in both its natural and political dimensions—but, rather, how to instill masses of data efficiently. Systematic instruction interested them as much as developing new, scientifi-cally rigorous methods to comprehend the relations among the earth's surface forms, its flora and fauna, its inhabitants, and its political divisions. Their works, of course, were not dissociated from broader intellectual or scientific trends. Antebellum geographies bear witness to the eighteenth- to nineteenth-century epistemic shift by which relational, especially visual, taxonomies be-came fundamental to grasping the biological, zoological, and physical aspects of the globe and its history. They also, however, drew upon a repertoire of stock knowledge about race, the effects of climate, and the supposedly Western path of civilization discursively in place from at least the earlier decades of the eighteenth century.

The prefatory tags the pedagogues gave to their titles ("A New System of" or a "A Modern System of") promised not advances in geography as a scientific discipline, but rather new methods of instruction that might—all the more important because of the increasingly lucrative schoolbook trade—recommend their volumes for family and schoolroom use. Thus William Channing Woodbridge in the preface to *A System of Universal Geography, on the Principles of Comparison and Classification* (1824), for example, eschews what he thought too common in his competitors' texts, the mere amassment of "insulated facts, scarcely connected by any association but that of locality." The mingling of data about any particular country's "rivers and climate—mountains and productions—government and manners in the same page" might aptly convey the salient features to be noted within its boundaries, but this technique according to Woodbridge also obscures important relations among countries. He therefore favors, instead, separate comparative sections and charts, with each devoted to a different genre of information—zoological, topographical, and, as he puts it, the "intellectual and moral state of a country." Woodbridge here elides the gulf between empirical items (river length, say) and those having less tangible contours, but he supplies a visual aid that works to reduce the flagrant conflation of discordant categories, a "Moral and Political Chart" in which the "degree of light or shade marks" each nation's relative position. Graphic knowledge, that is, the tautological authority of the visual, enjoins immediate assent, a point Woodbridge himself implicitly makes when, drawing upon post-Lockean assumptions about the primacy of the visual sense, he alludes to the need for the "durability of impression."[23] Woodbridge unlike Jedidiah Morse's German correspondent, Christoph Ebeling, avoids speculating upon the protocols of geography as a science. More concerned about pedagogic utility than mimetic fidelity, he does not entertain questions about what geography *is*, only about how it may be taught. The burden was no longer, as with Morse, how to select appropriate descriptive items to generate an accurate representation of a country or region, but how to arrange them in a pattern calculated to impress itself readily upon the reader. And usually, the writers of geographies coming after Morse did not suffer from the latter's diffidence. In the preface to a geography designed for family use, *The World: Geographical, Historical, and Statistical* (1853), the author asserts that his volume may be relied upon as having successfully selected the most visually apt details: it will "seize upon those prominent points which should best present the characteristics of each country, and daguerreotype for the reader's eye their past and present condition."[24]

In part, geographical fluctuation did not alarm these pedagogues because improvements in print technology and the production of textbooks by major publishing houses made modifying them from year to year less expensive. If

Morse feared that mutability would antiquate any textual representation, Samuel Goodrich's family geography, *A Pictorial Geography of the World* (1840), begins by confirming that geography "has, of course, kept pace with the progress of mankind in surveying the surface of the globe."[25] Augustus Mitchell (the first to write texts sequentially tallied to educational level), in the preface to his *Geographical Reader: A System of Modern Geography* (1840), acknowledged the "recent changes" in various regions of the globe, but the guarantee of revisions "introduced as the progress of discovery and science demands" underscored that his texts would keep mimetic pace with the ever-expanding field of their attention. Revision, rather than testifying to the impossibility of making a text commensurate with the world's unfixed or newly discovered features, became itself a sign of Western "progress."[26] Evidently, moreover, the era would soon dawn when substantial revising would no longer be required. As the preface to *The World: Geographical, Historical, and Statistical* happily put it, "[T]here remains scarce a nook or corner on the entire globe which has not been penetrated, its history obtained, and its resources developed and appropriated to the service of mankind and the benefit of science."[27]

What led to Morse's misgivings, the continual gap between his texts and the "objects" of geographical flux, also less troubled antebellum geographers because eighteenth-century static models of interpretation were losing ground to more linear ones. The sense that the world was dynamically evolving and that knowledge about it was necessarily progressive replaced the idea that one might define principles eternally operative. Morse and his contemporaries believed in progress, but the latter meant less a teleological movement forward than the gradual elimination of obscuring prejudice and partial visions. The antebellum geographer's equanimity signaled, as well, a new attitude toward the growing archive of information itself. For Morse and Parish, collating innumerable travel texts in order to compose a geographical work posed a challenge both because the texts themselves might be inaccurate (being either out of date or biased) and because it was nearly impossible to absorb all the data available in them. Neither the archive nor the compiler's condensation of it could hope to compete with a ceaselessly mutable world. Several decades later, however, the archive even as it endlessly expanded could be regarded as a locus of stability. Goodrich, in "Past and Present State of the World," the last section of *The World and Its Inhabitants* (1845), concludes with a paean to "the PRESS,—the instrument by which human knowledge is recorded and disseminated." Only the press, Goodrich writes, "may reconcile us to that otherwise disheartening fluctuation, which is written on the face of all human things." He then presents us with a curious fact as he muses upon the sublime technology of paper-making: "A roll of paper a mile in length, and of any required width, may be produced. . . . The paper manufactured at a single [New England] mill in a single day, if spread out, would cover four acres and a half of ground;—ten days' work would cover Boston Common!" Here, as Goodrich complacently imagines it, the world-of-print begins to compete with the world itself, offering what seems to be an unassailable sanctum of knowledge always available for democratic circulation. The only event that would be sufficiently catastrophic to impede the press, accordingly, is one envisioned in terms of an archival holocaust: "Whatever is known is recorded in so many forms, that no event, unless it be one which is coextensive with the surface of the world, and which blots out mankind from existence, can quench its light."[28] Only an improbable global cataclysm could counter the power of the press (Goodrich's own writing in *The World and Its Inhabitants*) to replicate the world in its totality.

This confidence in mimetic fidelity helped to confirm a sense of geography's practical, social, and moral utility. In his preface to *A New Compend of Geography* (1816), John Smith states that the "diffusion of knowledge, in republican forms of government, is of vital importance."[29] Emma Willard, one of the more highly regarded educators of the period, in the preface to her *Rudiments of Geography* (1821) insists that in "none of the objects of education do I conceive that this system [of geography] is so peculiar, as in that which relates to the discipline of the mind; and none are, in my opinion, of so much importance."[30] And Mitchell in his *Geographical Reader* argues that because geography embraces "the manners and customs, the moral habits and qualities, the social combinations, and the institutions of the various communities and races of men," no other science tends so "much to enlighten and improve the mind, as well as to enlarge the understanding." Geography was an omnibus discourse, Mitchell indicated, equally suited to aid the "transactions and enterprise of the merchant and navigator," the "researcher of the philosopher," and the "exertions of the philanthropist."[31]

The geographer-pedagogues staked out the merits of their field. They seldom, however, doubted their own assumptions. The purpose of their texts was less to chart theoretical relations among the world's physical contours, climates, inhabitants, and social institutions than to create, as it were, a secondary virtual world in which troublesome questions about how climate determined racial-national character or how the latter revealed itself in historical epochs could be resolved via simple elision or abstract generalities. Geography, for them, mostly was a mnemonic tool for recalling a gamut of sociological points about places and populations. Although typically recycling traditional rubrics—savage, barbarous, semibarbarous, and civilized—used in earlier political science treatises, such as Adam Ferguson's *Essay on the History of Civil Society* (1767), their works do not (as did the latter) confront the complexity of ascertaining whether progress serially through the stages was possible for *all* races or nationalities besides white U.S. or European ones, thus making cultural advancement a temporal rather than moral matter. Instead, the stages become rigidly evaluative, with the last reserved only for the United States or European nations whose barbarous prehistories could conveniently be overlooked.[32] Samuel Goodrich's *Peter Parley's Method of Telling about Geography to Children* (1830), for instance, divides geography into three major divisions—"Natural Geography," "Civil Geography," and "Moral Geography." The latter section "treats of the conditions of society in various nations," and directs us to three engravings—depicting "savages [who] are generally poor, ignorant, and miserable"; "barbarous nations [that] have generally little humanity"; and "civilized" nations, especially the United States, that "are by far the happiest."[33]

For antebellum geographers, these broad categories of social development overlapped with racial ones, and they invariably included in their texts hierarchical synopses of what were then deemed to be the major races. The conventional divisions, established in the eighteenth century by scholarly texts such as David Hume's *Of National Characters* (1748) and popularized in later compendiums of natural history such as John Mason Good's *Book of Nature* (1831), easily withstood—and likely became more firmly entrenched by—the main ethnological debate of the period. Josiah C. Nott and George R. Gliddon in their widely read racist treatise, *Types of Mankind: or, Ethnological Researches* (1854), promoted the essentially anti-Scriptural notion of polygenesis, the multiple and geographically separate creation of racial types; but their theory of racial origin, albeit unorthodox, all the more strongly confirmed the notion of racial hierarchy.[34] The pedagogues conservatively adhered to the Bible's account of humankind's singular origin, and they uniformly skirted speculation about the precise interactions between physiognomy and environment; yet by their lights racial character seemed no less a fixture of the natural realm than the new sciences of comparative anatomy and ethnology boasted to have more rigorously determined it to be: "The human family form in fact but one species," one geographer reflected, but "custom, climate, and other circumstances or providences, have conspired to divide the human family into distinct races."[35]

All the geographer-pedagogues maintained, without going into detail, that racial features exhibited an inexorable declension as postlapsarian populations migrated farther and farther away from Eden and the supposed best racial type, Adam's perfect Caucasian form. Eden was often described, with some assurance, as being located in the mountains of Iran, but the exact history and pathways of racial declension did not need to be delved into because the results were palpable and obvious. Quite frequently, prefatory engravings of the types, usually with a picture of a Caucasian in the center, verify the racial hierarchy as plainly self-evident. Harriet Beecher Stowe's *First Geography for Children* (a little-known work, published in 1855, three years after *Uncle Tom's Cabin*), which pictorially presents a "specimen" of each type, summarily concludes for example that the "middle and best looking is [the] one of the European race" (Figure 2). Other races, she adds, can only appeal when their representatives are not representative, when Indians or Africans, for instance, "look as well as the European race excepting their dark skins." Similarly, Arnold Guyot's 1866 *Physical Geography* includes a section on "The White Race, the Normal or Typical Race," with an accompanying picture depicting the typical man "in unrivalled works of the ancient sculptures," and with the text confirming that a "comparison of the different tribes and races of men, reveals the fact of a *gradual* modification of types, on every side of the central or highest race, until by insensible degrees, the lowest or most degraded forms of humanity are reached."[36]

The facile assumption of consent manifested in these schoolbooks' racial optics can lead us to disregard them: knowing the habits of nineteenth-century racist thought, we are not likely to be surprised by their bigotry. The fact that they are not *complexly* racist, that they make critique all too easy, can obscure their cultural importance or effects. It is not the case, however, that geographical volumes merely reflected how the white majority and its ideologues saw and felt about racial hierarchies: they did not originate *new* discursive content in respect to racist thinking, but they did bring to the classroom a new mode of its transference, or rather brought into that pedagogic space new techniques of instruction that aligned geographical writing with the comparative visual schema so pervasive elsewhere in the century's scientific fields. Mitchell, Goodrich, and Guyot (whose weighty contributions to U.S. geographical teaching will require further discussion below), along with their peers, all depended upon a highly regimented use of visual data. Nineteenth-century geography, no less than the majority of natural and social sciences of the period, elaborated what Michel Foucault refers to as an ordering "spatialized" discourse:

From now on, every resemblance must be subjected to proof by comparison, that is, it will not be accepted until its identity and the series of its differences have been discovered by means of measurement with a common unit, or, more radically, by its position in an order. . . . The activity of the mind . . . will therefore no longer consist in *drawing things together* [as it did in the Renaissance], in setting out on a quest for everything that might reveal some sort of kinship, attraction, or secretly shared nature within them, but, on the contrary, in *discriminating*, that is, in establishing their identities, then the inevitability of the connections with all the successive degrees of a series.[37]

The figure above the African represents one of the Malay race. These have a brown skin, soft, curly black hair, and dark eyes. Some of them are not darker than some of the darkest-skinned people among us.

The picture of the Indian and African is like some of the worst looking of their kind, for there are some of them that look as well as the European race excepting their dark skins.

FIG. 2. Racial types in Harriet Beecher Stowe's *First Geography for Children* (Boston: Phillips, Sampson, and Co., 1855), page 175. (Courtesy of the Baldwin Library of Historical Children's Literature, University of Florida.)

The locus of power no longer was to be spied within these secretive, God-ordained interconnections, but obtained instead to the viewer's panoptical position. Although Foucault does not discuss geographical science in a sustained way in any of his volumes, his theory applies neatly to the texts at hand here, in which categorization strongly masters the unruly plurality of the world.

The hierarchical groupings of racial type that defined the non-Caucasian as heteroclite, so boldly profiled in pictures, was also naturalized by catechetical instruction. Although basic to nineteenth-century history textbooks and all-purpose primers as well, the method was especially suited to geographies because knowledge about the world and its inhabitants could be marshaled into a delimited set of questions of which there could be no exceptional answers. Colton and Fitch's *Introductory School Geography* (1856), for instance, asks "Where is [mankind] found most beautiful in form and feature?" and then immediately provides the answer, "In the mountain region [of Caucasia] between the Black and Caspian seas," thereby privileging the schoolchild's own race by decisively admitting no debate about its own normative procedures.[38] The catechetical methodology, applied across the board—to rivers, mountains, and climates; as well as to races, governments, and religions—placed social assessment on the same level as empirically surmised facts. The questions posed and answered about racial-national features arise autotelically. They emerge as absolutely authoritative, but seemingly authorless, statements about the globe's inhabitants.

Catechetical summary, "moral" comparative charts, and a biased aesthetics of racial type all served to demarcate, with radical clarity, racial and national divisions. At the same time that schoolchildren learned how they differed from the inhabitants of other, especially non-European, regions, they also learned how to conceive the republic's plurality of locales—and the particular lore of each state—as contributing to a cohesive national identity. Mitchell's *Easy Introduction to the Study of Geography* (1848), for example, presents among other engravings those of the "Landing of the Pilgrims, William Penn's Treaty with the Indians, and Pocahontas saving the life of Captain Smith." The pictures, Mitchell avers, will help "produce a [more] permanent impression" than could word-descriptions of New England, Pennsylvania, or Virginia.[39] They sacralize state stories as venerable nodal points within the more embracing, collective national narrative.

Given the desire to perceive regional locales and history as telling a nationally corporate story, representing the slave states posed, of course, something of a dilemma. The works written in the first several decades of the nineteenth century often denounce slavery in no uncertain terms, and judge the slave states to have deviated from the New England Puritan way. By the 1840s and

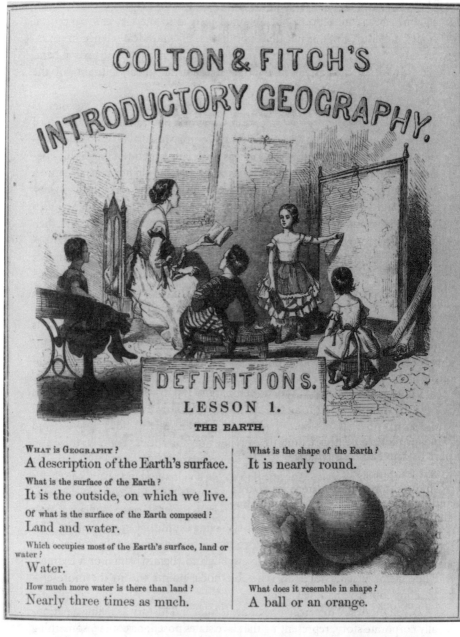

FIG. 3. Pedagogic scene in George W. Fitch and G. Woolworth Colton's *Colton and Fitch's Introductory School Geography* (New York: J. H. Colton and Co., 1856), page 1. (In the Nietz Textbook Collection, courtesy of the Special Collections Department, University of Pittsburgh Library System.)

1850s, however, New England authors recognized that, if they wished Southern educators to use their textbooks, slavery would need to be glossed over.
One convenient strategy was to condemn the slave trade but not the institution itself.[40] And in a number of the most popular texts, Colton and Fitch's
1856 *Introductory School Geography,* for example, the horrors of slavery could
be ignored altogether. Their text pays tribute to Georgia as "one of the most
flourishing of the Southern States" in its agricultural productions, and supplies a picture of a "Southern Plantation Scene," the point of which is to illustrate the South's agricultural industry, not the basis of that industry on slave
labor. (Not unexpectedly, Colton and Fitch denigrate Africans: "What of the
native inhabitants of Africa? They are generally of the negro race, and are ex-
ceedingly ignorant and degraded.")[41]

Antebellum geographers, we have seen, maximized difference in order to
intensify national self-conception. They also strove to minimize the possibility of contemplating legitimate alternatives to Protestant orthodoxy. Mitchell,
for instance, in *A General View of the World* (1859) tells us that the "remote regions" of Polynesia are "interesting," but only insofar as they have become
part of the "new Anglo-Saxon domain, whose foundations are already so
widely spread over the Pacific Ocean." Presenting "scenes of some of the most
striking moral events of the present age," that is, the conversion of idolatrous
natives, Polynesia compels attention from "all civilized nations, and especially
to those whose language, habits, and feelings, are kindred and congenial."[42] Because of these texts' nationalist chauvinism, we may safely conclude that the
ostensible intent of graphically depicting pedagogic scenes—to nominate the
subject to be studied—was not entirely innocent. These scenes serve, in fact, to
idealize the site of instruction and render images of compliant, middle-class
juveniles who should be emulated in order to maintain the republic's collective virtue (Figure 3). Stowe's geography incorporates the pedagogic site as
part of the narrative strategy of her text. A reviewer in *Putnam's Monthly* especially praised it for starting "with the town in which the learner is supposed to
live, teaching him all about the geography of that, and then advancing gradually to the country, the state, the nation, the continent, and finally the world."[43]
Before the lessons begin, Stowe presents an exemplary scenario: a "neat and
convenient" schoolhouse in which "there is a place to wash hands; and children take turns in bringing a clean roller towel every morning. O, what good
times that pleasant teacher and those obedient little children are having!"[44]

Goodrich, in *Manners and Customs of the Principal Nations of the Globe*
(1845), one of the volumes of his *Parley's Cabinet Library,* explains the connection between this bourgeois microspace and the moralized mapping of the
world's macrospaces. He notes that because of the Northern climate, New
Englanders' homes "cannot be permitted to decay, or to linger in a state of

barbarism." The "condition of society in hot countries," he adds for comparison, is one of "indolence, weakness, and raggedness": "Let a person turn round
an artificial globe, and mark the countries within the tropics, and observe that
there is not one among them all where the spirit of liberty, the light of learning,
the love of industry, the voice of piety, or the arts of refined life, pervade society—and he may then bless Providence that his lot is cast in the chill regions of
the Pilgrims."[45] Inquiry into the cultural effects of climate goes back to the
eighteenth-century French savant Montesquieu, who scrupulously (albeit still
ethnocentrically) attended to the tug of war between climate and institutions
as determining a nation's or continent's fate. In Goodrich's hands, however,
the Frenchman's nuanced calibration of the host of factors—weather, natural
law, written law, religion, political systems, and so on—that accounted for
European social superiority becomes reduced, literally, to a spin of the globe.
In the pedagogic context, geographical speculation hardens into unassailable
fact. For Goodrich, physical geography (hot or cold regions) inexorably determines national destinies, and the student is therefore enjoined to construe
the globe as a socially and morally comparative mnemonic regime. In these
examples, the Protestant home or schoolhouse, at once the site of pedagogical
instruction about the world and the sanctum of value that the pedagogic text
inscribes, becomes the privileged microspace by which all macrospaces, the
diverse countries and regions of the world, may be evaluated. Putting on display normative white bodies, whether in schoolroom scenes or in illustrations
of the racial types, these texts supplied cautionary reminders of how Americans should comport themselves in respect to a global moral-bodily economy.[46]

Racial-National Difference and the Peter Parley Conscience

In most of the geographies cited up to this point, markers of authorship are
minimal. Prefaces might foreground authorial labor or educational strategies,
and initial engravings might portray the pedagogic scene, with that scene as in
Stowe's geography being subsequently alluded to in the text proper. But the
catechetical questions-and-answers, the moral assessments of various countries and racial types, the specific descriptions of flora and fauna all emerge
autotelically, as if the textbook, rather than being authored by an individual
with a didactic intent, simply by itself reproduced the world and guided the
student's contemplation of it. With the congenial Peter Parley, Samuel Goodrich's persona, that position however becomes embodied. With the entry of
the discretely *located* pedagogue, what was elided—the subjective, moralizing
stance of the geographic compiler—becomes explicit. This embodiment entails, as well, the construction of what may be called the Peter Parley con-

science, a reluctance to endorse unqualified claims about any particular culture's alleged inferiority.

Born in Ridgefield, Connecticut, in 1793, Goodrich was the son of a Congregational minister.[47] He was largely self-educated, and as early as 1816 started a book-selling business in Hartford; it failed, but he began again in 1826 in Boston. From his Boston offices, Goodrich Enterprises, he flooded the market with educational texts under the pseudonym of Peter Parley. He wrote scores of juvenile geography and history textbooks, edited a children's miscellany, and oversaw the publication of family universal histories (including one written by Hawthorne and his sister, the *Universal History on the Basis of Geography* [1837]) and the twenty-volume family *Parley's Cabinet Library*—an encyclopedic series comprising biographies of Indians, famous women, and American benefactors; histories of Greece and Rome and modern Europe; custom-and-manners descriptions of the inhabitants of the major continents; and overviews of geology, astronomy, and geography. All told, before his death in 1860, he composed, commissioned, or edited more than a hundred volumes, with his Peter Parley series of juvenile books selling between 1825 and the Civil War some seven million copies.[48] Their popularity partially resulted from shrewd marketing, but Goodrich's astounding success also argues that how he saw the world and its inhabitants served a pedagogic need not fully satisfied by previous geographical textbooks.

What Goodrich did so well was to make geography interesting. He turned the plodding lessons of the textbooks into stories. Such would seem to diminish, by our standards, the disciplinary rigor of his works. In fact, though, Goodrich's geographical tales—although we cannot exactly say by intent—thereby reveal what modern theorists insist upon: that *all* geography or ethnography is compromised by subjectivity, that there is no "objective" space from which to observe the other, and that "objectivity" as such is really more an objectivity-effect, a strategic (whether acknowledged or not) covering up of ideological bias and agenda. Goodrich does not reflect a theoretical acuity about the Parley persona, but his works do become at times self-conscious about the grounds of their own authority.

In 1830, Goodrich published *Peter Parley's Method of Telling about Geography to Children*, revised in 1844 under the title *Parley's Geography for Beginners, at Home and School*; it sold, according to Goodrich, some two million copies. In the early 1830s he wrote, as well, geographies of specific regions—China, Africa, the Pacific Ocean, and Asia—structured as travel narratives that included landscape topography, concise manners-and-customs descriptions, and reference to major historical figures and significant buildings and monuments. These geographical tales were immensely popular, and they went through a number of editions up through the mid-1850s. What made the

Goodrich volumes unique was their Peter Parley persona, an avuncular pedagogue whose image accompanied the young reader as she or he plied through the sections or lessons of the textbook. *Peter Parley's Method of Telling about Geography to Children*, for instance, roughly proceeds as a travelogue. The first engraving shows Parley surrounded by children, and then after he announces that "I am now going to tell you of my travels," subsequent engravings (of a wharf, stagecoach, and so on) and lessons follow his itinerary through various countries.[49] Peter Parley's distinguishing physical attribute was his lameness, and the texts depict him using a set of crutches. *The Tales of Peter Parley about Asia* (1830), for example, begins with Parley saying, "Yes, here I am, alive and well, but I am more lame than I was last year. . . . But if my legs are stiff, my tongue is free."[50] The debility was a simple mimetic marker that individualized Goodrich's persona. It vouchsafed the wearying extent of his travels, made him a sympathetic figure, and indicated that, in the place of further traveling, he would now talk about his adventures. What the Parley persona constituted, then, was the opening up of an especially congenial textual space in which to speak, as his name indicates, about the multifarious world.

Crucially, that world is reproduced within the normative context of the site of instruction. Parley is a globe-hopping traveler, but the primary locus remains the hearth or schoolroom where eagerly receptive, and pliant, children listen to his tales. Certain hierarchies inform each of the Parley textbooks—the amenability of idolatrous populations to conversion, the level of a nation's industry and commerce, and, of course, the biased descriptions of racial types. And, as with the bulk of geographies designed for schoolchildren in the period, the questions appended to each chapter or section, or appearing beneath the text, routinely solicit that the student repeat the information and Parley's evaluation of it. The simplifying of the descriptive material, with a few sentences devoted to each group encountered, while necessary because Goodrich wrote his geographies for juveniles, functioned precisely to nominate foreign populations as having one or two essential qualities.

Although Parley himself is individualized, and sometimes melodramatically presented as having fallen captive to hostile natives or marauding pirates, all non-Europeans are invariably described en masse. Parley habitually collapses distinctions among tribes or groups encountered within a broad region down to one blanket appraisal. Of Polynesia, in *Peter Parley's Tales about the Islands in the Pacific Ocean* (1831), we hear that the "climate . . . is very agreeable, seeming to combine the beauties of spring and summer. The trees, fruits, and animals, are nearly the same in all. The inhabitants are very similar in complexion: almost all practice tattooing, are given to thievery, and, on common occasions, go nearly naked. There are shades of difference between them; but there is a general resemblance in their appearance, their customs, opin ions, and modes of life."[51] The economy of the geography primer demands this blurring of specifics. Yet, at the same time, the erasure of more discrete locales to highlight "general resemblance[s]" discourages impertinent questions about variegated polities, social histories, or belief systems. Abstraction works here, obviously, to render the diverse world knowable (we should not object to categorization per se); but it also serves to avert the eye from particularity. The Parley texts fashion all non-European bodies, unlike the body of the persona himself, as representative; and in that sense, individual native bodies—with, if you will, complex, human interiority or motives—do not appear at all. The native body, always generalized, always stereotypical, precludes the possibility that it might actually be seen for other purposes, for nonmonological discoveries about "difference," as Goodrich phrased it in *Peter Parley's Tales about the Islands in the Pacific Ocean.*

In these geographies, the most notable motif becomes the distinction between the beauty and bounty of the natural habitat and, by Parley's lights, the unattractiveness both morally and physiognomically of the inhabitants. Sometimes Parley assumes a causal relation between terrain and morals, but more often the dissimilitude is what most strikes him. Typically, he pauses to note the ironic disjunction between a pastoral land and its repulsive inhabitants. "This is, indeed, a land in which everything is lovely and beautiful," Goodrich writes, "except the people. These are among the most degraded of mankind."[52] In *The Tales of Peter Parley about Africa* (1830) we learn that "Nature has done everything to make" the regions of the Barbary States "one of the most charming portions of the globe. But the inhabitants are for the most part, cruel, vicious, and unprincipled."[53] Or in *The Tales of Peter Parley about Asia* we are reminded that however picturesque and fertile the countryside of China is, it is "still rather painful, than pleasant, to contemplate it. However beautiful is the aspect of nature, still, if the people of a country are degraded, by the influence of a despotic government and an idolatrous religion, that country is unhappy."[54] Such descriptions can be dismissed as being only didactic and ethnocentric, but in doing so we will ignore the two aspects that most strongly distinguish Goodrich's geographies from those of his contemporaries. First is the use of a Lockean aesthetics of visual pleasure and repulsion, a continual effort to evoke a visceral response, either "painful" or "pleasant," to the land or people being studied. And second, more surprisingly, is the countercompulsion to distrust his own ethnographical practices. Having created the Peter Parley character, Goodrich seems to have endowed him with a conflicted conscience, a voice capable of registering doubt.

In *Peter Parley's Tales about the Islands in the Pacific Ocean* he observes that the natives of one island group "live indeed almost like brutes. They have few tools, or utensils of any kind. Their warriors have spears and shields, and paint themselves in a hideous manner. There is very little to please us, in the description of these people." But then, continuing, he reverses his appraisal: "They have been represented by the English settlers, as brutal and savage to the last degree. But I am inclined to think they are not a very bad people after all."[55] Likewise, in *Peter Parley's Method of Telling about Geography to Children*, he refers to the Hottentots as being "ignorant and barbarous," "weak," and "indolent"; but then he confesses that he is "inclined to think, however, that they are a better people than they have been generally represented to be."[56] We could say that Goodrich recognizes the inadequacy of his own moral-aesthetic categorizing that produces "little to please us," or that he feels obliged to lean toward Christian liberalism, however condescending. What finally becomes apparent in the Parley geographies, though, is their author's discomfort with the almost mechanical reiteration of descriptive tags ("brutal and savage," "bad," "happy") deployed. These geographical tales oscillate between asserting difference and trying to foreshorten it. They intermittently disavow racialist judgments, producing a descriptive conscience that cuts athwart, and at times almost destabilizes, their more overt didacticism.

That conscience rebels against the assumption (in Stowe's *First Geography for Children*, among other texts) that physiognomy accurately indexes a culture's moral-political behavior. "The appearance of the people of New Guinea," Goodrich remarks, "is far from pleasing, they tie up their hair on the top of their heads, in great bunches, sometimes two feet high; they are, indeed, the ugliest people I ever saw." Again continuing, however, Goodrich confesses that his own sketch may be misrepresentative:

These people appear to have few religious notions, and they are said to be very savage and brutal, but the truth is we know but very little about them. When white men first go among savage nations, they are looked upon, and treated as enemies; sometimes the white men are killed or perhaps used very cruelly. They then go away and give a bad account of the inhabitants. Perhaps, after all, if they knew these people better, their character would appear different, and they would therefore tell a very different story about them.[57]

Because the Peter Parley persona differs from the voiceless authority behind nearly all other antebellum geographies, we might be tempted to attribute his liberal disposition merely to Goodrich himself, to his own benevolent regard for "savage," foreign cultures. We would be remiss, however, to assume that Goodrich alone was capable of seeing the demerits of U.S. culture or the merits of non-U.S. ones. There were like-minded writers of the period—Lydia Maria Child, for example—who penned juvenile tales about non-Europeans that largely escape crude ethnocentrism. Goodrich edited dozens of stories for *Peter Parley's Magazine* and *Robert Merry's Museum*, and these, although given to bourgeois sentimentality, often present non-Europeans in a favorable light.

An 1847 issue of the latter, for example, carried a seventeen-page redacted version of Melville's *Typee* (1846) that did not feature the natives as being only cannibalistic savages.[58] Nonetheless, the very popularity of Goodrich's geographies argues that the liberal-minded Peter Parley in fact embodied, Goodrich's intent aside, a singularly compelling subject-position, one nicely coordinate with the goals of the teachers or parents who used his texts to instruct children.

It was compelling, we may conjecture, because if the Peter Parley persona seems to open up a discursive space in which a "different story" about non-Europeans might be told, the profile of that story nonetheless does not emerge. Instead, typically, the space quickly closes, and Goodrich retreats to a vision of the world transformed by Christian philanthropy. In *The Tales of Peter Parley about Africa*, for example, after lamenting that "for the purposes of providing some excuse, for the barbarous and cruel treatment of the Negroes, the Europeans have been accustomed to misrepresent their character," Goodrich deflects detailed inquiry away from, say, the horrors of plantation life, and instead offers a generalized appeal to conscience: "How much more delightful would it be, to see all christian people united with heart and hand, to spread the light of education, and religious knowledge, among the unfortunate millions of Africa, rather than to send people to drive away the inhabitants, by violence and treachery, and their attempt to excuse this mean and dastardly conduct, by representing them as brutes, rather than as men."[59] Goodrich's motives can be deemed laudable, but his vague, utopic injunction, which forestalls change to an indefinite future, blunts his abolitionist zeal. The liberal Christian gaze, although it entails a critique of scopic, stereotypical looking, cannot quite void racist denigrations of their graphic, suasive power. Goodrich makes a political or evangelical point of global magnitude yet the text nowhere proffers a specific instance of seeing Africans as discrete or dignified "men."

Such formulations, as postcolonial theorist Abdul R. JanMohamed proposes, are essentially "specular." Instead of difference enabling what he calls "syncretic possibility," it here becomes only a "mirror that reflects" the first-world culture's high self-regard.[60] What Goodrich ultimately means by a "different story" may be clarified by turning to the musings of his brother, Charles, in the conclusion of *The Universal Traveller* (1838). He ends his travel compendium with a glance backward to the preceding chapter on Africa, and then exhorts Christians to more energetically advance the "Redeemer's kingdom":

The land of freedom, science, and religion!—shall America be wanting in efforts to diffuse abroad these blessings, which she so universally enjoys, and which she so highly prizes? May the day come . . . when every vessel from her coast shall carry the missionaries of the cross to publish the glad tidings of salvation on pagan shores. . . . May that day come; and when it shall have come, how different a story will the traveller tell, when he shall return, as we now return from our long wanderings to our own land. What is dark and dreary in our pages will in his be bright and beautiful. He will have the pleasure to record a truth, which we have not yet found:

We expect the "truth" to follow upon the colon. Instead, the text ends here; or not quite, for intervening between the colon and the last, centered word of *The Universal Traveller*, "END," are several inches of blank space.[61] This oddity of an anticipatory colon without any text following might be a typographical accident; but the syncope seems to invite the reader to supply, from his or her own conscience, the "truth" that the text itself omits. In the context of the previous African chapter and the reference to "dark and dreary" pages, the portended "truth," which the reader must fill in as he or she scans the page's remaining blank space, seems to be one in which racial difference will no longer be an issue for conscientious representation, because Protestant, Anglo-Saxon piety and, implicitly, Protestant, Anglo-Saxon customs will have been spread over the face of the globe. The blank space represents the nonrepresentable homogeneity of a future "truth," by which all present racial-national differences will disappear and the foreign, now the same, will proffer a perfect mirror "bright and beautiful" for the Christian conscience to see its own effects. Goodrich's texts, by foregrounding the Parley character, obliged the student to see through his eyes. Still, even if the narratives told at times betray a certain uneasiness with the authority of the geographer-observer, what they ultimately reveal is a social-moral optic in which agency resides only in the spectator, never in the seemingly barbarous or dolorous realms elsewhere.

Panorama and Physiography in Arnold Guyot's *The Earth and Man*

The geographies thus far focused upon achieving definite ideological ends as they survey the world's diversity. They instill orthodox values by passing judgment on the heterodoxy of other, especially non-Western, peoples and regions. Totalizing claims about a society's degraded state might, as we saw with Goodrich, momentarily become destabilized by the liberal voice of conscience, although even then the problem of racial-national difference, of telling a "different story," is elided by resorting to utopic imaginings of global conversion, whereby difference everywhere promises to become Protestant sameness. Goodrich and the other pedagogues devised, in sum, a set of techniques (the aesthetics of race, for example) that reinforced white, Protestant norms and ensured that all non-European cultures would be perceived as being, in varying degrees, heteroclite. Their works construed the world and its cultures in a nationally self-confirming manner by evading more precise, vexing questions about how the physical features of the globe related to the moral, cultural dimensions of the communities inhabiting it.

When it came to more sustained description (avoided by necessity in primers) in family or adult volumes, however, the attentive reader might have detected that antebellum geographical practice bordered on the inchoate. Evaluations could be made, but their basis was ever shifting. Take, for instance, a typical passage in Goodrich's full-scale *Pictorial Geography of the World*, published in 1840:

> The color of the *Hottentots* is a yellow-brown, and their formation is peculiar. . . . To European eyes, the women are objects of horror; lean and gaunt, except over the hips, where all the flesh seems to be piled. A Venus, drawn from the Hottentot model, would have little resemblance to that of Florence. . . . The language of the Hottentots, is harsh and shrill. Their dwellings are rude. . . . The Hottentots, who have been called a stupid race, seem to be so, only from their oppressed condition; they are gentle, and faithful, when trusted. They are filthy in their persons, and indolent in their habits, but they make good servants to the Boors, who have many of them as slaves, or attendants.[62]

Here, virtually every statement, whether pertaining to anatomy or cultural habit, initially seems to self-sufficiently encapsulate the Hottentot character; yet each remark receives qualification or is corrected as being a misperceived and superficial estimate. First, we learn that the Hottentots have a "peculiar" appearance, but is the framing perspective of "European eyes" and the oblique citation to George Cuvier's description of the so-called Hottentot Venus intended to be taken as authoritative, biased, or merely droll?[63] The Hottentots' "peculiar" physiognomy, together with their repugnant speech, would appear to be the exterior traits that warrant the abstraction—they are a "stupid race." That appraisal, however, is made only tentatively; and it is equivocally designated as being the result of their "oppressed condition," which may be interpreted as referring either to their enslavement or to their precolonized natural state, before their apparently innate tendency to "indolence" had been countered by the Boers, who made them into "good servants." Only the reader who read, as it were, in slow motion might have discerned the paratactic gaps of Goodrich's text or the confused manner in which history (that is, colonialism) erupts into the otherwise smooth flow of visual data, and then further reflected that a less than clear portrait of the Hottentots had been offered for contemplation.[64]

The passage's vacillations echo the ethnographic flip-flops in Goodrich's primers, and bring to light that if ethnography and geography seemed compatible sciences, linked together by a scopic preoccupation with race, the two also could be at odds. As an emergent discipline, ethnography during this time period had not yet fully disencumbered itself from the humanitarian impulses of liberal Christianity. Christian sentiment deemed the "native" as a fit subject for conversion, less intrinsically inferior than stunted by (to modify Goodrich's phrase above) oppressive conditions. Although geography textbooks collapsed regions and peoples into racial types (*the* Polynesian, *the* African, and so on), fusing geobodies to generic racial bodies, the sociological aspects of geographical writing obliged some degree of reflection upon determinative circumstances, which especially in the case of Goodrich came close to disrupting simple equations between the visuality of racial feature and a population's cultural attributes. Although the terms were not yet in currency, we may say that as ethnography (the study of particular cultures) shaded into, or was taken to exemplify, ethnology (the general theories of race or humankind's cultural history), the latter was increasingly coming to harden the racist absolutism of the former. What repulses Peter Parley, pigmentation and other markers of race, during the 1850s lost their potential uncertainty and instead became infallible signs of intrinsic racial differences that seemingly were in place from the beginning of time. The American polygenesists whom I alluded to earlier argued that the major races did not evolve over time or devolve from Adam's perfect Caucasian form but were caused by the original, separate creation of racially distinct peoples. The notion did not take full hold on anthropological theory in the United States, but it and other emphases on racially innate, as opposed to geographical (which is to say, accidental), features increasingly displaced the more liberal tendency of Goodrich and like-minded pedagogues to fluctuate between sociological sentimentality and the bigoted aesthetics of racial typology.

I do not intend my previous comments to suggest that Goodrich or other antebellum authors of geographical books were deeply anxious about their discipline in the manner that Jedidiah Morse was. The tensions I have been addressing are more submerged than directly apparent. But the consequent disjointedness of which Goodrich's *Pictorial Geography of the World* gives us an example, although not disturbing to most readers, did irk pedagogues such as Woodbridge, who dismissed texts that forced the student to contemplate mere "insulated facts." A more regimented, comparative approach was needed, one that might reconcile the potential disparities among the sociological, racial, and topographical aspects of geography writing.

Not surprisingly, then, educators extolled the more holistic method employed by Arnold Guyot in his *The Earth and Man*, a text that swept the field, easily becoming the most popular geographical work of the next three or four decades. Guyot, born and educated in Europe, was more cosmopolitan than Goodrich and the other U.S. geographer-pedagogues. He taught in Paris from 1835 to 1839 and became a professor of history and physical geography at the Neuchâtel Academy in Switzerland in 1839. When the academy closed in 1848, because of revolutionary upheaval, he immigrated to the United States under the urging of Louis Agassiz, the famed naturalist-geologist. Sponsored by Agassiz, he offered a series of lectures, in French, at Boston's Lowell Institute in 1849. They were then printed the same year, after being translated, in the *Boston Daily Traveller*, and finally appeared after more editing in full-title as *The Earth and Man: Lectures on Comparative Physical Geography, in its Relation to the History of Mankind*. Guyot's text established him as the pre-eminent American in his field. For five years he lectured on geographical methodology at the Massachusetts Teachers' Institutes, and starting in 1854 until his death in 1884 he held the chair of physical geography and geology at Princeton. In the late 1860s, he began the *Guyot Geographic Series* of primers, all of which went through multiple editions; one was even translated into the Dakota language.[65] In the words of James D. Dana, writing in 1886, he became "though European in equipment, an American in his labors."[66]

The first edition of *The Earth and Man* included encomiums by sundry luminaries of the day, who praised it for its seemingly seamless yoking of the natural, political, and moral dimensions of the world. George Ticknor found the lectures an "excellent foundation for the study of all geography as it is now taught, and especially of that higher geography which connects itself with the destinies of the whole human race." Charles Sumner saw it as making a trio with Alexander von Humboldt's much-famed *Cosmos* (which appeared in its first American edition in 1850) and Mary Somerville's *Physical Geography* (the best-selling geography before 1860 in Britain, and frequently used in American schools), which together have interpreted "the past fortunes of mankind, and . . . the grander destinies which are their inheritance on earth."[67] The volume was noteworthy enough for *Putnam's Monthly* six years later to laud Guyot as one of the "order of sound popular writers," along with Humboldt and Charles Lyell, who have "placed themselves between the public and the closets of the philosophers."[68]

Guyot was, in the main, less an original thinker than a conduit of ideas already proposed by Humboldt, Carl Ritter, and Agassiz in the natural sciences, and by G. W. Hegel in the philosophy of history. He had studied under Ritter and Humboldt at the University of Berlin and adapted their teachings to come up with what seemed to be a thorough and novel explanation of how the regions of the earth had a primary agency in determining human history. From Ritter, he developed and fine-tuned the notion of the causative role of the globe's massive dynamics, especially the effects of weather and physical contour; and from Humboldt, he took the idea of an all-encompassing, vital organic unity displayed in the various strata of nature, from particular organisms to the cosmos itself, and applied it to the earth's major geoforms.[69]

Humboldt's forte was the detection of harmony in nature not as a static

condition but as an evolving mechanism. Increasing diversity, for him, led not
to chaos but to superior forms of complex unity, to universal perfection. This
unfolding natural-historical telos, although directed by a providential hand,
could be understood simply as how Nature worked (the capital is needed to
convey the sense of self-agency).[70] Guyot took Humboldt's ideas a step further,
applying them to inanimate geobodies. He transferred by analogy what could
be seen in the vegetable and animal realms, the progression upward to more
elaborate anatomies, to the vastness of the entire globe. Different continents
have distinct physical contours, some simple and some complex, and each is
eminently suited by virtue of its physical character, he argued, to play a role in
the worldwide drama of civilization's advancement.

The readers of Guyot's volume, however, did not need to pull tomes of
German metaphysics from the shelf to grasp its points. It is not philosophically abstruse; instead it weds grand abstractions to empirical observation and
the conventional U.S. pieties of the day: that the physical world was morally
revelatory; that civilization advanced as it passed from the East, to Europe, and
then on to America; and that Providence intended for U.S. Anglo-Saxons the
spotlight role in ushering the world toward the Millennium. For Guyot, the
lessons of natural history, history proper, and metaphysics all combined to
show that geographical forces operate morally: the world itself is visionary.

The Earth and Man differs in format from the previously analyzed geographies, both because it was composed as a series of lectures for adults and because of its Hegelian predilection for charting an evolving metaphysical telos.
Guyot, in fact, deplores the geographical practice of immersing the reader in a
plenitude of referential detail. He denigrates "mere description" and the habit
of "partial observations" that results in little more than a "barren confusion"
(3). Rather, proceeding through a sequence of panoramic overviews, his text
solicits the student to relate natural fact to natural processes and, in turn, the
latter to their sociological ramifications. For Guyot, the job of the astute ob-
server of the global mechanism is to avoid compartmentalizing what might be
known about it, to see instead all of its components—landmasses, weather
patterns, distribution of races, governmental forms—as a magnificent, interrelated ensemble.

Oftentimes, the rhetorical effect is the text's continual spinning out of vast
webs of sheer interconnectedness, as in this abbreviated instance: "[We
should] seize those incessant mutual actions of the different portions of physical nature upon each other, of inorganic nature upon organized beings, upon
man in particular, and upon the successive development of human societies"
(3). This Humboldt-like or Hegel-like push toward synthesis is premised
upon a trope that enables the book's basic argument: the anthropomorphizing
of particular global areas and how they work in tandem. Each major landmass,

although nonsentient, exhibits a discrete "assemblage of physical characters and functions" that "really give[s] it something of individuality" (7). The geographer's task, accordingly, is to analyze how this ensemble—climate, coastal contours, type of mountain ranges and extent of plateaus, and so on—collectively defines the overall profile of any particular continent or region; and then, in turn, to show how these major landmasses interact to create "what might be called the life of the globe . . . its physiology" (3).

Conceiving the entirety of the globe as a *living* mass had two consequences that likely explains why *The Earth and Man* became the best-selling geography textbook of its era. Its emphasis on functional analysis (as opposed to itemized description) justifies the willingness of modern geographers to accept Guyot as a legitimate forefather in their field. They have, however, misread the true import of Guyot's functionalism, for, in fact, he was not solely an empiricist. He scorned science that did not transcend its materialist base; his volume insists that truly grasping this global physiology as an ordered totality entails more than tallying up surface phenomena. Although global interactions drive humankind's destiny, they cannot be divorced from a supreme intelligence who directs them and who indeed deploys the earth as a sort of macrotext for inscribing moral lessons. Just as bodies are spiritually animated, so too is the globe itself, obliging the student therefore to "elevate" him- or herself "to the moral world to understand the physical world" (11). Geography, in Guyot's reckoning of it, becomes a spiritual as much as physical science. The key notion that the globe's diverse parts corporately interact also, though, justified a less benign idea: to look upon the globe as an ordered whole moving teleologically forward allowed him to scorn what he took to be its debilitating, inferior parts (unfortunate climates, unfortunate races) or to argue for the proper subordination of those parts to more superior ones (the civilizations in temperate climates).

Guyot devotes the first third of *The Earth and Man* to examining the continental forms as "the anatomist would examine the body of an animal," and the next third to seeing "these great organs in operation . . . acting and reacting upon each other" (71). The final lectures trace how geographical features affect those of the world's cultures and how those cultures have, over the epochs, influenced each other. The detailed lessons advanced in each lecture need not be reviewed, but several of Guyot's conclusions along the way warrant consideration. Drawing upon analogies from animal life, which demonstrate complexity to be the "condition . . . of a richer life, of a completer growth for the animal," he asserts that in respect to both continents and their inhabitants "homogeneousness, uniformity, is the elementary state, the savage state" (76). Europe, for instance, exhibits a highly variegated coastline, an intermingling of sea and land. Its complexity of contour, Guyot maintains, encourages trade, which in turn results in an "exchange of thoughts" (77) and thus a more diversified and complex citizenry. Africa, on the other hand, "is far the most simple in its forms." Its mass, "nearly round or ellipsoidal, is concentrated upon itself. It projects into the ocean no important peninsula, nor any where lets into its bosom the waters of the ocean. It seems to close itself against every influence from without" (27). The moral lesson of coastal contour then follows. The consequence for Africans of Africa's physiographic structure, Guyot remarks, is inevitable: "Unhappy [is] he who . . . refuses to enter into those relations of intercourse with others which assure to him a superior life. He deprives himself voluntarily of the nutritive sap intended to give him vigor, and like a branch torn from the vine, dries up and perishes in his egoism" (78).

Conveniently enough, *The Earth and Man*'s account of how the major landmasses' physical contours correlated with, and caused, racial-national difference matched the older notion of racial declension, of deviation away from Adam's flawless form. One passage, alluding to an accompanying illustration, will suffice to convey the tenor of Guyot's taxonomy of racial types and his theory of their global dispersion:

Let us take for a type of the central region of Western Asia, this head of a Caucasian. What strikes us immediately is the regularity of the features, the grace of the lines, the perfect harmony of all the figure. . . . Such is the type of the white race—the Caucasian, as it has been agreed to call it—the most pure, the most perfect type of humanity.

In proportion as we depart from the geographical centre of the races of man, the regularity diminishes, the harmony of proportions disappears. . . . On the [western] . . . coast of Africa, more remote from Asia, the degeneracy of form is still more rapid. The Berbers of the Atlas still evidently belong to the Caucasian race; but their prolonged head, a tendency in the mouth to pouting, the spare and meagre forms, a deeper color, already herald a marked degeneration. The Fellatahs of Soudan, and still more the inhabitants of Senegal, bring us to the pure type of the Congo negro. In the latter, the retreating forehead, the prominent mouth, the thick lips, the flat nose, the woolly head, the strongly developed hind-head, announce the preponderance of the sensual and physical appetites over the nobler faculties of the intellect. At the extremity of Africa, the miserable Bushmen are still lower than the Hottentots; and, placed by the side of the Caucasian, make us see the immense distance which separates them. (232–38)

Guyot here couples anatomical, aesthetic, and moral evaluations to confirm what he takes to be the stark declension of African societies as they inhabit territories farther and farther from the originary locale of Creation. Africa embodies the nadir of social being, but in *The Earth and Man* all non-European regions, whether Polynesia, the Near East, Asia, or tropical America, also show inferiority in their racial-geographical contours. Reading the globe anatomically, whereby racial physiography metonymically stands in for entire cultures, the student of geography—in fact, in the above passage, a student of comparative anatomy or ethnology—in essence repeats the lesson of the more strictly juvenile geographies of Goodrich: some cultures are "painful" to contemplate visually.

According to Guyot, we have seen, geography constrains the social advance of non-Europeans. His theory even managed to account for what cruder theories of climate could not: anomalies such as the mature civilizations that had emerged in non-Northern regions. Some locations, through Guyot's deft geographical sleight of hand, turn out to be nonidentical with themselves: "The ancient civilization of the Quichuas, at the summits of the Andes of Peru, scarcely seems itself indigenous to South America. It belongs elsewhere by its elevated position; it belongs to the temperate zone" (240). The felicity of being an American, however, is to occupy *the* privileged "temperate" land that paradoxically determines national character by not determining it. The most striking attribute of the "nation which is forming on the soil of America," he asserts, is its "greater emancipation from the dominion of nature":

Man, the master, now explores [the New World's] vast territory. . . . The American uses things without allowing himself to be taken captive by them. We behold everywhere the free will of man overmastering nature, which has lost the power of stamping him with a local character, of separating the nation into distinct peoples. Local country, which has so great sway in the Old World, no longer exists, so to speak, beyond the limits of the city, itself an association determined by man's free will, and not by the force of external nature. The great social country wins all interest, and all affection; it overmatches entirely geographical country. (300–301)

Guyot, heir to Hegel and other late-Enlightenment thinkers, reads history as the process of escaping the binding perspectives of local place and circumstance. U.S. citizens, he concludes in his last section, need to help liberate from bondage those inhabitants of countries where geography still stamps, and delimits, their character. In "this way, alone, will the inferior races be able to come forth from the state of torpor and debasement into which they are plunged, and live the active life of the higher races" (307). If U.S. citizens willingly undertake the mission that their exceptional geographical location prepares them for, Guyot rhapsodizes, the "whole world" (307) will "appear as a sublime concert of nature and the nations, blending their voices into a lofty harmony in praise of the Creator" (308).

The Earth and Man was reprinted in yearly editions up to 1854, with only minor revisions, and intermittently thereafter, up to the 1890s, when it was still considered an authoritative, standard text. Its currency late in the century, when its effusive piety was somewhat outdated, can be explained by its comporting with imperialist thought and the interest in vast historical teleologies. (Brooks Adams in *The New Empire* [1902] explained, for instance, that "geographical conditions have exercised a great, possibly a preponderating, influence over man's destiny.")[71] Its popularity, we may conjecture, was largely based upon the sustained use of panoramic description, which elevated one's view, it seemed, to a godly perspective. Geography, as Guyot conceived it, allowed one to "embrace with a glance" the "past and future destinies of the nations" as "traced in ineffaceable characters by the finger of Him who governs the world" (16–17). His text surmounted what he believed to be the "barren confusion" of paratactic description by enjoining the reader to see the world and its inhabitants in successively more lofty panoramic arcs. At the same time, he grounded his pious and philosophical reflections in the solidity of empirical evidence. Here were no transcendental, vaporous musings, but the keen observations of a scientist who surveyed the actual earth. Here rigorous science, as in the case of Guyot's public lecture series in New York in 1852, which seemed to square geological theory to biblical cosmology, became the handmaiden of piety.[72] If geography was always good theater for the nation to see itself advantageously, Guyot made it a more sublime spectacle. The secrets of providential history appeared to be divulged in the very contours and interactions of the globe's regions.

Antebellum geography insisted upon the scopic as the means by which the non-European could most legitimately be understood. In this respect Guyot's *The Earth and Man* did not differ much from the works of his less professional contemporaries, Goodrich, Stowe, Mitchell, and the rest. They all equally disallowed the possibility of a more dialogical interpretive mode or attitude, one not shut off from the potential for perceptions of the foreign to destabilize bourgeois Protestant cultural norms—in the case of Guyot, because his text promised to elevate the reader to a position scopically mastering the totality of the globe itself; and in the case of Goodrich and the others, because graphic tautology (the visceral assent given to the visual) on the one hand, and descriptive disjointedness on the other, regardless of whether such was noted at the time, kept the reader from becoming immersed within the dense materiality of non-European lands or peoples.

The habits of the scopic gaze may be endemic to all geographical or anthropological writing, of whatever period, but the visual taxonomies so pervasive in the works of Guyot and the other pedagogues were, as I proposed earlier when I alluded to Foucault, part and parcel of one predominant mode of knowledge in the nineteenth century: the systematic hierarchies that fused together sociological "fact" and racial optics. The hierarchies could take many forms: juxtaposing racial types in anatomy or ethnological texts, seeing cultures ranked in a progressive continuum in museum exhibits, and, of course, evaluating "civilized," "barbarous," and "savage" lands in geographical volumes. Although in terms of their nationally chauvinistic theatrics, the geo-

graphical textbooks examined in this chapter are not dissimilar to those written in Britain or Europe, they also arguably held a more essential role in helping citizens position themselves against other, non-European peoples and
places. In England the citizen, whether rural worker or metropolitan aesthete,
knew that he or she was living in the nation-as-center from whence empire
extended outward. In the United States, because of democratic mobility, there
were less stable affiliations to locale and class; and, of equal importance, there
was no center, for either Washington or other cities or the frontier might be
deemed the motor-force driving the republic's ongoing history. For Alexis de
Tocqueville, democracy's solvent ethos was not an unmixed blessing: for "it
throws [the citizen] back forever upon himself alone, and threatens in the end
to confine him entirely within the solitude of his own heart."[73] Antebellum
geographical textbooks, though, transmuted this "solitude" into a grandiose
national self-regard, accomplishing what could not be done by the actual
geospatial coordinates of the republic: to stand citizen and nation at stage
center, playing the lead, in the theater of world events.

Guyot's volume remained influential until the end of the nineteenth century because its geographic gaze abstracted away from the impurities of local
history and description. Void of the detail that we have noted in Goodrich's
adult geography, nor concerned to itemize the "Changes" and "revolutions"
that so threatened the mimetic practice of Morse, *The Earth and Man* enjoyed
a fame that the latter's texts only had, briefly, by virtue of inaugurating an
"American" geographics. The fear that geographical writing would become
outdated almost as soon as it saw print plagued Morse, but what would have
dismayed him perhaps even more is how what he believed to be an essential
discipline for educating future citizens has lapsed, two centuries later, into a
nearly defunct subject. Spatial studies (a field comprising, among other disciplines, literary analysis of travel texts, eco-criticism, urban sociology, architecture, and geography proper) has become a new vehicle in the academy to
cross parochial lines and to posit new modes of historical and contemporary
inquiry, and my study falls within its interdisciplinary orbit. Yet geography
per se, regardless of whether it might muster enthusiasm among students, has
largely been dropped from the curriculum of most schoolchildren: in ad hoc
tests, according to routine news reports, students typically fail most miserably
when it comes to knowing basic geographical facts. So, if we were to assess geography's appeal today, we would have to say that it is very interesting on the
level of theory but exceptionally dreary on the level of pedagogy. (I have, of
course, left out of the picture the enduring popularity of the *National Geographic* magazine, copies of which may be found piling up on television-room
bookshelves across the country. The magazine caters to a touristic-minded
audience: the articles and glossy photos are browsed for their vibrant depic-

tion of non-Europeans, who from month to month change, as it were, color and locale. But each issue of the journal—as it is shelved beside copies of last month's, or last year's, or last decade's issues—quickly, like old geography textbooks, also becomes cultural ephemera.)[74]

There are, no doubt, a number of sociological factors behind geography's decline as a routinely taught subject in grade school or high school, at least in the fashion that this chapter has charted. Travel magazines, television, and, more recently, the Internet: all perhaps have subsumed the function of the geography primer, although plainly such media have not lessened the ignorance of the average citizen in respect to the world about him or her. Several other reasons can be proffered. The sheer complexity of ethnic and national alignments, following the reshuffling of boundaries during imperialism's heyday, and, conversely, the reduction of such complexity (seemingly) during the Cold War, when the world was either "Red" or not, made the classic hierarchical divisions, of both races and continents, a less viable mode of geographic instruction. Less easy to trace is the gradual loss of cultural power that adhered to tropes of the body politic, which made race, nation, and citizen virtual synonyms. We still require, in subtle and not so subtle ways, confirmations of how the United States differs from elsewhere. "Our" culture—it is, of course, not singular—still relies upon sundry modes of othering, whether in the form for instance of anti-Muslim news reports, resurgent nativist/anti-immigrationist movements, or shocking but never lingering focuses on African political problems (the other is there, but not deserving sustained meditation or mediation). Yet given a consensus, more or less at least, among most U.S. subjects that the American way *has been* the right way, we no longer depend upon the celebrations of national identity that nineteenth-century geography textbooks typically supplied. Having done its tasks, geographic pedagogy (I do not speak of revisionist geographical theory, still mostly the province of university teaching and research) is no longer needed.

CHAPTER TWO

"Precepts Graven on Every Breast"

Melville's 'Typee,' Polynesia, and the Forms of the Law

> The lawyer and the anthropologist, the both of them connoisseurs of cases in point, cognoscenti of matters at hand, are in the same position. It is their elective affinity that keeps them apart.
> —Clifford Geertz, *Local Knowledge: Further Essays in Interpretive Anthropology*

> The Chief Justice! We contemplate him as the East Indian does his wooden-headed idol,—he knows that he is ugly, but he feels that he is great.
> —Rufus Choate on Judge Lemuel Shaw

> Here speaketh the conscience of the State restraining the individual will.
> —Entryway inscription, Massachusetts State Courthouse

THIS AND the next two chapters study U.S. travelers whose encounters with the non-European world extend beyond the abstractions of the geographical gaze. Their works more conflictedly stage U.S. national narratives or ideologies: specularity, the aesthetics of race or the globe, gives way to more vexed somatic reactions; and immersion in a foreign locale, in turn, complicates the articulation of nationally self-serving agendas. In these texts the scopic drive—Herman Melville's fixation on Polynesian bodily marks, Ephraim G. Squier's quest for the archaeological sublime in the ruins of Central America, and the desire of a variety of Holy Land travelers to see signs of the numinous—will be apparent, but that drive will also find itself linked to other, more unsettling confrontations or exchanges between the U.S. subject and non-European realms. Both authorial self-fashioning and the fashioning of U.S. national topoi, in the absence of the lofty geographic gaze, are enabled through the reporting of travels elsewhere; yet what gets told—about the law (via Polynesia), the religiously luminous (via the Holy Land), or archaeological inquiry (via the tropical New World)—hazards the potential for ideological impasse as much as consolation. As I suggested in my introduction, the indigenous cultures per se will rarely be seen *an sich*: we will not discover a strong give-and-take of human relations when borders are crossed. Nonetheless, the authors appearing in the following chapters tell stories, as they travel through foreign domains, that are both nationally inflected and shaped by the specific regions that they describe. In varying degrees of interest or repulsion, they cathect with the materiality of the foreign, whether relics, monuments, topographies, or the bodies of the inhabitants themselves.

I begin with Melville's *Typee: A Peep at Polynesian Life* in part because of its familiarity and in part because, as the most narratively self-reflexive and yet also ethnographically oriented work in this study, it usefully foregrounds the *constructedness* of the non-European, that is, the tension between representation and what lies behind it. The most recent scholarship on the text emphasizes not just its anti-imperial stance but, as well, how it sees through or stages imperialistic mimesis.[1] If it peeps at exotic Polynesians, it does so self-consciously, highlighting the limits of what the Western viewer can know about them. In my reading, however, those limits will pertain less to Melville's intent to critique colonialist, imperialist modes of looking than to his sense, which preludes the gnostic ambivalence of his later works, that even sympathetic ethnography cannot penetrate the barriers of cultural difference. Melville's skepticism does not make him a voice of *our* worries about ethnography (to present him as being postcolonial would be anachronistic), but it does lead him or his narrator Tommo to enter provisionally and with a degree of ideological risk into the density of the foreign tribe, the Typees, that he describes. Such does not mean that he crosses over, in other than physical terms, to their culture. It does mean, though, that the materiality of that culture—bodily marks, rituals, and so on—takes on a resistant thickness, a nonabstract reality, especially at those moments when narrator or author are most concerned to explicate the tribe for the book's readers. Paradoxically, in *Typee*, the natives will be most real when they are least understood.

A comparison will help clarify these initial points about *Typee*'s geoenthographic optics. In her *First Geography for Children* (published in 1855, nine years after Melville's novel), Harriet Beecher Stowe bluntly directs us to an engraving of island natives accompanying her text: "[Here] is a picture of a chief of one of the islands of Polynesia, with his chief men around him. You see how stupid and brutal they look" (Figure 4).[2] Tommo's thumbnail sketch of his Typee valley companion, Kory-Kory, although obviously less dismissive, could also be said to place the Polynesian native under the dominating gaze of the Western viewer:[3]

FIG. 4. Polynesians in Harriet Beecher Stowe's *First Geography for Children* (Boston: Phillips, Sampson and Co., 1855), page 163. (Courtesy of the Baldwin Library of Historical Children's Literature, University of Florida.)

[Kory-Kory] had seen fit to embellish his face with three broad longitudinal stripes of tattooing, which, like those country roads that go straight forward in defiance of all obstacles, crossed his nasal organ, descended into the hollow of his eyes, and even skirted the borders of his mouth. . . . His countenance thus triply hooped, as it were, with tattooing, always reminded me of those unhappy wretches whom I have sometimes observed gazing out sentimentally from behind the grated bars of a prison window; whilst the entire body of my savage valet, covered all over with representations of birds and fishes, and a variety of most unaccountable-looking creatures, suggested to me the idea of a pictorial museum of natural history, or an illustrated copy of 'Goldsmith's Animated Nature.'

Statically framed as a "Portrait of Kory-Kory" and concluding with the allusion to Oliver Goldsmith's compendium, the passage secures Kory-Kory within the knowledge apparatus of Western textuality, offering him as a natural specimen for our scopic pleasure. To reduce the sketch, or the book from which it comes, to a straightforward example of othering, however, will not quite do it justice. In the previous chapter, I suggested that Samuel Goodrich's embodied persona, Peter Parley, began to complicate the ethnocentric hierarchies of geographical discourse by introducing an element of authorial subjectivity. Yet that subjectivity, the voice of tolerant or liberal conscience, ultimately did not destabilize his own texts' privileging of Western or U.S. bourgeois practices and spaces. With Melville's *Typee* I turn to a work that, although filtered through a semifictional persona, nonetheless represents a genuine cross-cultural encounter. That encounter as told in Melville's travel novel may, in the final analysis, be rhetorically self-serving, with the Typees for Melville becoming less interesting in their own right than in their capacity to provide a mirror by which he can critique U.S. cultural norms. The Typees as given in the text do not, however, thereby become merely spectral: the materiality of their social practices holds a purchase on its ideological issues and conflicts. *Typee* falls into the category of what Abdul R. JanMohamed generically labels as "symbolic" as opposed to "imaginary" imperial-colonial texts. Both types depict native cultures for ideological purposes, but whereas the latter only denigrates the native subject to confirm the values of the home culture, the former more willingly, JanMohamed argues, "examine[s] the specific individual and cultural differences between Europeans and natives" and "reflect[s] on the efficacy of European values, assumptions, and habits in contrast to indigenous cultures."[4]

We can begin to highlight some of those differences in *Typee*'s case by returning briefly to the "Portrait of Kory-Kory" quoted above. The passage ambiguously locates Tommo's native friend within both the natural and social realms. The tattoos of fish, fowl, and a "variety of most unaccountable-looking creatures" link Kory-Kory to the former, whereas the rectilinear ones obscuring the natural physiognomy of his face seem more to associate him with the latter. The striking image of the jailhouse window goes even further to confuse which realm, natural or social, Kory-Kory may be thought to most inhabit. Tommo here pictorially envisions some presocial Kory-Kory straining to peer out through his culture's binding constraints (the tribally prescribed marks of tattooing) and commune with him via the transcultural language of sentiment. Tommo does not articulate these ideas to himself, and they would likely be unfathomable to Kory-Kory and the other natives who, according to Tommo, lack "legal provisions" (200) and have not become technologically split off from nature. The text does not grant us access to Kory-Kory's mind, much less to the cultural intersubjectivity of the real Typees that Melville lived with in 1842. We therefore cannot know what the tattoos might have meant to the *actual* Kory-Kory (if there was one), whose textual stand-in I should add elsewhere gives no sign of feeling estranged from his own culture. Yet precisely this asymmetry between how Kory-Kory might interpret his tattoos and how the "Portrait" encourages us to interpret them makes it all the more pertinent. Tommo sees Kory-Kory as being *unknowingly* self-imprisoned because the latter cannot conceive of being in or out of jail, of dissenting or assenting to the laws or cultural codes of his community. In the Lockean tradition, true liberty means having the conscious freedom either to resist or not to resist the law, and thus the prison metaphor is apt from Tommo's perspective just to the extent that it is inapt, indeed unimaginable, from Kory-Kory's.[5]

Tommo's reference to Goldsmith should remind us that he elsewhere habitually translates Typeean culture in terms of nonindigenous imagery, through the glass of the already familiar. Frequent citations—to Benzoni, Egyptian hieroglyphs, Stonehenge, the Venus de Medici, Trajan's column, a Turkish seraglio—draw us away from the experiential perplexity and seriality of his story toward the intertextual domain of other travel works, art guides, and encyclopedic volumes (such as Goldsmith's or John Murray's Home and Colonial Library series, in which *Typee* first appeared) that put the exotic world in the cabinet bookshelves of the middle class. These citations, which bespeak Tommo as a well-read, postadventuring author, stand opposed to his sense of alienation while living with the natives, of being "[c]ut off . . . from all intercourse with the civilized world" (104). In *Typee*, the narrative in fact looks two ways: at once toward the literal Typees, in the time antecedent to the act of telling; and toward them as a rhetorical means, at the time of telling itself, to work out the narrator's discomfort with his own culture.

The Typees' language and customs remain opaque to Tommo, yet if the native culture frustrates ethnographical exegesis, it also allows him to exult in the timelessness of heart-law, what he will refer to as the "precepts graven on every breast" (201). Not unlike Samuel Goodrich, in the guise of Peter Parley, Tommo wants to look kindly upon the natives, although Polynesian difference resists, even as it invites, his effort to cross over into the Typeean mind. We can find this desire to breach the veil of cultural marks (tattoos) as being admirable, but it should not be forgotten that the liberal disposition to surmise a shared humanity can also become an excuse not to see otherness as such, to avoid reckoning with, in this instance, the full complexity of Typee culture. The flip side—which we observed mainly in geographers other than Goodrich, Arnold Guyot especially—was to harden otherness by way of geophysiognomic hierarchies. In Melville's travel novel, native anatomy does not betray an essential racial character of the sort that we have seen posited by geographical textbooks. Instead, the Typees are portrayed as either exceptionally handsome or decrepit, with the latter signaling not biological inferiority but rather the tribe's *cultural* stagnation.

A careful reader of *Typee* will note, however, that my previous remark is not entirely accurate, for in fact, one generalized passage about South Sea natives echoes the geographers' taxonomies of race. Tommo comments that the Typees'

> great superiority over all other Polynesians cannot fail to attract the notice of those who visit the principal groups in the Pacific. The voluptuous Tahitians are the only people who at all deserve to be compared with them; while the dark-hued Hawiians and the woolly-headed Feegees are immeasurably inferior to them. The distinguishing characteristics of the Marquesan islanders, and that which at once strikes you, is the European cast of their features—a peculiarity seldom observable among other uncivilized people. (184)

To the extent that we judge Tommo's voice here to be Melville's, the lines are damning. Even if we distinguish author from character, it seems unlikely that Melville wanted us to reflect upon Tommo's ethnocentricism. The best that can be said, and it stills seems like fudging, is that the young Melville ventriloquizes racist sentiments, not because he himself is racist per se, but because he well knew what would appeal to his audience.

I summon the unfortunate passage to mind to suggest that, in *Typee*'s case, it is the exception to the rule: otherness in Typee is not physiognomic, but instead a matter of social practices—tattooing, cannibalism—that threaten Tommo's sovereignty, his status as a sort of anticitizen, a social position that makes him content with neither the United States nor Polynesia. The distinction between Tommo as the often confused, embodied actor in the story and Tommo as its alternately droll or angered narrator holds a troublesome relation to the distinction between Tommo in either aspect and Melville: for Tommo's memories, while not exactly reprising Melville's, resubjectify them. In an unstable, interstitial genre of its own—somewhere between autobiographical travelogue, novel, and sociocomparative treatise—*Typee* presents us with a very interesting case for applying recent theories about the rhetoricity of ethnographical writing and, obversely, how literary texts subsume its discourses.[6]

Pursuing such a line of inquiry, which would presumably entail more than looking en passant at the actual Typees, lies beyond my goal in this chapter, however. By arguing, as I will, that Western eighteenth- and nineteenth-century legal-philosophical debate mediates how Tommo describes the Typees and, conversely, that his depiction of the Typees negotiates problems of historicity and the law, I necessarily beg the question of how the Typees circa 1842 reflected upon their own culture. *Nature, culture, assent, dissent*—these are resonant terms for our understanding of what the social contract, or its absence, means; for the actual prototypes of Kory-Kory, Fayaway, Chief Mehevi, Mow-Mow, and the other Typees, such terms may be entirely irrelevant. We might wish to assert that Melville, in a metacritical fashion, exposes the ethnocentricism of his persona; but efforts to distinguish the author from his character so that the second, but not the first, can be challenged for instrumentally using the Typees to castigate aspects of antebellum society strike me as a tactic to preserve the *novelistic* status of the book. All that is lost by positing a link, which is not to say an equivalence, between the authorial Melville and the character Tommo, or by presuming that *Typee* invests itself not entirely in metacommentary or irony about Tommo's self-aggrandizing authorship, is a notion that Melville always transcends the conflicted positions voiced in his texts. What is gained, on the other hand, is an obligation to attend with greater political-historical specificity to the milieu contributing to those conflicted positions.

Tommo celebrates Typeean culture as a nonjuridical tropical Arcadia, yet he also plainly shows us in the course of his story that the Typees have rigorous laws too. The question of whether Polynesians were somehow blithely free of burdensome legal or social restraints or, in fact, subject to intensive proscription in the form of taboos guiding the very minutiae of their daily lives was hardly new with Melville. Defining to what degree social laws regulated native cultures had exercised philosophers, political scientists, and literary writers ever since the Renaissance. The controversy, however, took on a greater immediacy following the discoveries and reports of Captain Cook and his epigones, which provided a new arsenal of protoanthropological lore crucial to the late Enlightenment nature-versus-culture debate initiated by Rousseau, Bougainville, Diderot, and other European savants. *Typee* may be deemed a late entry into that debate, and it may profitably be studied in terms of the Western fixation on the figure of the noble savage that stretches back at least as far as Montaigne and became recycled, in its primary U.S. guise, in the Leatherstocking tales of James Fenimore Cooper.[7] In this chapter, however, I wish to look at a more contemporary context. I explore how the news of the day in respect to United States–Polynesian relations, the exportation of American law to Hawaii in the early 1840s, bears upon the legal issues that shape Tommo's story at crucial junctures. Melville's portrayal of the Typees, I shall argue, mediates his concerns with a rhetoric of natural legalism, a rhetoric that while increasingly obsolete when it came to the pragmatics of legal practice, nonetheless still informed social and political theorizing during the antebellum period. Tommo's ambivalent attitude toward Typeean law, we will see, reflects not only the contradictory opinions many Americans who visited the Polynesian islands had when appraising native customs, but also more fundamentally, Tommo's and his culture's basic uncertainty about what best grounds authority: an explicit and historically determined set of positive law codes, or a transhistorical and transcultural law of the heart, the "precepts graven on every breast."[8]

Hawaii and the Exportation of American Law

Tommo's adventure, which lasts about four months, takes place on Nuku-heva Island, one of the Marquesas group, roughly one thousand miles north-east of Tahiti and twenty-five hundred miles southeast of the Hawaiian Islands. Melville himself, having fled the whaling ship *Acushnet* (along with his crewmate Richard Tobias Greene) on July 9, 1842, unintentionally stumbled into the Typee valley of Nukuheva and lived with the natives for less than four weeks. The Typees, reputedly ferocious cannibals, had repulsed intruders before; but it is unlikely that they intended to either harm or hold captive their visitors. Scholars have shown that Melville liberally drew upon a number of sources to fill in ethnographical detail about the tribe's customs. Those cited in the first chapter—Captain David Porter's *Journal of the Cruise of the U.S. Frigate Essex* (1815), Charles S. Stewart's *Visit to the South Seas, in the U.S. Ship Vincennes, During the Years 1829 and 1830* (1831), and William Ellis's *Polynesian Researches* (1833)—all furnished accounts of Nukuheva and its inhabitants, but they were all out of date by the time *Typee* appeared.[9] Although eager to hear the tale of a man who had lived among cannibals, Melville's readers probably would not have had these earlier books in mind when they opened his travel novel. The more immediate context would have been the sundry reports of the commercial, political, and religious activity on the Hawaiian (or, as they were then called, Sandwich) Islands in the years directly preceding *Typee*'s publication.

New England merchants had established Hawaii as a key commercial center for the exportation of sandalwood and other valuable commodities to the Far East during the last decades of the eighteenth century. Missionaries soon followed.[10] The first major group, sponsored by the American Board of Commissioners for Foreign Missions, arrived in 1819; and over the next thirty years, with fresh recruits from the mainland, they quickly came to dominate the political scene. In July 1842, the same month in which the events of the narrative transpire, *The North American Review* carried an article by Richard Henry Dana, Jr., that charted the progress of Protestantism in Hawaii. Dana disputes claims about the ameliorating effect of commerce upon the Hawaiians. He concedes that Western traders helped abolish superstitious and "arbitrary" taboos; and yet, he writes, "No Gospel had been preached to [the natives], and they had only substituted complete atheism and unbounded license to do evil in the place of their old idolatries." Only the subsequent arrival of the Protestant missionaries and their "preaching of the Gospel" successfully "counteract[ed] the evil effects of commerce." For Dana, however, the missionaries did not merely import the text and thus the spirit of the Gospel. They introduced a comprehensive legal system as well. Whereas "commerce gave [the natives] no laws," the missionaries "instructed their chiefs in legal science, and assisted them in forming a constitution and criminal civil code." As of the moment, Dana happily concludes, a "constitution and a complete code of laws are [being] prepared."[11] Such beneficent instruction had already been noted by the *American Jurist and Law Magazine* (July 1841) in a reprinted article from the island newspaper, the *Hawaiian Spectator*, written by James Jackson Jarves. The chiefs of Hawaii, having felt their "incompetence" to devise modern laws, had to defer to their "friends in the United States" and request that a civilian be sent upon "whom they might rely as a correct teacher of the science of government, in the same manner as religious teachers had been sent to teach them the truths of the gospel."[12] The document produced, the Hawaiian Constitution of 1840, limited the power of the reigning monarch, established a judiciary, and secured the continuity of a legislative body. One missionary proclaimed it nothing less than "the great magna charta of Hawaiian liberty," to be "hailed by every lover of freedom."[13] Two decades later, Dana observed the enduring salutary effect of this exportation of Western law. While on a tour of the Hawaiian Islands, he reported to the *New York Tribune* that the "missionaries have largely influenced the legislation of the kingdom, and its police system; it is fortunate that they have done so. . . . [In] no place in the world that I have visited are the rules which control vice and regulate amusements so strict, yet so reasonable, and so fairly enforced."[14]

That missionaries had brought the law to the Hawaiian Islands was nothing less than the fulfillment of what Scripture foretold and dictated. Hawaii was the spearhead of the evangelical movement in Polynesia, what the Reverend Henry T. Cheever in his popular *Life in the Sandwich Islands* (1851) called the "religious Protestant Heart of the great Ocean."[15] The evangelical project of exporting Christian law had its theological basis in Isaiah 42:4: "He shall not fail nor be discouraged, till he have set judgment in the earth: and the isles shall wait for his law." It was this text that inspired Hiram Bingham, the most influential New England Congregational missionary in Hawaii, when he gave his first sermon there in 1823. Not surprisingly, Bingham's recollection of the early years of missionary endeavor, his massive *Residence of Twenty-One Years in the Sandwich Islands* (1847), invariably casts the story of evangelical triumph in terms of biblical analogy. He sees, for example, the importation of the law as rendering him and his fellow missionaries as analogous to Moses, though with the antitype outdoing the Old Testament predecessor. Scanning the village and valley of Honolulu from atop the rim of a dormant volcano, the minister is granted a view of a superior sort: "[It was] a novel scene, not indeed like that presented to Moses when he ascended to the top of Pisgah, and surveyed the land of promise, with the earnest desire, but forbidden hope of entering it, even to exterminate its insufferable idolatry, and to establish there the seed of

Abraham." Bingham, continuing, envisions Honolulu as the future "seat of government."[16] Under his ministrations, that government would abide by Mosaic injunction, and, in suitable republican fashion, it would be one of rational consent.

In summing up his mission of bringing both law and the salvific Word to the islands, Bingham recalls in his volume's penultimate paragraph that a "nation has been raised from blank heathenism to a rank among enlightened nations, to the enjoyment of letters and laws, of Christianity and the hope of heavenly glory" (616). He anticipates that, under the continued tutelage of the missionaries and the "impress" of the "foster parent" of the Protestant church, the Hawaiians will "form a mature, symmetrical, and efficient character" (579). His Lockean and Christian tropes redefine political control as a family matter, by which the Hawaiian masses are cast as children improperly reared by tyrannical chiefs and who now need the better parental governance of the Protestant clergy. The other chroniclers of the advance of Protestantism in Polynesia used a similar familial rhetoric. Cheever, for instance, referred to the Marquesas Islands, where the missionary project had failed, as the "least Christianized, or weaned from cannibalism and barbarity of all Polynesia."[17] And Jarves, turning to the subject of the threatening "artillery of France and the spiritual decrees of the Pope" in his *History of the Hawaiian or Sandwich Islands* (1843), warned that the region might, without U.S. protection, become but "the nursery of a bigoted creed."[18]

The Hawaiian scene of a transition from superstition and legal benightedness to Protestant Christianity and constitutional felicity likely consoled American observers in two ways. First, in a period in which Christian precepts often seemed mismatched with codified law, most agonizingly in regard to slave laws, the recent history of the Hawaiian Islands showed that the two could be reconciled. Second, whereas Native Americans by and large resisted being either converted or assimilated, the Polynesians (at least those living in Hawaii) appeared receptive to U.S. influence and thus helped assuage guilt over expansionist policy. Contact with sailors may have brought contagious diseases that decimated the Hawaiian population—reducing it, by Jarves's calculation, from about 300,000 in 1779 to 100,000 in 1836 (403)—but the remnant, with the aid of Bingham and his fellow missionaries, had spurned their idols, formed an independent and semirepublican Protestant state based upon a written constitution, and thus confirmed the promise of the United States to re-create the world or a portion of it in its own image, to be among, in Jarves's words, those "great powers [that] give law to the globe" (368). That in the process of American politicocultural exportation the "nationality of the Polynesian race" might be lost, Jarves concluded, would disturb only those with a "blind adherence to a sentiment, which has nothing beside sympathy with the past to recommend it." Polynesian "perpetuity" depended upon Hawaiian national customs not surviving, upon the Hawaiians fully "adopt[ing]" the "virtues, language and knowledge, of the anglo-saxon race" (371). In Hawaii, Cheever bluntly summed up in 1851, "liberty and law are everywhere gaining force ... which will insure good government and equal rights, if only the people survive to enjoy them" (71).[19]

Dana, Jarves, and Cheever reflect the consensus opinion about the pedagogic role of the missionaries. The evangelical habit of thinking in Manichean terms may have struck some citizens interested in Polynesian affairs as being a bit extreme. Doubtless some readers may have been more archaeologically or ethnographically curious than repulsed when hearing Bingham's reaction to native monuments (he calls, for instance, one "frowning structure ... so large and prominent, that it can be distinctly seen with the naked eye, from the top of Maunakea, a distance of about 32 miles" a "fortification of Satan's kingdom" [84]). Yet few could resist, theology aside, the story of the Hawaiian community's rapid social and moral progress so amply testified to by Dana and other visitors. Even Bingham himself, when he refers to the natives' "blank heathenism," could forgo the stark chromatics of the bright Kingdom of Christ and the dark Kingdom of Satan, emphasizing not so much a negative state of absolute depravity but rather a cultural tabula rasa upon which the vivifying Word as well as lessons in rational government could be inscribed. Although the missionaries were occasionally accused of a too zealous expectation that the Hawaiians abide by the Decalogue, of self-aggrandizing meddling in governmental affairs, and of enriching themselves through native labor and appropriation of native land, for the most part they were extolled because of their influence in matters of state as well as Protestant social morality.[20]

The theological melodrama that justified the missionaries to themselves must, in short, be separated from the ideological value their proselytizing of the American way had to a republican, Protestant audience at home. Only those who had complaints about the American way itself, radical abolitionists or communitarian reformers, unreservedly aligned themselves with Tommo's didactic stance in *Typee*, of presenting the precolonized Polynesians, the Typees, as an alternative to what seemed an American dystopia. A writer for the *National Anti-Slavery Standard*, for instance, recommended that readers who "are sick at heart" at the "daily outrages upon the rights of humanity practised by Christian judges and lawyers in our Halls of Justice ... turn for relief to the amiable savages of Typee." And John Sullivan Dwight, former Brook Farm resident, mused in the Fourierist *Harbinger* how wonderful it was that in a "mere state of nature they can live together in a degree of social harmony and freedom from vice, which all our jails, and scaffolds, and courts of justice, and police officers, and soldiers, and schoolmasters . . . cannot procure for us."[21]

These reviewers' envy of Typeean democracy, harmony, and seeming freedom from legal prohibition is largely rhetorical, deriving from the conventional fall-into-civilization topos that privileges "primitive" societies only for the purpose of antithesis. Typee culture, of course, was not devoid of social regulation. Pierre Bourdieu (he is referring to the tribal, agrarian people of Kabylia) usefully reminds us that the "absence of a genuine *law*—the product of the work of a body of specialists expressly mandated to produce a coherent corpus of juridical norms and ensure respect for its application, and furnished to this end with a coercive power—must not lead us to forget that any socially recognized formation contains within it an intrinsic power to reinforce dispositions symbolically."[22] Going by the research of twentieth-century ethnohistorians, however, the sense that the Polynesian tribe Tommo described was egalitarian did have some basis in fact. The Typees and the other native groups in the Marquesas Islands maintained a polity considerably unlike that of the Hawaiian Islands.[23] The Marquesas had not only a different history of foreign intervention but also a different internal history. The Hawaiian archipelago was ruled by a monarchic and priestly caste. Through the late 1840s no monarch controlled even an individual island within the Marquesas. It was largely because the missionaries could not ingratiate themselves with a dominant ruler that their efforts to establish viable colonies on Nukuheva failed. Hawaii was conceived as a realm where republican and Christian values contested with and were supplanting those of heathen despotism, but a variant dichotomy applied to Nukuheva. Its polity was at once more democratic and more barbaric, a "republic *en savage*," as Charles S. Stewart pithily said, "in which every man is the representative of his own rights, and the only lawgiver."[24] On the one hand, each of the Marquesas Islands was a utopia of natural democracy that might be destroyed by British, American, and French colonizers. On the other, each was the site of such bizarrely irrational customs, dissociated from any social structure however despotic and benighted, that Christian morality and Western law could simply not gain a foothold, or, as in *Typee*'s depiction of Nukuheva, only temporarily on the tribes that lived near the beach.

Written and Unwritten Law

In *Typee*, of course, Tommo scorns the putative successes of the "republican missionaries" (188) and sustains a posture hostile to colonial-imperial agendas. Being no agent of either church or state, he would elicit our laughter at both. Before his story begins, therefore, he retells an anecdote about the

French colonial outpost on the primary bay of Nukuheva. Paired with a companion set-piece, in which the curious natives offend an American missionary's wife by trying to disrobe her, the anecdote lampoons colonizers' attempts to reform native sexual behavior, to make their character, as Bingham would say, more "symmetrical" (a key phrase used in the antebellum era to designate harmonious, moral relations between the body and the mind's faculties). The episode also debunks the "newly constituted authorities" (13) when they try to impose their law. Wishing to display the "beneficial effects of their jurisdiction, as discernible in the deportment of the natives" (7), the local French naval commanders parade the king and queen of Nukuheva before the officers of an American man-of-war. Embarrassingly, the native body hardly supplies a blank slate for the law's writing. The queen, when she boards the American ship, is only scantily draped by a "gaudy tissue of scarlet cloth" which "expose[s] to view her bare legs, embellished with spiral tatooing, and somewhat resembling two miniature Trajan's columns" (8). The Trajan column commemorated the Roman emperor's imperial victory over the Dacians and the extension of the Roman polity. Here, however, as in the next part of the scene, a monument of imperialism is ironically refigured as what scandalized nineteenth-century colonizers and travelers: the native's unclad body. To the chagrin of the French dignitaries, the inquisitive queen turns aside to inspect an old salt whose limbs are "covered with as many inscriptions in India ink as the lid of an Egyptian sarcophagus"; and worse, "eager to display the hieroglyphics on her own sweet form" (8), she leans forward to reveal her tattooed buttocks. The Trajan column memorialized subjugation of a weaker nation through imperial, military power; the Egyptian past was reconstructed and absorbed by the discourses of nineteenth-century Orientalism when the Rosetta Stone was discovered after Napoleon's Grand Army invaded Egypt in 1798, taken in turn by the English when they routed Napoleon from Egypt in 1801, and decoded by Jean François Champollion in 1822. These multiple incidents of appropriation are conflated and transformed into a military debacle. From the sight of the hieroglyphics on the queen's "sweet form," the "aghast Frenchmen" must retreat "precipitately, and tumbling into their boat" flee "the scene of so shocking a catastrophe" (8). The French officers do not read as they run. Rather than asserting their own Code Napoleon, they are rebuffed by what they take to be an all too sensual code. Discomfited by the queen's lack of decorum, they do not linger to scrutinize her bodily inscribed hieroglyphics.

The episode is similar to later ones intended to arouse readerly (male) desire and highlight the tension between eros and civilization, such as when Tommo, to his delight, sees the pretty figure of Fayaway undrape herself and perform the office of mast and sail on a small boat. We could go further, suggesting that what really compels Tommo to jump ship is his wish to flee bad forms of male bonding: the despotic rule of its commander, Captain Vangs, and the alarming prospect of sodomy (hinted at by a line about Vangs's use of "the butt end of a hand-spike" [21] to quell dissent, and by an allusion—which Melville's wife, in a later edition, saw fit to excise—to sailors endlessly circling "Buggerry Island, or the Devil's-Tail Peak" [23]).[25] In that respect, the bond that Tommo forms with the darkly attractive Toby—the fact that Tommo does not so much flee with him, but flees *to be with* him—might well stand in as an egalitarian, gay critique of shipboard, compulsive homosexuality. If a counterimaginary to prudish, bourgeois norms or a too dominant type of male bonding appears to be emerging in these early scenes, however, it does quite come into textual clarity. Melville seems to have propelled himself into a story line that he cannot conclude; for interestingly, even as he severs their alliance (in the plot, so that Toby might bring aid back from the shore to rescue Tommo, who has been immobilized by a leg injury), he suggests that Tommo's later angst derives as much from his separation from Toby as it does from being left to contend with cannibals by himself. The absence of the not-quite lover gets filled in, to some extent, by the ever-companionable Kory-Kory and the handsome valley migrant, Marnoo; the ambivalent erotic force of their bond—sealed in the strange, almost ritualistic sharing of food crumbs and tobacco stowed away in Toby's pockets (a "soft, pulpy, and discolored . . . villainous compound . . . engendered in his bosum" [42])—also resurfaces, once the text has repressed their relationship via Toby's departure, in Tommo's lurid obsession with cannibalism, with those who have a *lustful* proclivity for human body parts, an aberration kindred, in the Western imagination, to homosexual desire itself. Leaving his friend, Toby leaves him to lovers of human flesh—to the fate of becoming a body that, as a dismembered corpse, will have no desire. My latter comments, partially drawn from other scholars, may very well get at the deeper erotic or psychogenetic currents of *Typee*, and, when I return to Melville in Chapter 3, in an analysis of his late epic-scale poem *Clarel* and its fascination with the Dead Sea as a sexually transgressive site, I will have occasion to revisit Melville's concerns with sexuality more extensively. In the text at hand, however, the significance of the homosexual/cannibalism linkage remains mostly inchoate, affording more speculation than sustained interpretation.[26]

Consequently, although doubtless issues of eros are at play in *Typee*, especially in respect to Tommo's incapacity to surrender fully to the sensuality of native life, I believe Melville's agenda more explicitly puts in tension different forms of social—that is, nonerotic—liberties and constraints. The prefatory scene about the Nukuheva queen, after all, primarily stages a tableau in which one Polynesian body resists the ceremonious, symmetrical display of the Polynesian body politic. The disruptive force of the queen's body, ornamented with markings, implicitly contrasts with various types of legalistic writing and documents of authority referred to in *Typee* that control and regulate: the "written instructions" that sanction French, British, and American men-of-war to "burn, slaughter, and destroy" (27) in reprisal for native uprisings; the "musty parchments and title deeds" (202) that secure land to the privileged classes; the "bill[s] in Chancery" (192) that impede ready access to divorce; and finally, from the appendix, the codified "severe penal laws" (258) that govern the behavior and practices of the Hawaiian natives. According to eighteenth- and nineteenth-century social theorizing, posttribal cultures require written law because of their plural and divergent interests.[27] Tommo, however, stresses legalism's coercive force rather than its capacity to protect individual rights and liberties, and, in the passages of diatribe from which the above citations have been culled, he mounts a strong case against the brutality and injustices of his own culture and its regulatory machinery. Yet Typeean life as Tommo portrays it will scarcely seem unbridled, nor will Western law in all instances simply be deplored as a tool of oppressors who desire to assert cultural discipline or social hegemony.

The narrative action begins not as a consequence of interdiction, but because the law's writ has not been sufficiently constraining. Tommo's initial problem is that there is too little rather than too much law aboard the *Dolly*, the whaler upon which he has taken voyage in search of exotic adventure. His commander, Captain Vangs, has exhausted the crew in an unusually protracted whale hunt. More repellent, however, is Vangs's overbearing manner and habitual use of physical threats ("the butt end of a hand-spike") to restrain dissent. Tommo explains that he jumped ship because he lacked hope of "apply[ing] for redress" against such tyranny, the *Dolly* having "left both law and equity on the other side of the Cape" (21). He and his companion, Toby, desert because they cannot turn to a court of appeal that could enforce the written contractual obligation between captain and crew, "the ship's articles" that "legally" (20) bind them.[28] Whether or not Vangs has contravened the letter or the spirit of that contract in abusing Tommo, Toby, and their fellow sailors and, conversely, whether or not Tommo sanctions his desertion on the basis of the letter or spirit of the contract is finally a moot issue. Aboard ship, where there is no supervening authority higher than the captain, Tommo has felt the truth of John Locke's maxim—"Where-ever Law ends Tyranny begins."[29]

The interval between Tommo's escape from his captain's despotic command and his retreat back to the confinement of another ship at the end of *Typee* may be construed as a liminal state, as what Victor Turner defines as being "betwixt and between successive lodgments in jural political systems."[30] The consequences of being unlodged appear to be twofold. First, Tommo feels confused both during his trek into Nukuheva's interior and later when, living with the Typees, he can "comprehend nothing" (177). And, second, a sexualized self previously inhibited by the sterility and rigors of shipboard life begins to emerge. During his and Toby's arduous flight from their ship, Tommo receives a strange injury that causes his leg to swell. Critics agree that Tommo's leg pain, which will intermittently diminish and intensify during his captivity, somatically expresses at once his desire to enjoy the relaxed sexuality of the Typees and his inability to do so because he cannot fully divest himself of his own culture's sexual inhibitions.[31] As Tommo and Toby make their way from the shoreline village up through and across Nukuheva's mountain ranges, the topography refracts both the allure of a recovered sexuality and the disorientation of being "betwixt and between." At one stage of his escape, for instance, Tommo scans down upon the "bosom of a valley" to see an Edenic landscape so "ravish[ing]" that he is scarcely "able to comprehend by what means" he has "thus suddenly been made a spectator of such a scene" (49). This conjunction of a diffused sexuality and a lack of personal agency carries over to Tommo's stay with the Typees and can be seen in terms of his often-noted infantilization—his dependency on the native family of Marheyo, Tinor, and their son Kory-Kory both because of his leg debility and because of his naïveté in respect to Typee social customs and day-to-day life. He flees from Captain Vangs's hypocritical "paternal solicitude" (30), but he does not thereby become an adult. Rather, he regresses into an infantile state in which the natives cater to all his needs, except that for freedom.

The psychoanalytical aspects of Tommo's sojourn in the land of the Typees and the sexual symbolism of his aching leg are important, but overemphasizing either will obscure the narrative's sociopolitical embeddedness.[32] Earlier, I proposed that Tommo's problem with Captain Vangs is that he has abrogated the writ or spirit of the law. Tommo has been refused the right of rational consent to the law. That right, understood in the antebellum period to apply only to adults, has been denied him. And his reaction, explicitly one of revolt, is implicitly to take on the childlike attributes of the role in which he has been cast by the captain. This being the case, Tommo enters the Typee village to find what children typically seek, parental approval and authority. He wants, in brief, to be relodged within another, but more nurturing, jural-political system. Consequently, we should now see a more complex etiology for Tommo's afflicted leg. His injury becomes most excruciating not only when he feels sexual guilt but also when he becomes apprehensive about Typeean law: about whether it is benign, natural, and innately known, or a social mechanism historically constructed, although to him unfathomably so, and thus oppressive and menacing.

The question of whether Tommo and Toby have escaped from a jural realm or merely journeyed to another, but radically different, one is raised as soon as they enter the native village. Confronted by "eight or ten noble-looking chiefs," Tommo tells us that the one (Chief Mehevi, he later learns) "who appeared to be the highest in rank, placed himself directly facing me; looking at me with a rigidity of aspect under which I absolutely quailed. . . . Never before had I been subjected to so strange and steady a glance; it revealed nothing of the mind of the savage, but it appeared to be reading my own" (70–71). Tommo's anxiety before the judgelike scrutiny of the chief subsides when he responds correctly to Mehevi's inquiry—"Typee or Happar?" (71)—mainly because the opaque "mind of the savage" becomes transparent when Mehevi pantomimes enthusiastically in response to Tommo's condemnation of the Happars, with whom the Typees are at war. Here, as later in the story, Tommo oscillates between deeming the natives' subjectivity and intent as being plainly (and childishly) evident in facial and bodily gesture and as being inscrutable. His nervousness about the rules governing the behavior of the natives will return, however, at key junctions and belie his more overt appeals to the reader that the natives are idyllically free of prohibiting legal formalities and institutions.

Typee provides some facts about Nukuheva's geography and climate, its distinctive flora and fauna, its peculiar geological and man-made landmarks, the artifacts and material culture of the Typees, including food preparation, technological level, and so on. These details fulfilled genre expectations for customs-and-manners description and natural history. These were the authenticating aspects of travelistic writing that Melville knew would make his work more salable, and so he composed it with one eye turned toward Ellis, Porter, and other authorities. Customs-and-manners description in *Typee*, however, is spare and mostly anecdotal; and Tommo's main point of distinction between his own and Typeean culture is that the Typees abide by an essential law of the heart. The Typees, according to Tommo, do not require the formal apparatus of the law to sustain peaceful relations among themselves. They entirely lack "legal provisions," whether "courts of law or equity" or "municipal police for the purpose of apprehending vagrants and disorderly characters" (200). They need not secure their lands by "musty parchments and title deeds," because they "hold their broad valleys, in fee simple from Nature herself" (202). And, finally, the chiefs who spend their days in the Ti, a "sort of Bachelor's Hall," rather than making law, sleep "for the good of their constitutions" (157), the double meaning of "constitutions" underscoring a perfect correspondence between the natural regulatory dynamics of the body and the social contracts that bind individuals together. One explanation for such passive harmony is environmental: living in a natural economy of abundance rather than scarcity ("which God in his wisdom," Tommo speculates, "had ordained for the support of the indolent natives" [196]), the Typees enjoy a communal, noncompetitive mode of life. Waxing philosophic, though, Tommo furnishes another and opposed reason. In lieu of the "statute-book" (203), a judiciary, and penal institutions, the Typees are "governed by that sort of tacit common-sense law which, say what they will of the inborn lawlessness of the human race, has its precepts graven on every breast" (201). The natives need neither the letter of "established law" to promote "social order" (200) nor courts to interpret that law, because they already have natural law scripted upon their hearts.

The idea that the Typees can rely upon an interior heart-law draws upon the widely disseminated beliefs of Thomas Reid and his fellow Scottish Enlightenment philosophers in an innate, benevolently disposed faculty of common sense. When applied to native groups, the notion fitted conveniently with traditional assumptions, from Locke and other political-legal theorists, about a fundamental natural law anterior to all forms of civil law, codified or not. From the time of Cook, the perception of Polynesian natives was filtered by and contributed to arguments about natural conscience. Eighteenth- and early nineteenth-century travelogues are often couched in a rhetoric that distinguishes eternal principles of law and conscience from secondary customs and specific legal-social practices that are, at best, an effort to approximate first principles and, at worst, a repulsive corruption of them.

The most famous eighteenth-century American voyager addressing the tension between particular and universal law is John Ledyard, in his *Journal of Captain Cook's Last Voyage* (1783). Therein he remarks that superstitions among Polynesian natives are not surprising, since even the ancient Israelites deviated "frequently into downright idolatry, and all the vanity of superstition and unbridled nonsense from the imbecility of human policy when uninfluenced by heavenly wisdom and jurisprudence." Social customs that dictate morality, he adds,[33]

may be local and indigenous to particular times and circumstances, both in the civilized and uncivilized world, but far the greater part are derivative and were originally bestowed on man by his supreme Governor; those that we find among the civilized and wise, measured on a philosophic scale, are uncorrupted, while those that we find existing in parts remote from civilization and knowledge, though they have a resemblance which plainly intimates from whence they came, are yet debased, mutilated, and by some hardly known.

Thus one index of any society's level of morality was the degree to which the law of conscience divinely installed in all groups of people, originating from the first parents, was either manifested or effaced. Ledyard presupposes an originary, transhistorical "jurisprudence" that can either be rediscovered or maintained by the reasoning faculty of the "wise" or, through historical declension, be obscured by noxious social practices.

It was, of course, not uncommon for republican thinkers to cite native groups within the United States for evidence of the viability of more *natural* polities. The apparent superfluity of written law was evident to William Bartram and Thomas Jefferson when they reflected upon the social conditions of Native Americans. Bartram praised the Cherokees in his *Travels* because the "constitution or system of their police is simply natural." It "seems to be nothing more than the simple dictates of natural reason, plain to everyone . . . which in effect better maintains human happiness, than the most complicated system of modern politics, or sumptuary laws, enforced by coercive means." And Jefferson, directly evoking commonsense philosophy, in *Notes on the State of Virginia*, wrote that the natives "never submitted themselves to any laws, any coercive power, any shadow of government. Their only controuls are their manners, and that moral sense of right and wrong, which, like the sense of tasting and feeling, in every man makes a part of his nature." That "species of coercion" might be "[i]mperfect," Jefferson noted, but "crimes are very rare among them."[34]

Natural law, made known to humankind through what Ledyard calls the deity "Governor," was needed ethically and philosophically to keep manmade law, which it supposedly underwrote, from seeming merely arbitrary—a matter of power and political contingency. Embedded within the ideal of natural law was the antianthropological, essentialist notion of an equivalence among the races and nations of the world. It warranted that the native, whether in Polynesia, tropical America, Africa, or the United States itself, be accorded the rudiments of humanity, but it also sanctioned the defaming of all cultural practices that seemed to deny the inward, Godly enjoined, common nature. Comparative sociology, in the Enlightenment era and for nearly two centuries afterward, tended therefore to see indigene customs and beliefs as "mutilat[ions]" of a Eurocentric, more "natural" norm. The native, it was nearly always assumed, should know better, should be able to see the folly if not downright evil of his or her own cultural practices, because the monitor of conscience always resided within to speak the truth. The individual native succumbs, through a willful refusal to hold counsel with the inward conscience, to horrific tribal customs and rituals. Geographical thinking, as we have seen in the last chapter, added spatial coordinates that somewhat contradicted the Enlightenment assumption of natural law. If, as Ledyard himself implies, natural law inevitably becomes corrupted in those peoples "existing in parts remote from civilization and knowledge," they could not exactly be blamed for the geographical accident of their birthplace.

Of course, this was a contradiction always troubling to the missionary enterprise, manifest mostly in the clergy's equivocal mix of empathy and scorn for the native populations whose souls they felt had been entrusted to them. What many missionaries saw in the South Sea islanders was how totally natural conscience or law could be contravened or overwritten; what shocked them was both the morally "barbarous" practices they observed or heard about (lewdness, infanticide, and cannibalism) and how such practices showed that God's law had been supplanted by the irrational law of taboo. Bingham felt that the natives' "stereotype and misguiding tabu" had erased the "natural conscience, which God implants in every human breast, to be the expounder of moral law" (21); and, after a visit to one of the Marquesas Islands, he could only infer from the natives' "rudeness, lasciviousness, shouts, and uncouth movements" that there remained "very little of the *law* of God legible" on their "heart[s]" (460). The Polynesians appall Bingham not because they essentially differ from himself, but because they once were and should be essentially the same. They were dispensed the natural conscience that has become, through time's passage, a mere vestige of its original.[35]

Unlike the missionaries, Tommo cannot coherently explain the relationship between native morality (the innate "precepts graven on every breast") and the intricacies of taboo law. Bingham believed that taboo "misguided" what otherwise would have been the islanders' instinct, as God's creatures, to abide by divinely instilled conscience. But Tommo bifurcates what rules the Typees into a benign law of conscience or nature and a set of arbitrary, irrationally prescriptive customs. He comments that the taboos "guide and control every action of [the native's] being" (221), and yet he is left entirely "at a loss where to look for the authority which regulates this potent institution" (224).[36] Tommo's bafflement is intensified because he also tries to conceive native law in terms more appropriate to American and British common law.[37] Tommo nowhere directly compares the two, yet the rhetoric by which the latter was described by both its advocates and detractors shadows his understanding of native legalism. A few metaphorical descriptions of the common law should suffice to suggest the parallel. Jesse Root in 1798 argued that it is "within us, written upon the table of our hearts, in lively and indelible characters." The eminent jurist James Kent opined that "we meet with [the common law] when we wake and when we lay down to sleep, when we travel and when we stay at home; it is interwoven with every idiom that we speak." And Theodore Frelinghuysen, a Whig politician, spoke of the common law as "emphatically the law of the people. . . . [T]hey carry it about with them unconsciously: it waits like an invisible spirit on their secret thoughts: the monitor of the breast speaks to them in its language."[38] Common law, like native law, appeared to have emerged from the communal conscience rather than being coercively mandated.[39]

Elsewhere, however, the way in which Tommo describes native taboos ends up sounding very similar to how detractors of the common law portrayed it. At one point, for instance, Tommo recalls Chief Mehevi's exegesis of why Fayaway must be forbidden from sporting with him in a canoe. Mehevi offers a "very learned and eloquent exposition of the *history and nature of the 'taboo' as affecting this particular case*; employing a variety of most extraordinary words, which, from their amazing length and sonorousness, I have every reason to believe were of a theological nature" (133, emphasis added). That the taboo can have both a transcendental origin ("a theological nature") and a "history" is somewhat contradictory, but that contradiction was basic also to common law, at once having an elaborated provenance in precedent and commentary, yet ultimately not originating with any definitive written text. The antiquity of common law and the difficulty of sorting through its complexities led some reformist lawyers to compare it to the law found among native cultures. William Sampson, in *The Origin, Progress, Antiquities, Curiosities, and Nature of the Common Law* (1824), for example, vilified the common law's "barbarous jargon" and its "roots in savage antiquity," and he concluded that it only deserved "to be praised and worshipped by ignorant and superstitious votaries."[40]

We may safely assume that Melville was quite familiar with these troublesome aspects of antebellum law and was likely thinking of the mixed virtue of the common law when his character Tommo reflects upon the natural legalism of the Typees. Melville had studied law intently before shipping out on his first whaling voyage. Both of his brothers were attorneys, and they probably regaled him with the esoterica and rhetoric of their profession. And, of course, Melville was close to the Chief Justice of Massachusetts, the distinguished Lemuel Shaw, whose daughter he was to marry a few months after *Typee's* publication. Shaw, who once admitted "the state of perplexity in which the law still remains in this country," no doubt pronounced at length his own opinions about proper jurisprudence.[41] My concern, however, is less to demonstrate a precise parallel between the "immemorial practice," as the renowned Supreme Court justice Joseph Story put it, and the unwritten taboo system, than to argue for its haunting presence when Tommo contemplates the legal codes of his captors.[42] The foreignness of those codes confuses Tommo, but we should also note that this bewilderment results from his interpreting native customs in terms of the conflicting notions of antebellum law. When Tommo talks about Typeean law, he also talks about the law of his own country.

History, Custom, and the Legal Talk of the Typees

Tommo's failure to grasp the rationale behind the canoe taboo does not especially distress him. Similarly, when he recalls that even "Sir William Jones himself would . . . have despaired of mastering" (225) the "puzzling" (224) features of Typeean language, Tommo will not strike us as being alarmed by what he cannot fathom. Elsewhere, though, his confusion over native linguistic and legal rules appears to be directly linked to the painful swelling of his leg. In the preface to *Typee*, Melville abjures "rules of spelling" that would cause the "most beautiful combinations of vocal sounds" in Polynesian speech to be "altogether lost to the ear of the reader" (xiv). In two episodes, however, native language physically irritates Melville's embodied persona. Apparently, the talk of the Typees most pleases Tommo when it is devoid of legal, political, or theological content. The complexity of such content demands more complicated speech, which Tommo cannot understand simply because of the linguistic barrier between himself and the Typees. Yet his confusion also seems derived from an unconscious wish not to comprehend their language, when it would articulate the set of rules, customs, and rituals, in sum the "jural political system," governing the behavior of his captors. The talk of the Typees pains Tommo not so much because to him it makes little sense, but because it might make too much sense.

After a bloody fracas between the Typees and Happars, Kory-Kory launches into a harangue against his tribe's enemies and then drifts, Tommo says, "in emulation of our more polished orators . . . rather diffusely into other branches of his subject, enlarging, probably, upon the moral reflections it suggested; and proceeded in such a strain of unintelligible and stunning gibberish, that he actually gave me the headache for the rest of the day" (103). The image of Tommo getting a headache from listening to Kory-Kory's disquisition ends chapter 13; chapter 14 begins with his lament that he "still continued to languish under a complaint the origin and nature of which were still a mystery. Cut off as I was from all intercourse with the civilized world . . . [I] became a prey to the most gloomy thoughts" (104). Larzer Ziff contends that Tommo's leg ache grows most intolerable when he feels confined within a culture that seems to lack history and that has "no language; no means, that is, of communicating thoughts and sufferings that are the products of history." He believes that Tommo finally flees, at the end of the narrative, because he "opts for history and for language, [though] knowing full well the pain he must resume."[43] In support of Ziff's point about the timelessness of the Typees' culture we might adduce such evidence as Tommo's musings when he compares the valley's massive stone ruins to the "mighty base of the Pyramid of Cheops": "There are no inscriptions, no sculpture, no clue, by which to conjecture its history: nothing but the dumb stones." Tommo surmises that because Kory-Kory "attribut[ed] the [stone monuments] to a divine origin" neither he "nor the rest of his countrymen knew anything about them" (154–55). Ziff's argument is astute; yet it is not entirely precise, for the Typees' take on their ancestral monuments does not imply that they live in a state of historical amnesia, but rather that Tommo simply does not have access to Typeean historicity. Although the Typees may appear to live by the foundational law of the state of nature, their culture subscribes to rules that have evolved historically. Kory-Kory's account of the antique stone blocks and Mehevi's explanation of the "history and nature of the [canoe] taboo" may be faulty in Western archaeological or ethnographic terms, but that does not mean that the Typees lack a functional or archival concept of their own culture. We need not, however, try to determine what the actual Typees considered to be valid history. Instead, we should appraise to what use Tommo puts his understanding—or, as we shall see, misunderstanding—of Typeean discourse about law, historicity, and the historicity of the law.

Denigrating native historiography was not unusual.[44] Bingham, for example, scorned the oral traditions of the Hawaiians—"How imperfectly, then, were those stupid, unlettered, unsanctified heathen tribes furnished for making out a trustworthy history of their country for ages back or even for a single generation!" (18). Script and Scripture go hand-in-hand either to enlighten the natives or to chastise them for their lack of historical self-knowledge. For the missionaries, as I discussed earlier, those cultures far from the core of Christianity—either separated from biblical revelation or not part of the "civilized" world—debased themselves by engaging in cultural practices that seemed irrational because so distant from the logocentric merging of wisdom, writing, and Christian faith. Tommo, willing to label as innocence what the missionaries would condemn as ignorance, often seems more amused than irked by what he takes to be unreliable history. Nonetheless, no less than the missionaries, he cannot imagine the Typees as living beyond the moment, and to live only in the moment is to live primarily in the realm of the senses, where one ages but does not understand ages past.

Most powerfully, perhaps, Tommo's feeling that the Typees are ignorant of but not immune to history comes through by means of imagery: in the instance, above, of the "dumb stones," but more palpably in how upon one occasion he describes, in chapter 12, the denizens of the Ti:

As we advanced further along the building, we were struck with the aspect of four or five hideous old wretches, on whose decrepit forms time and tattooing seemed to have obliterated every trace of humanity. Owning to the continued operation of this latter process, which only terminates among the warriors of the island after all the figures sketched upon the limbs in youth have been blended together—an effect, however, produced only in cases of extreme longevity—the bodies of these men were of a uniform dull green color—the hue which the tattooing gradually assumes as the individual advances in age. Their skin had a frightful scaly appearance, which, united with its singular color, made their limbs not a little resemble dusty specimens of verde-antique. Their flesh, in parts, hung down upon them in huge folds, like the overlapping plaits on the flank of a rhinoceros. . . . These repulsive-looking creatures appeared to have lost the use of their lower limbs altogether; sitting upon the floor cross-legged in a state of torpor. (92–93)

The tribal elders' senility, their immobility, their sinking flesh: all symbolize a culture stagnating. The Typees here are not somehow anterior to time, in an Edenic la-la land as Tommo sometimes imagines, but suffering from the full weight of time, as it passes them by. More flesh than sentience, the elders seem to have become part of the natural, animal realm—and thereby essentially nonhuman. But, of course, the Typees are no more or less natural, or human, than Tommo himself; and more careful scrutiny of the scene shows an opposed concern being voiced. For what leads to the horrid "dull green color" is, in fact, a superabundance of culture: the tattoos spread about the entire surface of the skin.

The passage, in short, betrays Tommo's discomfiture in contradictory terms. The Typees lack the driving energy of his own culture, have become immobile in time, and thus seem closer to nature. Yet that which has "obliterated every trace of humanity" is the code of culture inscribed upon their bodies. Tommo without being philosophical about it thereby replicates, in his scopic obsession with how the natives look, what we have seen in Ledyard in respect to "debas[ing]" practices obscuring an essential, shared humanity.

What applies on the strictly imagistic level, applies as well when Tommo more explicitly ponders the *meaning* of native customs. Not the absence of native historicity, but its radical opacity to his own intellect disturbs him. This may be confirmed by a look at one crucial scene in which he fuses together his linguistic, historical, and legal befuddlement, epitomizing what could be called a leitmotif of deliberate incomprehension. Chief Mehevi explicates the purpose of a ritual, the Feast of Calabashes; but Tommo remains mystified, so Kory-Kory takes him on a guided tour of the Taboo Groves:

On leaving the Ti, Kory-Kory, who had as a matter of course accompanied me, observing that my curiosity remained unabated, resolved to make everything plain and satisfactory. With this intent, he escorted me through the Taboo Groves, pointing out to my notice a variety of objects, and *endeavored to explain them in such an indescribable jargon of words, that it almost put me in bodily pain to listen to him.* In particular, he led me to a remarkable pyramidical structure some three yards square at the base, and perhaps ten feet in height, which had lately been thrown up, and occupied a very conspicuous position. It was composed principally of large empty calabashes, with a few polished cocoa-nut shells, *and looked not unlike a cenotaph of skulls*. My cicerone perceived the astonishment with which I gazed at this monument of savage crockery, and immediately addressed himself to the task of enlightening me: but all in vain; and to this hour the *nature of the monument remains a complete mystery to me*. (160, emphasis added)

Here again Tommo belittles native speech, but why should he also insist, specifically, that Kory-Kory's lecturing almost literally hurts him? The symmetry between his remark about the odd pile of calabashes and coconut shells ("the nature of the monument remains a complete mystery to me") and his earlier comment about his aching leg ("the origin and nature of [the pain] were still a mystery") hints that the etiology of the latter may be associated with the former. Tommo's "bodily pain" here originates not from his being burdened with an historical consciousness in a land that time forgot, but rather from the abstruse language of the rituals of those who hold him captive. Not the mindlessness, or primitiveness, or timelessness of Typee culture irritates him, but his incapacity to penetrate the Typee mind in its cultural and historical dimensions. His observation that neither Kory-Kory "nor the rest of his countrymen knew anything about" the ruins may thereby be seen more as a willed misrecognition of the historical as opposed to naturally given status of Typeean culture. Rather than being an originary, prelapsarian society, the Typees, no less than Tommo, exist in time and are ruled by an intricate sociojuridical apparatus that is constructed through time. And if Mehevi's repeated questions about the "Franee" (79), the French invaders on the island, are a proper indication, they are, moreover, attuned to the ongoing history of their relations to interlopers upon their lands.

The passage on the Taboo Groves is pointedly revelatory mostly in respect to what does not quite come into full consciousness for Tommo. The episode is peculiar because he, through the litotes of the pyramid structure looking "not unlike a cenotaph of skulls," at once raises and represses anxiety about the sacred ground's being a possible site for cannibalistic banquets. Here, incomprehension may be matched by a desire *not* to comprehend: were Tommo to understand Kory-Kory he would learn he has nothing to fear (Kory-Kory presumably would not expound a tribal ritual of cannibalism to its next victim); by not understanding Kory-Kory, he subconsciously feels threatened but also skirts the import of the native's technical monologue. Tommo prefers his insecurity about the Typees' being cannibals to the more dreadful recognition that, if they are cannibals, their cannibalistic practice is in their terms legally and systematically regulated. Not being able to grasp Kory-Kory, while ostensibly a failure of communication, thus serves a psychological purpose. It allows Tommo to deem native law as either entirely natural and benign or too barbarically irrational to be designated as law in the first place. What Tommo cannot countenance, apparently, is that the laws of "natural" societies might be just as coercive, cruel, and culturally scripted as those of so-called civilized ones. Or, to put it in slightly different terms, what he cannot tolerate is the idea that native social life—and an abhorrent ritual such as cannibalism—evolves through choice, through communal acts of assent. Disgusted with the historical and imperial actions of Western nations, Tommo wants the Typees to be subject to, not agents of, history and the social practices that develop over time.

Typee distinguishes itself, oftentimes, by the narrator's refusal to follow the conventions of exploratory travel literature, one of which is to elaborate at some length upon archaeological and ethnographic features. Tommo cannot be expected to evaluate the function of taboo when he is an actor in the narrative: he is not exactly in the position to do extensive fieldwork. But at that other time, when he inhabits the moment of retrospective storytelling, when he draws upon Ellis, Porter, and Stewart, this refusal to speculate upon the meaning of Typeean customs and taboos turns out to be not only a reluctance to make ethnographical statements, which he believes usually are inaccurate, but the result as well of not wanting to know, even retrospectively, that the Typees do in fact subscribe to formal regulations, however puzzling to himself. When Tommo says he "saw everything" but could "comprehend nothing" (177), he states what perhaps could not be otherwise. We should also note, though, that this posture of ethnographic humility serves on the strategic level to bracket-out how his experiential encounter thwarts his efforts to appropriate native culture to his own ends.

Tommo seeks to contain or stabilize the problems of American law and the historical subject, of the historicity of the law, by representing the Typees tendentiously; what slips out of those brackets, though, is the vexing historicity and not-so-natural law of the Typees. His impediments to theorizing satisfactorily about native law likely explain why he resorts to envisioning Chief Mehevi as the supreme ruler of the tribe. When Tommo insists that "Mehevi was in fact the greatest of the chiefs—the head of his clan—the sovereign of the valley," the repeated appositives signal less a matter of ascertained fact (we never learn the exact extent of his rule) than wishful thinking. Only by so conceiving Mehevi's regality and thereby contradicting his sentiments about the Typees' republican polity can Tommo foresee himself successfully "pay[ing] most assiduous court" to the chief, which in turn would give him hope of "obtain[ing]" his "liberty" (187).

Tommo's desire to discern extralegal or prelegal sources of social authority leads him, almost paradoxically, to adopt legal phrasing when describing strictly natural phenomena. He brings to the Typee valley a consciousness that cannot quite disencumber itself from history and issues of legality, and that consciousness sticks with him, in time present, even as he informs us about trivial matters. Thus he rather oddly interpolates legal argot into nonlegal contexts. After speculating upon the stone ruins, for instance, Tommo lapses into legalese when accounting for the origin of the island, "that the land may have been thrown up by a submarine volcano is as possible as anything else. No one can make an affidavit to the contrary, and therefore I will say nothing against the supposition" (155).[45]

Such jokingly verbose diffidence is a measure of Tommo's self-consciousness about the tension between fact and myth in respect to Polynesia, but it also displays how the main source of confusion, the Typees' cultural behavior, contagiously affects what otherwise would receive straightforward exposition. At such points Melville comes close to highlighting the discursive artifice, the sheer theatricality, of his text's anthropological optics. A more telling instance occurs at the outset of the story, when Tommo offers us a peep show of anticipated Marquesan exotica: "What strange visions of outlandish things does the very name spirit up! Naked houris—cannibal banquets—groves of cocoa-nut . . . sunny valleys planted with bread-fruit trees—carved canoes dancing on the flashing blue waters—savage woodlands guarded by horrible idols— *heathenish rites and human sacrifices*" (5). Tommo's italicized emphasis in the last phrase, a sort of tonal smirk, undermines as much as it intensifies the passage's prurient intent. I believe we would be mistaken, however, to read our contemporary postcolonial, poststructuralist skepticism back into Melville's text. Its equivocations about Typeean cannibalism—is the tribe guilty of the practice? Is there an ethos that palliates its horror?—should not lead us to reckon the narrative as transcending its time period, in which the fact of cannibalism's being practiced somewhere in the Polynesian island world (actual sightings were another matter) was not seriously disputed. In Melville's case, the urge to disclose the *truth* of cannibalism anticipates the hermeneutic, questing drive of his later works, in which the gnostic motive is severely embarrassed by, but does not finally become a fatality to, the deceitfulness of words or competing claims of truthfulness.

What cannibalism most forces Melville to meditate upon is his worrisome belief that natural law, rather than being a bulwark against transgression and a protector of individual sovereignty or the right of an intimate selfhood, can also be fundamentally invasive: he wants heart-law, the scripted "precepts" within, to remain metaphoric or emerging from the heart, not imposed upon it. Most alarming to Tommo during his captivity is, of course, the threat of being tattooed and eaten by the natives. His strongest impulse to flee arises from his fear, as he says, that he might be "disfigured in such a manner as never more to have the *face* to return [to his] countrymen, even should an opportunity offer" (219). He dreads that he might be incarcerated in a body that no longer represents him and that his identity would be inseparable from the ritualistic marks of a foreign culture. The law's unerasable markings, encoded on the body, horrify Tommo because he does not want to be facially mutilated; they also horrify him because Typeean society now strikes him as being a community of docile bodies upon which is inscribed a form of law that, while invasive, skirts being either consensual or nonconsensual. Tattooing, as with the panoply of taboos, does not exist as an ideological option, something that one might elect to adopt or resist: Tommo may have "perfect liberty" (220) to choose among different tattoo patterns, but he has no liberty to decide not to be tattooed, since the practice appears to be tied to the "all-controlling" "system of the 'Taboo'" (221). We can usefully gloss the bodily markings of the Typees, some of which are inscribed across the eyes, "the windows of [the] soul" (218), by what Nietzsche refers to when he speaks of the "prehistory of man" before the advent of writing. He describes such customary markings as a legalistic mnemotechnics: "If something is to stay in the memory it must be burned in: only that which never ceases to hurt stays in the memory."[46] Whether or not the Typees perceive their tattoos in that way we cannot know, but it seems to be how Tommo thinks about them, as he witnesses a native "suffering [the] agony" (217) of their application.

Increasingly anxious about his fate, which he believes hinges on whether the Typees are or are not cannibals, Tommo feels compelled to peek into a suspicious wooden vessel. The natives shout "Taboo! taboo!" at the very moment he lifts its cover to glimpse the grisly contents within: "[My] eyes fell upon the disordered members of a human skeleton, the bones still fresh with moisture, and with particles of flesh clinging to them here and there!" (238). The native admonishment at once signals the infraction Tommo is about to commit and equates, by contiguity, the name or essence of the law—"Taboo! taboo!"— with a cannibalized corpse. Now, it is not the natural or interior "common-sense law" that regulates the Typees, but an inexplicable network of taboos that has no discernible foundational principle guiding it. Tommo does not know, and thus cannot articulate, what particular law he has broken. Just so, earlier in the story he had impugned a "lately adopted" law for destroying men, in his metaphor, "piece-meal, drying up in their veins, drop by drop, [their] blood" (125), but does not divulge the specific law itself. In both cases the withholding of what law has been transgressed—the one recently passed, the other sanctioned by historical but (to him) mysterious custom—amounts to a momentary fit of aphasia on Tommo's part. In both instances, the rationale of the law cannot be accounted for, and interdiction appears simply to arise in human affairs for interdiction's sake.

Until recently, scholarship on the theme of cannibalism in *Typee* has centered mainly on the issue of veracity: about whether the actual Typees were, in fact, cannibalistic and in turn about how we are to regard Tommo's reckoning of them as such. More adventurous exegesis, which I alluded to earlier, has seen the Eurocentric fantasy about the aberrant craving for human flesh as being linked with unutterable sexual practices—that is, homosexuality. Rather than expand upon such a reading, however, I want to look at cannibalistic ingestion in a manner more in line with the thematics of the law. Ledyard and those who carried on the tradition of counterbalancing interior heart-law against external, noxious customs would judge cannibalism, as did the missionaries, as the most depraved of social practices: as a mutilation of the cannibal's and, more literally, the cannibalized's humanity.

Metaphorically, Typee tattooing and cannibalism represent for Tommo what might be called gothicized, corporealized forms of the law. The trope of incorporating the common law (to have it "within us, written upon the table of our hearts," in Jesse Root's phrasing) figuratively works to conjoin the material body, with all the prerogatives of Lockean selfhood, to that reified abstraction of the body politic and the principles of governance that sustain its political-social health. The subject's internalization of authority is, we know, one of the master themes of the nineteenth century. Cannibalism, as Tommo imagines it, is the nightmarish trope of the subject interiorized within the law. It renders literal, and demonizes, what eighteenth- and nineteenth-century Western theorists of the law, including those in the United States, all hoped the law would do: fully enfold the individual citizen. Its all-too-visceral enactments grotesquely invert the relation of inside to outside. Tommo jumped ship because he had felt estranged from a realm of legal rule that might otherwise have preserved his sovereignty against the threats of Captain Vangs; he now wishes to escape the Typees because their practices, tattooing or cannibalism, would estrange him from his own body. Having fled Vangs, a name suggestive of *fangs*, Tommo discovers—or thinks he has discovered—a more voracious brutality at the hands, or mouths, of his captors.

The duress of paranoia becomes too much for him, and so he musters the strength, although still hobbled by his injury, to take flight. In the final episode, he takes vengeance against the linked sources of his anxiety: his inability to master the Typee language, his failure to fathom native legality and historicity, and his uncertainty about the hidden motives of his captors. When the one-eyed native Mow-Mow tries to thwart Tommo's escape by pursuing the longboat in which he is being rescued, Tommo shoves a boat-hook into his throat. Of all the significant, named natives in the novel, it is Mow-Mow whose voice we least hear. At this juncture, so radical is the native's foreignness, that the text simply cannot let him speak at all, but rather depicts him as a brute savage with only cannibalistic intent:

After a few breathless moments I discerned Mow-Mow. The athletic islander, with his tomahawk between his teeth, was dashing the water before him till it foamed again. He was the nearest to us, and in another instant he would have seized one of the oars. Even at the moment I felt horror at the act I was about to commit; but it was no time for pity or compunction, and with a true aim, and exerting all my strength, I dashed the boat-hook at him. It struck him just below the throat, and forced him downwards. I had no time to repeat my blow, but I saw him rise to the surface in the wake of the boat, and never shall I forget the ferocious expression of his countenance. (252)

Conversely, as Tommo rushes toward the longboat, he begins to tune out native voices altogether: "[In] the blended confusion of sounds," he says, "I almost fancied I could distinguish the voices of my own countrymen" (248). Passing from marginal ground, the beach, into the longboat that will carry him to an American ship, which in turn will take him back to his country, Tommo reaffiliates himself with nonnative consciousness and conscience. And whatever qualms the latter gives him, he barely pauses as he devoices his pursuer, quite literally. All he sees, as he jabs Mow-Mow in the throat, is what he needs to see since he now implicitly posits an absolute communicative gap between himself and his previous captors: Mow-Mow's "ferocious expression," the countenance of dark savagery that sanctions Tommo's only aggressive act in the narrative.

The passage above and the one I began with, the "Portrait of Kory-Kory," stand as paradigmatic bookends to *Typee*. The Mow-Mow scene represents the native stereotypically; he is looked upon just long enough to confirm his barbaric typicality (the "ferocious expression" Tommo cannot "forget"). Kory-Kory, trapped behind the prison-bars of his own culture, invites sentimental musings on Tommo's part, musings which at least implicitly suggest a desire to gaze beyond the stereotype, even though the object of that gaze, Kory-Kory's essential (by which I mean individual, not cultural) selfhood cannot quite be reached. The first scopic encounter symbolizes or sets in motion the novel's troubled meditations on the law; the second represents, if we wish to pull forth a metaexegetical point, the violence of the stereotype itself, or the violence that the latter sanctions.[47] This last scene also caps the necessary telos of all travel volumes, the eventual return home after an itinerary through a foreign setting, and the publication of the travel-report which, as Janet Giltrow notes, "announces [the traveler's] reincorporation into a familiar community and the end to his provisional alienation."[48] The episode nonetheless does not fully conjoin Tommo's subjectivity to the community of his countrymen. Hearing a "confusion of sounds," he is left confused.

The Disembodied Narrator and the Hawaiian Body Politic

Because of that confusion, I believe, the end of Tommo's story is not the end of the book. Melville includes an appendix. Although a late addition written at the behest of Melville's British publisher to make the work more topical, it is not thematically superfluous.[49] Tommo has violently devoiced Mow-Mow. Now the appendix must reconcile the narrator's conscience to that act and, more broadly, to a conception of the law with which he can live. The narrator of the appendix does so by speaking for the collective conscience of the Hawaiian natives and by envisioning the British commander, Lord Paulet, as the perfect lawgiver. Except for occasional outbursts of diatribe, the relations between the colonizing powers and Polynesia have been secondary to the narrative of Tommo's adventures. In the appendix, those historical relations fully emerge, while simultaneously, the narrator extricates himself from the time frame of his own story.

He reviews the baleful outcome of the Hawaiian government's being run by a "junto of ignorant and designing Methodist elders in the councils of a half-civilized king" (255). Lord George Paulet had arrived in Honolulu to redress injustices that this "iniquitous maladministration" (255) had committed upon the local British population. Taking "measures which unusual exigencies . . . [had] rendered necessary" (258), he had forced the provisional cession of Hawaii to Britain (on February 25, 1843) and then entered, we are told, "upon the administration of Hawiian affairs, in the same firm and benignant spirit which marked the discipline of his frigate, and which had rendered him the idol of his ship's company" (256). Five months later, upon the arrival of Paulet's superior, Rear-Admiral Thomas, native rule was summarily restored:

[His] Majesty announced to his loving subjects the re-establishment of his throne, and called upon them to celebrate it by breaking through all moral, legal, and religious restraint for ten consecutive days, during which time all the laws of the land were solemnly declared to be suspended.

Who that happened to be at Honolulu during those ten memorable days will ever forget them! The spectacle of universal broad-day debauchery, which was then exhibited, beggars description. . . . It was a sort of Polynesian saturnalia. Deeds too atrocious to be mentioned were done at noon-day in the open street . . . [and] Kekuanoa inform[ed] the white men, with a sardonic grin, that the laws were "hannapa" (tied up).

The history of these ten days reveals in their true colors the character of the Sandwich islanders, and furnishes an eloquent commentary on the results which have flowed from the labors of the missionaries. Freed from the restraints of severe penal laws, the natives almost to a man had plunged voluntarily into every species of wickedness and excess, and by their utter disregard of all decency plainly showed, that although they had been schooled into a seeming submission to the new order of things, they were in reality as depraved and vicious as ever. (257–58)

Never having fully taken to missionary rule, yet not having an indigenous polity of rational consent to fall back upon, the body politic of the Hawaiians devolves into mobbish disorder and "voluntar[y]" individual "excess."

The intended effect of the tone of revulsion, of the hypermoralized diction, is difficult to assess. In the haze of outrage, the censure of corrupt rulers fuses into a condemnation of the pre-evangelized Hawaiian "character."[50] The hazy tone is matched by a hazy reconstruction of history. The "saturnalia" preceded rather than followed the restoration of native government, or occurred under as well as after the last days of Paulet's administration.[51] Moreover, the recession of the laws and the revoking of penalties by King Kamehameha III applied mainly to transgressions committed by the native populace under the duress of Paulet's imposed government. July 31, the date of the king's proclamation, in fact remained for many years the foremost national holiday in Hawaii. The appendix, imagining it can now voice the mass sentiment of the Hawaiians, concludes nonetheless with unstinting praise: "[To] this hour the great body of the Hawiian people invoke blessings on his head, and look back with gratitude to the time when his liberal and paternal sway diffused peace and happiness among them" (258).[52]

Rivalry and mutual jealousy between the major sea powers had thus far kept the Hawaiian Islands from coming under the rule of either the United States, France, Russia, or Britain.[53] So the outrage of Americans at Paulet's usurpation—the wife of one of the missionary power brokers called him a "surly mastiff"—was merely self-interest posturing as altruism.[54] Nonetheless, what the appendix leaves unsaid is that Paulet's martial law abrogated the authority of the Hawaiian Constitution of 1840. What it elides is that Paulet ignores the authority vested in a document no less than Captain Vangs had ignored, by Tommo's account, the contract between sailor and commander. The action of *Typee* began with tyranny overriding contractual law, with force supplanting the letter of the law. Now force also supplants the letter of the law. In this case, however, the usurpation is interpreted positively because the alternatives explored during Tommo's stay among the Typees have proven to be repugnant.

Melville's special pleading on behalf of Paulet—he calls it a "mere act of justice" (254)—may have stemmed from his friendship, while he was in Honolulu, with an English merchant who took the commander's side against the missionaries. But given his skepticism about the benefits of any intercourse—commercial, religious, political, or sexual—between American-European and Polynesian cultures, and given that even in Britain, where *Typee* was first published, Paulet's actions were hardly sanctioned (the naval ministry sent out his superior to restore native government immediately), we must suppose that the appendix's peculiar tonal inflections and rhetoric work to address conflicts originating in the previous narrative as much as they mirror a sentiment of youthful loyalty. The "bluff and straightforward" Paulet (255), Melville insists, manages to command his ship crew without recourse to the corporal punishments habitually resorted to by the British navy. His charismatic character "mark[s] the discipline" of the sailors; so the mnemonic marks of the whip are simply not required. The narrator's encomiums on Paulet, on his "paternal sway" and his being revered as the "idol of his ship's company," neatly replace Tommo's rebellious gesture against the disciplinary "paternal solicitude" (30) of Captain Vangs and his anxiety over the superstitious rule of taboo. Tommo had occasion to allude to Rousseau when speaking of the "continual happiness" of the Typees, which springs from the "mere buoyant sense of a healthful physical existence" (127). A different quotation from Rousseau will serve to highlight the motive behind the Paulet accolade. In *The Social Contract* he speaks of the lawgiver who "can lead without compelling and persuade without convincing." Such power, neither coercive nor rational, depends upon the lawgiver's being exalted to the status of a mythic figure or god, an idol, so that the "people [will] obey with freedom and bear the yoke of public well-being with docility."[55] Tommo, as embodied actor in the narrative, initially had fled the *Dolly* because its commander ruled by brutal physical force, by the "butt end of a hand-spike"; and he had fled the Typee valley because he had been threatened by "disfigur[ing]" tattoos and the puzzling rule of uncodified taboo, whose main ritual would lead to bodily dispersion ("disordered members"). Now, in the appendix, Tommo abstracts himself out of his own story and escapes his body altogether. He dissolves into the disembodied, retrospective narrator of "the author of this volume" (254), whose subjectivity blurs with what he takes to be the memory of nonnative consensus ("Who that happened to be at Honolulu during those ten memorable days will ever forget them"); and who then abstractly extols Paulet's "benignant spirit" and tells us how the "body" of the Hawaiian natives "invoke blessings on his head."[56]

What comes next upon *Typee*'s completion from that narrator's, or Melville's, perspective is to dedicate the book to an American magistrate, "LEMUEL SHAW, Chief Justice of the Commonwealth of Massachusetts," who literally appears in name only. We could interpret this last gesture as being tongue in cheek.[57] It certainly confounded the novel's first reviewers, who, not knowing that Shaw was soon to be Melville's father-in-law, saw the author as mocking the judge's sober morality and staunch legalism.[58] But the dedication functions much like the near idolization of Lord Paulet: by deferring to an author or figurehead of the law, the narrator or Melville evades resolving whether or not natural legalism, the "precepts graven on every breast," constitutes a less or more coercive form of social rule than that which is based upon written law codes. Indeed, to defer to a benign (benign, at least, in the absence of some textual counterclaim) external authority such as Shaw may very well differ little from submitting to an internalized heart-law. In either case, one relinquishes the possibility of dissent, since true liberty presumably would mean having the freedom or willpower consciously to resist the law. When authority is irresistible—because it is internalized, charismatic, or perceived as benign—dissent and consent simply have no meaning. The dedication when read as the final act of composition should remind us that Melville's impulse to rebel against authority uneasily and tensely coexisted with the opposite, conservative impulse to submit to it. That conflict is the hallmark of virtually all of Melville's subsequent novels. *Typee* may lack those works' high artistry; but, by focusing Melville's attention upon the mixed blessings of different forms of the law, this first major publication with its narrative of his encounter with the Typees inaugurated and made possible his later inquiries into the complexities of power and authority.

Melville's travels through Polynesia in the early 1840s and the writing of *Typee* helped him to establish a critical posture of wariness toward his own culture's claim, as Bronson Alcott put it, of having "monopolized the best of time and space." In his next two works, *Omoo* (1847) and *Mardi* (1849), he continued to draw upon his adventures in Polynesia, and he continued, even more vehemently, to satirize the pretensions of the Protestant missionaries. But neither, unlike *Typee*, sustainedly registers its complaints about antebellum society through the depiction—however self-serving—of actual Polynesians. In neither do we feel, via their protagonists and narrators, situated vicariously within a palpably rendered foreign realm. These texts, instead, resist the binarism of *Typee* and, as anthropologist James Boon observes, open up a discursive domain where "all cultures, histories, languages, and rhetorics theatrically, parodically, semiotically, and apocalyptically collide."[59]

Not surprisingly, then, when Melville went on the lecture circuit a decade later, he could not make sense, entirely, of his previous life as a sailor touching on Polynesian shores. He recollected the history of discovery in the Pacific; described the sundry enchantments of balmy days and attractive natives; and wrapped up his lecture with a request, "beg[ging] as a general philanthropist" that the Hawaiian Islands not be annexed to a nation that presented so many ailments of its own. Nothing in the lecture is discordant with the views he expressed in *Typee* either about the Typees themselves or about his own culture; what is discordant is his strained effort to cater to public taste. In one striking passage, he luridly tantalizes the audience: "I would direct the gas to be turned down, and repeat in a whisper the mysterious rites of the 'taboo,' but the relation would so far transcend any of Mrs. Radcliffe's stories in the element of the horrible that I would not willingly afflict any one with its needless recital."[60] Tommo's grisly description of what he assumed were the scraps of a cannibal feast lapses into a similarly self-conscious gothicism, but the passage here is utterly phantasmagorical—at once conveying that the rites are, as it ostensibly states, too "horrible" to be told; and yet also, by virtue of its extravagant theatricality, distancing the audience from any *real* encounter.

Melville's intensely formative experience while living with the Typees becomes, twelve years after the publication of *Typee*, the fictitious claptrap of the gothic novel. This is not to say that Melville's own memory of his life with the Typees had become drained of significance. Rather, he overplays sensationalism because he could no longer count on his auditors being very interested about the South Sea islands or their inhabitants. His uneasiness in the lecture results from the fact that for his audience, by and large, narratives about Polynesians did not elicit quite the same response they had from the time of Cook's narrative to the time of *Typee*'s publication. Highly gratifying reports of missionary accomplishments would continue to be published, and all of Polynesia would continue to exert what one could call a long half-life, or afterglow, of the exotic. But the very success of the missionaries in converting Hawaii into a semirepublican, Protestant nation made it less the fascinating arena it once had been, when the emissaries of American Protestantism, as it were, heroically battled the forces of pagan darkness. As Mark Twain half sarcastically, half nostalgically summed it up in *Roughing It* (1872), the latter fourth of which recounts his tour of Hawaii in 1866–67, such were "those old bygone days."[61]

The discursive community interested in issues of the law—missionaries; social commentators such as Richard Henry Dana, Jr.; U.S. lawyers and judges themselves; and, of course, Melville and his contemporary readers—came into ideological conjunction around Polynesian affairs in the middle of the nineteenth century. Other U.S. narratives, other national topoi, could be told. I have, for instance, not remarked upon *Typee* as a version of American pastoralism; nor have I commented, except in passing, upon the links between it and novels or travel reports about the republic's own indigenous native population. James Fenimore Cooper's Leatherstocking series, for example, sustains a running theme on the tension between natural, immemorial law (the law of the Indian native's woods practiced by Natty Bumppo) and positive law, tallied to the political necessities and convenience of a nation in flux. And a novel such as Cooper's *Crater* (1847)—which condenses the history of the United States and indeed, in a sense, universal history itself, by charting the fortunes of its hero, Mark Woolston, as he attempts to found a colony, battles with indigenes, and sees his new home overrun by a democratical rabble—has significant overlap with the issues of freedom and constraint at stake in *Typee*.

At base, no less than in many of Cooper's novels, *Typee* is about the cost of historicity: about what gets left behind in time's tracks, not so much indigenous cultures and their intrinsic merits—though that, too—but an alluring realm seemingly absent of artifice, before the elaborate push and pull of contending democratic, political forces; before, most fundamentally, the time of dialogue mediated by the vexations of written culture (Cooper's native characters, although at times absurdly verbose and stilted in their diction, are intended to exemplify natural eloquence). When Tommo crosses from the European-dominated shore to the hidden valley of the Typees, he wants to believe that he enters into an exotically foreign, Edenic time. In the next two chapters, we will witness kindred desires for a sublimity that can be found only elsewhere, far way from Western historicity: that of travelers to the Holy Land, who scanned its sacred geography for signs of the Word's numinosity; and that of archaeological-ethnographical explorers, whose U.S.-Eurocentric longing for a "pure" space outside of the debilitations of temporality will from the start be blocked, even as it is defined, by their phobic reaction to the hybrid races and history of tropical America.

CHAPTER THREE

Desire, Transgression, and the Holy Land

> What is found in the profane world is a radical secularization of
> death, marriage, and birth; but, as we shall soon see, there remain
> vague memories of abolished religious practices and even a
> nostalgia for them.
>
> — Mircea Eliade, *The Sacred and the Profane:*
> *The Nature of Religion*

> The Almighty withheld from the Israelites all knowledge of the
> final resting-place of their great lawgiver: may not the same
> Supreme Wisdom have left us in ignorance of the exact position of
> places infinitely more sacred, to preserve them from desecration,
> whether of wanton malice or intemperate zeal?
>
> —William F. Lynch, *Narrative of the United States'*
> *Expedition to the River Jordan and the Dead Sea*

> Whitish mildew pervading whole tracts of landscape—bleached—
> leprosy—encrustation of curses. . . . Is the desolation of the land
> the result of the fatal embrace of the Deity? Hapless are the
> favorites of heaven.
>
> —Herman Melville, *Journals*

> [In] the anguish of death, something is lost and eludes us, a dis-
> order begins within us, an impression of emptiness, and the state
> which we enter is similar to that which precedes a sensual desire.
>
> —Georges Bataille, *Literature and Evil*

THE IDEOLOGICAL anxieties that *Typee* sounds emerged out of a
widespread concern about the status of natural or foundational law. They
are also, though, intensely Melvillean. A more venturesome reading would
have delved into what in the previous chapter I had mentioned only in passing: the foreign realm eliciting or echoing the otherness within—that is, homoerotic difference which, in the narrative, becomes split into the *non*-story
of the bond between Tommo and Toby on the one hand, and the bodily thematics of cannibalism on the other. The parallels and crossovers, to come into

view, would require a more theoretical, psychoanalytical lens—one that would magnify *Typee*'s preoccupations with the law (albeit at the cost of skirting its specific legal or contextual milieu) into an ahistorical probing of the Law of the Father. In such a reading, the bad Captain Vangs would stand in as the Father whose authority is simply a given, a prohibitive regime that pressures the rebellion of desire (Tommo's and Toby's affection and flight); and cannibalism would symbolize the monstrosity of the Law itself, when it becomes grounded in no certain person, is everywhere and nowhere, and in fact merges with appetite; for the Law, writ large, wants to be pervasive, externally operative in specific taboos but internally informing all dispositions and desires. At the same time, the secretiveness of cannibalism and the shock value of its *almost* discovery would represent a transgressive epiphany that, going against the bourgeois order of normality, would also be aligned with homosexual knowledge (if not quite acknowledgment), although here, too, we can give these issues a final twist: for in Melville the urge to "peep" is an urge directed toward both the forbidden (cannibalism and homosexuality) and the genealogical roots of the law, whether formulated as natural law, taboo law, or, more psychoanalytically, the Law of the Father.

The law/homoerotic/cannibalism nexus is barely visible in *Typee*, and so I have resisted a more than cursory sketching of its contours. Transgressive sexuality and a concern about Fatherly prohibition will however be partially the subject of this chapter, when I turn to the somber meditations of Melville's outsized, omnibus *Clarel: A Poem and Pilgrimage in the Holy Land*, in which the Dead Sea as a personal and cultural trope collapses together otherness in multiple forms. It at once stands as the Levant's blighted epicenter; the topographical correlative of the absent, unknowable Protestant God (or, rather, one knowable only through the catastrophic effects of divine judgment); and the geographical symbol of Melville's own psychosexual self-identity, the enigmatic inward corridors that haunted him and became the subject of his most elusive fiction, especially *Pierre; or, the Ambiguities* (1852).[1] Although composed after the Civil War and not published until 1876, *Clarel* is based upon Melville's trip to the Levant in 1857–58, a period of deep personal crisis, of social and theological anomie, that his post–Civil War years neither substantially changed nor mollified. He was, to be sure, attuned to new developments in science and sensitive to a transformed cultural and political landscape, but he tended to see the tokens of incipient modernity as confirming the old story of America's lost promise, the darkening of its beacon of hope, of its not recreating the world.

Melville's poem—one of the most complex (and certainly underestimated) works of the nineteenth century—could stand on its own as exemplifying a certain crisis in what I shall refer to as theological mimesis, the effort to coordinate the Word, the world of the Holy Land, and words about the latter. I wish, though, to broaden my case study approach to include several other primary authors, both to illumine Melville's neglected late work and because their texts deserve analysis in their own right. This chapter examines a diversity of writers with varying political interests who cathect with the Holy Land's ruinous but biblically surcharged topographies and histories. In the Levantine context, otherness becomes doubly vexatious: a matter of confronting not just non–Anglo-Saxon peoples but also a disturbingly offensive landscape littered with holy shrines and relic sellers, which—precisely because it was the original home of Christianity—all the more uncannily registered the Protestant distrust of and secretive yearning for physical emblems of the Godhead. Repulsion, though, will be balanced by sentimentality, in two forms, which conjoin to link the way of the Protestant heart to the American way itself: the utopic motive to convert non-Christians and redeem a cursed landscape, and the urge of the Protestant pilgrim-traveler to fill in inward desolations with the heart-knowledge of Christ. If Melville and his contemporaries often portrayed the Marquesas Islands as an Edenic realm outside of time, U.S. travelers to the Holy Land saw it as containing *all* of time, a region uniquely resonant with the most personal and public aspects of the Protestant ethos, speaking both to its haunting voids or exaltations and to the nation's role in redemptive history.

Consensus opinion held that Hawaii offered the absorbing spectacle of a U.S.-led ascent out of benighted barbarism. Other non-European realms— Latin America and Africa (or, at least, the regions surrounding the Liberian settlement)—also appeared destined to be awakened by Northern, white-ruled ones. The "inferior races," Arnold Guyot predicted in his 1849 textbook *The Earth and Man*, will "come forth from the state of torpor and debasement into which they are plunged, and live the active life of the higher races" (307). By his lights, the continents were providentially disposed to guarantee that glorious elevation:

History seems to be advancing towards the realization of these hopes, towards the solution of this great contrast. Each northern continent has its southern continent near by which seems more especially commended to its guardianship and placed under its influence. Africa is already European at both extremities; North America leans on South America, which is indebted to the example of the North for its emancipation and its own institutions. Asia is gradually receiving into her bosom the Christian nations of Europe, who are transforming her character, and beginning thence to settle the destinies of Australia. (307–8)

The Near East (today, more commonly labeled as the Middle East), though, posed something of a dilemma. Guyot lauds the "true Western Asia, the Asia of history" as the "original country of the white race, the most perfect in body and mind" (269), from whence ancient civilization and Christianity spread.

Yet he has trouble showing how Caucasian culture, transported through the epochs to the West, would redeem the sacred territory now in his own era under Turkish rule. Although his volume includes sections on "Eastern Asia" and "Western Asia," the Levant per se receives the least attention of all the major geographical regions in *The Earth and Man*. The text's near occlusion of the Holy Land suggests how antebellum Americans regarded it: immensely relevant for mapping the geotemporal origins and destiny of their own land, but barely approachable politically.

In fact, the Holy Land—unlike Hawaii, other Polynesian islands, Latin America, or Africa—held slight political or commercial interest for U.S. citizens. It lacked major centers of government or global trade, and, except for nearby Egypt, could boast of few impressive ruins. The conflict at the turn of the eighteenth century with the so-called Barbary States over the payment of tribute had helped bolster nationalist sentiment, especially during the Tripolitan war of 1801–5, in which U.S. marines exercised the might of the young republic. But the hostilities—although entering the cultural archive via Susanna Rowson's *Slaves in Algiers* (1794), Royall Tyler's *The Algerine Captive* (1797), and other Early Nationalist texts—by midcentury had become a distant memory.[2] The U.S. Navy's vessels only occasionally stopped at ports along the southeastern coast of the Mediterranean; and diplomatic efforts were little more than halfhearted (a treaty of friendship with the Ottomans, which President John Adams had initiated in 1799, took some thirty years to complete). Protestant missionaries adopted a more active stance. The American Board of Commissions for Foreign Missions in 1818 dispatched Pliny Fisk and Levi Parsons to posts in Palestine, and they were followed by a steady stream of capable ministers. If tolerated, however, they won few converts. Muslim apostasy was a capital offense under Ottoman law; and "Oriental" (Greek or Coptic) Christian and Judaic sects simply were not interested.

Throughout the nineteenth century, the bulk of the area that Americans and Europeans loosely designated as the Holy Land—Palestine, Syria, and other eastern Mediterranean locales associated with the Bible—putatively lay under Turkish control. The Ottomans had dominated it since the sixteenth century, but it had become a backwater to the moribund empire whose preoccupations of state lay elsewhere. Centralized authority from Istanbul barely extended to the region, and real power resided in the provincial governors. Egypt, once Napoleon's army withdrew, was strongly ruled by the pasha Mohammad Ali, an Albanian-born Ottoman soldier, who after a dispute with the Ottoman sultan, Mahmud II, invaded and seized Syria in 1831, occupying it for nine years. He was a reformer, and under his reign bureaucracies were modernized, greater tolerance was granted to non-Muslims, and the desert Bedouin tribes were curbed from preying on local farmers and foreign travelers. Eventually

rule passed back to the Ottoman Empire, with the reformist lead of Mohammad Ali being continued by Abdul Medjid I (Mahmud II's son), who also
cautiously began to seek diplomatic relations with the West and to court
European military and industrial expertise. In 1844, Secretary of State John
Calhoun appointed Warder Cresson, a Philadelphian Quaker, as the first U.S.
official consul in Jerusalem. Subsequently, foreigners could expect some degree of security when traveling through the Levant. From the late 1840s, tourist
pilgrimages became increasingly commonplace and, indeed, a routine part of
an itinerary abroad (the indefatigable British publisher of travel guides, John
Murray, issued one on the Holy Land in 1858). Travel conditions would continue to be forbidding—roads were poor, rail service inadequate, and disease
rampant; but packet tours since the late 1860s had laid out standard travel
routes. During the latter third of the century, a trip to the Holy Land had become less a novelty than a tourist commodity, supported by the marketing in
the United States of innumerable guidebooks, stereoscopic views, popular
lecture series, and assorted religious bric-a-brac.[3]

In the middle of the century, however, the area still could be reckoned as a
strange blend of the fabular and repugnantly familiar. On the one hand, popular
travelogues and potboiler novels—George William Curtis's *Nile Notes of a
Howadji* (1851); its sequel, *The Howadji in Syria* (1852); and Marturin Murray
Ballou's *Circassian Slave: or, the Sultan's Favorite* (1851), for example—drew
upon the previous Romantic era's stereotypes of a sensual, mysterious Orient.
"Damascus is a dream of beauty as you approach it," Curtis wrote; but "the secret
charm of that beauty, when you are within the walls, is discovered only by penetrating deeper and farther into its exquisite courts, and gardens, and interiors, as
you must strip away the veils and clumsy outer robes to behold the beauty of the
Circassian or Georgian slave."[4] On the other hand, many antebellum texts also
invoked the customary republican aversion to what seemed to be Old World
depravity. The Orient's seductions required debunking, and thus in a coeval
text, John Ross Browne's *Yusef; or the Journey of the Frangi* (1853), we get an antithetical gloss on harem delights: "Every vestige of enchantment vanished in a
moment. There was not a single passable face in the crowd. The features were
coarse and sensual . . . the costume slovenly and unbecoming. . . . The fact is, life
in the Harem is one of absolute servitude, and disgusting sensuality."[5] This
strain of negative Orientalism, no less stereotypical, continued into the postbellum period, most notably in Mark Twain's satiric *Innocents Abroad* (1869), a
text that figures the Near East under Ottoman subjugation as the very antipode
of the nation of progress: "They never invent anything, never learn anything."[6]

Whether prudential or prurient, these texts approach the Holy Land as a
realm to be exposed to bourgeois view. Sites, legends, relics: all had to be tallied, their authenticity measured against the word of Scripture. To travel

through the Levant, or to read travelers' volumes about it, was to engage more tangibly a spiritual terrain already intimately known from Bible study and the typological reading of U.S. history. Puritan typology had cast the incipient republic as the New Israel, and that tradition, by the nineteenth century subsumed into the more amorphous rhetoric of the Redeemer Nation, profoundly shaped antebellum attitudes to Christianity's birthplace. The United States, many devout Protestants felt, held a special obligation to resurrect a Jewish homeland and convert the Jews as the crucial prelude to ushering in the Millennium. The more fervid of the latter, compelled by a sense of what we could call a U.S.-sponsored Zionist Manifest Destiny, immigrated to the Levant to establish Jewish/U.S. settler-colonies. Among the most celebrated of those who had their eyes toward Zion was Clorinda Minor, a strong-willed Philadelphian woman whose belief in the Second Coming led her to sacrifice the comforts of home for the hard work of establishing an agricultural, evangelical colony in Palestine.[7] Less grandiosely, U.S. pilgrim-travelers, carrying in hand the only book deemed requisite to orthodox faith, traversed the land in order to distinguish the numinously resonant from the claptrap of holy icons and legends purveyed by monks and the local citizenry.

What was called the study of "sacred geography" held a widespread, but paradoxical, appeal. It helped render the biblical story more concrete; yet only by relying on the pristine Word itself could one separate bona fide data from the morass of half-truths built up over the centuries by deluded Catholic commentators. To take a trip through the Holy Land, or to read about one, was to follow a path at once doubling and emphatically distinct from the sacrosanct narrative itself. Protestant scorn for European Catholic idolatry applied as well to Levantine sites, most especially that of the Church of the Holy Sepulchre, which with its gaudy decor and reliquaries seemed to vivify faith all too palpably.[8] Not surprisingly, then, nearly all U.S. Protestant-authored texts on the Holy Land abound in inconsistencies: simultaneously seeking to anchor faith in reverential locales and yet also repulsed by the shocking corporealization of spiritual matters.

The most respected biblical geographer of the era was Edward Robinson.[9] Erudite and meticulous, he set the standard, in both the United States and Europe, for Holy Land archaeological and geographical inquiry. Robinson was a faculty member at the conservative Andover Theological Seminary, an academy devoted to battling the tide of European post-Enlightenment skepticism that judged the Bible to be a flawed, at times contradictory, document. He came to regard the accurate mapping of biblical geography as crucial to explaining otherwise obscure and conflicting passages, and when he joined the Union Theological Seminary in New York City as the chair of biblical literature in 1837, he requested a sabbatical that would allow him to explore sacred territory firsthand. Setting forth in 1838, Robinson journeyed through the Holy Land for nine months, studying archeological ruins, topographical features, and Arab place names; and afterward, in 1841, he published his three-volume theological masterpiece *Biblical Researches in Palestine, Mount Sinai and Arabia Petræa*. The latter uses an elaborate calculus of biblical and ecclesiastical citation, inference, and geographical scrutiny either to determine the falsity of traditions about Scriptural episodes and sites or to amplify those traditions' value by validating their historical plausibility. In a chapter on Jerusalem's topography and antiquities, he spells out his wish to purge the Levant of false lore: a "vast mass of [ecclesiastical] tradition, foreign in its source and doubtful in its character," has "flourished luxuriantly and spread itself out widely over the western world." All knowledge of "Palestine, the Holy City, and its sacred places" has been, unfortunately, transmitted by the dubious "topography of the monks." Their commentary, he insists, "IS OF NO VALUE, *except so far as it is supported by circumstances known to us from the Scriptures or from other contemporary testimony*." He then follows with valid and invalid examples. The legend "which points out the place of our Lord's ascension on the summit of the Mount of Olives . . . is obviously false" because "it stands in contradiction to the Scriptural account, which relates that Christ led out his disciples 'as far as to Bethany,' and there ascended from them into heaven." By contrast, Robinson continues, he would not "venture to disturb the traditional location of Rachel's grave on the way towards Bethlehem . . . mentioned by . . . Jerome in the fourth century," because the "Scriptural narrative necessarily limits the spot to that vicinity."[10]

Robinson regards himself, in proper Protestant fashion, as clearing away ecclesiastical rubbish from the purity of Scripture on the one hand; and, on the other, as using empirical means to render Scripture more precise. The intent, as Herbert Hovenkamp observes, was "not proving that the Bible was true" so much as to "demonstrat[e] that it was not false."[11] Through his and his colleagues' labors in the field, Americans felt that they could lay proprietary claim to the region. "We know far more about the land of the Jews," a writer in *Harper's New Monthly Magazine* remarked, "than the degraded Arabs who hold it."[12] Such topological presumption bordered itself on being unorthodox, as we see in the best-selling *The Land and the Book* (1858), written by William M. Thomson, who spent some twenty-five years of missionary work in Syria and Palestine.[13] Thomson endorsed Robinson, not tongue in cheek, as "the greatest master of measuring tape in the world," and in his introduction avers that the "land where the Word-made-flesh dwelt with men is, and must ever be, an integral part of the Divine Revelation." Sensible enough, but then he more boldly asserts, without recognizing his own idolatry, the necessity of a secular, material supplement to the Bible: the "Land and the Book—with reverence be it said—constitute the ENTIRE and ALL-PERFECT TEXT, and should be studied together."[14]

The authors of biblical geographies reveal, more implicitly than explicitly, some of the insecurities of mid-nineteenth-century U.S. Protestantism. This chapter explores the tensions arising from the effort to locate congruities between the "Land" and the "Book," but I also wish to focus on more subtle, subtexual forms of what I call hermeneutical desire. To chart the multiple paths of that desire we will need to rely upon a different set of texts, ones less restricted to the staid empiricism of Robinson's volumes. The thematics studied will extend well beyond the strictly theological, for what is most fascinating about the U.S. imaginary of the Holy Land, of its sites and scenery, is the polymorphous features of its hermeneutics. Hermeneutical desire, in the texts subsequently examined, routes itself through a conflicted psychotheological terrain, interweaving both the libidinal and the religiously luminous. Desire will find its destination not so much in specific foreign bodies, or in the mirror of a non-European other per se, but rather in the topographies, relics, and monuments of the Levant—a haunted, uncanny landscape that does more than just in a chiaroscurolike way illuminate the U.S. Protestant subject or nation. Holy Land travel boosted U.S. patriotism and piety; it also, though, invited inquiry of varying degrees of profundity into the nature of an American selfhood whose main claim would be its capacity to ward off the sins, or consciousness about the sins, of history.

I begin with John L. Stephens's immensely popular *Incidents of Travel in Egypt, Arabia Petræa, and the Holy Land* (1837). The wasteland of Edom (the part of ancient Palestine located between the Dead Sea and the Gulf of Aqaba) simultaneously elicits Stephens's anxiety over his own physical debilities and motivates a masculinist quest to follow in the track of Moses, to visit, more particularly, originary sites of transgression and Old Testament wrath. His narrative of masculine hermeneutics, the working through of obstacles that transcode the geographical into the physiological, sets up the terms of discussion for the next three sections: the first on one of the more curious U.S. military-scientific ventures of the period, Lieutenant Commander William F. Lynch's expedition to survey the River Jordan and the Dead Sea; the second on Maria Susanna Cummins's intriguingly complex, though almost entirely forgotten, story of love in Lebanon, *El Fureidîs*, which, published six years after her 1854 *Lamplighter*, extends that novel's concern with Christic power—domiciled in the U.S. household and Protestant female heart—into new territory, to the reclamation of idolatrous terrains and the male subject; and, the last, on Herman Melville's *Clarel*, which reflects the psychotheological crises of the previous texts and yet also denies their sentimental resolutions, for in Melville's poem, as figured by its main character, there will be no return itinerary to the ideological consolations of American innocence. The Dead Sea, under which supposedly lay sunken the cursed cities of Sodom and Gomorrah, symbolizes for Melville the ne plus ultra of transgressive or proscribed knowledge. It is a nodal locale responsive to his twined investment, evident throughout his career, in homoerotic spaces or relations and the numinous yet wrathful Law of the Father. Melville nervously renders the Dead Sea's fatal seductions, what Curtis in *Nile Notes* referred to as its "bewitched desolation" (239), as the unutterable alternative to Clarel's blocked love for Ruth, the young half-Jewess who dies before the two seal their passion in nuptial rite. The texts of Stephens, Lynch, Cummins, and Melville, although diverse in genre and agenda, collectively chart the troubled Protestant effort to reconcile Scriptural antitheses: the Old and New Testaments, the Father and the Son, vengeance and love. In what follows, however, my interest lies less in these works' theological contours than in their limning of a more intimate response to the Holy Land. My emphasis is not on U.S. Protestants so much as on the Protestant body in the land of Scripture.

Groping in the Dark

In his partially autobiographical early novel *Redburn* (1849), Melville recalled having sighted while in church the "person who had been in Stony Arabia" and who had "passed through strange adventures there."[15] He probably was alluding to John L. Stephens, who, next to the prolific Bayard Taylor, was likely the most well known American traveler of his age. Stephens's *Incidents of Travel in Egypt, Arabia Petræa, and the Holy Land*, first published in 1837, earned him some $25,000 within two years, and within less than a decade it had gone through ten editions. The volume made him a celebrity, and its royalties helped bankroll subsequent travels to Central America (I will address his later Yucatán travelogues in the next chapter). It was praised as an American original, superseding the outdated, impressionistic accounts of the European Romantics, such as François Chateaubriand's *Itinéraire de Paris à Jérusalem* (1811). The book was novel on other grounds as well. Stephens's journey took him through the biblically banned land of Edom and to the site, only vaguely known about in the West, of the ancient ruined city of Petra. The intaglio city had been discovered in 1812 by the Swiss explorer Johannes Burckhardt, but the latter's mysterious death in Cairo in 1817—some thought he had been punished for going through Edom—only added drama to Stephens's own venture.[16]

Stephens was born in 1805 in Shrewsbury, New Jersey. He at first planned for a career as a lawyer and was admitted to the New York Bar in 1828 after studying at the Tapping Reeve Law School in Litchfield, Connecticut. The tasks of an attorney, however, little appealed to him. "This profession is no fairy-land in which a person can indulge his heart," he wrote his father; and so he turned instead toward politics, serving as a stump speaker for Cornelius W. Lawrence's bid for the New York governorship in 1834.[17] During his speech-making he came down with a virulent case of strep throat, and his doctor advised a trip abroad to regain his health. Stephens toured through England, France, Italy, Greece, Turkey, Russia, and Poland the next year and was about to depart for the United States when he came across a copy of Léon de Laborde's *Voyage de l'Arabie Petrée* (1830). Given his lingering illness, the prudent choice would have been to return home, but the book's exotic descriptions so enthused him that he decided to explore the Levant for himself.

When Stephens started out, his goal was uncertain, and only later did the specific project of traversing Edom and locating Petra dawn upon him. His travels, taking almost a year, had three stages. After landing in Alexandria, he quickly went on to Cairo, where he visited the pyramids, chartered a small sloop sailed by a crew of Egyptians, and then, accompanied by a Maltese dragoman, Paolo Nuozzo, proceeded up the Nile as far as Aswan, exploring the ruins of Gizeh, Dendereh, Thebes, and Luxor. Surfeited with Egyptian sites, he then sought the more arduous adventure constituting the most dramatic part of his volume. He hired a caravan and embarked toward Jerusalem through the perilous desert route of Judea, with the intent of tracing the Israelite flight through the wilderness and, more particularly, finding the secluded site of Petra. After he had accomplished the exploit, he wrapped up his tour with a brief visit to the Dead Sea and Jerusalem. The appeal of his travel story to its American audience is easy to see. Stephens cut a romantic figure. Once outside of Egypt, he traveled under disguise, dressed in the garb of a Cairo merchant; and the volume, written in an urbane style, contains a number of droll anecdotes (as when, for instance, sailing up the Nile, Stephens shoots toward some pigeons and accidentally places a "shot . . . smack into the beautifully sculptured face of the goddess [Isis]"; or when his factotum, Paolo, serves up an unexpected meal of "Irish stew" to the delight of some British guests aboard his Nile sloop).[18] Readers, doubtlessly as well, would have concurred with Stephens's proposals for civic improvement. Habitually juxtaposing the antiquity of the land to its contemporary squalor, he at one juncture— inspired by the "genius of my native land"—muses on how, with the proper resources, he would transform an Alexandrine ghetto into "fine buildings, fine country houses, and gardens" (4).

Adventure and American panache or ethnocentrism: such are the surface features that potentially may keep us from seeing *Incidents of Travel in Egypt, Arabia Petræa, and the Holy Land*'s more nuanced psychotheological currents. Stephens, apparently, was fairly complacent in respect to his own faith. Yet he also reveals a longing to gaze upon sites of ancient idolatry, to penetrate into hallowed recesses, and to assume the mantle of an explorer-prophet retracing the path of Moses in the wilderness. If, on the one hand, the work displays a nearly compulsive seriality (over and over again he notes the speed of his progress), it also, on the other, lingers along an opposed, vertical axis. Stephens tries to superimpose his own itinerary upon the biblical narrative itself and thereby bring the latter into temporal intimacy. The goal of gaining access to some inner core or temenous of Scriptural luminosity takes on as the narrative proceeds what can only be called a certain visceral, alimentary dimension. The book traces a trek through, as it were, the very penetralia of the Bible. At one telling moment, he rues the lack of scholarly guidebooks to help him chart his way. Bereft of such texts, which might "illustrate[e] obscure passages in the sacred book," he finds himself, metaphorically, "groping in the dark" (190).

Stephens, in fact, foregrounds ocular and kindred somatic blockages, as if to travel across the blighted landscape to view sacred spots amounted to a physiological rite-of-passage through a cloacal terrain. Initially, he has troubles, in particular, navigating his way across the "fallen city of Alexander" and its squalid habitations—populated by "dirty, half-naked, sore-eyed Arabs, swarms of flies, [and] yelping dogs"—in order to survey sites that might recall the past "glory of Egypt" (4). Emphasizing his hurried "movements" (4) as he crosses a ghetto with its "poverty, and misery, and famine, and nakedness" (5), he finally finds himself on the outskirts of the city, whereupon "one glance" at the "majestic height" of Pompey's Pillar informs him "that this was indeed the work of other men and other times" (5). The appeal of past Egyptian grandeur, a masculine solidity, becomes more explicit later. Investigating a pyramid's interior, Stephens must fend off some young Arabs, who insist upon his patronage as he enters the darkened tunnels:

It is not the least interesting part of a visit to the interior of the pyramids, as you are groping your way after your Arab guide, to feel your hand running along the sides of an enormous shaft, smooth and polished as the finest marble, and to see by the light of the flaring torch chambers of red granite from the Cataracts of the Nile. . . . Having no janissary with me to keep them off, I was very much annoyed by the Arabs following me. . . . I shouted to them to go back, but they paid no regard to me; so, coming out of [the shaft] again, I could not help giving the fellow next to me a blow with a club, which sent him bounding among his companions. (34–35)

In these passages Stephens sets in place a network of oppositions—Arab sloth, disease, or mere intrusiveness versus his own ascetic diligence and eagerness to explore monuments—that comes to structure the remainder of his account. Oftentimes, what most seems both to repulse and fascinate him is the sheer otherness of the Arab body, which, as he puts it in one of many similar formulas, "seemed particularly black, naked, and hairy" (66). We can easily find this racial animus in other contemporary Western texts about the Near East,

but Arab bodies, especially dying and dead ones, also hold a personal resonance for Stephens. At key junctures, diseased Arabs and desiccated landscapes
remind him of his own bodily infirmity, evoking fears that he might fail to
survive his (according to Scripture) impious sojourn through Edom's cursed
terrain and thus replay, as legend had it, the story of his predecessor, Johannes
Burckhardt. Edgar Allan Poe wrote a long review of *Incidents of Travel in
Egypt, Arabia Petræa, and the Holy Land* in which he argued that following its
author's path through biblical geography would help Scripture "tak[e]" a
"palpable hold" upon the reader.[19] The subtext of Stephens's volume, however,
is the Levant's own repugnant and strangely alluring palpability.

Reading Stephens's Holy Land volume in tandem with his later Yucatán
works, which also fetishize hidden or idolatrous spaces, might argue the need
for a more psychoanalytical approach, one that would divulge the psychogenetic source of this wish for the darkly numinous. I am not opposed to such an
interpretive path (my discussion of Melville below will take it), but we in fact
know very little about Stephens's private life. With slight pertinent biographical fact to go on, we can only speculate why he felt compelled to cast his Holy
Land trip as an heroic test of his own virility. He began his journey as a tourist,
but once he elected to travel through Edom he seems to have re-envisioned it
as a more dramatically surcharged one. His direct inspiration came from con-
versing with a group of British tourists about the prophet Isaiah's injunction
that "None shall pass through [Edom] for ever and ever" (Isaiah 34:10). The
exploit—to "follow the wandering footsteps" (138) of the Israelites; to visit
Petra, for "more than a thousand years buried from the eyes of mankind"
(139); and, finally, to climb the "holy mountain of Sinai, where the Almighty,
by the hands of his servant Moses, delivered the tables of his law to his chosen
people" (138)—seems, in part, opportunistic. Yet Stephens could hardly, while
in Egypt, have predicted the spectacular success of the published volume,
which launched his career as a writer and archaeologist. The question of motivation seems to have puzzled the author himself. He repeats in kindred
phrasing my preceding citations or at least half-a-dozen times in the text alludes to the Edom curse, partially no doubt for melodrama's sake, yet also as if
he cannot articulate the inward rationale for the chosen route. Traveling to the
Levant with his health impaired, with, more particularly, his powers of oratory stifled by his swollen throat, Stephens, we can perhaps surmise, sought
renewal by hoping to pass through what seemed a diseased land to the very site
where the prophet Moses had received, and proclaimed to humankind, the
tablets of the Law. Lawyering, he had told his father, little delighted him: to
retrace the footsteps of the first lawgiver, however, might better allow him to
"indulge" his heart's desire. He was skeptical about the threat of Isaiah's
prophecy, but he nonetheless seized upon the ban to underscore his own he-

roic undertaking. The "route through Idumea was difficult and dangerous," he writes, "requiring all the energy of mind and body" (207) that he could summon forth. "[B]rav[ing] the malediction of Heaven" (284), he recollects near the book's end, he applauds himself as the "only person, except the wandering Arabs, who ever did pass through the doomed and forbidden Edom" (306).

The hazards were to some extent real. Bedouin tribesmen preyed upon hapless travelers, and the terrain itself, desolate and hot, was enervating. In crossing through it, however, Stephens came to see himself as reinvigorating his ailing body. What most defines him somatically is a compulsion for speed in the land of the "Mussulman," where everything is going to "ruin" (8). "I pointed towards Aqaba," he tells us, "and gave the brief and emphatic order, 'Forward!'" (213). *Incidents of Travel in Egypt, Arabia Petræa, and the Holy Land* oscillates between urgent movement and panicky immobility, the latter sometimes caused simply by the contingencies of travel, but also by Stephens's sheer physical agony. If the main impetus behind his trip abroad had been to restore his health, the Edom adventure, at least as he reports it, nearly killed him.

At one point, his illness resurging, he seeks refuge in a desert monastery. He falls asleep and awakes the next day to find himself "as if pinned to the floor . . . startled and alarmed at the recurrence of a malady, on account of which I was then an exile from home" (120). At Aqaba, he becomes utterly "prostrated" (227), feeling "sick in body and soul" (228). Paralysis, however, inhabits more than just Stephens's body. We have seen how he regarded Alexandria as a decrepit city. In the subsequent stages of his journey, he continues to mark the decay of the Ottoman Empire; he also obsessively notes more literal deathly sights. At Suez, for instance, he looks out a balcony window one morning to discover in the courtyard below "directly under me a dead Tartar" (159). The man's corpse exerts a strange fascination; "I gazed," Stephens writes, "long and steadfastly upon [his] face" (159). To be sure, fears of dying far from home are natural enough; but such morbid sights begin uncannily to apply more specifically to Stephens's throat ailment, to his speech impediment. We thus hear him, at another juncture, worrying about the prospect of dying in the desert wasteland "alone, and beyond the reach of help, where" his "voice can never reach the ears of . . . distant friends" (289). These alimentary anxieties, projected upon a topography of barren land and sickly or dying Arabs, coalesce grotesquely when, camping on the plain of the Red Sea, he comes upon a "thin, ghastly figure," an Arab on the verge of death. The poor man "open[ed] his mouth and attempt[ed] an inarticulate jabber," whereupon "there fell out a tongue so festered to the very throat, that the sight of it made me sick" (220–21).

Stephens's conflation of corporeal self with the landscape and its inhabitants serves, though, not just to remind him of his precarious health. Disease, sterile terrains, death: these are the elements of Edom's malignancy against which he measures his own askesis, his willingness to drive his pain-racked body through the supposedly cursed landscape. Such becomes especially clear when he ponders the masochistic habits of desert fanatics. After his encounter with the Arab with the infected throat, he meets an abject, aging hermit: "[H]is skin was dry, horny, and covered with blotches resembling large scales . . . and he looked like one who literally crawled on his belly and licked the dust of the earth" (222–23). Stephens cavalierly claims that he cannot "imagine the possibility of existing in such a dronish state" (223), but as made evident from an earlier passage he does not quite dissociate his own self-mortification from that of the Sinai hermits. "[S]trange as the feeling may seem," he remarks, "my very soul cleaved to the scene around me" (189):

In the East, the fruitful parent of superstition, occurred the first instances of monastic life. A single enthusiast withdrew himself from the society of his fellow-men, and wandered for years among the rocks and the sands of the desert, devoting himself to the service of his Maker by the mistaken homage of bodily mortification. . . . [The] lashes and stripes he inflicted upon his worn and haggard body excited the warm imaginations of the Christian of the East. Others . . . followed his example . . . [and the] . . . deserts of Thebaid were soon covered with hermits; and more than seventy thousand anchorites were wasting their lives in the gloomy wilds of Sinai, startling the solitude with the cries of their self-inflicted torture. (189)

Stephens obtains a surrogate thrill. He is, though, no masochist manqué of the Sinai desert: for what most attracts him about these scenes of stark privation, all the more in retrospect, is his virile feat of passing through them unharmed. His sojourn in the desert is a peculiarly insouciant one. For the hermits, external, physical abjection calls forth an inward sense of humility; punishing the flesh, presumably, necessarily preludes divine ecstasies. Yet nowhere in the book does Stephens dwell upon some pained sense of personal turpitude. Traveling in the desert, he at most only fitfully enters into, and ultimately resists, the inner domain of self-torment. He slums, if you will, in the bleak wilderness of asceticism.

At the same time, this corporeal doubling or tripling—of his body, the landscape, and the Bible—affords him a satisfyingly intimate access to Scriptural antiquity, to the core of religious numinosity, upon which he wishes to gaze. Several passages may serve to illustrate this compulsion to penetrate the sites of biblical illumination and wrath. During the first leg of his journey, while sailing up the Nile, Stephens went ashore to inspect the royal sepulchers in the Theban Valley of Kings:

Travelers and commentators concur in supposing that these magnificent excavations must have been intended for other uses than the burial, each of a single king. Perhaps, it is said, like the chambers of imagery seen by the Jewish prophet, they were the scene of idolatrous rites performed "in the dark"; and, as the Israelites are known to have been mere copyists of the Egyptians, these tombs are supposed to illustrate the words of Ezekiel [Ezek. Viii:8–10]: "Then said he to me, Son of Man, dig now in the wall; and when I had digged in the wall, behold a door. And he said unto me, Go in, and see the abominable things that they do there. So I went in, and saw, and behold, every form of creeping thing and abominable beasts, and all the idols of the house of Israel, portrayed upon the wall round about." (112–13)

What impels Stephens's curiosity, it seems, are idolatrous sights, which he here figures via Ezekiel as being corporeal and bestial. As I suggested earlier, gaining access to these dark, transgressive recesses transcodes alimentary anxieties. Seeking out loathly spots, he rises from abjection to virile power. His most jubilant moments, not unexpectedly, come later in the narrative when he retraces the footsteps of biblical heroes and prophets. Ascending Mount Sinai, for example, he locates what, pulling out all the stops, he imagines to be the site where Old Testament law, God's inscribed Word, was given to Moses: "Can this naked rock have been the witness of that great interview between man and his Maker?" Stephens exults, where "amid thunder and lightning, and a fearful quaking of the mountains, the Almighty gave to his chosen people the precious tables of his law?" (188). In yet another passage, having trekked into the heart of Edom, he enjoys a resurgence of vitality as he penetrates a hallowed interior. He climbs to the top of Mount Hor to seek out the cavernous tomb of Aaron who, according to Scripture, had been punished for disobedience. Stephens dwells on the "desolate and dreary scene" where Aaron was "stripped . . . of his garments . . . [and] died . . . in the top of the mount" (274). He then plumbs the depths of the tomb, finding a descending staircase: "At the foot of the steps was a narrow chamber, at the other end an iron grating, opening in the middle, and behind the grating a tomb cut in the naked rock, guarded and reverenced as the tomb of Aaron. I tore aside the rusty grating, and thrusting in my arm up to the shoulders, touched the hallowed spot" (275). "[G]roping in the dark," to borrow Stephens's earlier phrase, amounts to a remarkably overdetermined activity—a genealogical motif involving a return to originary sites of transgression as well as a more corporealized desire to contact the alimentary source, the "spot," of his own disease. To travel through the blighted biblical landscape, to grope in the dark, ends up sounding like a phantasmagoric replay of the occasion of his trip to the Holy Land in the first place: his bout of strep throat, which obstructed the inward channels of speech and impeded his career shift from the law to New York politics. Having conquered that debility as he journeyed through Edom, Stephens triumphantly assumes the role of prophet-explorer: pursuing the path of Moses, spying out hidden idolatries, and bringing, if not the Word, at least the report of his feat back home.[20]

Phrasing it thusly, I have acceded to Stephens's own penchant for hyper-

bole. It is in fact difficult in his case to distinguish genuine anxiety from rhetorical theatrics. His Holy Land excursion, as written, became an act of self-
fashioning, a large element of which was irreverent urbanity. *Incidents of
Travel in Egypt, Arabia Petræa, and the Holy Land* does not end on Old Testament terrain. The last stage of his journey took him to Jerusalem and its environs, and there, too, he experienced sensations of paralysis, but of a more
comic order. He visited the notorious Church of the Holy Sepulchre, the
elaborate reliquary memorializing Christ's life, which virtually all Protestants
deemed an idolatrous travesty because it embodied spiritual matters all too
concretely. John W. De Forest in *Oriental Acquaintance; or, Letters from Syria*
(1856) was struck by the "air of absurdity about most of the sacred localities
and traditions which abound at Jerusalem," and Reverend J. T. Barclay in *The
City of the Great King; or, Jerusalem as It was, as It is, and as It is to be* (1858)
lamented that "angel[s]" would "weep to see the misdirected, superstitious,
idolatrous devotion paid to sacred localities by the overwhelming majority of
pilgrims."[21] Relic peddlers, all American visitors agreed, offensively seemed to
importune one on every corner—such was sacrilegious as well as indecorous.
As Curtis smugly observed in *The Howadji in Syria*, if "Jerusalem were nearer
Europe or America, it would be different, at least it would be more decent"
(190).

Jerusalem could not be moved, but antebellum sightseers could study
proximate renditions in their home country. John Banvard, building upon
his fame from his vast panorama of the Mississippi River, painted one of the
Holy Land following a trip there in 1850. The panorama was so long that
Banvard when he first showed it in New York City in 1852 had difficulty
finding a building that could contain it. Favorable press reviews and the artist's own tireless promotion made the work a hit with the public in several
other major cities, including Boston, where it was put on display. No small
part of its appeal was the segment that carried viewers on a virtual tour
through the lurid splendors of the Church of the Holy Sepulchre. Stephens's
text predates Banvard's painting by over a decade, as well as other popular
artistic works depicting the Church, such as a set of Currier and Ives lithographs published in the late 1840s, and so we should regard his narrative's
peep into the chambers of exotic worship as setting up the spectatorial thematics that likely informed how audiences viewed the site as well as later artistic versions of it.[22]

No locale in Jerusalem elicited stronger reactions. There, in the most morbid of holy places, a shrine anathema from the standpoint of reformed Christianity, one could enjoy the frisson of traversing tabooed spaces or of focusing
religious emotion, surreptitiously, upon visual embodiments. Stephens's
revelatory itinerary—into the Church proper, and then into particular

shrines—heightens hermeneutical desire, even though from the start he describes his visit as something of a captivity tale in which expectation mixes with revulsion. Rather than aggressively seeking entry into the site's interior, he is nearly forced in against his will by a mob of pilgrims: "I was carried almost headlong into the body of the church. The press continued behind, hurrying me along and kicking off my shoes; and in a state of desperate excitement both of mind and body, utterly unsuited to the place and time, I found myself standing over the so-called tomb of Christ" (346). The reliquary, though, clearly fascinated him. A "day seldom passed," he writes, "in which I did not visit the Church of the Holy Sepulchre" (349); but that tabooed desire, the wish to scan the spaces and sights of corporealized theological interest, requires in the telling the alibi of exposé. Stating that he "chiefly [intended] to observe the conduct of the pilgrims," he beckons the reader to "accompany" him "into the interior" (349). Over five pages are spent reviling what he takes to be the site's garish, fraudulent religious apparatus and relics: the "stone of unction" where "the body of our Lord was laid when taken down from the cross and washed"; the sundry chapels of different Christian sects; the "tombs of Joseph and Nicodemus"; the "pillar of flagellation, to which our Savior was tied when he was scourged"; the "pit in which the true cross was found"; and so on, until he brings us before the "inner chamber, the holiest of holy places," the Sepulchre itself (349–53). Earlier in the narrative, Stephens had rejoiced in the chance to contact tangible hallowed sites, but the sacred precincts of Christ's body are, it seems, too holy to touch, deserving in fact only incredulity. The investment he had in touching Old Testament sacred interiors cannot be fully translated into a New Testament equivalent; instead he merely concludes that Christ's divinity "is too holy a thing to be made the subject of trickery and deception" (354).

Iron Expeditions, Decadent Emperors, and the Search for Sodom

Stephens finds himself at once captivated and repulsed by the spirit made too fleshy when he enters the Church of the Holy Sepulchre. Old Testament scenes of wrath and idolatry excite his hermeneutical desire, but the zone of Christ's body requires Protestant circumspection—U.S. "decen[cy]," as Curtis phrased it. That these dilemmas of Scriptural mimesis are not unique to Stephens's text becomes apparent when we turn to one of the odder military-scientific expeditions of the nineteenth century, that led by Lieutenant Commander William F. Lynch to the Levant, and more particularly, the Dead Sea, in 1847–48.

A Virginian, born in 1801, Lynch was a pious and well-respected officer of the U.S. Navy. Fresh from his service in the Mexican-American War, and in search of new fields of heroics, he persuaded the head of the navy to send him on an exploratory mission to the Holy Land. Lynch and his crew—a group of five officers and nine seamen—sailed for Smyrna late in 1847. They then took a steamer to Constantinople, where Lynch visited the sultan, Abdul Medjid I, to obtain permission to pass through Syria. Using camels, the sailors hauled two portable vessels, one of galvanized iron and the other of copper (constructed to withstand corrosion), eastward from Haifa across some thirty miles of hilly terrain separating the Mediterranean from the Sea of Galilee. With the Sherif of Mecca as a guide and with Arab soldiers as guards, the expedition made its way down the Jordan, and then upon arrival at the Dead Sea spent a grueling two months surveying its waters and shoreline. Lynch returned to Washington in early 1849, and in the same year published *Narrative of the United States' Expedition to the River Jordan and the Dead Sea.*[23]

The expedition, which involved sketching topographical charts, calculating barometric changes, and so on, was of some scientific value. Previously, both the Jordan and the Dead Sea had been unmapped, and for centuries the latter had posed something of an enigma. Accounting for its high salt content and its eerily desolate terrain had vexed amateur and professional geologists. Yet neither science nor diplomacy can satisfactorily account for Lynch's motives. His venture lacked any real political agenda besides that of establishing friendly relations with the Ottoman sultan (in the 1860s, somewhat lamely, Lynch promoted the notion that gold might be found in Palestine and that the entire region was ripe for U.S. commerce).[24] The scientific data garnered, moreover, yielded little practical knowledge. The main discovery, that the Dead Sea was as many had suspected indeed below sea level, and thus antipodally related to the heavens, was more theologically than scientifically pertinent. The expedition, quite likely, would not have been mounted had it not been for Lynch's having urgently solicited John Mason, the navy secretary. As historian David H. Finnie comments, "Lynch simply got a bee in his bonnet" and "persuaded the Navy to back him."[25] The public, however, found the spectacle of sacred territory being traversed by the marines of "this great Republican country," as one of Lynch's officers put it in his own narrative, altogether compelling. The New Israel through its ingenuity had mapped a venerable portion of the antique world, uniting—however nebulously—modern science and religion.[26] By the time he submitted the more complete *Official Report* of the expedition to Congress in 1852, the popular version had already run through seven American and two English editions.

The Dead Sea, of course, was legendary for being, as Scripture told, the locale where once stood the iniquitous cities of Sodom and Gomorrah, now hidden beneath its waves. Scholars both in the United States and abroad debated at length precisely how the cataclysm occurred (Edward Robinson spent an entire subsection of his *Biblical Researches* on the topic, arguing that godly wrath worked indirectly, through the secondary agency of volcanic activity).[27] Haunting descriptions of the sea and its environs were reiterated in almost all European travel narratives pertaining to the Holy Land. Travelers invariably sought to glimpse the fated cities supposedly sunken below its surface. In his 1697 *Journey from Aleppo to Jerusalem*, for example, Henry Maundrell reported his frustration that he could not "discern any heaps of ruins" that would evidence "so dreadful an example of the divine vengeance."[28] That such ruins would not likely be located became clear a century later when a German naturalist and physician, Ulrich Jasper Seetzen, circumnavigated the lake in 1807 and found no submerged edifices. And, indeed, when the Frenchman Louis Félicien de Saulcy in 1850 claimed a small, dilapidated lakeside building to be from the remains of the sunken cities, European savants and clergy were incredulous. Spying the cities' vestiges would have satisfied biblical literalists. But *not* seeing them was also theologically apt. Such tardy revelations would, no doubt, have had an air of impiety, as if one wished to see too tangible exempla of God's actions in history. The ineffable could best remain ineffable by leaving the signs of His wrath buried beneath the waves.

That is—for those not impatient to reveal God's ways. Robinson was strictly orthodox, yet there is an element of "American" grandiosity in his effort to comprehensively chart the topographical and geological features of the Holy Land, as if the vast apparatus of his research could satisfy doubt simply by rendering the Godhead more empirically knowable. Science, U.S.-style, seems to have posed little threat to faith. Stephens, for instance, whose itinerary took him to the site, immediately follows his statement that "modern science has solved all the mystery about this water" with another one about his urge to witness the deity's puissant handiwork:

I never felt so unwilling to leave any place. I was unsatisfied. I had a longing desire to explore every part of that unknown water; to spend days upon its surface, to coast along its shores, to sound its mysterious depths, and search for the ruins of the guilty cities. . . . I can see no good reason why it should hide forever from man's eyes the monuments of that fearful anger which the crimes of the guilty had so righteously provoked. (394)

Such scopic thrills correlate with Stephens's quest, as seen earlier, to penetrate or uncover transgressive sites and yet remain innocent, and this passage perhaps more so than ones I had occasion previously to cite conjoins his drive toward mobility (here, as he skims along the water's surface) and his drive to gaze, more lingeringly, on hallowed or idolatrous locales. The Dead Sea prompts a characteristic response from Stephens, but we may surmise that one of the site's appeals in the antebellum era was just this tension between geo-metaphysical depth and surface. The wish to see God's ways or to sense the imprudence of that desire was not disingenuous. It was, rather, superficial. Stephens's passage signals an eighteenth- to nineteenth-century shift in theological or metaphysical mimesis: from a focus, often taking the form of the jeremiad, on the Father's wrath, the signs of which typically could be representationally depicted; to one on the more sentimentalized, however elusive, representations of the Son's heart-knowledge. The Holy Land provided ample testimony of God's ire. To wish to locate the body of Christ, though, was tantamount to idolatry: the "Almighty," to cite the epigraph from Lynch at the start of this chapter, rightly "left us in ignorance of the exact position of places infinitely . . . sacred," that is, the site of Christ's burial.[29]

The Dead Sea's signal virtue to nineteenth-century readers of Holy Land travel volumes, I hazard to guess, resided in its odd blend of representational or theological dynamics. Hidden depravities could be summoned to mind, yet to describe its lifeless surface and shores was, in effect, to represent nothing at all. The artist Edward Troye, for instance, in 1858 displayed a large canvas featuring the Dead Sea in the Apollo building of New York City; but the stark painting, with no vegetative forms or human figures, appears virtually devoid of conventional pictorial interest (Figure 5).[30] To represent the Dead Sea was simultaneously to skirt the impiety of corporealizing spiritual matters, to invoke implicitly the traditional genre of the jeremiad, and yet also to remind Americans how their nation had transcended such colossal communal slips into sin. In brief, the Dead Sea did not raise anxieties about national crime and punishment, but repressed them, allowing one a theologically nonchalant response, especially in Stephens's case, to the spectacle of Old Testament anger.[31]

Lynch, however, to whom I now wish to return in full, cannot quite regard the Old Testament's theology of godly vengeance with Stephens's trademark urbanity. What makes his report intriguing, in fact, are the signs of his discomfort as he attempts to straddle both the Old and New Testaments, to locate himself on their antithetical theological divide. Early in his *Narrative*, he tells us that the trip consummated "yearnings of twenty years" to "look upon the country which was the cradle of the human race" and see "the soil hallowed by the footsteps, fertilized by the blood, and consecrated by the tomb, of the Saviour" (18). Yet the text equally, if not more so, coordinates itself with the Old Testament and its scenes of righteous chastisement. In the interstices of its day-to-day account of the expedition and the progress of recording geological, meteorological, and zoological data, the report reveals less Lynch's desire to follow the footsteps of Christ than to witness the death throes of an immoral culture doomed to the dustbin of history.

F I G . 5. Edward Troye, *The Dead Sea* (c. 1856). Oil on canvas, 66 x 124 inches. (Stan Franzos, photographer; courtesy of Bethany College, West Virginia.)

The *Narrative*, accordingly, often adopts a censorious tone as it sounds out ill-governed communities. Those communities it seems are located everywhere but in Lynch's contemporary homeland. He initially signposts the contrast between Ottoman decadence and U.S. national purity by recollecting his insistence that the expedition's marines needed to be "young, muscular, native-born Americans, of sober habits" (14), a guarantee, presumably, that they would not succumb to the torpor, both physical and moral, of the region. His concerns about corruption went beyond the crew. Lynch called his two metallic boats the *Fanny Mason* and the *Fanny Skinner*, deriving their names from "two young and blooming children, whose hearts are as spotless as their parentage is pure" (19). Subsequently, the two craft are figured as characters in the melodrama of the expedition, requiring chivalric protection as the crew guides them down the Jordan's cataracts. The *Fanny Mason* we hear at one moment of crisis "fairly trembled and bent in the fierce strength of the sweeping current" (189); and in another instance, several sailors must leap overboard, to usher the *Fanny Skinner*, a "graceful" vessel, "down the perilous descent" (214).

Lynch counterpoints these masculine heroics with hypermoralized obloquy against the Ottoman authorities. He contradictorily sees Turkish rulers as being too patriarchally rigorous and too decadent in their administration of the law. Stephens, we will recall, frequently underscored Near Eastern indolence and decay, and other antebellum writers concurred. "The life of the Orient is nerveless and effete," Bayard Taylor wrote in *The Lands of the Saracens* (1854): "[T]he native strength of the race has died out, and all attempts to resuscitate it by the adoption of European institutions produce mere galvanic spasms, which leave it more exhausted than before."[32] In the hands of some American authors, to be sure, the imaginary of Oriental languor offered a refuge from mid-Victorian masculine competition. A countertradition or genre most notably in the texts of Curtis and Nathaniel Parker Willis emerged at midcentury. Willis, Curtis, and lesser-known "bachelor" authors constructed their personae as idlers, given in Sandra Tomc's apt phrase to "exaggerated ennui."[33] Their texts routinely luxuriate in the diffused eroticism of voluptuous fabrics, odors, and decors, or in the more polymorphous joys of the bath, administered by half-clad young Arabs.

Lynch himself at times approximates the style, but his unease with such effusions and their often lurid content is plain. In one passage, he recollects his tour of the seraglio of the sultan, Abdul Medjid I. The tonal quirks signal an awkward attempt to mimic the salacious Orientalist idiom:

> The harem looks out both upon the court and the water, but to the windows were fitted gilt arabesque gratings, to screen the sultanas within. What scenes have been enacted in these apartments! What intrigues, murders and sewing up in sacks! Alas, poor woman!
>
> Here are marble baths with alabaster fountains, and domes thickly studded with glass-lights overhead—the bath of the harem! where many a Circassian form has laved! (94)

Lynch cannot decide whether to divert us with "Circassian form[s]" or to disgust us with sinister plots directed against feminine chastity. The passage's oddity arises from more than an inept handling of an incongruent genre, however. Its conflicted yoking of curiosity about and repulsion over the most notorious of patriarchal privileges registers the *Narrative*'s almost sadistic, albeit fitful, obsession with scenes of punishment.

These concerns are nowhere more evident than when Lynch takes us through a tour of universal history, which, according to him, stages moral dramas of the deity deploying strong rulers as the instruments of providential wrath. The *Narrative* compulsively cites historical, as well as mythical and religious, exempla of transgressors receiving inexorably just discipline. Lynch becomes engrossed, for instance, by the Brahmin representation of "Punishment as the son of the Deity" who, "with his dark countenance and fiery eye, presses forward to extirpate crime" (42). All epochs of history exhibit the sure outcome of national depravity, for "whatever may have been the immediate cause of national calamities, licentiousness of morals has always preceded and precipitated the [punitive] catastrophe" (42). Thus the era of Cromwell, "the stern and formal Puritan," followed that of Charles, the "licentious cavalier" (43); and the French Revolution, as the "Avenger of crime," justly repaid the "crimes of the French people," which "were permitted to accumulate until Paris rivaled Sodom in iniquity" (43).

When Lynch turns away from providential history, however, juridical severity becomes more troubling. The preceding history lessons he now divulges were required to prepare the genteel U.S. reader to grasp what he calls a "dire necessity" (43). During his stay in Constantinople with the sultan, Lynch had beheld the grisly execution of a criminal. The transgressor, Lynch writes, "was led forth into one of the public streets, and duly prepared. The clumsy executioner, unable to strike off the head with repeated blows, deliberately, with a saw, severed the hacked and disfigured head from the convulsively writhing trunk" (44). Confusingly, the spectacle is offered as an instance, however hideous, of crime's consequences *and* as an example of how despotic countries conduct themselves in the absence of enlightened codes of due process and constitutional restraint. The punishment meted out, Lynch concludes, "would have shocked all England, even when her penal laws, like those of Draco, were written in blood" (44).

The brutality, Lynch later suggests, in fact stemmed not from the sultan's tyrannical rule, but rather from his deficient iron-handedness. He apparently has lost, to recall Taylor's phrase, the "native strength"—even if too patriarchally rigid—to oversee his own subofficials, who routinely keep him in the dark about such juridical occasions because his "humane heart" would "shrink with horror" (44). Lynch, in these passages, cannot separate his ambivalent attitude toward Ottoman absolutism from his satisfaction at seeing the omnipotent deity of the Old Testament sternly punishing communal transgressors. According to him, the real problem with the Ottoman Empire is that it seems to lack the perfect balance between the Old and New Testaments, between wrath and love. Knowing the law only in the figure of the Father, in the Koran's Muslim ordinances, Ottoman authority, it appears, rules either too despotically or too weakly. Tyrannical harshness and decadent misrule, Lynch comes to believe, are the only alternatives.

Not surprisingly, when he recollects his interview with the sultan, what he most notes is the latter's brooding sensitivity, which, if it makes him likable, also betrays his lack of virility and the ebb tide of Ottoman rule. The year previously Lynch had fought in the Mexican-American war, and now he stages his meeting with the sultan in terms of that war's most salient prefigurement—the rueful agon between Montezuma and Cortés:

My feelings saddened as I looked upon the monarch, and I thought of Montezuma. . . . His smile was one of the sweetest I had ever looked upon,—his voice almost the most melodious I had ever heard; his manner was gentleness itself. . . . Through him, the souls of the mighty monarchs who have gone before, seem to brood over the impending fate of an empire which once extended from the Atlantic to the Ganges, from the Caucasus to the Indian Ocean. . . . The expression of his features . . . was that of profound melancholy. (77, 92)

The sultan's failing, Lynch implies, lies in his inadequate masculinity. He has become a sovereign not of his predecessors' vast domains but only of morbid memories (the Eastern version, one might say, of Alexander von Humboldt, whom we will recall from my introduction was lauded by Bayard Taylor for the wide world that he had surveyed). Pondering the genealogy of past powerful emperors, he has forgotten how to rule.

Given Lynch's partiality for stories of national crime and retribution, we might anticipate that his descriptions of the Dead Sea would be the most morally overwrought of the *Narrative*. In fact, they are not. He avoids the didactic rhetoric elsewhere so prominent in his account. What most strikes him, instead, is the Dead Sea's sheer lifelessness, its inactivity:

It was indeed a scene of unmitigated desolation. . . . To the south was an extensive flat intersected by sluggish drains, with the high hills of Edom semi-girdling the salt plain where the Israelites repeatedly overthrew their enemies; and to the north was the calm and motionless sea, curtained with a purple mist, while many fathoms deep in the slimy mud beneath it lay embedded the ruins of the ill-fated cities of Sodom and Gomorrah. The glare of light was blinding to the eye, and the atmosphere difficult of respiration. No bird fanned with its wing the attenuated air through which the sun poured his scorching rays upon the mysterious element on which we floated, and which, alone, of all the works of its Maker, contains no living thing within it. (310–11)

We would expect Lynch to linger on the crimes of the Cities of the Plain; yet what we get is not the vengeance of the Father, but rather his own paternal concern about the crew's welfare. The extreme heat and consequent lassitude threatened to halt the effort to map the Dead Sea's topography, and Lynch worried that his crew, however virile, might succumb to a fatal listlessness (one member, in fact, died from heat exhaustion). At one point, he becomes alarmed when he imagines how the "fierce angel of disease seemed [to be] hovering over them" (338). Then in a remarkably inapt image—inapt because the crew is guilty of no crime, of no impiety—he inserts himself and his subordinates into a Dantesque tableau: "The solitude, the scene, my own thoughts, were too much; I felt, as I sat thus, steering the drowsily-moving boat, as if I were a Charon, ferrying, not the souls, but the bodies, of the departed and the damned, over some infernal lake, and could endure it no longer" (338). Here, paternal solicitude mixes with agonized guilt: Lynch suffers, not unlike the insufficiently iron-willed sultan, from a "humane heart."

The cruise-to-Hell analogy indicates that for all of Lynch's semisadistic fascination with scenes of the Father's wrath, he was equally, but uncomfortably, disposed toward the more gentle, empathic dispensations of the Son. In the *Narrative*, however, he cannot reconcile the duality of the Protestant Godhead, as is seen in two crucial instances. Toward the end of the account, when the expeditionary party had begun its return trip by way of Jerusalem, Lynch recollects his wish to trace the final footsteps of Christ along the Via Dolorosa, the "route traversed eighteen centuries before by the Man of Sorrows" (396). The *Narrative* devotes several pages to describing the path taken by Christ on his way toward the Crucifixion, but he does so indirectly, by borrowing extensively from the journal of one of his officers. Apparently, he felt uneasy about rendering Christ's story too concretely or, perhaps, about identifying too closely with Christ's gentleness (elsewhere, he says that Christianity "acts first upon woman, because . . . she is more susceptible [to] . . . its law of purity and love" [70]). Lynch cannot, in short, coordinate Old and New Testament versions of the deity. More specifically, what he has trouble conceptualizing, or can conceptualize but cannot convey, is how the Son, as it were, can be treated cruelly by the Father. During a theological debate with an Arab guide, Lynch at the key moment retreats into the ineffable. The Arab queries, "[Why] do you insult the God you believe in, by supposing that He died the ignominious death of a criminal?" (236). Lynch does not respond; instead he begs the question, leaving Christian mysteries mysterious, and concludes by telling the reader that the Arab, "sensually imaginative," is "incapable of a refined, spiritual idea" (236).

In the face of such imponderables, Lynch takes refuge in the clarity of his status as a U.S. citizen. Near the end of the *Narrative*, he more successfully reconciles the Old and New Testaments by conceiving the United States as a charitable, pastoral New Israel, pitying the misfortunes of the geographically distant, old Israel. America's "hills and plains . . . lowing herds, the bleating flocks . . . the clustering fruit-blossoms, the waving corn" make it a "glorious land" in which each citizen should "thank God that his lot is cast within it" (390). Having inscribed himself as a citizen of a nation typologically uniting the Old Testament (as the New Israel) and the New Testament (as the Redeemer Nation), Lynch can soften jeremiadic obloquy into sentimental lament. "And yet *this* country [the Holy Land]," he concludes, "scathed by the wrath of an offended Deity, teems with associations of the most thrilling events recorded in the book of time. The patriot may glory in the one,—the Christian of every clime must weep, but, even in weeping, hope for the other" (390–91).

Converting the Heart: The Holy Land Sentimentalized

Maria Susanna Cummins's *El Fureidîs* of all the texts considered in this chapter is the most Christic, that is, sentimentally oriented. Ann Douglas in her important study *The Feminization of American Culture* argues that the era's literary-religious culture suffered a declension from the rigors of the jeremiad to a more consolatory theology, at which only a few authors, such as Melville, bravely balked. Her perspective though not her scorn informs my following analysis of Cummins's novel: its New Testament thematics are sentimental, but the latter term as I apply it should not be regarded as pejorative.[34] *El Fureidîs*, published in 1860, draws upon Cummins's studious reading of biblical geographers and Holy Land travelers (she cites Edward Robinson, among others, in her preface), but it also relies upon Victorian plot conventions in which the right man, after much travail, finds the right woman. Through the novel's heroine, Havilah, daughter of an expatriate U.S. businessman living in Lebanon, the thirty-year-old British aristocrat Meredith is awakened from religious apathy—he is more "attuned to classical than to religious emotion"—to love of Christ.[35] Havilah's father has adopted Lebanon as his home country and Havilah herself, whose mother is Greek, regards the region as her native land. Cummins regularly alludes to her Near Eastern beauty and spirituality, yet her mixed heritage frees her from specific ethnic or national affiliations. The novel, in fact, operates on an allegorical level, with Havilah figuring as a womanly paraclete conducting Meredith to his religious enlightenment.

Because the plot line interweaves a crisis of faith and a crisis of the heart, we might suppose that *El Fureidîs* matched the success of Cummins's earlier novel, *The Lamplighter* (1854), a text that powerfully rewrote woman's domestic subjugation as Christlike valor and thereby earned it an unexampled cultural longevity in the nineteenth century.[36] Apparently, however, reviewers barely noticed it, and it was seldom reprinted. In *The Lamplighter*, readers thrilled to the heroine's much-suffering lessons in Christian humility; in *El Fureidîs*, Meredith also must learn humility, yet his story lacks the earlier text's psychological pathos. With his tight-lipped British reserve, chivalric habits, and wealth, Cummins has trouble making his one setback in life, the delayed reciprocated love of Havilah, dramatically compelling, and Havilah herself is too cloyingly perfect in body, heart, and soul. Yet if *El Fureidîs* seems short on the melodrama that made *The Lamplighter* so appealing to its audience, it does repay analysis for its remarkably canny exploration of religious sublimation itself. The novel offers, as well, an interesting preface and contrast to Melville's *Clarel*, the focus of my next section: for if Melville's poem foreground's Clarel's hermeneutical quest as a vexed reaction-formation against frustrated, compulsory heterosexuality (Clarel's love for Ruth), *El Fureidîs* foregrounds Meredith's quest for the beautiful body of Havilah as a prelude to religious epiphany. According to Cummins, Meredith does not so much sublimate eros into Christic agape. Such transcendent love, rather, is the subliminal motive that drives the hero's affections for Havilah, although it takes the entire progress of the novel for him to discover the source of his own compulsions. Once Meredith relinquishes his strictly erotic attachments, he can redirect his heart to both Havilah and Christ. Before the two marry, and in the conclusion embark for England, Meredith must also work his way through the perplexing sensorium of the Near East.

Meredith's journey, no less than that of Stephens, involves hermeneutical excursions. Indeed, his love for Havilah gets mediated through successive architectural scenes or enclosures: a monastery that the two visit on their rambles through the Lebanon hillsides above the town of El Fureidîs; a desert harem, where resides Havilah's Arabic friend Maysunah; and the ruined cities of Balbec and other ancient sites. In each of these locales, as well as the pastoral landscapes of Lebanon at large, Meredith learns lessons of the heart that finally guide him to a revitalized faith that will, in the end, warrant Havilah's faith and love in him. When we first meet him, he is on the last leg of a Grand Tour that has taken him to Lebanon in his hope of satisfying "unuttered longings" (1). His response to the country's landscape splendors—upon which he "feast[s] his eager eyes" (2)—suggests that the young man's subsequent itinerary will be a libidinal one. Yet Cummins, obviously aware of the Orient's sensuous blandishments, also quickly qualifies her hero's scopically erotic pursuits. He has requisite "manly vigor" (7) yet also is quite "fastidious" (5); his "imaginative and poetic enthusiasm" is "aroused" not "only to see Eastern lands" but also "to imbibe their spirit" (5). Following the call of this twined libidinal and, as yet, only protoreligious motivation, Meredith hires a young Arab guide, Abdoul, who leads him to the "lovely and picturesque village" (14) of El Fureidîs nestled in the mountains of Lebanon, where he meets Havilah, a figure—in the first of many similar epithets—of "seraphic loveliness" (17). Her maidenly, Orientalized body at once figures forth and transcends the stereotypical sensual allure of the Near East. Her exotic beauty, Cummins directs us to understand, symbolizes the pure piety of her disposition. When Meredith learns to distinguish the two, or rather once he can see through her body to Christ, she in turn falls in love with him in the multiple nuances of the term (Cummins is not a prude).

Havilah herself is something of a Lebanese wunderkind. "Music," for instance, "had come to her as an inspiration, and most of the modern languages had been familiar to her ears from childhood" (95). Cummins no doubt intended her polynationality and polyglot faculties to comment upon the limitations imposed upon womanhood in the United States. In one scene her scholarly aptitude and cosmopolitan sensibility empower her to enter unharmed into heterodox spaces. Havilah and Meredith visit a nearby Catholic convent, and Havilah, ever studious, settles in:

Had Meredith been less familiar with the impulsive and independent movements of the young girl, he would have felt some anxiety for her safety among the lonely corridors and dim archways of the half-dilapidated convent; and it must be confessed that, even with his knowledge of her self-reliant habits, he was somewhat relieved . . . [after] having passed through the chapel, refectory, and dormitory, [and having] explored the subterranean vaults . . . [because] he was at length ushered into the antique library, and beheld her quietly seated on the low sill of a deep-set Gothic window, the floor around her strewn with strange old books and manuscripts, while Father Anastase was seeking amid his musty archives for some hidden volume which he had reason to believe would suit her erratic tastes. (89–90)

Later that day, Havilah even refreshes Meredith with a lecture on the "remarkable ruins and archaeological curiosities" abounding in the region of the convent, which she informs him were the "remains of temples erected in the high places by the ancient Hivites for the worship of Baal" (92). Rather cleverly, Cummins both evokes the threat of Catholic captivity and shows that self-reliant womanhood can navigate these "erratic" textual, psychic, and literal corridors without fear of contamination or impiety. Unlike Stephens, who felt compelled to penetrate Holy Land spaces of numinosity or idolatry to fulfill hermeneutical longing, Havilah can imperturbably gaze on the "musty archives" of heteroclite traditions. Spiritually self-reliant, she seeks to fill no inward lack by disclosing hidden, hallowed, or transgressive locales.

In *El Fureidîs*, in fact, the real void turns out not to be idolatrous spaces or loathly terrains, such as the Dead Sea, but the desert within Meredith's own heart. Havilah, by the "intuition of her own pure spirit," we learn, "had probed the depths of his unsatisfied soul, and had beheld the void within" (97). Indeed, it is her sense that the prideful Meredith has not yet turned his heart to Christ that keeps her from turning her heart to him. He "could never be," she tells her mother, "the husband of my soul" (126). In a key passage that dangles before us the prospect of Meredith's redemption, Cummins indicates that his love for Havilah is but the antecedent to religious love: "We have not yet probed the depths of his secret heart. We do not know the true man. He does not yet know himself" (117–18).

Meredith comes to know himself, it turns out, through a sequence of episodes taking him deeper into Near Eastern terrains and architectural spaces. Mr. Trefoil, Havilah's father, although born in America has been reared in the East, and he wishes to rejuvenate his adopted land—specifically by introducing industry, a silk-worm factory, to Lebanon. The factory, in a long subplot, is catastrophically flooded. Trefoil becomes monetarily embarrassed; and he, his daughter, and Meredith must seek out an associate of Trefoil's, Mustapha Osman, a "rich Turkish merchant at Damascus" (257), to assess his financial options. Trefoil is benevolent, but also fiscally careless; and Cummins tacitly suggests that he has become too Orientalized, apparently forgetting supposedly Occidental skills in managing property and industrial concerns. There is, Meredith says, a "mystery which clouds his affairs" (257). During the entourage's journey to Damascus, Cummins in the voice of a Trefoil family counselor indulges in a tirade against "Ottoman misrule" (271) and improvidence. The cozy village of El Fureidîs pleases, but the rest of the territory requires foreign intervention to stir it out of its lethargy:

[T]here, to the northeast of us, almost overlaid with rubbish and vegetation, are the sole remains of a city over which Ptolemies and Herods have been proud to bear sway. Two or three miserable hovels with their wretched occupants now represent the wealth and royalty of an almost forgotten past. . . . Another cycle of God's providence has nearly run its course in this land. . . . It needs no prophetic eye to see that this age is ripe, and that Syria is soon destined to be rid of her tyrant. I look confidently forward to the time when men shall cease to curse the land which God has blessed,—when commerce shall flourish on our shores, agriculture disclose the teeming wealth of the soil, and Christianity flourish in the land of its nativity. . . . Asia, until now a jealous recluse, is flinging open her doors to the stranger. Syria is the key to the whole continent; and who can question that the son of the West will make for himself a highway through her deserts? (271–73)

This is about as explicitly political as the novel gets, for Cummins's main purpose is to conceive Occidental-Eastern political relations in terms of romantic conventions, which in turn are the vehicle to allegorize her pious message of a heart restored to its proper, Christic home.

If she tames Meredith's sexuality, sublimating it into his intense appreciation of Havilah's wondrous spiritual beauty, she also conveniently provides him with a villainous double, the young Abdoul, who we learn also is an aristocrat, "a prince in his native desert" (65). Abdoul harbors in his "wild and untamed breast" (119) an alternatingly fawning and fiercely passionate regard for Havilah, and as the story proceeds his jealously leads him to despise Meredith as an interloping suitor for her affections. The last third of the novel allows Meredith at once to gain ascendancy over Abdoul and to find Christ. The "son of the West" masters, we might say, the son of the East, because the former acquires the heart-power of the Son himself.

Meredith agrees to invest capital in Trefoil's factory to restore it. Havilah, although grateful, refuses to repay such chivalrous gestures with a self-surrendering affection: he still must learn humility. Meredith's probity makes him a good businessman, but if the "son of the West" can easily rectify Trefoil's improvidence, he requires a much sterner mastery to reroute his own libidinal impulses. The travelers make their way to the residence of the merchant Mustapha and his daughter Maysunah; and, after enjoying the "elysium" (287) of an Oriental bath, Meredith falls half asleep and sinks into languorous reveries:

From the canopied alcove where he lay, he looked up at the domed ceiling, whose azure tint was relieved by paneling of gorgeous arabesque, and draped with a fretwork of gold. A gilded cornice, with delicately carved pendents, ran around the walls of the court. . . . As his eye ranged up and down the lofty walls, he felt himself lost amid mazes of coloring, and bewildered by architectural forms. Arches with fluted pillars, niches from which streamed a subdued light, slabs of marble and porphyry, on which inscriptions from the Koran were engraved in graceful Arabic characters, light galleries and colonnades festooned with the passion-flower and jessamine in full bloom,—all these elements of beauty assailed his senses at a glance, and, reflected in innumerable little mirrors inserted in the wainscoting, were repeated in endless perspective. . . . It was enough to gaze in dreamy wonder, sunk in an apathy of Oriental delights. (288–89)

The passage continues in a similar vein for several pages, up to the point when Meredith spies his beloved Havilah and her friend Maysunah, the "lonely child, reared in the desolate harem" (292), preparing each other's toilette: "'Rest here, my drooping lily, my panting dove,' said Havilah, as, seating herself amid the cushions, she pillowed Maysunah's head upon her lap" (291). We can read nineteenth-century texts anachronistically, seeing sex where there is none. But here Cummins fairly clearly positions herself behind Meredith's gaze to elicit what we must assume she took to be her readers' fantasies of harem eroticism.

She does so, however, to purge our interpretation of its own sensual proclivity. The decor is real, but the reverie makes it seem more like a textual trompe l'oeil—whose allure the reader must resist. Havilah and Maysunah's bond, of course, is pure; and there are no semiclad houris here. We soon hear that the harem was "such only in name" (292). Maysunah's father has forsaken his prerogatives several years earlier upon the death of his wife, for whom he still lovingly mourns. Cummins, it should be underscored, sees sensuality as harmful only when it is not subordinated to spiritual love. She does not scorn eroticism per se, and if in one sense Meredith must learn to distinguish eros from agape, in another the first propels him to the second. The scene just rendered occurs in the twilight zone between wake and sleep, when Meredith's moral guard is down. After he fully awakens, he sees Havilah in all her immaculate glory and his libido becomes purified: "[As] soul masters sense . . . so Meredith's throb of homage soon gave place to a resolute calm; a beam of holy light shone upon the night of his spirit, and the star which he worshipped became to him a guiding star" (293). In *El Fureidîs*, it seems, Western male libido inexorably through Christ's agency, which is also to say through Havilah, becomes transmuted into religious desire.[37]

The full redirecting of Meredith's erotic affections does not occur, however, until the party on its return trip from Damascus "penetrat[es]" (329) into the middle of the Syrian desert, into what Cummins earlier had called the "heart of this stony creation" (279). Meredith's double, Abdoul, also must be humbled or, rather, humiliated. In the progress of the trip, the Arab youth becomes increasingly vicious; and now, in his homeland, his murderous impulses are given full vent. Meredith lies innocently asleep, but "over his unprotected breast leaned one with a savage face, a sharpened dagger, and a soul thirsting for blood" (353). Havilah at the crucial moment intervenes and shows us a superior form of power. "[T]riumphing in the very meekness of the love which she proudly professed" (358) for Meredith, she subdues Abdoul, who sinks "lower and lower at her feet" (360). The hero learns his lesson: physical power does not conquer, but Christic love does. The two now confess their mutual regard, and Meredith is utterly transformed, no longer estranged from his soul-mate and the inward geography of his own soul: "His old world lay around him a desert; his new world was in his arms" (366). Amid the novel's last architectural mise-en-scène, the ruins of "Baalbec, with its giant record of the past" (369), the two commit themselves to each other and to Christ, "join[ing] hands in the cause of humanity and the active service of God" (369). In the conclusion, with the day "waning, and the sun . . . declining towards the west" (378), Meredith and his bride depart El Fureidîs and set sail for England and his vast estate. Meredith's transformations—from religious anomie to religious fulfillment, from bachelorhood to marriage—required what, in the final analysis, must be taken mainly as a necessary detour through the Near East. His itinerary ultimately takes him back to England, which at the ending is simply labeled "the west," allowing the U.S. reader to map the story's coordinates in an Occidental-Eastern opposition that implicitly encompasses America as well. In the sentimental tradition, inward space is what counts, and so that literal geographical traversal from East to West should be taken equally as an allegory of the Protestant soul's fate: the New World, if it is in "the west," is also in the "new world" of the redeemed heart, purified by its Christ-led or Havilah-led trek out of the wilderness of spiritual torpor.

Iniquity, the Uncanny, and the Dead Sea

Libidinal and religious perplexities in *El Fureidîs*'s sentimental economy are resolved with heart and soul harmoniously yoked and the happy couple returning to the West to enjoy their Christ-inflected heterosexual companionship. The novel, as I mentioned earlier, did not sell well. This may seem odd, since in addition to the sentimental theology that earned Cummins fame in the case of *The Lamplighter*, it held the appeal of Oriental exoticism, was contemporary with the nascent, but not entirely negligible, movement to establish a Protestant foothold in the Levant, and told a powerful love story. Perhaps, though, for all its conventionality, it was also perceived as being too atypical at least in one regard: the male hero suffers, but the female heroine transcends anxieties over faith or proper gender roles. Havilah—a strong, gifted woman throughout the tale—simply lacks the tortuous piety that made the heroine of *The Lamplighter* so viscerally stirring to its audience.

Herman Melville I suspect would have disliked *El Fureidîs*; for in his long poem about the Holy Land, *Clarel*, the libidinal and theological are more tensely intertwined, with no quietude reached by its end. Cummins in both her novels, whatever agon of the heart expressed, whether religiously or in terms of finding a suitor to love and return love, ultimately discovers an accessible God—one knowable within, and sentimentally responsive to those who religiously crave to fill in, as Meredith learns through Havilah's tutelage, inward voids. For Melville, however, the Godhead was a figure of eclipse, known only (if at all) through wrathful judgment—in for example the cursed environs of the Dead Sea—or more inwardly through a personal sense of transgression, which led him to fixate upon, as I will highlight later in the context of my discussion of *Clarel*, unspeakable sins.

The linkage between libido and gnostic looking is pervasive in Melville's oeuvre, but we might well begin with a direct citation to the Holy Land. In *Redburn*, we will recall, Melville remembered having spied an exotic looking traveler who most likely was Stephens. The passage, which I would now like to quote more fully, conflates the scopic, the textual, and the somatic:

I . . . star[ed] at . . . [the] man myself, who was pointed out to me by my aunt one Sunday in Church, as the person who had been in Stony Arabia, and passed through strange adventures there, all of which with my own eyes I had read in the book which he wrote, an arid-looking book in a pale yellow cover.

"See what big eyes he has," whispered my aunt, "they got so big, because when he was almost dead with famishing in the desert, he all at once caught sight of a date tree, with the ripe fruit hanging on it."[38]

The anecdote prepares us for Redburn's wanderlust, although given the actual story of his trip to Liverpool, which includes a visit accompanied by his aristocratic friend Harry Bolton to a bordello, the "Palace of Aladdin," it is difficult not to read the later episode's libidinal contours as being anticipated in the church scene. The aunt's comment, which seems as much monitory as explanatory, tacitly makes looking a libidinal activity, both enticing and threatening. Such early nurture pays off in Redburn's phobic reaction, when in Liverpool, to the Palace's seamy, overblown decor, especially the sundry lewd paintings "such . . . as you may still see, perhaps, in the central alcove of the excavated mansion of Pansa, in Pompeii—in that part of it called by Varro *the hollow of the house.*" Later, he recoils in a fit of sexual nausea: "All the mirrors and marbles around me seemed crawling over with lizards; and I thought to myself, that though gilded and golden, the serpent of vice is a serpent still."[39] In both passages, albeit in the opening one less directly, scopic knowledge becomes overdetermined by sexual anxiety—or longing, for the hyperbole of the aunt's remark and Redburn's lingering revulsed gaze at the bordello's furnishings come across as defense mechanisms blocking full identification with what is desired.

My goal in this section is not to fill in that cryptic "what" with specific epistemological or corporeal content. Although several Melville scholars, most notably Robert K. Martin, have persuasively argued for the centrality of homoerotic and homophobic imagery and themes in Melville's major works, the nature of desire in his texts remains ultimately elusive and can be tied neither to sexuality per se, masculine power (or its opposite, fraternal bonding), nor religious-philosophical seeking.[40] Yet we can, I think, usefully trace in relief the Melvillean enigma by looking at several of his Holy Land texts. Drawing upon Eve Sedgwick's notion of homosexual-homosocial panic, I suggest that Melville's Holy Land writings exhibit a fascination with hermetic enclosures and tabooed knowledge, which if not about homosexual affiliations per se, follow paths that conspicuously skirt the conventions of the heterosexual love plot that we have seen, for instance, operating in Cummins's *El Fureidîs.*[41] My intent is not to "out" Melville but rather to trace, without reducing the libidinal to the religiously numinous or vice versa, their intriguing if often baffling transcodings of desire and knowledge.

Nearly all of his texts make use of Orientalist lore, especially in respect to Egyptian mythology. Discoveries about hieroglyphics and the story of Giovanni Battista Belzoni, the most famous Westerner to gain access to the pyramids, especially intrigued him. Egyptology was in its heyday in the 1840s and 1850s. George R. Gliddon, one of the first U.S. consuls in Egypt, lectured on the subject around the country in the early 1840s and in 1843 wrote *Ancient Egypt,* which went through ten editions within only four years. His fame was sufficient for Poe to satirize him in a short story, "Some Words with a Mummy," first published in 1845. The appeal of the Egyptology fad is not difficult to surmise: it gave another forum to voice racial ideas; arcana of biblical times and places could be studied without fear of prying, sacrilegiously, into holy matters; and Egyptian culture was exotic, but the architecture relatively stark (it expressed the pomp of state, but not flamboyantly so). As John Irwin has shown, Egyptian mysticism and hermeticism spoke to Melville's epistemological questing, and the mythology of ancient Egypt figures in a number of his major works, including *Moby-Dick* (1852). Egypt or the Near East provided symbolic motifs, useful in a variety of thematic contexts; conversely, his hermeneutic obsessions in part derived from his brooding, from the early stages of his career, on Oriental mythology and travel reports pertaining to the region.[42]

For my purposes, the most relevant of Melville's shorter works employing Egyptological symbols is the comic story "I and My Chimney," published in the March 1856 issue of *Putnam's Monthly*. The tale's premise is a simple one. The narrator proudly celebrates the massive chimney of his house, "a huge, corpulent old Harry VIII. of a chimney" that his wife wishes to remove in the interest of home remodeling.[43] The phallic masculine emblem, however, also contains in its midsection an hermetic, interior space—a "mysterious closet" (360). Its warmth, the narrator muses, might make his "wife's geraniums bud there. . . . Her eggs, too" (360). The fertile hidden chamber, the chimney's bulk, and its foundation in the house's gloomy cellar likened to the "cob-webbed mausoleum of the great god Apis" (365) coalesce as a feminine-masculine space of conception. But the narrator, when he explores the chimney's cavernous foundation, is motivated by more than a literal genealogical drive. He also seeks the solid evidence of past numinosity. He is "obscurely prompted by dreams of striking upon some old, earthen-worn memorial of that by-gone day when, into all this gloom, the light of heaven entered" (357). The wife hires an architect, a Mr. Scribe, who informs the narrator in a letter (penned from "New Petra") that it may not be entirely "Christian-like knowingly to reside" in a house whose chimney hides a "reserved space, hermetically closed" (369).

The symbolism of the story is richly allusive, a tongue-in-cheek interpretive tease (the chimney stands, among other things, for Melville's creative talent, largely unrecognized by the magazine audience to whom he needed to cater). Beyond its anatomical suggestiveness, the chimney also seems to represent what Mircea Eliade would designate as an instance of the myth of the "cosmic pillar" (Jacob's ladder is a variation) or *axis mundi* that expresses a desire for "communication with heaven."[44] Melville, however, locates his version of the myth within the stereotypic gender dynamics of his period: such theological or phallo-eccentric pursuit, apparently, is the domain of the male only. "The truth is," he writes, "women know next to nothing about the realities of architecture" (360). The husband wishes to preserve the token of his "masculine prerogative" (362), but the wife wants to dismantle it. He irately declares that "[i]nfinite sad mischief has resulted from the profane bursting open of secret recesses":

"[If the chimney has a closet] it is my kinsman's. To break into that wall would be to break into his breast. And that wall-breaking wish of Momus I account the wish of a church-robbing gossip and knave. Yes, wife, a vile eaves-dropping varlet was Momus."

"Moses?—Mumps? STUFF with your mumps and your Moses!"

The truth is, my wife, like all the rest of the world, cares not a fig for my philosophical jabber. (376)

Here, through remarkable concision, Melville replays the story of Edenic transgression. Momus, who mocked Vulcan for creating a man without a window into his interior, seems to stand for those who would profanely seek godly knowledge of good and evil, and through such profane seeking Eve fell from grace ("a vile eaves-dropping varlet was Momus"). Eve's lapse in turn brought forth disease, "Mumps" (which, in Melville's time, could refer to inflammation of the mouth, testes, or ovaries), and the need to cover one's now shameful sexuality with a "fig" leaf (Melville also anatomically puns on the chimney's "queer" "secret ash-hole"—"'Don't you know,'" he asks his wife, "'that St. Dunstan's devil emerged from the ash-hole?'" [372]). No doubt, these double entendres and allusions should not be pinned down to one, singular interpretation. But when the husband declares his wife's indifference toward his "philosophical jabber," what is plainly emphasized is the isolation of those with, as it were, extradomestic psychotheological concerns.

In March of 1856, when "I and My Chimney" was published, Melville could speak humorously of the foibles of the artist who seeks "the light of heaven." But poorly compensated for his short stories, and with the reading public scorning his larger efforts, he became increasingly cynical and morbid. In October of the same year, suffering from nervous exhaustion, he sought relief by taking a trip abroad, and for seven months between 1856 and 1857 toured Europe and the Levant. He kept a journal of his travels, observations from which he later recycled into *Clarel*. The journal deserves study for its commentary, however clipped, on the cosmopolitan, multicultural scenes of the Levant, and for what it tells us about the Protestant ethos when abroad.

No less than Curtis or Stephens, Melville scorned the claptrap of the relic peddlers and, especially, that in the Church of the Holy Sepulchre:

Smells like a dead-house, dingy light. . . . [Near the entrance] is a blind stair of worn marble, ascending to the reputed Calvary where among other things the showman point you by the smoky light of old pawnbrokers lamps of dirty gold, the hole in which the cross was fixed and through a narrow grating as over a cole-cellar, point out the rent in the rock! . . . The door of the church is like that of a jail—a grated window in it.—The main body of the church is that overhung by the lofty & ruinous dome whose fallen plastering reveals the meagre skeleton of beams & laths—a sort of plague-stricken splendor reigns in the painted & mildewed walls around. In the midst of all, stands the Sepulchre; a church in a church. . . . First passing a wee vestibule where is shown the stone on which the angel sat, you enter the tomb. It is like entering a lighted lanthorn. Wedged & half-dazzled, you stare for a moment on the ineloquence of the bedizened slab, and glad to come out, wipe your brow glad to escape as from the heat & jam of a show-box. All is glitter & nothing is gold. A sickening cheat.[45]

Jenny Franchot, in *Roads to Rome: The Antebellum Protestant Encounter with Catholicism*, shows that U.S. Protestantism, as a cultural dynamic, depended upon an oscillating attraction/repulsion to the more corporealizing tenets and practices of Catholicism; and Melville here expresses a typical mixture of loathing and longing.[46] The passage guides us through a parade of idolatrous horrors, not memorials of the Son of God, within a corpselike architectural enclosure. The most striking line, the "ineloquence of the bedizened slab," should prompt us, though, to see that more is going on in this passage than stereotypic defamation of non-Protestant religious customs. If Melville excoriates the pretense that the site's ghostly paraphernalia might embody the presence of Christ, he also seems to wish to *hear* a voice from the tomb. I do not think, however, that Melville keens for an affirmation of faith so much as he would want the dead per se to speak. As I will propose below, we have a strong warrant for interpreting such deathlike spaces in psychoanalytical terms, as being more about unreconciled feelings toward the Father-as-father than toward the actual spiritual Father.

What most seems to distress Melville, in the passage on the Holy Sepulchre and in the following one about his visit to the Egyptian pyramids, is that death and gnostic knowledge haunt the same corridors:

A feeling of awe & terror came over me. Dread of the Arabs. Offering to lead me into a side-hole. The Dust. Long arched way,—then down as in a coal shaft. . . . I shudder at idea of ancient Egyptians. It was in these pyramids that was conceived the idea of Jehovah. Terrible mixture of the cunning and awful. Moses learned in all the lore of Egyptians. . . . As with the ocean, you learn as much of its vastness by the first five minutes glance as you would in a month, so with the pyramid. Its simplicity confounds you. . . . It refuses to be studied or comprehended. It still looms in my imagination, dim & indefinite. . . . A dead calm of masonry. (75–78)

Melville actually tried with the help of an Arab guide to enter a pyramid, to re-enact physically the genealogical urge he had described in "I and My Chimney." But he ran out quickly, feeling an intolerable sense of claustrophobia. Rather than uncovering the "light of heaven" he found only a paralyzing void. Paranoia, a sense of suffocation, gloomy bewilderment: these were the keynotes of his remembrance of the massive ancient tombs.

"I and My Chimney" and the Holy Land journal—the first humorously; the second, more somberly—echo Stephens's desire to explore hallowed, interior Levantine spaces. In *Clarel*, we will also see a similar motive in respect to the transgressive site of the Dead Sea. Before we turn to this longer, poetic meditation on the Holy Land, however, the psychological dimensions of Melville's

hermeneutical concerns, which I alluded to earlier, require additional un-
packing. Melville's father, Allan, died abruptly of pneumonia when Melville
was eleven years old, and critics have seen much of his fiction as working
through his yearning for, and resentment against, father-figures (evident to
some extent in his first novel, *Typee*). Neil Tolchin, more particularly, speculates that Allan's death and the formality of early Victorian mourning rituals
led to a protracted trauma of obstructed grieving. Melville was neither able to
lay his father to rest nor conquer adolescent fixations on fatherly authority or
the father's body. Traumatized in effect by the weight of the father's corpse,
Melville subsequently conflated the search for the father with the search for the
Father, a frustrated desire encoded in various genealogical quests and an obsession with internalized spaces of patriarchal power.[47]

The space and body of the absent or ghostly father/Father goes, in Melville's
haunted thematics, by the name of both Death and God. This trauma, though
idiosyncratic, may be glossed in more psychologically universal terms, as suggested by Jean-Joseph Goux's reflections on the law, idolatry, and sexuality in
Symbolic Economies:

> Idols, therefore, can be destroyed only when this law is recognized and internalized, for
> the law is what enables the subject finally to tolerate the sanctuary's holy emptiness
> without clinging idolatrously to fetishes. It is not by chance that Moses, bringing the
> Tables of the Law, can in one and the same gesture prohibit figurative representation.
> ... The law commands desire for a woman that is not the mother. Distilled in the emp-
> tiness of the sanctuary is the acceptance of the law of the dead (invisible, unrepresent-
> able) father as a necessary condition for nonincestuous desire for the female *hollow*.
> The imageless temple is, on one hand, the Father's vault, but it is also the void of femi-
> ninity, now tolerable and even desirable: the woman's cavity.[48]

Goux's insights are rather heady, but their sense is borne out when applied to
Melville. Following Goux, we may say that his hermeneutical urge, his fetishizing of hermetic/patriarchal spaces, resulted from an insufficient internalization of the fatherly presence (a consequence of blocked mourning). Subsequently, that failure leads to a restless desire for materialized forms of both the
father and the Father and a refusal to accept, as Goux puts it, the "emptiness of
the sanctuary." These epistemological-genealogical pursuits also, however,
disrupt normative heterosexual relations. As we will see in *Clarel*, Melville's
psychotheological quests which make unacceptable the void of the "Father's
vault" also make heterosexual relations not quite "tolerable" or "even desirable."[49]

Although a postbellum text, probably begun in 1871 when Melville was employed at the New York Custom House, *Clarel* reflects long-standing epistemological and sexual preoccupations and resonates with many of the aspects
of the previously discussed Holy Land works.[50] The poem's link with the post–

Civil War utopian politics of U.S. millennialists as well as the specific groups of the faithful that established colonies in Palestine is important, and recent studies have insisted that, far from being a self-reflexive text, *Clarel* shows Melville's enduring commitment to critiquing nationalist, New World ideologies. My more psychoanalytically inclined inquiry, however, largely elides this later context, emphasizing instead the poem's effort to find a topographical corollary for the issues of transgressive knowledge and sexuality that vexed its author.[51]

Very lengthy (divided into four parts, it runs to some eighteen thousand lines), excruciatingly inwrought, and clunky and snarled in prosody, *Clarel* presents formidable barriers to our grasping its profound insights about identity, eros, and religious knowledge. Its basic plot, however, is straightforward. Clarel, a young American divinity student, travels to Jerusalem to revivify his lapsing faith. He is smitten by a part-Jewish woman, Ruth. But when her father, Nathan (an expatriate U.S. citizen), is murdered by raiding Arabs, Clarel must forgo courting her because Jewish custom forbids extrafamilial relations during the period of bereavement. So, instead, Clarel elects to join a band of pilgrims whose route takes them to the Jordan River, the Dead Sea, the famous Greek monastery Mar Saba, Bethlehem, and finally back to Jerusalem. The excursion lasts only a few days, but when Clarel returns to Jerusalem in the evening, he finds Ruth dead and about to be buried by torch-light. The poem ends with Clarel, left alone in his solitude, numb with grief.

Exceptionally cosmopolitan, the pilgrim group permits Melville to raise a dauntingly diverse set of issues from an equally daunting diversity of perspectives. Clarel, the poem's eponymous focus, more often than not remains an auditor to his companions' monologues and debates. He is, however, no mere cipher even though the nuances of his dilemmas must be read less in his own exposition of them than in his responses to the Holy Land terrain and the other travelers' disputes. The poem begins with Clarel ensconced within a Jerusalem hostel, brooding within his "chamber low and scored by time, / Masonry old, late washed with lime—/ Much like a tomb new-cut in stone."[52] It ends with Clarel—his ordeal of faith unresolved and anguishing over Ruth's death, for which he feels vaguely culpable—watching Greek Christians in "rite / Commemorative" (4.33.2–3) of Easter gather about "THE TOMB" (4.33.18) in the Holy Sepulchre. Vernal rains refresh the worshipers, but Clarel reflects in this aptly numbered canto that the "cheer, so human, might not call / The maiden up; *Christ is arisen:* / But Ruth, may Ruth so burst the prison?" (4.33.64–66). The poignant juxtaposition highlights the poem's most salient thematic strand: Christ's resurrection, given the heavy quiddity of death, is voided of significance. Clarel has lingered too long in the interior mazes of doubt, sacrificing his chance to clasp Ruth physically and perhaps wed her. If the aging narrator of "I and My Chimney" sees his wife as a scold denigrating his genealogical or theological impulse, Clarel obversely shows the cost of pursuing those urges: the loss of domestic, matrimonial bliss.

Unlike Meredith in *El Fureidîs*, Clarel finds neither Christ nor maiden. Melville's poem, though, does more than rewrite Cummins's story as tragedy. It also probes whether the alignment of heterosexual love and love of Christ— the core of the earlier tale—conquers the dilemmas of all religious-sexual seekers. Whereas Meredith's love of Havilah leads him to love of God, Clarel's religious journey, as Nina Baym astutely argues, may properly be seen as an elaborate flight, intensely ambivalent, from physicality itself—from, more specifically, a woman's body.[53] At key junctures, what seems to be a tale about Clarel not getting Ruth because of her father's death and then her own may be read as an alibi, a cover story, for a counternarrative. Women, traditionally associated with carnality and, because of Eve's transgression, mortality itself, impede access to the numinous. In the course of the poem, however, Clarel has a chance to deflect his desires away from Ruth. By envisioning fraternal unions between men, and a shared Godhead via the concord of male souls, he essays a different avenue out of his morbid turmoil, one that leads him to eschew what he fretfully deems as his all-too-carnal interest in his prospective bride. My previous points in the main have been drawn from Baym. I wish now, though, to shift her emphasis: the poem, I propose, *pivots* around homoerotic bondings and spaces as much as it alludes to them as an inevitable corollary to Clarel's uneasy relation with Ruth. In *Clarel*, the Dead Sea becomes an uncanny, transgressive locale, a site that both evokes and represses homosexual panic.

Neither the poem's narrator nor its main character is Melville, of course, and so we should not ignore the critical distance that Melville maintains toward all of the actors in the pilgrimage drama. With that caveat in mind, however, let us begin with what in the poem is staged as the originating moment of desire. Clarel, initially described as "feminine" (1.1.16), seems to discover male-female passion for the first time when he meets Ruth: "in emotion new and strange, / Ruth thrilled him with life's first romance" (1.23.47–48). Clarel becomes privy, then, to his own desire, but its consummation is thwarted by her seclusion, during her bereavement for her dead father, Nathan. His death, which at once breaks up one family and delays its potential reconstitution—a "Pure home of all we seek and prize" (1.23.67)—in what otherwise would have been the nuptials of Clarel and Ruth, prompts the young man to take his pilgrimage. Yet if Clarel (if we assume that Nathan's death *is* an alibi) flees the physical entrapments of conjugality, his Holy Land itinerary takes him to a more vexatious deathly and carnal locale. In the poem, Clarel's identity comes into focus not by the specular mirror of a human other, in this case Ruth, but by one of the most resistantly alienating topographies on the planet: the sterile region of the Dead Sea, where desire, if it may exist at all, will in Clarel's imagination turn toward the antithetical, that is, the nonheterosexual.

Book II, amid much twisted theological disquisition, obsessively alludes to the Dead Sea and its environs. The Sinai desert, through which winds the ravine Kedron that "Conduct[s] unto Lot's mortal Sea" (2.11.76), is utterly desolate; and Melville, seemingly in *propia persona*, ponders "why does man / Regard religiously this tract / Cadaverous and under ban / Of blastment?" (2.11. 78–81). He answers, in the first of many indirections, that "to pure hearts it yields no fear; / And John, he found wild honey here" (2.11.90–91). At this moment Melville cannot clarify the nature of the transgression "under ban." He merely asserts that the proscribed terrain can be negotiated only if one is holy and celibate. The Dead Sea's significance in the poem may first be disclosed by correlating it with a straight reading of Clarel's and Ruth's alliance and with my earlier comments about the effect on Melville of his father's death. The narrator has reminded us that the Dead Sea also goes by the name of "Lot's mortal Sea," and we should recollect that if the biblical story was about the fated Cities of the Plain being punished for communal sin, it was also about Lot's loss of his mate, whom God had turned to a pillar of salt because she could not forsake her memories of the town from which she was instructed to flee. The psychological motif of the biblical legend would, then, appear to be about the mourner who impiously and paralytically refuses to come to terms with death. Clarel, forbidden from participating in the funeral rites of Nathan, who would have become his father-in-law, naturally enough becomes haunted by death's topographic icon—the Dead Sea. More precisely, to follow the coiled logic of blocked mourning, Clarel (and, by extension, the narrator or Melville himself) wishes to return to the primal site of death itself. The Dead Sea accordingly becomes an idée fixe representing a thanatonic drive, indeed a site nostalgically longed for. Yet, of course, it is also the site of the Father's wrath. To gaze imprudently on death; to look back on Sodom and Gomorrah, as Lot's wife does; to pursue any scopic-hermeneutical enterprise—all act to imprison one in the fatal, inward spirals of unrelieved mourning and to risk the punitive judgment of the Father. The poem also rewrites Lot's story, for whereas in Scripture Lot loses his wife when she casts a last, lingering look backward on her doomed hometown, Clarel will have lost Ruth, by the poem's end, because *he* has dallied too long in sterile, deathlike terrains.[54] Thematically, the poem recoils upon itself. Clarel, dimly haunted by the prospect of her death throughout his journey (he habitually alludes to an Armenian funeral procession, which he had seen before departing from Jerusalem), in effect proleptically mourns for her, which—insofar as he cannot escape his fixation on the Dead Sea—turns out to cause the occasion of his final grief, his too late return to his not-bride-to-be.[55]

Thus far I have assumed that Clarel sustains his passion for Ruth. The nature of his desire, however, can be interpreted differently, with the unavailability of Ruth's body (both as a tabooed other and because of the mourning customs that restrict Clarel's access to his beloved) being seen in fact as a pretext to give impetus to desires that will lead elsewhere. In Cummins's novel, Havilah's Orientalized body in effect serves in the plot as a sort of masquerade, for if Meredith finds her splendid form exceptionally alluring in its foreign costumes, his desire eventually cathects not with the Orient or Oriental woman but with the maiden's simple, transcultural piety of the heart. Not unlike, say, Cooper's good savages, inward ethics outweigh the more superficial pageantry of costume or exotic locale, although the habits or racial difference of the native or, in Cummins's case, Havilah helps pull the protagonist (Natty Bumppo or Meredith) away from the realms of white Protestant comfort, away from a blasé attitude toward nature or religion. Ruth is perhaps one shade darker than Havilah, yet she lacks the racial frisson hovering about the mysterious Jewess elsewhere in the antebellum imaginary (for instance, the leading character Miriam in Nathaniel Hawthorne's *The Marble Faun* [1860]). She has a Mediterranean complexion, but her body never comes into focus sufficiently to make credible Clarel's supposed libidinal attachment to her:

> Hebrew the profile, every line;
> But as in haven fringed with palm,
> Which Indian reefs embay from harm,
> Belulled as in the vase the wine—
> Red budded corals in remove,
> Peep coy through quietudes above;
> So through clear olive of the skin,
> And features finely Hagarene;
> Its way a tell-tale flush did win—
> A tint which unto Israel's sand
> Blabbed of the June in some far clover land.
> (1.16.176–86)

Offstage for most of the poem, moreover, Ruth barely emerges as one of its dramatis personae. She pulls so little on our attention that it at first seems unremarkable that Clarel when away from the precincts of her body—which the poem, read bluntly, wants to bury—entertains thoughts resisting what Eve Sedgwick refers to as compulsory heterosexuality.

Clarel, in Ruth's absence, seeks communion with the other pilgrims, hoping to allay his religious anxieties by probing their more seasoned experiences. He also, though, intermittently dwells on more problematically intense—because not exclusively spiritual—fraternal unions with his fellow travelers, in particular the reticent and mysterious Vine.[56] The entourage camps overnight at Jericho, and he listens intently to a debate between two of the party—Rolfe, a kind, well-traveled American sailor; and Derwent, an English clergyman—on sundry religious issues. "Disturbed by topics canvassed late," Clarel cannot sleep:

> He rose, stood gazing toward the hight
>
> . . . .
>
> When Rolfe drew near. With motion slight,
> Scarce conscious of the thing he did,
> Partly aside the student slid;
> Then, quick as thought, would fain atone.
>   Whence came that shrinking start unbid?
> But from desire to be alone?
> Or skim or sound him, was Rolfe one
> Whom honest heart would care to shun?
>
> . . . .
>
> How frank seemed Rolfe. Yet Vine could lure
> Despite reserve which overture
> Withstood—e'en Clarel's late repealed,
> Finding that heart a fountain sealed.
>
>   But Rolfe: however it might be—
> Whether in friendly fair advance
> Checked by that start of dissonance,
> Or whether rapt in revery
> Beyond—apart he moved, and leant
> Down peering from the battlement
> Upon its shadow....
>
> . . . .
>
> But Clarel turned [to Rolfe]; and anew
> His thoughts regained their prior clew;
> When, lo, a fog, and all was changed.
> Crept vapors from the Sea of Salt,
> Overspread the plain, nor there made halt,
> But blurred the heaven.
>   As one estranged
> Who watches, watches from the shore,
>
> . . . .
>
> See here the student, repossessed
> By thoughts of Ruth. . . .
>
> . . . .
>
> The mist before him, mist behind,
> While intercepting memories ran
> Of chant and bier Armenian.
>   (2.17.1–50)

We could easily take this episode as an instance of Clarel's cruising for a fellow spiritual traveler, but the gestural nuances and interrupting Dead Sea fog indicate, however obliquely, that Clarel here broaches more tabooed terrain—male-male unions that exceed the merely spiritual. Melville leaves undeterminable whether Vine's hermetic self-possession elicits erotic or brotherly affections in the young Clarel, but it is precisely the contagion between the physical and spiritual, the possibility that you cannot have one without the other, that seems to call forth the monitory, malignant vapor, the portent that transgressive precincts have been entered. Clarel's "thoughts of Ruth" pull him back toward safer (that is, heterosexual) territory. Yet we cannot be sure given the poem's confusing overall causal syntax whether, inversely, Clarel's "thoughts" of heterosexual conjugality signal the death of a wished-for homosexual or homosocial alliance. In the densely inbred logic of the poem, the Dead Sea simultaneously symbolizes the homosexual or homosocial alternative to heterosexual relations, Clarel's *too* carnal desire for Ruth's body, and the author's own repressed act of mourning that drives his character's psychotheological quest in the first place.

The narrator, to be sure, attempts to cordon off the physical dimensions of Clarel's relationship to Vine by designating it in the language of innocent pastoral. The enigmatic Vine at one point meditates upon a group of Bedouins from whom he believes he "might espy, / For all the wildness, thoughts refined / By the old Asia's dreamful mind" (2.27.54–56). As Vine gazes at the Bedouins, Clarel gazes at Vine, who is embowered behind a "leafy screen, / Luxurious there in umbrage thrown" (2.27.12–13):

> Of true unworldliness looked Vine.
> Ah, clear sweet ether of the soul
> (Mused Clarel), holding him in view.
> Prior advances unreturned
> Nor here he recked of, while he yearned—
> O, now but for communion true
> And close; let go each alien theme;
> Give me thyself!
> (2.27.63–70)

Such spiritual bonding, though, Clarel deems unlikely because of the body's natural (for him, heterosexual) disinclination: "But for thy fonder dream of love / In man toward man—the soul's caress—/ The negatives of flesh should prove / Analogies of non-cordialness / In spirit" (2.27.124–28). He is not, however, fully convinced by his own argument, and it takes once again the intruding memory of Ruth to forestall a further pursuit of Vine. He concludes that "sick these feelings are" (2.27.139) for he cannot at this juncture conceive of what we today would call bisexual leanings. As Clarel poses it in a question to himself, how can he "findest place within thy heart / For such solicitudes apart / From Ruth?" (2.27.140–42).[57]

With Clarel's longings for Vine bracketed as "sick," what in the above canto 27 had been posed as an alluring companionship, in the next, canto 28 (named "The Fog"), becomes refigured as being grotesquely repugnant. The travelers approach the Dead Sea, and the vernal imagery previously associated with Vine—"while buds unroll; / So pure, so virginal in shrine" (2.27.61–62)—is replaced by that associated with the blighting fog itself. The repellent landscape is described as "Pluto's park" (2.28.1), a sort of antipastoral. Here, shrubs carry "Pippins of Sodom" (2.28.10) on "mildewed stunted twigs unclean" (2.28.5), and the branches of palm trees—"Spotted they show, all limp they be"—are saturated by the "bitter mist" of the "Bad Sea" (2.28.38–39). The remainder of the canto continues to describe the withered vegetation and dreary shores of the Dead Sea, and then in cantos 35 and 36 the narrator turns to the doomed Cities of the Plain themselves.

In canto 35 ("Prelusive"), though, the approach to the transgressive site—to knowledge of the homoerotic—requires a stratagem of indirection. The elusive horror or desire that Clarel cannot pin down evokes a bizarre detour into art history and the landscapes of paranoia:

> In Piranesi's rarer prints,
> Interiors measurelessly strange,
> Where the distrustful thought may range
> Misgivings still—what mean the hints?
> Stairs upon stairs which dim ascend
> In series from plunged Bastiles drear—
> Pit under pit; long tier on tier
>
> . . . .
> Those wards of hush are not disposed
> In gibe of goblin fantasy—
> Grimace—unclean diablery:
> Thy wings, Imagination, span
> Ideal truth in fable's seat:
> The thing implied is one with man,
> His penetralia of retreat—
> The heart, with labyrinths replete:
> In freaks of intimation see
> Paul's "mystery of iniquity:"
>
> (2.35.1–24)

Melville here, of course, could just be charting the murky corridors of a generic inner depravity, but the canto concludes with a forewarning, which indicates that he likely has more particular contents in mind. He requests that "As bride and suit let pass a bier / So pass the coming canto here" (2.35.40–41). To couples seeking the bliss of marriage, the specter of death must be warded off, but antithetical sexual relations must also be pushed out of sight. Mortmain, an erratic and morbid Swede, in the earlier canto 34 had tasted the waters of the Dead Sea in a sort of crazed ritual—"Did Mortmain his pale hand recall? / No; undeterred the wave he scooped, / And tried it—madly tried the gall" (2.34.65–67). Now, in canto 36, the acrid libation seems to offer him a peculiar insight into the legend of Sodom and Gomorrah:

> ... [He] made review
> Of what that wickedness might be
> Which down on these ill precincts drew
> The flood, the fire; put forth new plea,
> Which not with Writ might disagree;
> Urged that those malefactors stood
> Guilty of sins scarce scored as crimes
> In any statute known, or code—
> Nor now, nor in former times:
> Things hard to prove: decorum's wile,
> Malice discreet, judicious guile;
> Good done with ill intent—reversed:
>
> . . . .
>
> "But who the manifold may tell?
> And sins there be inscrutable,
> Unutterable."
> (2.36.25–85)

What, exactly, those "[u]nutterable" sins are the text no further divulges. *That* particular transgressive destination, of male-male couplings, simply cannot be articulated. It is the source, simultaneously, of aphasia and the text's all-too-ample meandering in a traumatizing terrain.[58]

My reading of the poem, up to this point, has tried to illuminate what I perhaps earlier too coyly called the Melvillean enigma. No less than in *The Confidence-Man* (1857), we lack certitude about Melville's own position on the dialogues exchanged; in this poem all interpretations, virtually, must be framed tentatively. Interestingly, however, his focus on the Dead Sea as a site simultaneously representing both the principles of eros and thanatos was not unique to himself. The literary retelling of the Dead Sea cataclysm became, it appears, a popular topos in the antebellum period. The *Ladies' Repository* in 1843 and 1845, for example, included respectively both a poem and a brief narrative.[59] But perhaps the most curious rendition was penned by the young Lucretia Maria Davidson, published in a deathbed edition of her poems in 1843. "The Destruction of Sodom and Gomorrah" devotes several stanzas to God's punitive wrath, yet what Davidson lingers on is less transgression per se than the pathos of unexpected calamity:

> In that city the wine-cup was brilliantly flowing,
> Joy held her high festival there;
> Not a fond bosom dreaming, (in luxury glowing,)
> Of the close of that night of despair.

For the bride, her handmaiden the garland was wreathing,
  At the altar the bridegroom was waiting,
But vengeance impatiently round them was breathing,
  And Death at that shrine was their greeting.

But the wine-cup is empty, and broken it lies,
  The lip which it foamed for, is cold;
For the red wing of Death o'er Gomorrah now flies,
  And Sodom is wrapped in its fold.

The bride is wedded, but the bridegroom is Death,
  With his cold, damp, and grave-like hand;
Her pillow is ashes, the slime-weed her wreath,
  Heaven's flames are her nuptial band.[60]

In the antebellum cultural archive, the Dead Sea apparently enjoined not just reflections about dark iniquities, but also sentimentalized, innocent musings on the precatastrophic pleasures of the bourgeoisie. In Davidson's poem the punishment for communal sin is less emphasized than the ironic and sad closure to otherwise anticipated conjugal felicities. The poem, in brief, becomes significant for exactly what it excludes: that among the sins punished were those involving homosexual congress, or at least practices going beyond the mere indulgence of "luxury."

Given a collective effort of repression, it is difficult to know what nineteenth-century men and women thought of when they dwelled on the crimes of Sodom and Gomorrah. We cannot, with absolute assurance, assume that the proscription against a generalized lasciviousness or depravity included that against illicit same-sex relations. Michael Warner, in a discussion of seventeenth-century New England jeremiadic literature, proposes that references to the Cities of the Plain functioned as "an argument not for what we would call heterosexuality but for public regulation. The fable of Sodom represented, in a way that no other image could, an entire society open to discipline and in need of saving."[61] Homosexuality or sodomy, according to Warner, was lodged in the Puritan mentality less as a sexual proclivity than as a pervasive, culturally serviceable trope—with its resonance emanating precisely from the steadfast repression of specific sexual content. The sermonic traditions that Warner examines had, to be sure, become attenuated by Melville's day; but the Dead Sea's unique allure, we might say, remained distinctly uncanny.

Non-U.S. writers later in the century such as the famous British explorer Richard Burton more explicitly named what they saw. He noted that the Near East and other regions (China, the South Sea islands, and Italy and Greece), comprising what he called the "Sotadic Zone," were notorious for a "Vice [that] is popular and endemic."[62] That the Dead Sea in antebellum America raised the potential of homosexual-homosocial panic is at least made clear by one traveler, Bayard Taylor, in his 1854 *Lands of the Saracens*. Taylor, who wrote several homoerotic Oriental poems and who, as Robert K. Martin believes, maintained at least protogay feelings toward a young correspondent, depicts the Dead Sea in the customary lexicon of desiccation, disease, and death familiar to us from Stephens's, Lynch's, and Melville's Holy Land texts: "The region is so scarred, gashed and torn, that no work of man's hand can save it from perpetual desolation. . . . The plants appeared as if smitten with leprosy" (64–65).[63] As Taylor continues, though, the Dead Sea carries a more intense threat: one of contagion. He decides to go swimming, to test the buoyancy of the salt water, and then after bathing seeks to "wash off the iniquitous slime of the Dead Sea" (68). Nothing remarkable thus far: many travelers tried the waters and responded similarly. How, though, should we interpret his subsequent anxiety that the "taint of Gomorrah was not entirely washed away" (68)? Should we hear him admitting homophobia or latent homosexuality? Neither possibility would seem warranted were it not for the fact that, in his volume's following section, he carefully describes his fairly overt attraction to a young Arab in a fashion calculated to reduce the threat of having entered the domain of tabooed sexualities. Now in Jerusalem, Taylor passes a youth whose "face was the most perfect oval, and almost feminine in the purity of its outline." The Arab lad's eyes especially haunt him—"shall I ever look into such orbs again?"—but he quickly rewrites his desire. "Large, dark, unfathomable," the Arab's eyes "beamed with an expression of divine love and sorrow" (82), reminding him, he sums up, of Christ.[64]

Davidson's and Taylor's Dead Sea descriptions, the first through sentimental denial, the second through diversion, help us to see why Melville in *Clarel* felt obliged to approach homosexual spaces so indirectly that we may conclude that we have not been led there at all. In that regard, *Clarel* returns us to one major crux of *Typee*: what cannibalism and homosexuality hold in common for Melville is not how either manifest desire—cravings for flesh—but the fact of their cultural proscription, the allure of tabooed knowledge. To the extent that cannibalism and homosexual urges stand as tropes for the *hidden*, it is apt in both the early and late work that neither is certifiably disclosed.

If it is ultimately unclear whether gnostic longing or dread and the knowledge of alternative sexuality fold together in the cantos pertaining to the Dead Sea, so is the narrator's or Melville's attitude, overall in the poem, toward proscribed unions. Mortmain is hardly himself a trustworthy guide about sex. For if the tirade in the passage cited earlier ("And sins there be inscrutable, / Unutterable") seems targeted against homosexual relations, what really disturbs him is sexual congress in general. As canto 36 proceeds, Mortmain lapses into a condemnation of woman as responsible for loathly biological generation itself. Looking upon bubbles in the Dead Sea's waves, he meditates: "Thee,

thee, / In thee the filmy cell is spun—/ The mould thou art of what men be: / Events are all in thee begun—/ By thee, through thee!—Undo Undo, / Prithee, undo, and still renew / The fall forever!" (2.36.98–104). All women are offspring of Eve, implicitly blamed here as the progenitor of humankind's liability to disease and mortality. Melville, however, appears to have little patience with Mortmain's misogyny or revulsion against all things biological. The rest of the travelers, Clarel included, simply turn away from his frenzied diatribes. When Mortmain explains to himself why the party disregards him—"because he open threw / The inmost to the outward view" (2.36.109–10)—we might be justified in sensing Melville's own lament about his audience's disinclination to respond to his own hermeneutical explorations. Or we might be tempted to view Mortmain's morbidity—his name is a giveaway—as equally valid (or invalid) as the alternative vision of woman's body proffered when the band of travelers has finally made its way to Bethlehem. In the Church of the Star they see in "A semicircular recess; / And there, in marble floor, they view / A silver sun" (4.13.184–86) inscribed with a "Latin text; which thus may run: / THE VIRGIN HERE BROUGHT FORTH THE SON" (4.13.192–93). Such fabular sites, the narrator implies, are shallow attempts to enlist credulity rather than profound testimonies to the virginal generation of humankind's Savior. A belief in the efficacy of the Incarnation—the poem refuses to choose—may mean that we are properly faithful or that we are simply fools.

Melville offers the reader some brief respite from such quandaries of faith and doubt earlier in the poem, when Clarel had envisioned the life of perfect asceticism, the seclusion of celibate monks whom the pilgrims visit at the Mar Saba cloister. Clarel is especially taken by one young monk who appears "an almoner of God, / Dispenser of the bread of light" (3.30.45–46). Such "Saba doves / Seemed natives—not of Venus' court / Voluptuous with wanton wreath—/ But colonnades where Enoch roves, / Or walks with God, as Scripture saith" (3.30.64–68). He finds an ascetic, not necessarily homoerotic, brotherhood compelling: "Can be a bond / (Thought he) as David sings in strain / That dirges beauteous Jonathan, / Passing the love of woman fond?" (3.30.149–52). But when he later in Book IV returns to these fraternal reveries, heterosexual desire strongly emerges: "he felt the strain / Of [Ruth's] clasping arms which would detain / His heart from such ascetic range" (4.26.308–10). The equivocal use of "strain" (as positive tug or negative constraint?) suggests the fine-tuned ambivalences through which the narrator or Melville regards the Mar Saba brethren. Yet perhaps the real problem with the monks is not their renunciation of passion, but rather the danger in the absence of social relations of a fatal, inward-turning narcissism. At Mar Saba, Clarel is ushered into an "inner grotto" (3.27.108) where a "crazed monk" (3.27.103) has spent his days, up to his death, marking the walls:

> "How like you it—Habbibi's home?
> You see these writings on the wall?
> His craze was this: he heard a call
> Ever from heaven: O scribe, write, write, write!
> Write this—that write—to these indite—
> To them! Forever it was—write!
> Well, write he did, as here you see.
> What is it all?"
>
> . . . .
>
> *'I, Self, I am the enemy*
> *Of all. From me deliver me,*
> *O Lord.' . . .*
>
> (3.27.112–25)

Such self-loathing Melville did not himself succumb to, although his own urge to "write" in *Clarel* led him to a kindred wilderness, in which the terrains to be explored, outwardly and inwardly, almost collapse together into feverishly obscure nonmeaning. For him, desire sutured the theological to the sexual; the questing toward some revelation, luminous or transgressive, could not be disentangled from more agitated longings. The crossovers between religious motives and knowledge and sexual motives and knowledge can be posed too glibly, but I think we can safely say that Habbibi's forlornness, his need to complete himself by getting out of himself, through the mediation of a superior power, is deeply resonate with what many readers find most compelling about Melville: his anguished longing for fraternity, to make himself whole through affectional bonds; or his sense that the arc of the self had dimensions of mystery, both sublime and dark, that were always unsayable. From that standpoint, to search the depths of the Dead Sea, to seek out heterodox unions, or to fixate on the unobtainable body of Christ (the "ineloquence of the bidizened slab" in the Church of the Holy Sepulchre) all amount to the same need: to fill in the desolations of the heart. In Melville's Levantine writings the genealogical, religious, and sexual fuse together, and no one category should be regarded as dominating the others.

Reviewers disliked *Clarel*. It was too overwrought, too perplexing, too, in short, metaphysical. The "reader soon becomes hopelessly bewildered," one critic commented.[65] Seven years earlier, in 1869, Mark Twain launched his writing career with the publication of *The Innocents Abroad*—a title which, given Melville's mining of deeper matters in *Clarel*, neatly signposts the sort of text that readers preferred. *The Innocents Abroad* holds, however, one similarity to Melville's work. If the poem seeks in the depths of the heart—of Clarel, Vine, and the other pilgrims—and in the depths of the Dead Sea to penetrate the labyrinth (call it metaphysical or sexual), it comes to no conclusion. Twain, the consummate satirist of surfaces, directs his scorn at nearly every object in sight. His work, too, comes to no conclusion, as he restlessly debunks venerated sites of both the Holy Land and, implicitly toward the end of this passage, America itself:

These gifted Latin monks never do anything by halves. . . . If it had been left to Protestants to do this most worthy work, we would not even know where Jerusalem is today, and the man who could go and put his finger on Nazareth would be too wise for this world. The world owes the Catholics its goodwill even for the happy rascality of hewing out these bogus grottoes in the rock; for it is infinitely more satisfactory to look at a grotto where people have faithfully believed for centuries that the Virgin once lived than to have to imagine a dwelling place for her somewhere, anywhere, nowhere, loose and at large all over this town of Nazareth. . . . There is no one particular spot to chain your eye, rivet your interest, and make you think. The memory of the Pilgrims cannot perish while Plymouth Rock remains to us. The old monks are wise. They know how to drive a stake through a pleasant tradition that will hold it to its place forever.[66]

Melville's problem was that he could find no scopic site that adequately could "rivet" his psychotheological desires. Lacking the cavalier disposition of Stephens, who was satisfied to skim upon the surface of the Dead Sea; lacking Lynch's righteous understanding of history; lacking, finally, Cummins's sentimental consolations—Melville was left with himself, composing for himself, much like the manic monk, Habbibi: "he heard a call / Ever from heaven: O scribe, write, write, write!"

Melville's tension-fraught agnosticism, his incapacity to read the Levant's literal or cultural landscape and *not* be struck by the Godhead's uncanny presence / absence, led him to refuse the easier routes that Cummins or Lynch took in their conjoining of Protestant faith and country. Melville's poem holds forth no exceptional role for the United States in the Holy Land or globally. In a canto near the end of *Clarel*, the narrator sums up several of the pilgrims' responses to the cynicism of Unger, a former Confederate officer, who excoriates the dawning "Dark Ages of Democracy" led by "America" (4.21.139–40):

> They gazed, nor one of them found heart
> To upbraid the crotchet of his smart,
> Bethinking them whence sole it came,
> Through birthright he renounced in hope,
> Their sanguine country's wonted claim.
> Nor dull they were in honest tone
> To some misgivings of their own:
> They felt how far beyond the scope
> Of elder Europe's saddest thought
> Might be the New World's sudden brought
> In youth to share old age's pains—
> To feel the arrest of hope's advance,

And squandered last inheritance;
And cry—"To Terminus build fanes!
Columbus ended earth's romance:
No New World to mankind remains!"
(4.21.144–59)

I have discussed Melville's attention to the Dead Sea in psychotheological terms, but more broadly *Clarel* holds a negating relation to Adamic possibilities, of the American promise to make the world new, for in the poem, albeit offstage, America, too, lacks newness, and has come to know the Old World's "pains."[67] Melville's irresolute faith—his failure to secure what Cummins would define as faith's heart-knowledge—was matched by a faithlessness in the American way itself, especially after the doleful carnage of the Civil War. Melville found some relief from sorrows personal and national in his verse collection, *Battle-Pieces* (1866). He did not lose interest in U.S. international affairs, or rather he could not, given his work for nineteen years as a customs inspector on Manhattan's docks. But those were dreary years, of exile from a fit audience, with no anticipation of traveling elsewhere, from the United States or himself, in the steamer ships that he could see loading and unloading passengers to and from other lands.

As Jenny Franchot poignantly puts it, in "circling back to a desiccated Asiatic origin, *Clarel* renounces the illusion of travel, the illusion that there is a space of belief, of otherness, into which one can journey and lose the burden of unbelief and of self."[68] The Dead Sea, though, could be relied upon to excite in attenuated (that is, innocent) form U.S. audiences up through the earlier decades of the twentieth century. In 1928, Melvin Grove Kyle, a minister-explorer hailing from Saint Louis, Missouri, published *Explorations at Sodom: The Story of Ancient Sodom in the Light of Modern Research*. One virtue of the Dead Sea story, he writes, is that unlike other biblical episodes that might be "jeered at by unbelievers," such "catastrophes" as Sodom and Gomorrah "leave remains, and remains do not move around." According to Kyle the expedition when proposed "aroused a widespread interest" and a "flood of aspirants for a trip to Palestine." The lure of the "horrible," he explains, "seem[ed] irresistible."[69] The bulk of *Explorations* is given to standard traveler fare—preparation, itineraries, sites to be noted, and so on—interspersed with droll, though always orthodox, sentiments. What most stands out, however, is Kyle's resilience to the theological or psychological (or sexual, for that matter) pertinence of his journey's destiny. When he speaks of the Dead Sea he ventures to ward off its darker numinosities. He was, as Twain would say with some acerbic bite, an American innocent abroad:

Those who have written of this place have done so under the spell of the dreadful tragedy which took place here. They have not been untruthful, but psychology sometimes makes people "see things." The truth is that, when Palestine becomes prosperous—and she is rapidly becoming so—an automobile line from Jerusalem to the Dead Sea and a motor-boat line on the sea will make this one of the finest winter health resorts in the world. . . . A Californian in our party said the climate was "just like home," and with a Californian there is nothing beyond that—except heaven.[70]

Kyle reminds us that over the long haul America's destiny lay westward, whatever fantasies various Protestant settler-communities and their stateside evangelical backers had in respect to reclaiming Palestine as an antecedent to the future glory days of the Millennium. The Holy Land experiences, real or imagined, of Stephens, Lynch, Cummins, and Melville preceded the onslaught of U.S. traveler-tourists in the Holy Land (although Melville wrote *Clarel* during a time period in which such tourism was becoming heavily promoted, its thematics hearken back equally to his pre–Civil War trip to the Levant). Because the texts appearing in this chapter neither rest on the Holy Land as commodity nor rely upon the interests of direct U.S. political involvement, we may take them as being, perhaps, more resolutely or purely ideological: that is, if the Levant had little claim on U.S. citizens in a low-level political sense, it did in the higher geometaphysical sense of arguing for the centrality of the nation in the theater of global history. The movement, literally, was across the Mississippi to the western frontier; but to the Protestant citizen, who took seriously his or her Bible, the passage of destiny encompassed a wider arc of time and nations, from the *old* Old World (which is to say, the Holy Land, not Europe) to the New World, the New Israel.

We will, however, misread this comparative geographical trajectory if we deem it tied exclusively to either piety, national boosterism, or the idiosyncrasies of authorial identities. My cast of writers in this chapter may or may not typify the bulk of U.S. travelers to the Levant; Melville in his passage on the Holy Sepulchre, for example, is both conventionally satiric and personally invested. Individual U.S. citizens encounter foreign terrains and their inhabitants not merely as subjects of the republic. National ideologies, in the case of the Holy Land and elsewhere, are not carried in some abstract portmanteau, unaffected by the wear and tear of contact with the materiality of the non-European other. Rather, they take form against, are informed by, and in turn inform not only what is seen but also the traveler doing the seeing. Ideology is never or not only national: it reflects psychonational crossovers, and is a matter of both macro (geographical) and micro (psychogenetic) conjunctures.

The U.S. geographical imaginary entailed thinking about non-European regions and peoples. But no particular region—whether Polynesia, the Near East, Africa, or tropical America—was exceptionally positioned against the United States: no particular dialectical bond of othering took precedence in the antebellum imaginary of other lands. Different discursive communities, in various constellations of assent or dissent, made appeals to the nation by way of those differing non-European realms. In the chapter on *Typee* the community comprised, besides Melville and his readership, specific missionaries and their sponsors as well as sundry political observers; in this chapter, likewise, there has been no dominant professional group with its own peculiar agenda, for Melville, Lynch, and so forth all pursued dissimilar careers. It is instructive, though, to witness how particular group affiliations filter the U.S. imaginary of particular non-European locales. In the next chapter, therefore, I focus on how a specific region—tropical America—challenged even as it enabled the ideological goals of a singular set of professionals, antebellum archaeologist-explorers, whose investments in the archaeological sublime linked, as we will see, personal and U.S. national, New World glory.

CHAPTER FOUR

The Archaeological Sublime of Tropical America

Ephraim G. Squier and John L. Stephens

> But while the degenerate and amalgamated sons of the Conquistadors excite only mingled pity and contempt, the traveler cannot resist a feeling of admiration for those iron adventurers who raised here, in the midst of a vast tropical wilderness, before the Puritan landed at Plymouth . . . those massive fortifications which, even in their ruins, seem to bid defiance to the destroyer, Time!
> —Ephraim G. Squier, *Harper's New Monthly Magazine*

> I know not what to think of the [Mayan] ruins, they leave my mind in a kind of mist, which I shall not attempt to dispel.
> —William H. Prescott to John L. Stephens

THE LEVANT interested U.S. Protestants both as the cradle of Christianity and as a fallen realm that contrastively showed why America was the rightful heir to the true faith. "Palestine sits in sackcloth and ashes," Mark Twain observed; over "it broods the spell of a curse that has withered its fields and fettered its energies."[1] Maria Susanna Cummins in *El Fureidîs* called for the "son of the West" to awaken the Holy Land from its torpor and subjugation to Ottoman rule, yet such a task, according to Twain, would be left to non-U.S. nations: "I never disliked a Chinaman as I do these degraded Turks and Arabs, and when Russia is ready to war with them again, I hope England and France will not find it good breeding or good judgment to interfere."[2] Closer to home, the lands south of the border offered a fairer field for U.S. intervention. The Monroe Doctrine, proclaimed in 1823, had carved up the globe, discouraging if not quite forbidding European attempts to spawn new colonies or reassert monarchical rule in states recently independent of Spanish power. The New World, disencumbered from the final vestiges of the Old World, would become all the newer.

The lush scenery, agricultural diversity, and rich mineral deposits made the other Americas almost erotically enticing: they were not virgin territories, but did hold a seductive allure for those wishing to exercise northern virility or indulge a dream-memory of the Conquistadors' quest for gold and glory. Fantasies of a southern El Dorado were catered to by spurious travelogues such as *Rambles in Brazil; or, A Peep at the Aztecs* (1854), which purports to recount the narrator's discovery of a lost city of living Aztecs, resplendent with marbled halls, pillars and mosaics inlaid with gold, and maiden natives bedecked with jewels. The title (the Aztecs did *not* inhabit Brazil) suggests the public's willingness to suspend historical accuracy for wish-fulfillment when it came to thinking about gold-laden lands. For expansionists, Central America in particular beckoned as an area where a new commercial empire might arise, transcending the splendor of the old Spanish dominions. "Let northern energy" exert itself there, Representative Samuel S. Cox of Ohio mused, and "the gold mines of Upata would gleam with their olden treasures . . . and that mart of the golden age of Spain and her viceroys will teem with a wealth which no buccaneers in a thousand caravels can bear away." "These tropical wastes ought to give us coffee, indigo, and cocoa," he went on; and in return "they will take our flour, pork, machinery, fabrics, and a thousand other articles which they need, and which every State of this Union produces." Especially if the United States controlled access to an interoceanic route, commerce between the Union's coasts would be facilitated (crucial after the discovery of Californian gold in 1848), and the nation would be able, Cox envisioned, to "encircle the earth with a white zone of argosies."[3]

The admonitory evidence of the cyclic rise and fall of nations, for those with an historical conscience, might have belied such heady prospects. The Conquistadors had laid to ruin and supplanted the ancient Mayan and Aztec civilizations, but the Spanish Empire by the nineteenth century now barely shadowed its former glory. Out of the debacle of Spanish rule arose aspiring young governments, novitiates of republicanism. Those new nation-states, however, reflected in a glass darkly both the promises and dangers of revolutionary upheaval. They often modeled their polities upon the U.S. Constitution and the Enlightenment political principles that informed it, and their patriots were routinely lauded as incarnations of the heroes of the American Revolution. The ark of liberty, happily, seemed to be progressing southward beyond the border. That was the message celebrated, for instance, in John Neagle's *Portrait of Henry Clay* (1843). The painting commemorates the senator's diplomacy on behalf of Peru, which in 1826 gained official U.S. recognition as a nation independent of Spain. Peru emerges from under the protective aegis of the iconic flag, as if the United States, with Clay as political midwife, has borne a new realm replicating its own republican virtues (Figure 6).[4] Yet if the revolts against Spanish tyranny replayed the revolution against Britain, the fact that they kept recurring did not provide tidy closure to the story of the

FIG. 6. John Neagle, *Portrait of Henry Clay* (1843). Oil on canvas, 111 1/4 x 72 1/2 inches. (Courtesy of the Union League of Philadelphia.)

first episode of New World nationalist liberty begetting subsequent liberations. Moreover, the heterogeneous population of Spaniards, indigenous natives, blacks, and mulattoes—an admixture that seemed partially to account for Latin America's notorious political instability—exacerbated anxiety over the Union's own racial conflicts. Republicanism was to be promoted; but the spectacle of bloody revolution, all the more so if led by black insurgents, alarmed nearly all commentators. The forebodings of Chaplain C. S. Stewart when the U.S. ship *Vincennes*, the first American naval vessel to make a tour around the globe, took port in Rio de Janeiro in 1829 are typical:

> Nothing contributes more to the offensiveness of a first impression, than the large proportion which the half naked negroes and mongrels, of every tint and degree of blood, make of the persons seen in the streets. . . . [T]heir number to the eye of the stranger is fearfully great; and were I an inhabitant of the city, there would be times at least at which I should tremble in the fear of witnessing the development of a tragedy like that of St. Domingo. . . . [T]here is ample room for apprehension on the point, and to dread eventually some fearful retribution at the hands of the afflicted and oppressed. . . . The foundations of the empire, from all I can learn, are far from being sure. It is morally and politically corrupt, and filled with ignorance and superstition; and the leaven of republicanism is scattered so extensively through the dominion, that it is not improbable that Brazil, in her order, will be the theatre of that turning and overturning which for twenty years has kept the neighboring states in agitation and distress.[5]

Cuba especially troubled Northerners and Southerners alike. The House-not-yet-Divided became increasingly fractured because of the proximity of a neighbor with a slave-based economy. Northerners were suspicious of conspiracies to expand slave territory; and many Southerners, in turn, dreaded the prospect that Spain might eventually liberate and enfranchise the Cuban slave population, opening the way for a black free state perilously nearby. The Louisiana legislature, in fact, sent a request to Congress in 1854 urging action against so-called Spanish Africanization policies that would "create almost in sight of our shores a government administered by an inferior and barbarous race."[6]

The specter of Cuban black insurrection linked together a pan-American, indeed transatlantic, politics embracing the United States, Central America, the Caribbean, as well as Africa. Herman Melville's "Benito Cereno" (1856) is the text that for a modern audience most familiarly brings the issue of black revolution to mind. It re-creates the vexed geopolitics of New World slavery within the confines of one slave ship, and critiques, by means of the theatrics performed by the black ringleader Babo, all the soothing panaceas about black docility that kept alarums of revolution from becoming too alarming in the antebellum white mind. In Melville's narrative, the representative U.S. citizen, Captain Delano, comes aboard and walks the deck of the *San Dominick*, a foreign ship symbolizing the complexity of international and interracial relations that he must *not* fathom if he is to maintain his (and his nation's, Melville implies) historical-political innocence. Delano hails from the country that had, in Bronson Alcott's phrasing, "monopolized the best of time and space"; and it is that lofty conceit that Melville puts to the test when Delano remains blind to what is before him: the unyielding ferocity of black vengeance. I will return to Melville's text briefly in the next chapter, where I discuss Martin R. Delany, whose efforts to promote the cause of African-American nationality led him to scrutinize U.S. politics in terms of Africa, the African diaspora, and the wider hemispheric New World scene.[7] Both authors illumine the complex, triangulated relations among the United States, Africa, and tropical America, but my main concern in this chapter has to do with how U.S. citizens responded to the latter's more indigenous scenic, political-racial, and temporal dimensions.

Those dimensions almost invariably echoed each other. Nervousness about political instability and race warfare was matched by qualms about how the sensuous scenery might affect the white viewer. The strange foliage, exotic fauna, and geological dynamism warranted devoted study. Yet both the dynamism and seductiveness were unsettling, and enjoyment needed to be curbed. The author of an article in *The Knickerbocker* (June 1849), for example, described at length the "romance" of the "torrid zone" where the traveler might "indulge in . . . [a] thousand delights"; but he ended by reminding his readers of their own "native land" where "Truth, goodness and virtue flourish in far greater beauty."[8] Nathaniel Parker Willis, in his travelogue, *Health Trip to the Tropics* (1853), remarked that the southern tropical region "was not the clime for prudence."[9] Tropical climates, virtually all U.S. writers agreed, led to indolence, to debilitated faculties that, apparently, were inheritable. The "race" of the Spanish rulers, Julia Ward Howe wrote in her travel-memoir *A Trip to Cuba* (1860), has "suffer[ed] and degenerate[d] under the influence of the warm climate."[10]

The thematics of North American virility and tropical American effeminacy, not surprisingly, got played out as well in how viewers scanned vast natural tableaux. Take, for instance, Bayard Taylor's fantasy of white domination in the penultimate chapter of *Eldorado*, in which the landscape gets projected in the form of what W. J. T. Mitchell calls, in a discussion of scene painting as history by other means, the "'dreamwork' of imperialism":[11]

We were now on the borders of paradise. . . . As we came out of the deep-sunken valleys on the brow of a ridge facing the south, there stood, distinct and shadowless from base to apex, the Mountain of Orizaba. It rose beyond mountains so far off that all trace of chasm or ledge or belting forest was folded in a veil of blue air, yet its grand, immaculate cone, of perfect outline, was so white, so dazzling, so pure in its frozen clearness, like that of an Arctic morn, that the eye lost its sense of the airy gulf between, and it seemed that I might stretch out my hand and touch it. No peak among mountains can

be more sublime than Orizaba. Rising from the level of the sea and the perpetual summer of the tropics, with an unbroken line to the height of eighteen thousand feet, it
stands singly above the other ranges with its spotless crown of snow, as some giant,
white-haired Northern king might stand among a host of the weak, effeminate sybarites of the South. Orizaba dwells alone in my memory, as the only perfect type of
mountain to be found on the Earth.[12]

One of the most famous paintings of the period, Frederic Church's *Heart of
the Andes* (1859), likewise offered geographical gender lessons. "Mr. Church
has been helping us to a complete knowledge of the exciting and yet indolent
beauty of the tropics," Theodore Winthrop wrote in a contemporary guidebook; but if he has "learned the passion of those Southern climes," he has "not
unlearned the energy of his own."[13] The threat of tropical seduction even when
just looking at Church's canvas perhaps explains why, when reshown in 1864
at the New York Metropolitan Sanitary Fair, it was staged with three portraits
of the Founding Fathers hung above its frame (Figure 7).[14] Standing before it,
the viewer could only gaze at the vista depicted—of geological upheaval—
while becoming, in turn, subjected to the severe gaze of the republic's past
leaders.[15] Shown in the midst of the Civil War, the painting indirectly commented on the convulsions besetting the nation (ironically, Winthrop's guidebook to the masterpiece had on the eve of war complacently linked the topographical and political in respect to American countries *elsewhere*: "We of the
northern hemisphere have a geographical belief in the Andes as an unsteady
family of mountains in South America—a continent where earthquakes shake
the peaks and revolutions the people").[16]

    Church's art and that of his contemporaries contributed to a national sym-
bolic order, to what art historian Katherine Manthorne calls an "awakening
inter-American consciousness," at once encompassing and positing itself
against the other Americas.[17] A range of works helped variously to fill out the
gendered, racial, and temporal contours of that symbolic order. Historical
romances or potboilers, such as William Gilmore Simms's *Damsel of Darien*
(1839), toyed with tabooed cross-racial sexual relations; William H. Prescott's
History of the Conquest of Mexico (1843) and other epic histories as well as
novels restaged scenes from the Spanish Conquest, figuring Cortés and Montezuma in a fatal agon of iron virility and effete melancholy; and, of course, a
deluge of news items covered the U.S.-Mexican War or followed the exploits
of the filibusters, the most famous being William Walker, who obsessively
mounted a series of hapless campaigns in the 1850s with the goal of establishing a personal empire radiating out from Nicaragua.[18] Running through all
these genres was the need, as well, for the Protestant psyche to define itself and
the nation against the simultaneously alluring and menacing Catholic other
within the country's own boundaries.[19]

F I G . 7 . Frederic Church, *Heart of the Andes*, as exhibited at the Metropolitan Sanitary Fair, New York, April 1864, stereograph. (Photographer unknown; courtesy of the Collection of The New York Historical Society, negative number 61263.)

The effort to locate the history of the United States within a broader New World context, of course, was not novel at midcentury. Joel Barlow's epic poem, *The Vision of Columbus* (1787, revised twenty years later as *The Columbiad*), for instance, looks back to the checkered story of Columbus as a cautionary *ur*-text to the unfolding drama of U.S. utopian aspirations. The republic will fulfill its New World promise only, Barlow suggests, if it can surmount "blinded faction" and give the "palm of praise" to other values than "Wealth pride and conquest."[20] It was not until the Spanish sway in the New World had more or less eroded, however, that U.S. travelers and writers were freely able to inscribe U.S. national topoi upon the regions south of the border. The market, starting roughly in the 1840s, began to be flooded with texts that both supplemented and complicated the tales of what Samuel Goodrich called the "bless[ed] . . . chill[ed] regions of the Pilgrims." Although the trajectory of liberty from founding moment at Plymouth Rock to futurity was not in the final analysis disrupted by texts about tropical America, these narratives about non-U.S. America held a key role in filling in the temporal contours of a nation whose history, it appears, needed to extend continually beyond itself, literally by means of the expanding frontier and mythically by the appropriation of non-European, non-Protestant bodies, spaces, and cultures.

There are multiple pathways we might take to chart how U.S. ideology took form in respect to tropical America. In this chapter, I have elected to focus upon the careers of two writers that, arguably, most *materially* engaged its realms and peoples. The texts of the archaeologist-explorers John L. Stephens (whom we will remember from the previous chapter) and Ephraim G. Squier traverse the literal, ethnological, and temporal cartographies of Latin America, providing a fascinating lens refracting both the attraction and repulsion that it held for antebellum travelers and historians. I believe both deserve to be better known. If we are to make good our claims for expanding American studies in a fashion that does more than, say, compare different styles of New World epic writing or the modernist/postmodernist aesthetics of William Faulkner and Latin American writers, we need first to know the initial occasions of, in Manthorne's phrase, an "awakening inter-American consciousness." Comparative studies have their virtues, but the latter examples involve *our* desire for transgeographical connections, not the concrete, historical traversals from the United States to the other Americas (by way of U.S. authors traveling) and vice versa (by way of U.S.-authored texts representing tropical America being read in the United States).

Although unknown today by most lay readers, Squier and Stephens were seminal in their own time, virtually inaugurating the sciences of Amerindian archaeology. Stephens's accounts of his two voyages to Central America in search of native antiquities became overnight bestsellers, and Squier's works, though granting him considerably less fame, still are accorded respect by archaeological scholars. In this chapter, however, the scientific merits of neither author will be championed, for whatever illumination their texts might offer in respect to pre-Columbian civilizations is so intermixed with racist or jingoistic musings that we would be hard-pressed to laud their achievements un-reservedly. Indeed, we can easily regard their writings as divulging how U.S. archaeology in respect to indigenous populations from the start had motives less than honorable. To correlate a profession's intrinsic protocols with its practitioners' ethos during any one specific era, though, is a dubious enter-prise, based upon the assumption that all knowledge is filtrated by power. Sci-entific discourses and knowledge evolve historically and are not immune from historical effects—of power relations, of ideology, of professional status-seeking. But we may still posit, if we do not wish to subjectify science entirely, that an ideologically uncontaminated substratum runs parallel to the often all-too-tangible racist affects of nineteenth-century archaeological, geographical, and ethnological sciences.

Consequently, the analysis here although highlighting U.S. archaeology's bigoted inception will not seek to critique archaeological science per se. Rather, as with the earlier chapter on Melville's *Typee*, I am interested in how the imaginary of a non-European foreign region simultaneously evokes and helps resolve key cultural anxieties bred at home. Specifically, I show that the quest for archaeological sublimity—the epiphany of discovery—coalesced vexing antebellum concerns over gender, race, and historical consciousness. The white history of the republic, so nascent, could barely be called history as such: the service that Squier and Stephens rendered the nation was to append to it the longer duration of a different, yet "American," region of the globe. Appropriation of indigene history in their careers and texts was a masculinist enterprise, often conceived in military tropes, as we will see especially with Stephens. At the same time, though, the attempt to recover the tropical Ameri-can past and conjoin it with U.S. history was for both authors frustrated by the resistant materiality of Amerindian cultures: either because the hieroglyphic remains of those cultures could not be interpreted or because the contempo-rary tribes they met seemed to lack adequate memories, it seemed, of their forefathers. Nonetheless, both Squier and Stephens sought to disclose and mimetically co-opt in their texts, for personal as well as U.S. national glory, the antique monuments of Mesoamerica, whose sublimity resided precisely in their temporal opacity—their unfathomable historicity.

Squier, the son of a Methodist minister, was born in 1821 in Bethlehem, New York. He was largely self-educated and became qualified in civil engi-neering, but the economic panic of 1837 limited his chances for suitable em-ployment. In 1839 he began training as a teacher, yet found the prospects of being a pedagogue dreary, and so instead elected a career path, journalism, that might give him a name in the world. He worked as a confident, aggressive journalist, first in Albany between 1841 and 1844, where he promoted Whig causes in the *New York State Mechanic* and other papers, and then later in Chillicothe, Ohio, where he moved in 1845 to help edit the *Scioto Gazette*. He became intrigued by the large pre-Columbian mounds of the area, which he began excavating under the tutelage of Edwin H. Davis, a physician and amateur archaeologist who had been studying the mounds and collecting artifacts since 1831. Seeking financial backing for his research, Squier traveled to New England, where he met William H. Prescott and several scientific luminaries, including Professor Benjamin Silliman of Yale College, Dr. Samuel G. Morton, and Albert Gallatin, president of the American Ethnological Society. He returned to resume his study of the mounds with an agreement that the young Smithsonian Institute (founded in 1846) would publish his findings, and in 1848 *Ancient Monuments of the Mississippi Valley* became the first monograph to obtain the imprimatur of the "Smithsonian Contributions to Knowledge" series.

Squier's research led him to surmise an affinity between the earthworks that he had excavated and the Mayan ruins in Central America. He solicited the aid of Prescott, who successfully recommended him to President Zachary Taylor for an appointment as chargé d'affaires to Central America. He embarked in 1849 and was able to combine his diplomatic mission—to negotiate with the Nicaraguan government over the right to build an isthmian canal—with some modest investigations of antiquities located around Granada and on Lake Nicaragua's small islands. Squier lost his diplomatic post, however, when he opposed Daniel Webster's policy of tolerating British colonialist designs in the region, and for the next twenty years he sought a variety of other assignments that either would allow him to pursue his wish to oversee the construction of an interoceanic canal or railroad or, in his free time, return to the field for further study. He served in 1853 as secretary of the Honduras Interoceanic Railway Company (a route was planned, but the railroad was not built), between 1863 and 1865 as U.S. commissioner to Peru, and in 1868 as the Honduran Consul General in New York City. The effort to sustain a diplomatic career fatigued him, and financial distress obliged a return to journalism; during the Civil War he edited Frank Leslie's *Illustrated Weekly*, a job he held through the 1870s. Nonetheless, he managed to publish an array of major, still highly regarded volumes—among others, *Nicaragua: Its People, Scenery, Monuments, and the Proposed Interoceanic Canal* (1852) and *Notes on Central America; Particularly the States of Honduras and San Salvador* (1855)—as well as a number of articles in *Harper's New Monthly Magazine*, the *Democratic Review*, and the *American Whig Review*, besides those in scientific journals. Squier's accomplishments all told were significant: he had been elected an honorary member to a host of learned societies abroad; in 1871 he had become the first president of the Anthropological Institute of New York; he could count Alexander von Humboldt and Francis Parkman (with whom he corresponded for some thirty years) among his friends; and by the time he died in 1888 his oeuvre, in total, came to more than one hundred published articles, monographs, and books.

The anomaly, and the focus of my last section, is his mostly fictional travelogue *Waikna; or, Adventures on the Mosquito Shore*, published under the pseudonym of Samuel A. Bard in 1855. The immediate motive behind *Waikna* (besides, perhaps, to capitalize on the public's insatiable appetite for travel works) was sheer propaganda. Squier in fact had little if any direct contact with the tribes living on the Mosquito Shore, a region encompassing the eastern coastline and lagoons of Nicaragua. Rather, he relied upon previous accounts of the area to fabricate a travel text intended to malign the Mosquitos, who had become pawns, or so it seemed to Squier, servile to British imperial designs. England had established a protectorate over the Mosquitos and maintained that their king, George William Clarence III, held a valid claim to San Juan del Norte, Nicaragua, the most likely eastern terminus for an interoceanic canal route. By demonstrating the illegitimacy of the Mosquito kingdom in terms both of the king's lineage and his people's status as a nation, Squier hoped to debunk the pretense that Britain had used, in 1848, to invade the port city.

Waikna's narrative, however, considerably exceeds and at times conflicts with its putative agenda. It engages the aforementioned contest over New World imperial management, although on a more personal level than its author's magazine diatribes against British policy in the *Democratic Review* and elsewhere. Squier's persona does not travel back in time, but he does meet indigenes whose lineage may be traced back to the pre-Columbian era, allowing Squier to fantasize himself in a cultural space free of what he regarded as hybridized history. The text also served, I believe, to compensate Squier for his checkered political-diplomatic career and, more so, for his sense of being a belated, postheroic archaeologist. His first publication on the prehistoric Indian mounds of the Mississippi valley and its sequel, *Aboriginal Monuments of the State of New York* (1851), were well received by reviewers and guaranteed his reputation in scientific circles; but he never enjoyed the accolades (much less the financial reward) that fell for instance upon John L. Stephens when the latter published *Incidents of Travel in Central America, Chiapas, and Yucatan* (1841) and *Incidents of Travel in Yucatan* (1843). Not until 1863 was Squier able to fulfill Prescott's call that Peruvian antiquities be explored with a "kindred spirit of enterprise," and his narrative, *Peru: Incidents of Travel and Exploration in the Land of the Incas*, an important study of the pre-Inca Chimú civilization, did not appear until 1877.[21] By then, though, Squier had suffered through three years of intermittent insanity. His wife, Miriam Florence Folline, had divorced him to marry his employer, Frank Leslie, in 1873; and an inquiry the following year at the New York City Courthouse found him to be "a lunatic, not having lucid intervals, so that he was incapable of the government of himself or of the management of his goods and chattels."[22]

John L. Stephens and the Classic
Ground of the Conquistadors

When in London in 1836, about to return home from his trip to the Levant, Stephens had befriended Frederick Catherwood, the English artist then gaining fame for his exhibit of a vast panorama of Jerusalem. Catherwood showed Stephens a book by Antonio del Río, a captain in the Spanish army, who in 1786 had stumbled upon the ruins of Palenque in southern Mexico. The Mayan cities, buried by the dense debris of the Mesoamerican rain forest, had before Río's account remained the subject of only vague rumor. The soldier's discoveries excited Stephens, and once back in New York he came across several recently published studies that further piqued his interest, especially Jean Frédéric Waldeck's lavish folio volume *Voyage Pittoresque et Archéologique dans la Province d'Yucatán* (1838). Catherwood joined Stephens in New York, and the two began planning a trip to visit the obscure ruins. Stephens solicited President Van Buren's administration and secured an assignment to negotiate a treaty with the government of the Confederation of Central American States. In 1839, the two explorers left New York by steamer, landed in Belize, and spent the next nine months on a half-official, half-archaeological trek on mule back tracking down Central American officials and Mayan antiquities. Their expedition took them to some forty sites, but further inquiry was aborted when Catherwood came down with a bad case of malarial fever.[23]

Stephens published *Incidents of Travel in Central America* in 1841. The two-volumed edition—with gold-stamped spines featuring Mayan hieroglyphs, seventy-seven engravings, and a fold-out map—went through nine printings in a mere three months. Its spectacular success, together with proceeds from *Incidents of Travel in Egypt, Arabia Petræa, and the Holy Land*, helped to fund a second expedition, in which he, Catherwood, and Dr. Samuel Cabot (an amateur ornithologist from Boston) were able more leisurely to explore Uxmal, Nohcacab, and other Yucatán sites. In 1843 he published, also in two volumes, *Incidents of Travel in Yucatan*, which equally garnered public and professional acclaim.

Discovering the past of Indian groups disinherited from their lands or the monumental remains of the cultures from which they were descended was one motive that animated Stephens, though he also appears to have longed to assume the powerful mantle of firstness: not just to be a *white* discoverer of Indian antiquity, but also to seek out archaeological secrets that would push him to that unrecoverable time predating the Spanish Conquest. Eighteenth- and nineteenth-century British antiquarians sought to root out the origins of Anglo-Saxon culture, to confirm a national lineage extending from the nebulous past to the contemporary multicontinented empire. In the New World context, the genealogical project of seeking origins involved working through the simultaneously enticing and blocking evidences (hieroglyphics, strange monuments, and so on) of the culturally and racially other so that a geotemporal locale of sheer newness might be inhabited. In terms of their more direct literary affiliation, Stephens's volumes took their place alongside the works of Henry Rowe Schoolcraft, James Fenimore Cooper, and a host of now lesser known authors who offered the reading public the curious lore—often more fabular than authentic—of Indian customs and history. Stephens's travel narratives, although not developing native "characters" per se, held a kindred aura in respect to Indian culture: a sense sublime of its ghostly density, a complexity of difference inexorably fading—and thus becoming all the more estranged and alluring—in time's passage or beneath imperialism's onslaught. The seduction of archaeology, ethnology, or stories of Indian tribes is, for us today, perhaps the same: not merely the promise of entering into the past, but also the presentiment of being on the scene first, which is to say, in the space open to pure futurity. When we travel back in time with Cooper or Stephens what we secretly wish for, we can speculate, is not to see history or the other (that is, indigenes not yet contaminated by white culture), but to find ourselves at a moment of beginnings, of singular power.

Stephens's texts, in their fixation on origins, could well be regarded as key documents in the history of the Romantic movement and its practitioners' preoccupation with original/aboriginal spaces. From the previous chapter, we will recall Stephens's longing to be an originary traveler. That concern even more so informs his Central America texts. An anxiety of influence, to borrow Harold Bloom's phrase about the burden of strong poetic predecessors, often surfaces in U.S. travel texts about the other Americas.[24] All explorers had to pay homage to the stunning achievements of Alexander von Humboldt. Joel Poinsett, after reading Humboldt's writings on Latin America, nearly saw fit to "abandon" his own travel journal: "[Humboldt] has seen more of the country, and described it better, than any other can hope to do, and he has left almost nothing for the future traveller, but the narrative of his own adventure, and a record of his own feelings and impressions."[25] One tactic to manage a feeling of belatedness, the one taken by Bayard Taylor, was simply to reconfirm one's own travel experiences in the eyes of the world-renowned scientist. In *At Home and Abroad* (1859) Taylor recollects a visit, discussed in a different context in my introductory chapter, to Berlin to meet Humboldt:

[Humboldt's] nose, mouth, and chin had the heavy Teutonic character.... "You have travelled in Mexico," said he: "do you not agree with me in the opinion that the finest mountains in the world are those single cones of perpetual snow rising out of the splendid vegetations of the tropics?"... "You remember Orizaba," continued he; "here is an engraving from a rough sketch of mine. I hope you will find it correct."... "You have travelled much, and seen many ruins," said Humboldt, as he gave me his hand again; "now you have seen one more." "Not a ruin," I could not help replying, "but a pyramid."... I looked into the eyes which had not only seen this living history of the world pass by, scene after scene ... but had beheld the cataract of Atures and the forests of the Cassiquiare, Chimborazo, the Amazon, and Popocatepetl, the Altaian Alps of Siberia, the Tartar steppes, and the Caspian Sea.[26]

Taylor's own impressions, rather than rivaling Humboldt's, are corroborated when the latter magnanimously defers to him. In this episode, though, Taylor does more than just validate his own travel narrative: Humboldt himself becomes a venerable site, because his capacious "Teutonic" intellect has absorbed the world in its entirety. Taylor wants his anecdote to register the greatness of a great man; and, perhaps, few Europeans of the day could match Humboldt's diverse and ample achievements. As much as Taylor is star-struck by the noble scholar, though, he also in the passage shows us that amassing non-European sights (in sketches or textually) took place in the context of a certain masculinist, well-healed fraternity of competitors, who earned the respect of their peers less by in-depth inquiry than by the comprehensivity of that inquiry. For Taylor, what suffices is that Humboldt has gazed, it seems, everywhere.

Although the field in respect to Central American antiquities was relatively new, Humboldt's fame loomed in Stephens's mind as well. He felt nervous about whether his audience would fully appreciate the novelty of his own historical tour de force. The issue is brought to the fore, one-fourth of the way through the first volume of *Incidents of Travel in Central America*:

I am entering abruptly upon new ground. Volumes without number have been written to account for the first peopling of America. By some the inhabitants of this continent have been regarded as a separate race, not descended from the same common father with the rest of mankind; others have ascribed their origin to some remnant of the antediluvian inhabitants of the earth, who survived the deluge. ... The first new light thrown upon this subject as regards Mexico was by the great Humboldt.... Unfortunately, of the great cities beyond the Vale of Mexico [in Central America and Yucatán], buried in forests, ruined, desolate, and without a name, Humboldt never heard, or, at least he never visited them. It is but lately that accounts of their existence reached Europe and our own country. These accounts, however vague and unsatisfactory, had roused our curiosity.[27]

Stephens stakes a claim to originality, yet he also betrays signs of discomfort as he scrupulously informs us that hitherto the ruins have been but the subject of rumor or tentative report. Later, in the second volume, when he speaks of competing accounts in more detail, he admits that they were not exactly as inadequate as he had initially suggested. Now his book's merit rests less on the primacy of discovery than on the quantity of sites that he describes and the greater accessibility of his text—its relative inexpensiveness:

Lord Kingsborough's ponderous tomes, so far as regards Palenque [one of the three major sites Stephens explored], are a mere reprint of Dupaix, and the cost of his work is four hundred dollars per copy. . . . As to most of the places visited by us, [the reader] will find no materials whatever except those furnished in these pages. In regard to Palenque he will find a splendid work, the materials of which were procured under the sanction of a commission from government, and brought out with explanations and commentaries by the learned men of Paris, by the side of which my two octavoes shrink into insignificance. . . . My object has been, not to produce an illustrated work, but to present the drawings in such an inexpensive form as to place them within reach of the great mass of our reading community. (2:298–300)

Stephens here recasts a problem, the U.S. government's reluctance to sponsor expeditions without the prospect of immediate benefit, into a testament of his own volumes' worth.[28] He makes his case for archaeological renown on the basis of his (and Catherwood's) singular effort, on that effort's not being funded by aristocratic governments, on finally, the result being authored by an amateur. He writes not for a coterie of savants, but for the "mass[es]." Later, in fact, he boasts of his role as a public benefactor, expressing his wish to bring home the spoils of excavation, to "remove the monuments of a by-gone people from the desolate region in which they were buried, set them up in the 'great commercial emporium,' and found an institution to be the nucleus of a great national museum of American Antiquities!" (1:115).

The sequel volumes of the second trip, *Incidents of Travel in Yucatan*, will suggest the toll exacted by this obsession with antiquities-as-commodities. Stephens, often quite glibly, substitutes a rigorous desire to penetrate the depths of history with the lesser satisfaction of having, with Catherwood's aid, successfully pictorialized surfaces—the floor plans and front perspectives that the latter laboriously drew or daguerreotyped as the two moved from site to site. The more immediate challenge facing him in his first expedition, though, had less to do with the hermeneutics of archaeology than the hermeneutics of seeking a governmental body with whom he could complete his diplomatic mission. *Incidents of Travel in Central America* comprises more than a narrative of an archaeological quest. Because of the tumult of civil war and revolution, the federal government had disbanded, and Stephens hastily traveled from region to region in pursuit of state officials. He recounts with a mix of anxiety and humor his "desperate chase after a government" (1:148) and the moments when he believes he has successfully "*treed*" (1:323) it. The story of his search for proper authority; the miscellaneous anecdotes about Catholic friars, bull fights, peasant women, and motley revolutionaries; and the evocative description of dense jungles, mountain ravines, volcanoes, and so on—all make, even today, *Incidents of Travel in Central America* a compelling travelogue.

The multiple registers—the political, the historical, and the picturesque—through which the text unfolds indeed shape it into something of an omnibus work. These different registers, however, are also discordantly out of phase. As he trekked through the countryside, Stephens traversed three diachronic strata: the time present in which he struggled with all the day-to-day contingencies of traveling through tropical jungles and avoiding the perils of warfare; the time of Spanish rule, betokened by old fortifications and monasteries, which he visited to inspect archives of documents relating to the era of the Conquistadors; and the opaque, undecidable time, predating the Spanish Conquest, of the original Mayan people. The most salient parts of the narrative pertain not to what we discover about the ancient Mayas, but rather to its author's efforts to skirt jarring temporal disjunctions. Stephens enjoys the beauty and sublimity of the scenery, yet that scenery, more often than not, is also an ironic backdrop to the chaos of civil war. "I was heartily sick of the country and the excitement of its petty alarms" (1:186), he writes in recoil. Even more lamentably, amid "all the convulsions of the time," there was "no flash of heroism, no higher love of country" (2:52) to be witnessed. In one remarkable descriptive sequence, however, all that is out of phase coalesces as Stephens inserts himself into a tableau out of the pages of imperial epic:

The situation was ravishingly beautiful, at the base and under the shade of the Volcano de Agua, and the view was bounded on all sides by mountains of perpetual green; the morning air was soft and balmy, but pure and refreshing. With good government and laws, and one's friends around, I never saw a more beautiful spot on which man could desire to pass his allotted time on earth.

Resuming our ride, we came out upon a rich plain covered with grass, on which cattle and horses were pasturing, between the bases of the two great volcanoes; and on the left, at a distance, on the side of the Volcano de Agua, saw the Church of Ciudad Vieja, the first capital of Guatimala, founded by Alvarado the Conqueror. I was now on classic ground. . . . The appearance of the country harmonized with the romantic scenes of which it had been the theatre; and as I rode over the plain I could almost imagine the sides of the mountains covered with Indians, and Alvarado and his small band of daring Spaniards, soldiers and priests, with martial pride and religious humility, unfurling the banners of Spain and setting up the standard of the cross. . . . After a brief rest in the convent, with a feeling more highly wrought than any that had been awakened in me except by the ruins of Copan, we visited a tree standing before the church and extending wide its branches, under whose shade, tradition says, Alvarado and his soldiers first encamped. (1:277–81)

Earlier, Stephens had dismissed the Spaniards as "illiterate and ignorant adventurers, eager in the pursuit of gold, and blind to everything else" (1:160).
Now, however, he re-envisions the imperial mise-en-scène by subsuming it
into a picturesque vista. The spectacle of the landscape and spectacle of Latin
American politics, up to this point at odds, become happily united when he
sees himself walking in the footsteps of Alvarado and the other Conquistadors.

Stephens relishes the epiphany that he has while standing on "classic
ground," we may hazard to guess, because the Mayan antiquities he unearthed frustrated historical decoding. Or rather, the archaeological sublime
for Stephens was a paradoxical matter. The Mayan hieroglyphical writing
and ruins became sublime *because* of their unfathomability. Over and over
again, he alludes to the hermeneutic opacity of the symbols he scans: "All
was mystery, dark, impenetrable mystery" (1:105) he says of the Copán ruins;
later, examining a wall tablet at Palenque, he remarks that to "us it was all a
mystery; silent, defying the most scrutinizing gaze and reach of intellect"
(2:354). Stephens, even after his second trip, admitted that he and Catherwood could ascertain very little from their discoveries, except for the notion
that the monuments, buildings, and idols were likely the product of an indigenous culture, rather than one that had migrated in the pre-Columbian
period from the Far East: "[We] cannot go back to any ancient nation of the
Old World for the builders of these cities; they are not the works of people
who have passed away, and whose history is lost, but of the same great *race*
which, changed, miserable, and degraded, still clings around their ruins"
(1:167–68).[29] The previous sentiment is a peculiar one, however, for Stephens
implies that his major finding—the *American* origin of the "builders"—
depends upon the presence of the contemporary indigenes whom he everywhere denigrates. In his Holy Land account Stephens often emphasized the
decay of the Ottoman Empire, but here the discord between past grandeur
and present squalor becomes more problematic because the project of the archaeological sublime cannot do without its obverse, the supplementary
spectacle of the present "degraded" natives. In a rather tricky fashion, Stephens converts a temporal dilemma into a solution: he negotiates the gulf
between time past and time present, between the sublime and his own ignorance, by insisting upon Mayan declension.

In the account of the later venture, *Incidents of Travel in Yucatan*, we witness him routinely lording it over the "degraded" descendants of the original
Mayas. He refers frequently, almost as a leitmotif, to the chasm between the
builders of the ruins and their contemporary representatives.[30] He tells us that
the natives en masse are debased and given to a deplorable "abject submission"
(1:120), which he exemplifies in several anecdotes. At one point, crossing a

courtyard, Stephens observes a luckless Indian peasant being whipped. We do not learn the infraction committed or the circumstances of his punishment. Instead, Stephens simply says that his "whole bearing showed the subdued character of the present Indians. . . . Indeed, so humbled is this once fierce people, that they have a proverb of their own, 'Los Indios no oigan si no por las nalgas'—'The Indians cannot hear except through their backs'" (1:82). The latter image is a suggestive one, for Stephens habitually thinks of the contemporary Indians as existing in a realm that is only bodily and temporally illiterate. Even their own language, according to him, does not quite congeal into meaning. This point is made most strikingly when he recollects an evening in the house of a local Spanish family in Merida, where he had slept before embarking the next day into the jungle:

While arranging ourselves for the night, we heard a loud, unnatural noise at the door, and, going out, found rolling over the pavement the Cerberus of the mansion, an old Indian miserably deformed, with his legs drawn up, his back down, his neck and head thrust forward, and his eyes starting out from their sockets; he was entertaining himself with an outrageous soliloquy in the Maya tongue, and at our appearance he pitched his voice higher than before. Signs and threats had no effect. Secure in his deformity, he seemed to feel a malicious pleasure that he had it in his power to annoy us. We gave up, and while he continued rolling out tremendous Maya, we fell asleep. (1:9)

It is, indeed, an odd passage. That Stephens can hear the vocalizations of the Mayan Indian only as nonsensical sounds is reasonable enough; but he also perhaps suggests that the "Cerberus of the mansion" is engaged in some bestial, "unnatural," self-absorbed sexual act, as if the problem with the autochthonous native is a degenerated virility. I do not, however, wish to linger upon the latter reading. What should be noted instead is how the Indian ironically asserts, in an almost Caliban-like fashion, the palpable form of his own grotesque abjection ("[s]ecure in his deformity") to irritate the foreign interlopers. Yet if Stephens evokes the native's resistant otherness, he also dismisses it, as he sinks into slumber.

The above episode links to others in which the contemporary Mayas are dissociated from the history of their forebears and judged incapable of conveying valid knowledge about the past. We have seen, in the chapter on Melville's *Typee*, Tommo's kindred dismissal of native historiography, by which he tried to keep himself from becoming immersed in the vexing genealogy of Typeean taboos. Here, highlighting what seems to be native babbling serves a different purpose. It may be equated with the jungle debris that blocks Stephens's access to, but also drives his desire to penetrate, the inner corridors of the Mayan edifices. At one juncture, for example, when investigating the ruins of Kabah, he tells us that to "many of these structures the Indians have given names stupid, senseless, and unmeaning, having no reference to history or tradition" (1:242). In contrast are the hermeneutics of discovery that engage Stephens, Catherwood, and Dr. Cabot. Stephens typically would hear rumors of some ruins cloaked in the depths of the jungle, proceed to the likely site, and begin to unearth it (with the aid of a large horde of native subalterns) from rubbish and entangled jungle growth. More often than not, however, Stephens and Catherwood found the structures to be either entirely solid or so filled with accumulated dirt as to be nearly impossible to excavate. He articulates his frustrated struggle to gain entry into these vaguely womblike or cloacal edifices via various roof-openings, holes, or tunnels in terms of a stymied archaeological sublimity. Each effort to dig deeply enough is thwarted: "[E]very step was exciting," he says, "and called up recollections of the Pyramids and tombs of Egypt, and I could not but believe that these dark and intricate passages would introduce me to some large saloon, or perhaps some royal sepulchre. Belzoni, and the tomb of Cephrenes and its alabaster sarcophagus, were floating through my brain, when all at once I found the passage choked up and effectually stopped" (1:126). We would be mistaken if we assumed that Stephens lusted after treasure, wished to fill private or state coffers (as did the Conquistadors) with mere lucre. He, in fact, never alludes to the possibility that the chambers might have contained buried gold relics. Instead of fetishizing gold, he fetishizes the hermeneutical quest itself, the very fact of *potentially* unburying that which has been hidden. All "the great mounds scattered over the country," he at one point muses, likely "contained secret, unknown, and hidden chambers, presenting an immense field for exploration and discovery" (1:128). In all of his field trips to the sites, we are later told, his one "great desire was to discover an ancient sepulchre" (1:163).

The motive concords with Stephens's goal in *Incidents of Travel in Egypt, Arabia Petræa, and the Holy Land* to penetrate the forbidden land of Edom and rediscover Petra or to spy within the inner chamber of Aaron's tomb. In the Central American books, though, the impetus to disclose interiors becomes more aggressively masculinized and racialized, especially in the second volume to *Incidents of Travel in Yucatan*, where he bespeaks the pleasure of commanding a crew of native diggers. Passing through a dark corridor, he observes that the Indians "held down their torches, and rendered obeisance to the blood of the white man" (2:17). "If anything could have added to the interest of discovering such a new field of research," he remarks, "it was the satisfaction of having at our command such an effective force of Indians" (2:30). Some seventy pages later, the idea of marshaling native labor still thrills him. He once again can "hardly imagine a higher excitement than to go through that country with a strong force, time, and means at command, to lay bare the whole region in which so many ruined cities are now buried" (2:107).

FIG. 8. Zayi ruins, Frederick Catherwood sketch for John L. Stephens's *Incidents of Travel in Yucatan* (New York: Harper, 1843), opposite page 27, vol. 2. (Courtesy of the Special Collections Department, Florida State Universities Libraries, Tallahassee, Florida.)

We blur important distinctions when we conflate military campaigns with white campaigns of knowledge seeking; and, in this case, the effort to recover the past may be deemed an honorable attempt to repair damage done in the past—the depredations resulting in "ruined cities." The paradox of the project of the archaeological sublime, though, is that it revisits even as it counters the masculinist power and pillage of the Conquistadors. And the glory, in any event, always applies to the home country. Stephens's quest to become an original, white discoverer of Mayan antiquities, it finally turns out, is at the service of U.S.-American mimesis. He anticipated, even when in the field, replicating his findings in a published volume for public consumption. Before Catherwood could sketch panoramic pictures of the sites, or use the cumbersome daguerreotype apparatus he had brought with him, intervening foliage and trees had to be cleared away. After a "strong force of Indians" laid "bare the whole of the front" (2:5) of the ruins at Zayi, for example, Catherwood was able to sketch one of the denuded scenes that were to make their way into the printed volumes (Figure 8). But that is all, in fact, the reader gets in respect to the antiquities as he or she plies through either of Stephens's accounts— surfaces only, floor plans, few interiors; ultimately, very little historical-archaeological *depth*. One English commentator astutely noted this failing in the first set of volumes from the earlier expedition: "He has given" but a "reflection of the Ruins ... simply a *fac-simile* resemblance,—light and shade ... only ... a specimen of Daguerreotype!"[31] In place of archaeological profundity, Stephens can provide only serial quantity, moving through the jungle in a nearly endless "track of ruined cities" (2:128), in the belief that he might "reach a point which might unravel all mystery, and establish a connecting link between the past and present" (2:128).

Such a goal is not ignoble: it is the main raison d'être of archaeology. Yet Stephens, as we know from his Holy Land narrative, also yearned to push his way into idolatrous spaces. The primal acts of Mayan ritual seem to have intrigued him as much as the antiquity of Mayan culture itself. He cannot explain to himself why trekking into the jungle to find sites of ancient idolatry so tantalized him. He merely in one passage fantasizes that in the "wild region beyond the Lake of Peten, never yet penetrated by a white man, Indians are now living as they did before the discovery of America; and it is almost a part of this belief that they are using and occupying adoratorios and temples like those now seen in the ruins in the wilderness of Yucatan" (2:134).

The urge to spy on primitive, exotic scenes of worship (something of a constant in the history of anthropology) cannot be readily pinned down to one source: the scopic drive fixates on non-European sites, physiognomies, or iconic writing out of conjoined gnostic, psychosexual, racist, and scientific motives, without one strictly dominating the other three. The emerging sciences of ethnology, comparative anatomy, professional geography, and archaeology all contributed to, and drew upon, the era's racist thinking. The racist scopic urge, which discerns the "purity" of whiteness by comparative means, nonetheless also carries within it another: the allure of passing beyond surface feature—pigmentation, continental contour, or an edifice's exterior—into a hidden, secretive interior, into arcanum as such.

This tantalization, however, also requires its own frustration if the archeological sublime is to maintain its seductive power. Stephens of course found no isolated tribe worshiping in the forms of the past; and so it is little wonder that he once again was obliged to resort to the filtering tactic—drawing upon the pageantry of New World, Spanish epic—that he had used in the account of his first expedition. This time, however, he seeks not to reconcile present political turmoil, the picturesque, and the "classic" times of the Conquistadors, but instead to recapture a heady instance of imperial luminosity. He sees through Spanish eyes, mimicking what in the first set of volumes he had called their "blind" "pursuit of gold" (1:160), even as he differentiates his own scopic drive.

Mr. Catherwood made two drawings at different hours and under a different position of the sun, and Dr. Cabot and myself worked upon it the whole day with the Daguerreotype. With the full blaze of a vertical sun upon it, the white stone glared with an intensity dazzling and painful to the eyes, and almost realizing the account by Bernal Dias in the expedition to Mexico, of the arrival of the Spaniards at Cempoal. "Our advanced guard having gone to the great square, the buildings of which had been lately whitewashed and plastered, in which art these peoples are very expert, one of our horsemen was so struck with the splendour of their appearance in the sun, that he came back at full speed to Cortez, to tell him that the walls of the houses were of silver." (2:32)

The archaeological sublime depends, for its transcendental resonance, on vulgar cupidity being repressed. Yet Stephens's point in the above passage is less to recollect how the shining plaster fooled the Conquistadors (their delusion is buried within the Dias quote) than to buttress the mimetic glory—the overlap between past and present—of re-creating the front surfaces of the stone ruins as they originally appeared to the Spanish soldiers. He adopts their desire, but evacuates it of its object, the gold ornaments used in the "adoratorios and temples." Such satisfactions are evanescent; and this shimmering effect, the mimesis of the archaeological sublime, ultimately fades as do subsequent, equally delusory, hopes of finding a revelatory key to the mystery of the ruins, monuments, and idols. At a crucial juncture, Stephens reflects upon the futility of his project. He refers to some hieroglyphic writing on the lintel of a doorway, which the local Indians "call Akatzeeb, signifying the writing in the dark" because of its obscurity in the shadows of the edifice: "The sitting figure seems performing some act of incantation, or some religious or idolatrous rite, which the 'writing in the dark' undoubtedly explains, if one could but read it. Physical force may raze these buildings to the ground, and lay bare all the secrets they contain, but physical force can never unravel the mystery that involves this sculptured tablet" (2:191). The image hauntingly echoes the earlier one of the squatting, "miserably deformed" Indian whom Stephens saw before entering the jungle in the search of ruins. There, Stephens demonized the figure whose babbling of "tremendous Maya" held an almost uncanny "power to annoy" the white, U.S. auditor. Here, the written tongue of the Maya also goads him, taunting him with the indecipherable materiality of Mayan difference, of, as he phrases it as he concludes *Incidents of Travel in Yucatan*, their culture being "absolutely and entirely anomalous" (2:313).[32]

The Irony of Nationalist Archaeology

Stephens's volumes did not adequately clarify ancient Mayan history for Prescott. The historian wrote a letter to Stephens in April of 1843 conveying that he did not know "what to think of the [Mayan] ruins" because "they leave my mind in a kind of mist, which I shall not attempt to dispel."[33] Prescott's statement seems less a sign of scholarly fatigue than of his wish to relish foggy knowledge, a sense sublime that he cannot bring himself to deflate by pressing Stephens to be more conclusive in his discoveries. Stephens himself, a self-proclaimed amateur, perhaps cannot be faulted for a lack of archaeological rigor. Squier, unlike his predecessor in the field, had affiliated himself with a coterie of elite New York and Boston ethnologists whose scholarly protocols demanded precision; and as he associated with them, he was pleased to be welcomed into their circle of learned inquiry.[34] Unfortunately, for the young man yet to earn his laurels, the practices of archaeology and ethnology did not square together well. As he worked on *Ancient Monuments*, he corresponded with Dr. Samuel G. Morton, George R. Gliddon, Louis Agassiz, Josiah C. Nott, and the other ethnologists who were advocating the anti-Scriptural notion of polygenesis, the separate and regional creation of racial types. Squier's investigations impressed his colleagues because they believed that the data he had collected would help verify their radical theory of racial evolution and global distribution. Nott, for one, pronounced that his discoveries roundly disproved not only the widely held opinion that the Mound Builders had descended from a biblical tribe, which supposedly had migrated from Asia, but also Scriptural history itself. Smugly satisfied by Squier's preliminary findings, Nott told him that he fully expected the published volume to "give the *coup de grace* to that venerable *HE brayist*, Moses."[35]

Squier's own conclusions in the published volume were considerably more diffident. Although apparently sympathetic to the polygenesis theory, he skirted conjectures that would directly offend orthodox belief. Consequently, the popular press could appreciate *Ancient Monuments* for its novelty and thoroughness without being disquieted by its anti-Scriptural implications. A reviewer for the *Literary World* applauded it because it offered national sentiment what hitherto had been lacking—a sense of the country's temporal duration. The volume rebuffed European belittling of the nation's "excessive modernness and newness": "We find we have here, what no other nation on the globe can claim: a perfect union of the past and present; the vigor of a nation just born walking over the hallowed ashes of a race whose history is too early for a record, and surrounded by the living forms of a people hovering between the two."[36] British archaeological and antiquarian pursuits attempted to recover and preserve the ancient Anglo-Saxon past, and thereby certify the magnificent racial lineage of the English people. Squier's work, however, allowed the history of a culturally and racially different people to be appended to the white history of the republic. For the reviewer, the meaning of the "nation" as a civil entity, which happens to be dominated by Caucasians, overlays the meaning of the "nation" as a geographical entity, upon which once lived an ancient, racially separate culture: so formulated, the "nation" takes ownership of the indigene past, but does not embrace or feel responsible for the indigenes themselves. The present white citizenry may thereby be glorified without tallying, in conscience, the depredations committed upon either aboriginal or contemporary Native Americans.

On the one hand, then, Squier's first work patriotically lent historical depth to the republic; on the other, at least in the orbit of the scientific avant-garde, it helped to relocate the final arbiter of historical chronicle from the Mosaic account to the disciplines of archaeology and ethnology.[37] His hedging kept him from being criticized by those who feared the impiety of the new historical sciences, and that hedging was appropriate for the son of a Methodist minister. He clearly recognized the potential heresy of his investigations; when he first undertook them, he wrote to his father that "I will show you some things 'you never dreamed of in your philosophy.' "[38]

Squier deferred to his older ethnological colleagues and permitted them, without fully committing himself publicly to the polygenesis theory, to use his discoveries to suit their own polemic. Ironically, however, if he thereby gained approval—and pridefully delighted in Nott's judgment that, when it came to accounting for the past, he had usurped Mosaic authority—other theories of the ethnologists cut athwart his archaeological ambitions. The archaeological and ethnological impulses to explore the vestiges of the ancient Amerindians were in tension rather than being perfectly coordinated, as witnessed by an article, "American Ethnology," that Squier published in an 1849 issue of the *American Whig Review*. The article promotes ethnology as "essentially the science of the age," a panoptical discourse which "neglects no subject of inquiry; and which brings the minutest points of the world, its most widely separated and diverse nations, with some knowledge of their history, institutions and conditions, at once under view." We have heard similar pronouncements of a discipline's all-encompassing mastery in the prefaces of geographical textbooks. Such boasts reflect a transitional moment in the establishment of disciplinary fields; each—whether geography, ethnology, or history—even as it delved more narrowly within its own domain, felt competitively obliged to refute its disciplinarian-sectarian status and to avoid separating professional discourse from a broad public audience. That discourse (again, we saw the same with geographical volumes) could take a stronger hold on the public if it could claim to confirm the primacy of the United States itself, and so not surprisingly Squier makes a second point about ethnology: he proudly announces that it is peculiarly an "American science," because within the "boundaries of our own country, *three* at least of the five grand divisions into which the human family is usually grouped, are fully represented." Puffing his colleagues, he notes that Morton's collection of crania (the evidence for the latter's racial theorizing in *Crania Americana* [1839] and *Crania Aegyptiaca* [1841]) "is not only the largest in the world, but neither public nor private cabinets in any country, contain a tithe of his materials or varieties."

The ethnological ranking of cranial capacity and racial disposition depended upon, in part, a pose of clinical detachment, an objective analysis of evidence at hand to be measured and tabulated. For Squier, however, the more intimate traversal of non-European spaces—his on-site digging of Native American mound structures—led to a wish to magnify rather than diminish the merits of nonwhite cultures. Consequently, when he reviews Morton's specific arguments in respect to Indians, he takes stark exception. He cites his mentor's disparaging comment: "It is my matured conviction that as a race they are decidedly inferior to the Mongolian stock. They are not only averse to the restraints of education, but seem for the most part incapable of a continued process of reasoning on abstract subjects." Squier, though, had concluded otherwise, and in his article grants both aboriginal and near-contemporary Indians a high degree of cultural development. The "nations which occupied the central parts of the continent . . . rank equally high," he observes, "with the people of Hindustan and the ancient Egyptians"; and the Iroquois Confederacy, he adds, should be deemed "nearly perfect as [a] machiner[y] of government and national organization."[39]

Squier, in short, had been let into the inner circle of a scientific group whose theories would likely tarnish the glory of his own archaeological exploits, because disclosing the sites of a relatively undeveloped civilization would hardly amount, in the world's eyes, to a very momentous achievement. What Squier had hoped to accomplish by his endeavors we may surmise by the musings of his friend, M. Lewis Clark:

> I cannot have a doubt, are not our mounds, the North American "Pyramids"? and may not their contents hereafter prove analogous to and perhaps identify with those of Mexico and Central America? From their remains perhaps some American "Rosetta Stone" may yet be exhumed to discover to the astonished savants of the Old Continent that on our side of the "great Water," nations of civilized human beings with Arts, Sciences, and religion have existed in the valleys, and peopled the banks of the American "Nile" thousands of years gone by; and probably prior to the "Nilotic" events themselves.[40]

Squier's *Ancient Monuments* had garnered him the esteem of his colleagues, and it was praised in the popular press. But it did not fully satisfy, we may suppose, his archaeological aspirations. Only by more definitively linking the culture of the Mound Builders to the ancient Indian inhabitants of the regions south of the border would he be able to astound the "savants of the Old Continent." That project, unfortunately, implicitly put him in competition with John Stephens, and embroiled him in political controversy about U.S. expansionist policy. The volume had placed him in the bind between how his ethnological colleagues assessed Indian culture and how he, as an archaeologist, needed to assess it if he wanted to become renowned. His diplomatic mission to Central America placed him in another bind: how to ride the coattails of expansionist fervor, which would require denigrating the indigenous inhabitants of tropical America, and yet also lay claim to original discoveries, which would require celebrating those inhabitants' magnificent past.

Squier's Obstructed Vision: The Interoceanic Canal and Postheroic Archaeology

The scientific community respected *Ancient Monuments*, but Squier had excavated no lost cities of ancient grandeur. The delight of discovery, of ushering before the public previously hidden monuments, became apparently an obsession that eventually manifested itself psychosomatically. For direct evidence of this syndrome of belated discovery, we need to turn to one of his post–Civil War volumes, *Peru: Incidents of Travel and Exploration in the Land of the Incas*, based upon the research that he had conducted while stationed as U.S. commissioner to Peru between 1863 and 1865 but not published until 1877.

The prefatory pages reckon with several of Squier's predecessors in historical inquiry. He recalls his visit in 1863 to the temporary grave site of George R. Gliddon, who had died in Panama in 1857. Gliddon's expertise in Egyptian monuments, relics, and craniology had made him world famous, and Squier properly pays homage to a friend and colleague:

It was a sad duty for me now to visit the grave of my old friend. I early directed my steps to the "American Cemetery." I found it literally a golgotha—"a place of skulls." The shrubbery which had covered it had been cut away, and from numerous little hillocks projected skulls and human bones; many others had been piled up in heaps and burned. . . . I sought in vain for the tomb of my friend; all that I could find were two or three half-calcined fragments of the marble slab which I had sent out. (18–19)

The passage might be monitory: a grotesque, all-to-apt assessment of the risks of the archaeologist in the field. Squier ironically envisions, whether by intent or not, the skeleton of one of the leading U.S. ethnographers, famed for his cabinets of skulls (used, we will recall, for racist comparisons), being promiscuously dispersed in the graveyard. More speculatively, though, Gliddon's death—that is, the citation of it—reduces the psychological pressure of being an explorer who had not yet fully come into his own professionally.

Squier copes with the anxiety of belatedness by, in effect, killing off a competitor; he also does so by mimicking the consequence of heroic, scholarly labor of another predecessor. In the preface, he speaks of his early desire to "visit the land of the Children of the Sun" (2). That wish originated, he explains, from hearing Prescott's invitation to future scholars in *The Conquest of Peru* (1847), which he quotes in his own volume: "[E]nough of the Incas remain to invite the researches of the antiquary . . . [and] we may hope that they will one day call forth a kindred spirit of enterprise to that which has so successfully explored the mysterious recesses of Central America and Yucatan" (2). Unfortunately, Squier confesses, his own personal history hampered the chance to follow Prescott's suggestion and match Stephens's accomplishments:

> Inexorable circumstances, distracting occupations, and the thousand vicissitudes which make us what we are, and often prevent us from becoming what we might have been, interfered to defeat my hopes and aspirations; till at length, owning to undue exposure and protracted over-exertion, the light began to fade before my eyes, and a dark veil fell between them and the bright and moving world without. The skill of eminent oculists was exerted in vain, and I was told that my only alternative lay between absolute mental rest and total blindness. (2–3)

Neurasthenic responses to overwork were, of course, common in the nineteenth century. Squier's somatic reaction, however, was tellingly keyed to his predicament, as becomes clear when we read Prescott's own preface to *The Conquest of Peru*. The historian had closed with an autobiographical note: it had been mentioned in reviews, he remarks, that "I have had the credit of having lost my sight in the composition of my first history."[41] Prescott goes on to detail the difficulties of sustaining the labors of research when his vision was debilitated; so, too, the younger author in his preface recounts the story of his loss of sight. Squier, wishing to emulate preceding historical scholarship in the heroic mode, ends up emulating the disorder that hindered the work of Prescott. Or rather, since Squier writes from the standpoint of having completed the Peru volume, he cites his own somatic ailment as implicit testimony of the herculean feats involved in any effort of historical recovery. Once he landed on the soil of Peru—the investigatory field that allowed him to complete a major work—the lapse into ocular impotence, neatly enough, abruptly subsided:

> [An] unexpected concurrence of circumstances enabled me to realize the hope which I had so long cherished. I received the appointment of Commissioner of the United States to Peru. . . . [H]ere, close by the spot where more than a hundred heretics had been burned alive, and more than three hundred had been beaten with rods—here the day came back to the failing vision, and the glorious light once more vibrated on responsive nerves, and filled the sinking heart with joy and gratitude. (3)

There are inward nuances to Squier's resurgent vision (does he align himself masochistically with the Indian martyrs or sadistically with the Conquistadors?) that perhaps could be further addressed. Antebellum historical texts such as the epics of Prescott and Francis Parkman depend upon the appeal of martial heroics, but also draw upon more subtle allegiances to the repressed content, in the Protestant mind, of Catholic or heathenish rituals and corpo-real suffering. Here, though, it will suffice to note that for Squier, not unlike Stephens, an originary scene of imperial dominance—the agon between con-querors and the conquered—opportunely intervenes to mediate his more contemporary sojourn in the other Americas.[42]

Squier's confessional remarks in *Peru* justify the assumption that neither *Ancient Monuments* nor his other 1850s professional works on Central Amer-ica satisfied his ambition. Under Prescott's urging, he had accepted in 1849 the diplomatic mission to travel to Central America; but the type of relics and monuments he had investigated, upon completing his official duties, had al-ready been described by Stephens, and subsequently, he lost the appointment that would have allowed him to undertake more substantial research. Before Squier departed for Nicaragua, Francis Parkman wrote to encourage him: "[Y]ou will have need of all your grit," he said, though "I do not doubt . . . that the result of [your diplomatic] success will be such as to repay you for all your toil and trouble. Only don't let Politics swallow up science."[43] Political in-trigue, as it turned out, engulfed Squier.

Ever since the Monroe Doctrine, of course, U.S. policy rested upon the na-tion's perceived right to exploit the natural resources of the southern Ameri-cas.[44] After the acquisition of California by the Treaty of Guadalupe Hidalgo, expansionists became especially perturbed by Britain's effort to maintain a colonial presence in the Nicaraguan regions judged most suited for an isth-mian canal route. The Whig party, however, tended to be pro-British and was reluctant to back up the Monroe Doctrine by force when, in January 1848, a British naval squadron seized the port city, San Juan del Norte (renaming it Greytown), under the pretense of supporting the territorial rights of the Mos-quito king, George William Clarence III. When Squier arrived, his task was to report on British activities and to begin negotiations that would, as he later re-called in his 1852 *Nicaragua*, without granting the United States an exclusive right to build and maintain a canal, nonetheless secure "every desirable priv-ilege" of "intercourse [with Nicaragua], commercial or otherwise." Squier likely overstepped his diplomatic assignment by actually having completed a treaty favoring the United States; but, in any case, upon his return it was ap-proved by President Taylor and his cabinet. When Taylor submitted it for ratification, however, the Senate—already much distracted, as Squier phrases it, by the "exciting and decennial task of 'saving the Union,'"—caved in under Sir Henry Bulwer's entreaties and decided to adopt the Clayton-Bulwer pact of 1850, the crucial clause of which stipulated that both countries would refrain from further attempts to dominate the area. Squier did not believe that the treaty would adequately protect U.S. interests, and he took particular umbrage against Webster, whom he believed had conspired with Bulwer, commenting that it "is perhaps well for the memory of the dead, it certainly is for the credit of American statesmanship, that the details of this surrender of American dignity, honor, and interests lie under 'the seal of secrecy.' "[45] Webster had been instrumental in getting Squier's treaty rejected in the Senate, and he disavowed Squier as well. When Millard Fillmore became the new president, Taylor having died in 1850, he made Webster the new secretary of state; and Webster promptly replaced Squier with a new chargé d'affaires.

Chagrined, Squier mounted a campaign in the major journals impugning British policy and the Mosquito people's legitimacy as a nation with territorial rights. In an 1852 article in the *Democratic Review*, for instance, he employed traditional arguments such as those made in John Locke's *Second Treatise of Government* and Emmerich de Vattel's *Law of Nations* about how insufficient use of a land invalidates possession of it: "The Mosquitos have none of the conditions essential to nationality, according to the standards of common sense and the requirements of the law of nations. . . . They are without fixed habitations, without a written language, without laws, the institution of marriage, or even a distinct idea of God. They have no conception of the responsibilities of government, nor are they capable of discharging its duties."[46] As for British colonizing efforts, not to mention the cabals of Webster, such were, as he later wrote in *Waikna*, "beyond the scope of sober history or serious recital," warranting only to be "properly illustrated by the appropriate pens of Charivari, or of Punch."[47]

Squier's motive for sustaining a three-year propaganda war against Britain and Whig policy is not entirely clear. He may simply have resented that Webster's intriguing with Bulwer had voided his laborious negotiations with the Nicaraguan government. Or, it may be that he hoped to capitalize— perhaps by receiving another appointment, this time from a Democratic administration—on the tide of anti-British feeling that resurged in the country after 1852. As the jingoistic first lecture to the American Geographical Society put it in that year, it was both a matter of pride and commercial necessity that the United States dominate Latin America. The lecture distinguished "the opening of an entire new world to our enterprise" in Paraguay and contiguous South American countries from "unprofitable commercial exploits in China"; and it proclaimed that the British presence could not be tolerated in South or Central America: "*Shame* should hinder us from permitting the English to be considered, on any part of our own continent, as the head of civilization and all progress rather than ourselves."[48] Stephen Douglas and other prominent leaders in the Congress, in fact, thought the Clayton-Bulwer treaty an act of folly. One pithily condemned it as "the diplomatic blunder of the century— stand[ing] as a huge gorgon in our path."[49]

Thwarted ambition does not adequately explain, however, the intensity of

Squier's anti-British attitude or his loathing of the Mosquito people, whom, we will recall, he mostly learned about secondhand. In his 1852 volume on Nicaragua, Squier's nationalist rhetoric is calculated to inflame expansionist sentiment, but the last sentence should give us pause:

The fortune of war has planted our eagles on the Pacific: across the entire continent . . . our Republic is supreme. Our trim built [ships] of the deep . . . sweep in the trade of Europe on one hand, and on the other bring to the mouth of the Sacramento the treasures of the Oriental world. . . . To gird the world as with a hoop, to pass a current of American Republicanism . . . over the continents of the earth, it needs but one small spot should be left free from foreign threats and aggression.[50]

Nationalist chauvinism, by Squier's lights, assumes the form of a Freudian family romance. The "one small spot" (the port of San Juan del Norte) becomes a fetishized locale, surcharged because the wondrous imperial destiny of the republic might there be fulfilled. If Squier disliked the Mosquitos because they were to his mind, as we will presently see, a repugnantly amalgamated race, what he likes about a future interoceanic canal is that it would conjoin the waters of the Pacific and Atlantic, and provide commerce between East and West. The canal builders, he wrote in an 1854 article for *Harper's New Monthly Magazine*, were "seeking to break down the barriers which divide [the oceans] and to mingle their as yet estranged waters." A traversing railway likewise struck him as an heroic conjugal union: with not "less of romance than attached to the figurative marriage of Venice to the Adriatic," the railroad would "bound the Atlantic to the Pacific with an iron band."[51] For Squier, these projects of northern masculinist energy would consummate a glorious wedding between East and West, a compact only to be achieved if the United States supplanted, in no uncertain terms, England as the power controlling the most likely routes for rail or canal construction.[52]

Of course, indigene claims to those areas would need to be invalidated as well. Groups that lacked the capacity to develop the natural resources in the region where they lived, Squier apparently came to believe by 1855, were simply inferior. And those groups comprised more than just the Mosquitos. Dramatically reversing his position on the merits of Native American cultures, which he had asserted in his earlier 1848 article on "American Ethnology," Squier now alleges that the "Indian does not possess, still less the South Sea Islander, and least of all the negro, the capacity to comprehend the principles which enter into the higher order of civil and political organizations. His instincts and his habits are inconsistent with their development, and no degree of education can teach him to understand and practice them."[53] And, yet more stridently, he writes that given the importance of Central America to the imperial powers, the Indians would need to be sacrificed on the altar of progress: "Short-sighted philanthropy may lament, and sympathy drop a tear as it looks forward to the total disappearance of the lower forms of humanity, but the laws of Nature are irreversible, *Deus vult*—it is the will of God!"[54]

Disparaging the descendants of the very people that as an archaeologist he had earlier lauded put, presumably, a strain on Squier. One solution, which he took in *Nicaragua*, was to maximize his own masculinist labor in unearthing various idols. Squier's diplomatic mission took him from San Juan del Norte to the seat of government at León, and along the way he pursued detours (the artist J. W. Orr accompanied him) to explore sundry jungle antiquities. On a series of small islands dotting several Nicaraguan lakes, he unburied and transported back to the Smithsonian a number of Mayan stone idols. The relics differed little from those that Catherwood had depicted in the engravings accompanying Stephens's accounts, and they were apparently well known, although not of much interest, to the local residents. Squier compensates by emphasizing the masculine feats required to bring the monuments to light. Typically, he and his crew of diggers uncover the idols with "every muscle swell[ing]" (475); or, he represents himself dwelling upon his "singular discoveries" with the "complacency of a father contemplating his children" (475). The idols merited investigation, to be sure. Squier was especially intrigued by the serpent symbols carved upon them, a clue that Mayan religious rites involved phallus worship. In 1851, he had published *The Serpent Symbol, and the Worship of the Reciprocal Principles of Nature in America*, in which he equated Amerindian serpent and egg icons with rites of generative power and sun-god adoration.[55] In *Nicaragua* he broaches the topic in veiled terms, referring to that form of "primitive worship . . . of common acceptance amongst the semi-civilized nations of America" (490). Most often, though, he articulates his fascination through lingering descriptions of the phallic-looking idols themselves: the "prostrate figure . . . represented a human male figure, of massive proportions" (450). Nonetheless, Squier did not discover any cities in ruin, as Stephens had, much less sites as fabulous as those reported in Austen Layard's *Discoveries in the Ruins of Nineveh and Babylon* (1851), one of the travel-archaeological volumes that he read while in Nicaragua, and whose Oriental imagery haunted his dreams.[56] As for the idols that Squier eventually shipped back to the Smithsonian, Francis Parkman's comment to him was apposite. They appeared, Parkman observed in a letter, "extremely curious" but also "unspeakably ugly."[57]

Waikna, Racial Declension, and the Psychopolitics of Purity

Waikna, Squier's only literary work, continues to reflect his animus toward British policy. It enacts as well an imaginary resolution to his fairly ineffectual efforts as an archaeologist up to 1855. In the antebellum archive it is, perhaps, a unique text. Although there are a number of other, more well known works—

such as *Two Years Before the Mast* (1840) by Richard Henry Dana, Jr., and Bayard Taylor's at the time much-vaunted *Eldorado*—that engage the scenes and sights of Spanish America, no other volume to my knowledge represents a sustained, however racist and in part fabular, encounter with the indigenous cultures. Sui generis in specifics, Squier's text is not so ideologically, however. It replays the fantasies and frustrations that compose the U.S. imaginary of tropical America, then and perhaps today as well: of an aggressive, masculine northern body that feels its strength by exerting itself against the engulfing political and ethnographic debilities of southern climes.

Squier published *Waikna* under the pseudonym of Samuel A. Bard. Bard, clearly a surrogate self for the author, is a poor artist residing in New York. He goes south hoping to gain fame by painting tropical landscapes, but his supplies are lost when the ship taking him to Nicaragua founders in a storm, leaving him shipwrecked on a small island off the Mosquito Shore. Bard gets picked up by a passing steamer, which lands him at Bluefields, the main settlement of the Mosquitos. He then decides, in lieu of painting the countryside, to explore it. He proceeds by canoe accompanied by two young Poyer or Paya Indians, Antonio and another who remains nameless (Bard refers to him only as "my Poyer boy" [123]), northward up the coast, through interconnected lagoons toward Cape Cracias, where the Wanks River leads west into the highlands of Nicaragua. Having "penetrate[d] into the interior" (77) of the country, Bard visits Antonio's mountainous homeland, the realm of "several tribes of pure Indians" (76).

Early Spanish imperialists had regarded the Mosquitos (a corruption of the name Miskitos) as a primitive, backward people; and, since they could locate no gold in the region, the tribe was more or less ignored. The lagoons along the Mosquito Shore did, however, later provide a haven for buccaneers raiding the Spanish Main, and the natives by the end of the eighteenth century had become racially mixed with them as well as with fugitive slaves.[58] Squier places in opposition the swamp-dwelling, hybrid Mosquitos to the noble indigenes he meets in the mountains, and thereby casts his topographical itinerary along racial lines. The Poyer Indians are not white, but their racial purity accords them for Squier an intrinsic virtue he finds utterly lacking in the Mosquitos. The split between the native groups involves more, though, than just the contrast between racial admixture and racial purity, a topic that much exercised Squier's "American Ethnology" colleagues. It involves, as well, a transcoding of race into history—for if the Mosquitos in Squier's eyes can appear in history only as caricatures, in their absurd half-adoption of British military garb (Figure 9), the Poyers are divulged in the conclusion to be heroic actors in history as they prepare to mount a full-scale rebellion in the hope of restoring their ancient empire. Antonio, it turns out, is a prince; he descends from "regal stock, [being] the son and lieutenant of Chichen Pat, one of the last and bravest chiefs of Yucatan" (55).[59]

CAPTAIN DRUMMER.

FIG. 9. Mosquito native in military British uniform, in Ephraim G. Squier's *Waikna* (1855; Gainesville: University of Florida Press, 1965), page 93. (Reproduced with the permission of the University Press of Florida.)

The episodic adventures and naturalist detours occurring along the path of Bard's journey helped make *Waikna*, as one reviewer wrote, a "savage idyll" that was both "entertaining and instructive."[60] Scenes such as his midnight fight with a group of Mosquito natives (Figure 10) and his detailed inventory of wildlife and sundry plants—from wild pigs and tapirs to bananas and herbs taken to counteract tropical fever—are among the devices Squier used to authenticate his travel volume. Readers, we imagine, would also especially have delighted in the simultaneously macho and urbane figure that Samuel Bard cuts. An opening sketch depicts the twenty-six-year-old adventurer as a virile, rough-and-ready artist-traveler (Figure 11), but Squier quickly lets us know that his persona hails from a U.S. metropolis, from New York and its cultivated milieu of art and patronage.[61] The adoption of the artist persona was clever, for it explained why Bard has elected to travel to a region that, except

THE FIGHT NEAR QUAMWATLA.

FIG. 10. Samuel Bard fighting with Mosquito natives in Ephraim G. Squier's *Waikna* (1855; Gainesville: University of Florida Press, 1965), page 153. (Reproduced with the permission of the University Press of Florida.)

for its landscape, he finds distinctly repulsive. While in New York, he had wished to "paint grand historical paintings... [especially of] Balboa, the discoverer of the Pacific, bearing aloft the flag of Spain" (16–17). But for the impoverished artist lacking patrons, "historical painting," he laments, is a "luxury" (17), and so he shifts to wishing to paint landscapes, fantasizing scenes of

tropical lands, where Nature had grander aspects, where there were broad lakes and high and snow-crowned volcanoes, which waved their plumes of smoke in mid-heaven, defiantly, in the very face of the sun; lands through whose ever-leaved forests Cortez, Balboa, and Alvarado, and Cordova had led their mailed followers, and in whose depths frowned the strange gods of aboriginal superstition, beside the deserted altars and unmarked graves of a departed and mysterious people. (18)

Echoing Stephens, Bard desires to follow in the tracks of the Conquistadors, and he likewise places much stock in his own mimetic talents. He confesses to having a "rare hand for landscapes—good flaming landscapes, full of yellow and vermillion, you know!" (17). Yet if he likes his pigments to be intensely chromatic, what he discovers when he first lands in Jamaica is a population whose mixed pigmentation, its racial admixture, deeply offends him: "[A] week had given me a surfeit of Kingston, with its sinister, tropical Jews, and variegated inhabitants, one-half black, one-third brown, and the balance as fair

MOSQUITO SHORE.

Chapter 1.

A MONTH in Jamaica is enough for any sinner's punishment, let alone that of a tolerably good Christian. At any rate, a week had given me a surfeit of Kingston, with its sinister, tropical Jews, and variegated inhabitants, one-half black, one-third brown, and the balance as fair as could be expected, considering the abominable, unintelligible Congo-English which they spoke. Besides, the cholera which seems to

FIG. 11. Sketch of Samuel Bard, hero of Ephraim G. Squier's *Waikna* (1855; Gainesville: University of Florida Press, 1965), page 13. (Reproduced with the permission of the University Press of Florida.)

as could be expected, considering the abominable, unintelligible Congo-English which they spoke" (13).

Bard, as ethnologist-cum-landscape painter, continues to descant upon the horrors of racial hybridity. The "manifest lack of public morality and private virtue, in the Spanish-American States," he asserts, "has followed from the fatal facility with which the Spanish colonists have intermixed with the negroes and Indians" (24). The entirety of Latin America, it seems, is composed of a "hybrid stock" with "most, if not all, of the vices, and few, if any of the virtues of the originals" (24). Lest the dangers of admixture be not clear enough, Squier includes a monitory vignette by having Bard visit an "ill-fated Prussian colony" (74), situated on the Mosquito Shore, that has succumbed to the racial-historical miasma of its tropical environs. He describes the rotting away of the colonists' fields, their rusting farm implements, and their "disappointments and sufferings" (74). The lesson he draws from the defunct enterprise was conventional in the antebellum period: it was "folly" to attempt "to plant an agricultural colony, from the North of Europe, on low, murky, tropical shores" (74). Squier's conclusions here concur with the blunt one Nott and Gliddon reached in respect to miscegenation in *Types of Mankind*: "*[M]ulat-toes* are the shortest-lived of any class of the human race."[62] The tone of Bard's final reflection on the colony's demise, however, registers an hysteria not quite congruent with the moralizing occasion:

[At] the time of my visit, two or three haggard wretches, whose languid blue eyes and flaxen hair contrasted painfully with the blotched visages of the brutal Sambos [Mosquitos], were all that remained of the unfortunate Prussian colony. The burying place was a small opening in the bush, where rank vines sweltered over the sunken graves, a spot reeking with miasmatic swamps, from which I retreated with a shudder. I could wish no worse punishment to the originators of that fatal, not to say, criminal enterprise, than that they should stand there, as I stood, that Conscience might hiss in their ears, "Behold thy work!" (75)

Here, rather than founding a plantation that subsequent generations will inherit, the otherwise virile Prussians have left a settlement to be overrun by the amalgamated Mosquitos, whose bodies we later learn suffer the effects of syphilis contracted from "their unrestrained licentious intercourse" (244) with beachcombers and sailors. The Prussians' mere inhabitance of the degenerative locale (Squier only implies that their vitiation follows from actual sexual congress with the "Sambos") suffices to defile pure lines of descent. Northern Europeans may rule and dominate tropical American peoples, but they must maintain a racial-bodily distance and avoid admixing themselves either with indigenes or, through agricultural labor, the land itself. The Prussian catastrophe follows from the breakdown of hierarchy: rather than lording it over, to recall Bayard Taylor's suggestive passage on Orizaba, a "host of the weak, ef-

feminate sybarites of the south," they have become engulfed by—in their demise, buried within—the rotting terrain.

Archaeology customarily involves digging up relics from burying grounds,
and Squier had done so in his researches for *Ancient Monuments.* In the hands
of the archaeologist, such sites are not the locales of death and decay, but rather
historical re-creation; out of such metaphorically womblike spaces the archaeologist engenders history (in this regard, we will recollect Squier's "complacency of a father contemplating his children" as he unearthed Nicaraguan relics). Gillian Rose, a theoretical-feminist geographer, suggests that for male
travelers the landscape often appears in antithetical guises, either as the "wel-
coming topography of the nurturing mother" or as "terrifying maternal
swamps, mountains, seas, inhabited by sphinxes and gorgons."[63] Such speculations seem to be borne out in Squier's repulsed fetishizing of the decaying
Prussian colony, which symbolizes not what I have called the archaeological
sublime, but rather its horrifying opposite: a loathly space of historical declension.

Squier's macho persona helps him to negotiate these troublingly gender-
ized terrains. His obsessions over racial amalgamation take on as he travels
through Mosquito topography an heightened sexual dimension. The natives,
each time Bard meets them, are described as being barbarous; but he is nowhere more repulsed than when he witnesses a drunken dance, in which the
revelers of both "sexes finally gave themselves up to the grossest and most
shameless debauchery, such as I have never heard ascribed to the most bestial
natives" (229). Counterpointing this Mosquito saturnalia is an earlier scene of
bourgeois intimacy, which Squier projects onto the landscape:

> By and by the night came on, but not as it comes in our northern latitudes. Night, un-
> der the tropics, falls like a curtain. . . . Reflected in the lagoon, [the stars] seemed to
> chase each other in amorous play, printing sparkling kisses on each other's luminous
> lips. The low shores, lined with the heavy-foliaged mangroves, looked like a frame of
> massive, antique carving, around the vast mirror of the lagoon, across whose surface
> streamed a silvery shaft of light from the evening star, palpitating like a young bride,
> low in the horizon. (81)

Stephens, too, needed to adjust how he pictured himself in tropical American
settings, and did so by reframing key scenes in terms of imperial tableaux. In
Squier's case, the otherwise foul lagoon becomes re-envisioned as a site of
erotic, spousal bliss. He looks into the mirror-lagoon to see an awaiting bride,
sexualized yet also presumably virginal. The purplish romanticism of the passage, however, should not just be read as being erotically suggestive: in the
nineteenth-century bourgeois imagination, these joys are heavenly as much as
libidinal.

These polarities—between sexual chastity and sexual defilement, between

racial purity and racial admixture—finally become epitomized in the two native prophetesses, or Sukias, that Bard encounters as he travels up the Wanks
River into the Nicaraguan interior with his ever-faithful assistant, Antonio.
The first he meets, in a squalid Mosquito village, is a "powerful *Sukia*, whose
commands were always implicitly obeyed by the superstitious Sambos" (230)
and who "possessed more power over [them] . . . than king or chief" (231).
Squier depicts this Mosquito Sukia as a decrepit matriarch, "almost fascinating in her repulsiveness": "Her hair was long and matted, and her shriveled
skin appeared to adhere like that of a mummy to her bones; for she was emaci-
ated to the last degree. . . . Her eyes were bloodshot, but bright and intense, and
were constantly fixed upon me, like those of some wild beast of prey" (228–
29). The "hideous old woman" (228), who as Bard says "disturbed my dreams"
(230), becomes the abhorrent type, we might say, of history-as-declension.

In contrast is the Poyer Sukia who greets Bard when he and Antonio venture farther upriver to the mountain region of Antonio's homeland. The Poyer
community, Squier asserts, "afforded an example of a purely patriarchal organization, in which the authority of paternity and of age was recognized in
the fullest degree" (297). And accordingly the Poyer Sukia, this time a "shy and
timid" young woman, "perfectly formed" (255), is the reservoir of the lore of
the elders. She tells stories about the patriarchal lineage of Antonio's ancestors,
and her prophecies speak of the restoration of the royal Mayan line and empire. Whereas the earlier Mosquito Sukia represented barren sexuality, and
figured forth history-as-declension, this Sukia inducts Bard into Mayan arcanum. She is an oracle of time's fulfillment. Bard, having just left the
"sanctuary" of the young Sukia, a pure female space, stands amid ancient
monuments and is granted an epiphany:

It was past midnight when, with a new and deeper insight into the mysteries of our
present and future existence, and a fuller and loftier appreciation of the great realities
which are to follow upon the advent of every soul into the universe, and of which earth
is scarcely the initiation, that [I] . . . left the sanctuary of the *Sukia*. . . . Immediately in
front of the hut from which we had emerged, stood one of the ruined structures to
which I have already alluded. By the clear light of the moon I could perceive that it was
built of large stones, laid with the greatest regularity, and sculptured all over with
strange figures, having a close resemblance, if not an absolute identity, with those
which have become familiarized to us by the pencil of Catherwood. (258–60)

Bard's occult "insight" replaces Squier's failure to bring to sight relics that
might have explicated the Mayan past. Prescott had written to Stephens that
the ancient temples and other edifices described in *Incidents of Travel in Yucatan* simply confounded him, "leav[ing]" his "mind in a kind of mist." And
Stephens himself lamented that the Mayan ruins would never be fully interpreted, mainly because of the present Indians' ignorance of their ancestors, no

"traditions [having been] handed down from father to son, and from generation to generation" (1:105). Squier, rather than competing with Stephens and
Catherwood, can graciously allude to the latter's sketches precisely because his
persona, Samuel Bard, has fathomed through the midnight séance a superior
form of knowledge, not about the past, but about futurity itself.

The history-discovering author, however, could not be content with that
illumination. The text continues with more revelations, which return it to a
less metaphysical, but nonetheless fabular, history. Antonio, previously a
rather enigmatic figure, divulges toward the end of the travelogue, after Bard's
meeting with the young Sukia, that he in fact directly descends from the ancient royal Mayan line. He, the Sukia, and the tribal chiefs, Antonio reveals,
have formed a "secret organization" (258) plotting a "complete subversion of
the Spanish power" (258): the "scheme of insurrection . . . was intended to include, not only the Indians of Yucatan and of Central America, but even those
of Mexico and Peru, in one grand and terrible uprising against the Spanish
dominion" (331). In 1847, the Maya of Santa Cruz had, in fact, launched a protracted but ultimately ineffectual rebellion against the Spanish Mexicans
known as the Guerra de las Castas; and smaller skirmishes, about the same
time, took place in the Belize region as natives tried to protect the last vestiges
of their territory against the encroachments of British logging companies.[64]
But the scattered tribes presented no united front against imperial power; so
we may take Squier's fantasy of indigene insurrection as being more psychopolitical theater than bona fide history. The full disclosure of the revolutionary plot and of Antonio's royalty occurs only when Bard and Antonio
have returned to the coast, on an island distinguished, appropriately, "as the
one whence Columbus first descried the mainland of America" (324). Here,
through Antonio's confession of the "great secret which [had] swelled in his
bosom" (242), Squier imaginatively compensates himself for his more or less
lackluster New World archaeological feats, for not having found, as his friend
Clark had put it, an "American Rosetta Stone" that would unlock archaeological secrets.

The fantasy sequence of discovering a pure descendent of the original Mayan chiefs, though, still did not apparently resolve all the issues of declension
and impurity animating Bard's narrative. Squier therefore supplied yet another denouement. The other, anonymous Poyer boy departs for the mountains, leaving behind a token of loyalty:

The reader may, perhaps, smile when I say that I strained my eyes to penetrate the
darkness, if only to catch one glimpse of my Poyer boy; and that I wept when I turned
back to the village. And when, on the following day, as I unrolled my scanty wardrobe,
a section of bamboo-cane, heavy with gold-dust, rolled upon the floor, I felt not only
that I had lost a friend, but that beneath the swarthy breast of that untutored Indian

boy there beat a heart capable of the most delicate generosities. Be sure, my faithful friend, far away in your mountain home, that your present shall never be dishonored! Washed from the virginal sands, and wrought into the symbol of our holy faith, it rests above a heart as constant as thine own; and, inscribed with the single word "FIDEL-ITY," it shall descend to my children, as an evidence that Faith and Friendship are heavenly flowers, perennial in every clime! (315–16)

Here, in place of memories of "mongrel" (67), lascivious Mosquitos, Squier's surrogate sees himself bringing home an icon fashioned from the Poyer lad's pure (yet suggestively phallic) gift. That icon, its gold mined from the mountainous realms of Nicaragua, becomes the very emblem of a masculinist obsession with pure genealogy, as Squier envisions his hero bequeathing it as a family heirloom that will "descend" unblemished through the generations. Coming at the end of *Waikna*, it stands for a clarified, unproblematic vision of imperial relations—one not sullied by the misfortunes of personal or political history.

Gold had motivated the brutal tactics of the Spanish invaders, and had led to the wholesale slaughter of Mexican and Central American natives. Both Squier and Stephens in their archaeological quests sought to recover the relics of the aboriginal past in a manner that at once transcended and replayed the masculinist aggression of the Conquistadors. Their uneasy refashioning of the story of the Spanish Conquest, in pursuit of the archaeological sublime, explains some of the tensions we have observed in the texts of both authors—between surface and depth or between the co-optation of the Amerindian past and wonderment over it. Ultimately, though, why either became so engrossed by the archaeological sublime remains just as unfathomable as the two explorers found Mayan culture to be. Anne McClintock reminds us that in the imperial context the relations "between the individual unconscious and political life are . . . neither separable from each other nor reducible to each other. Instead, they comprise crisscrossing and dynamic mediations."[65] To sound the psychogenetic nuances of *Waikna*'s final passage more fully would no doubt help us, in turn, to sound more thoroughly the latent content of U.S.–Latin American relations, at least in respect to Squier. Little, though, is recorded about his family life other than the few details I have alluded to earlier. He married Miriam Florence Folline in 1858, three years after *Waikna* appeared in print, and we do not know much about the history of their previous courtship. Ironically, the final scene proleptically contrasts with their later relationship, which was to end with a loss of "fidelity," when the two had become estranged from each other and when—it made a nice scandal for the New York newspapers—Squier's wife divorced him to marry his employer, Frank Leslie, in 1874. Earlier passages that I quoted—when Bard sees a virginal bride in the mangrove/lagoon mirror, visits the sanctuary of the Poyer prophetess, and holds the token of a young Indian's friendship in his hands—could well be regarded as a coded triangulation of Squier, his wife, and his employer's tangled relationship.

But the danger in pursuing such speculations further is that we will reduce Squier's conflicted encounter with Central America to a mere matter of psychobiography. A gesture toward avoiding that analytical trap is to take a cue from Squier himself, noting that the endings that I have just cited do not, in fact, conclude *Waikna*. Squier provides an "Historical Sketch of the Mosquito Shore," "Various Notes on the Topography, Soil, Climate, and Natives of the Mosquito Shore," and, finally, a "Brief Vocabulary of the Mosquito Language."[66] In a movement kindred to that which we saw in Melville's *Typee*, Squier takes us from personal anxieties and negotiations to more impersonal history, but for a different effect. In a travelogue-novel whose main burden has been to denigrate the Mosquito people, these appendixes and especially the last do not entirely make sense. The first two outline what Squier in the narrative proper had taken to be the tribe's absurd pretensions to nationality, but why in the last one should he also validate the native group via a lexicon of their language, a few entries of which follow?

English.	Mosquito.	English.	Mosquito.
Man,	waikna.	. . . . . .	. . .
Woman,	mairen.	Bread,	tane.
Father,	aize.	Maize,	aya.
Mother,	yapte.	Fish,	inska.
. . . . . .	. . . .	. . . . . .	. . .
House,	watla.	To drink,	diaia.
Thing,	dera.	To eat,	piaia.
Dory,	duerka-taira.	To run,	plapia. (363–65)

For the reader, what the "Brief Vocabulary" presages is a belief that ethnographers or archaeologists would be prepared to admit, or at least theorize about, only later in the nineteenth century: the intrinsic merit of all indigenous cultures. Karl Kroeber explains that the school of anthropology that emerged out of the teachings of Franz Boas in the 1880s came to see that "cultures are precious because diverse." That notion, Kroeber elaborates, in part depended upon coordinate developments in historical and comparative linguistics, which "strengthened American anthropology's emphasis on variety rather than hierarchy."[67] Stephens had concluded his second set of volumes by ruminating on his failure to appropriate the Mayan past or their language. Squier's lexicon, prefaced with only a short paragraph of his own words, begins to push the reader to the other side of the border, where one might hear what Squier himself in a rare moment of transcultural generosity willingly acknowledges: that the Mosquito language and, by implicit extension, their culture need not be deemed "deficient in euphony" (363).

Archaeology or anthropology served to append the ancestral time of indigenous populations to that of the relatively young republic, expanding its history anteriorly, but what the archaeologist-traveler, Stephens or Squier, could do only in passing moments of reverie was to recapture the originary, New World imperial enterprise of, as Squier put it in an 1855 issue of *Harper's New Monthly Magazine*, "those iron adventurers" trooping through the "vast tropical wilderness, before the Puritan landed at Plymouth."[68] To revisit the dramatic flesh-and-blood scenes of the contest between the two predecessor empires of the New World, Spanish and Aztec, required the historical imagination proper, which was so magnificently evidenced by William H. Prescott's monumental 1843 *History of the Conquest of Mexico*. Stephens and Squier regarded the indigenous tropical American natives under the guise of history-as-declension; the native body for them was one marked by abjection. I want to conclude by looking briefly at what, by all accounts, must be the most famous abject Indian represented in the era: the figure of Montezuma, abject because so supremely royal as well.

The archaeologists traveled across Latin American topographies to divulge the mysterious contents of densely historical sites, but as we have seen, especially in the case of Stephens, interiors were hardly disclosed at all. What his published volumes offer instead are mostly surfaces, with the facsimiles (the representations in travel volume or sketch) seldom conducting us to the inward spaces of archaic ritual, so strongly fetishized by the author. Prescott's text, too, may be seen as structuring its portrayal of the colonial agon between Cortés and Montezuma by way of surface and depth: as it, specifically, traces the route the armor-clad Conquistadors took across the Mexican plain into the heart of the Aztec kingdom; or as it follows Cortés's effort to discover the plots of the sweet-countenanced but inscrutably foreign Indian emperor. Prescott's virile hero was, the historian writes, the "young adventurer, whose magic lance was to dissolve the spell which had so long hung over these mysterious regions" (180). Toward the end of his work, Prescott sums up the essential meaning of the struggle, which, as with the previous quote's suggestive sense of lance equaling pen, echoes the challenge of heroic historical re-creation itself:

Whatever may be thought of the Conquest in a moral view, regarded as a military achievement it must fill us with astonishment. That a handful of adventurers, indifferently armed and equipped, should have landed on the shores of a powerful empire inhabited by a fierce and warlike race, and, in defiance of the reiterated prohibitions of its sovereign, have forced their way into the interior;—that they should have done this, without knowledge of the language or of the land, without chart or compass to guide them, without any idea of the difficulties they were to encounter, totally uncertain whether the next step might bring them on a hostile nation, or on a desert, *feeling their way along in the dark, as it were* . . . [A]ll this . . . [is] too startling for the probabilities demanded by fiction, and without a parallel in the pages of history. (818, emphasis added)

Prescott, as Jenny Franchot has argued, projected his own concerns about the pressures of being the author of grand epic histories upon how he envisioned the struggle between Cortés and Montezuma, at once cathecting with the masculine drive of the Spanish leader and with the defeated Aztec emperor whose dreary death in captivity became a mirror for the historian's own sense of debilitation from being overworked and nearly blind. If, on the one hand, Prescott becomes absorbed by the virile spectacle of iron soldiers campaigning, he is equally on the other absorbed by the effete Montezuma, the sad ruler who, he tells us, was "gentle even to effeminacy in his deportment" (582) and was the "sad victim of destiny,—a destiny as dark and irresistible in its march, as that which broods over the mythic legends of Antiquity!" (583–84). In his account, therefore, the appeal of describing grandiose campaigns—the motor, as it were, of New World history or epic—becomes conflicted by the wish to render the pathos of Montezuma's culturally different royal mentality.[69]

No less than in the case of Stephens or Squier, the study of the tropical American past for Prescott hauntingly conjoined personal anxieties and U.S. national ideologies. Abject regality in non-European, exotic realms fascinated him; Montezuma's grandeur and opacity to the historian might well stand as a metaphor for the melancholy of historical re-creation itself, of history's essential unwritability. In that regard, what Stephens, Squier, and Prescott most hold in common—notwithstanding all their phallic-military images of penetration—is their sense of how resistant history or non-European otherness is to interpretation. As with Herman Melville's *Typee*, though, representational crises (in the latter instance, over ethnographic knowledge) should not be entirely correlated with ideological concern (in *Typee*, in respect to the law; in this chapter, in respect to the masculinist appropriation of indigenous temporality). The juggernaut of U.S. destiny, expanding westward across the frontier states and incipiently imperialistic in terms of the non-European world, was hardly halted, or even slowed down, by textual or authorial befuddlement. From a certain perspective, then, even those texts that see through the ruse of American exceptionalism, such as Melville's *Typee*, or find the masculinist obligations of the New World, U.S. subject burdensome as much as privileging, such as in the key ones of Squier's oeuvre, can be deemed to be historically negligible, if we take history to mean vast, unidirectional national plots or national crises inscribed in the hearts and ideologies of the citizenry at large.

New Historicism and other modes of poststructuralist criticism seek to return agency to the text insofar as they make little distinction between text and history, or between archive and world. Or, rather, agency and angst are everywhere or nowhere, in a circulating, causally hazy social energy that neither derives from empirically verifiable origins nor concludes in definitive consequences. Many Americanists tend to be sympathetic to such a folding together of text and history because it magnifies the weight of the archive and—what cultural historian will not admit it?—the sheer pleasures of the aleatory, of making otherwise odd texts *count* in history. This is not to say, for instance, that Squier's *Waikna* for all its personal idiosyncrasies is just odd: indeed it condenses issues of gender dynamics, historicity, and othering as much as any antebellum text, and in that sense is representative of its age.

Representative, that is, of majority culture: for *Waikna*'s concerns reflect those of its peculiar discursive community (American ethnologists) and white U.S. citizens. To minority groups, those actors in history not of the majority culture where the operative term for the New Historian is always *anxiety*, the nervous sense of power's possible evacuation, texts hold a different purchase on the world. They serve to carve out spaces of real, even if only potential or psychological, freedom. The next chapter traces the geographies of power, both inward and outward, in the career and writings of Martin R. Delany, the visionary African-American separatist who sought both to articulate and be the agent of black spaces of national empowerment in and beyond the United States.

CHAPTER FIVE

Outgrowing the Boundaries of North America

Martin R. Delany, Africa, and the Question of African-American Agency

> The first thing which the native learns is to stay in his place, and not to go beyond certain limits. This is why the dreams of the native are always of muscular prowess; his dreams are of action and aggression. I dream I am jumping, swimming, running, climbing; I dream that I burst out laughing, that I can span a river in one stride.
> —Frantz Fanon, *The Wretched of the Earth*

> We love our country, dearly love her, but she don't love us—she despises us, and bids us begone, driving us from her embraces; but we shall not go where she desires us; but when we do go, whatever love we have for her, we shall love the country none the less that receives us as her adopted children.
> —Martin R. Delany, *The Condition, Elevation, Emigration, and Destiny of the Colored People of the United States*

> Africa and her past and future glory became entwined around every fibre of his being; and to the work of replacing her among the powers of the earth, and exalting her scattered descendants on this continent, he has devoted himself wholly.
> —Frank A. Rollin, *Life and Public Services of Martin R. Delany*

> Whatever we determine shall be, will be.
> —Martin R. Delany, *Blake; or the Huts of America*

THE CASE STUDIES in Chapters 2, 3, and 4 have explored how U.S. ideologies or national topoi were affected or came into being by traversals through non-European domains. Those domains' inhabitants, although in a sense *in* the texts, seldom obtain a more than ghostly narrative presence.

They are described but given little agency outside the confines of the stereotype (for instance, Polynesian expressiveness seems to occur mostly through the body: tattooing, pantomime, licentious indulgence, cannibalistic appetite). To be fair, though, I should add that stereotypic representation does not always rule the works previously analyzed. In *Typee*, for example, Kory-Kory and Fayaway are both to some extent individualized, respond empathically to Tommo's forlornness, and seem at times to be less restrained—and thereby less communally defined—by the strictures of taboo law. The image of Kory-Kory gazing out "sentimentally" through his facial tattooing, for instance, suggests a uniqueness, a discrete selfhood, trapped behind the prison window of tribal culture. He suffers, we might say, the melancholy of not wanting to be fully or stereotypically Polynesian, yet condemned to being so in respect to what his tribal affiliation will allow and, perhaps more important, in respect to what outsiders usually will see: Kory-Kory is sad because he knows that Westerners will regard him only as *representative*, as a subject—if he could frame the issue in this phrase—for textual reproduction.

The prison-bar trope is paradigmatic of the complexity of engaging the other when the geographic gaze becomes less abstract, that is, more focused on particular, concrete locales. Even in Stephens's Central American travel narratives a number of mixed Spanish/Indian landowners, revolutionaries, and guides participate in lengthy dialogues and exchanges with Stephens or Catherwood, are not depicted as abject, and in fact are seen beyond their use value in the project of the archaeological sublime. In "reality," Stephens's exploratory odysseys could not have been undertaken without continual contact, frictional or pleasurable, with an assortment of Central Americans, of different racial or class groupings. The latter, however, work mostly to posit a sufficient quiddity of "thereness," which keeps the texts in question from becoming mere mirages of the exotic; *othering*, it paradoxically seems, requires a degree of individuation beyond the stereotype. Were the lens slightly shifted, those individuals' presence might be magnified, deemed more prominent, more *in* Stephens's accounts. In his volumes, however, such a shift rarely if ever takes place. Whether with Stephens or other travel authors, what extra density some non-European characters seem to hold serves, in fact, mainly to give an authenticity effect to travel reportage and its thematics: the figures rarely become fully rounded actors in their own right.

The tension between the non-European invoking ideological crisis and not really being "there" most strongly manifests itself in Squier's *Waikna*. The Mosquito natives disturb the author, but we know that he had very little contact with them. What it means—and this applies to Melville's *Typee* as well—for a native population to be more ideologically troubling in the time of telling than the time of encounter is a question inviting speculation. The distance of memory, we might guess, allows for the psychic image of the other to become saturated with home-bred ideological concerns, although of course such concerns mediate the moment of encounter in the first place. Because of this fusion—of past and present, of "reality" and textual re-creation—we can either feel easy or uneasy about *not* attending to the originary other or impetus behind the representation. In my introduction, I suggested that not to reproduce (or attempt to reproduce) the other's self-seeing might well be deemed an act of ethical-critical negligence: to not juxtapose, for instance, Kory-Kory against real natives circa 1840 is to come dangerously close to replicating the optics through which *Typee*'s narrator looks at him. Of course, one legitimate task of the cultural historian is to make more visible what a text itself may incidentally or strategically occlude: to show the real political-historical relations, the full agency of all the actors, behind what otherwise comes across, in respect to the non-European, as being merely stereotypical. My intent is this study, though, has not been to re-create the lands and cultural mentalities of the non-European realms visited by U.S. subjects during the antebellum period. Its focus is not on Polynesia, Central America, the Holy Land, or Africa per se, but rather on how those regions and their inhabitants entered into the ideological stories that Americans, in the final analysis, felt compelled to tell about themselves.

These remarks preface the following chapter because, although it analyzes some of the contours of mid-nineteenth-century African-American identity, it will have very little to say about a factual, temporally specific Africa. Both region and those living there will remain offstage in this chapter. Rather than make a gesture toward inclusiveness (which, if it would give the subsequent discussion a better conscience, would also pull it out of the orbit of American studies), I will turn, quite exclusively, to how Africa was *regarded* by nineteenth-century U.S. subjects—in particular by Martin R. Delany, the most stalwart exemplar of minority separatist politics in the nineteenth century.

In the era's geographical literature, Africa was the foreign realm accorded the least agency, the least purchase on world affairs. Not all U.S. subjects, however, agreed with the pedagogues' contempt for the land and its people. Delany, in his late monograph, *Principia of Ethnology* (1879), offered an antithetical take on the continent: "[So] far from [being] stupefying and depressing, as popularly taught in our schoolbooks [the African] climate and inhalations of the aroma and odors with which the atmosphere is impregnated, are exciting causes, favorable to intellectual development."[1] What, Delany implies, did not minister to this "development" was the racist milieu of the United States itself. Nonetheless, in the long arc of his life he never completely disaffiliated himself from the United States nor fully bonded with his ancestral homeland. His

MAJOR MARTIN R. DELANY, U. S. A.
PROMOTED ON THE BATTLE FIELD FOR BRAVERY

FIG. 12. Portrait of Martin R. Delany as a Union major (c. 1865). Hand-colored lithograph. (Courtesy of the National Portrait Gallery, Smithsonian Institute.)

story is one of continual negotiation, of attempting to gauge—both for the black community and for himself—conflicting loyalties to the U.S. proper and a land elsewhere, where African-Americans might be granted the dignities of self-sovereignty, the foundational ethos of the republic that, for his entire career, he at once felt estranged from and loved.

In 1865, subscribers to *The Weekly Anglo-African* would likely have been struck by a lithograph of Delany in the regalia of a Union major (Figure 12). He had earned his commission in February of that year for his role in raising African-American troops, and the portrait (later made available as a postcard) honors his elevated status within the national body politic. Poised against a background of the U.S. flag and army field tents, he seems to have abjured separatist ideology to conjoin black selfhood to the nation at large. Indeed, one scholar refers to Delany as harnessing his soldierly "disciplined masculinism" to the national organism, thereby becoming its "willingly-governed subject and defender."[2] A second look at the portrait, though, might not entirely confirm this reading of a consolidated identity. Delany stands firmly erect in the foreground, overshadowing entirely the flag and pale-toned scene behind him. His dark uniform signals his state fealty, but it also visually distinguishes him, intensifying our recognition of his black body. As an instance of African-American hagiography, the portrait properly focuses on Delany's imposing figure; yet in doing so, it also disconnects him from the national enterprise. Even as the lithograph patriotically gestures toward linking him to the nation, it equally suggests his resilient detachment from it.

The portrait ambivalently presents Delany's national affiliation. History, too, seems uncertain where to place him.[3] His relevance to our understanding of nineteenth-century U.S. race relations is indisputable. In diverse genres— journal essays, political treatises, fiction, travel writing, ethnology, oratory— he fervidly asserted what virtually all of white America denied, African and African-American agency.[4] But he has not yet obtained canonical status, perhaps because his oeuvre lacks an iconic text such as Frederick Douglass's autobiography or his life story the high drama of the latter's ascension from slave to freeman.

Delany was born free in 1812 in Charles Town, Virginia (now Charleston, West Virginia). His family prided itself on its patrician African forebears, claiming lines of descent from both a Golah village chieftain and a Mandingo prince, and his mother, Pati, took special care to ensure the literacy of her children. The townspeople disliked educated blacks, however, and for safety's sake she was compelled to move North to Chambersburg, Pennsylvania, when Delany was ten (later, after purchasing his freedom, his father, Samuel, joined them). There and afterward in Pittsburgh, Delany worked hard to gain a solid

education. Under the tutelage of Dr. Andrew N. McDowell, he acquired sufficient medical training by 1836 to embark on a career as a physician (skilled in
"Cupping, leeching and bleeding,"[5] one of his advertisements ran), and, befit-
ting his own political aspirations, he became active in several antislavery and
black self-help organizations in Pittsburgh, such as the Young Men's Anti-
Slavery and Literary Society, the Temperance Society of the People of Color,
the Theban Literary Society (he became their expert on geography), and the
Young Men's Moral Reform Society. His membership in those clubs, along
with a trip in 1839 through the Southern states and the Texas Republic, in
which he witnessed firsthand the horrors of chattel bondage, impelled him to
a lifelong career as an outspoken advocate of black resistance and renewal.

Delany emerged on the national scene when in 1843 he founded and began
editing the *Mystery*. It was one of the first African-American newspapers, and
helped to foster black communal self-respect. Its stirring articles, in fact, led
one contemporary editor to remark that one "would almost think that he was
back in old Africa, surrounded by the noble fathers."[6] When the paper folded
because of inadequate funds four years later, Delany joined Frederick Douglass
as coeditor of the *North Star*. It seems to be the fate of African-American leaders to be paired off in stark contrast (Dr. King versus Malcolm X, for example);
such makes it easier, in the ideologies embedded in historical interpretation,
to grasp and delimit minority complexity. In the case of Douglass and Delany,
though, even the titles they gave their political journals testify to their polar-
ized visions. The *Mystery*, by name alone, anticipates Delany's later efforts to
preserve an African-American space unsullied by white intrusion; and the
North Star, with its title, focuses on (at least implicitly) the freedom path to be
pursued *within* the country.

The two leaders' discordant stances on the moral-political logic of black
emigration soured their friendship. Delany perceived Douglass as too much
an accommodationist, and Douglass, on his part, thought Delany too unwilling to work for racial integration within the United States. In 1849 Delany quit
his editorial post on the *North Star*, and he and his former colleague-in-arms
remained alienated from each other's perspectives for the rest of their careers.
His skepticism about the likelihood that black communities in the North,
much less enslaved blacks in the South, would ever be accorded equality and
garner respect within the borders of the United States was personally borne
out by two assaults of racial prejudice. He had successfully applied to the Harvard Medical School and had begun his first semester in 1850, but after only
one term the college's white students demanded that he and two fellow blacks
be expelled lest the school's reputation be tarnished. He also discovered in
1852, upon applying for a patent for an ingenious railroad device (designed to

help engines pull heavy loads up mountains), that black men were legally dis-
barred from holding patent rights. Such exclusionist acts were part and parcel,
Delany saw, of majoritarian bigotry.

He did not cease insisting upon the rights of blacks within the United
States, but he also vehemently believed, up through the first year of the Civil
War, that the road to political enfranchisement lay beyond the nation's bor-
ders. The black body politic, having been marginalized and downtrodden,
would need to separate itself from the coils of menialism within the United
States and seek advancement abroad. Toward that end, in 1852 he published
*The Condition, Elevation, Emigration, and Destiny of the Colored People of the
United States.* And in 1860–61 he led, along with the Jamaican-born naturalist
Robert Campbell, an exploratory expedition to the Yoruba and Nigerian areas
of West Africa. The subsequent document, the *Official Report of the Niger
Valley Exploring Party* (1861), earned its author laurels in Britain, albeit not in
the United States, for being one of the first reliable accounts of the region.
Both texts argue the need to found an independent black nation, a republic of
industrious African-American expatriates, which not only would demonstrate
to whites a capacity for self-governance but also compete with the South's
cotton kingdom. Delany also wrote a novel, *Blake; or the Huts of America*,
published serially in 1859 and again in 1861–62, a uniquely transnational text
that follows its hero's effort to incite a slave insurrection encompassing the
Southern states, Cuba, and Africa. When the Civil War began, he did not forsake a longing for a strong black nation-state; but his emigration projects, always planned with the attendant goal of bankrupting the Southern cotton
economy, largely became irrelevant, and so he directed his talents to marshaling U.S. black troops. After his stint as the Union's first black major, Delany
kept active in public affairs, working for the Freedmen's Bureau and holding
other appointments in the Reconstructionist South as well as becoming involved in the tangled web of South Carolina politics (he ran unsuccessfully
there for lieutenant governor in 1874). He died in 1885.

Delany's self-esteem was nearly boundless, evoking the remark from Frederick Douglass that he "stands up so straight that he leans back a little."[7] But
his pride or egotism, the sense of which pervades virtually all of his texts,
would not allow him to be satisfied with merely private or autonomous accomplishments. He was ambitious, both for himself and his people. The two,
as with all politicians, perhaps, need not be at odds, but in Delany's case this
double ambition crucially structured the civic thematics of his works, for as
much as he wanted to generate a geopolitical emancipatory space, a black nation, which would secure basic rights and engender respect from the world at
large, he also desired a black body politic in which he could insert himself as
the governing intelligence. Throughout his career, he fixated upon secretive

black enclaves whose rituals, mysteries, and organizational minutiae at once functioned to bracket out white oppressors and to privilege his role as the elite, inspired pedagogue teaching the lessons of black nationality. Calling for a stronger black agency in national and global affairs, he nonetheless remained suspicious of whether blacks, en masse, could fathom the pathway to their own rightful political destiny; and so, the various revolutionary councils and black political organisms that his texts depict invariably collapse into the singular figure of Delany himself or his personae. His fascination with the interior spaces of power, literal sites of authority as well as a more inward sense of self-sovereignty, can profitably be approached through a number of angles. Carla L. Peterson, in a mostly critical assessment, underscores what she takes to be a masculinist, competitive concern with white capitalist production; Robert Levine sees his entire career as playing out the thematics of maintaining against Douglass, in particular, a representative black identity; and Robert Reid-Pharr, in a rare psychoanalytical reading of *Blake*, detects a fixation on dyadic structures of domination and submission.[8] This chapter draws upon these perspectives, but focuses more specifically on the spatial metaphors in Delany's texts, on the dialectic between internal and external geographies of power. I suggest that his strength as a black spokesperson, his exemplary will-to-power, was premised on his charting the lineaments of a black nation: the promised palpability of that nation would solicit converts to his message; and yet its imperceptibility to the downtrodden masses, apparently, was also required to maintain the privileged command of the revolutionary theoretician.

The Denial of African Agency

Delany has been lauded as the forefather of the back-to-Africa movement of the later nineteenth and twentieth centuries; and, in current "canonical" pedagogic and scholarly contexts, he is coming into increasing visibility. Such recognition is long overdue, although one danger of his elevation into the canon is that we will forget the extent to which his vision matured through a long, active, and often contentious dialogue, directly or indirectly, with other African-American intellectuals who labored to redress both in word and action the plight of the country's black populace by promoting ventures outside of the continent. Alexander Crummell, born in the United States in 1819 and dying in 1898, was roughly Delany's contemporary, and the ideological positions of the two men warrant brief comparison to show how separatism, as an alternative to integrationism, had its own divisive agendas. Crummell, who took his training as an Episcopalian minister in England, first went to Liberia in 1853 as a missionary and then later held ministerial and professorial posts at the Liberia College. For him, the merit of the Liberian community was that it was a

Christian state, poised to spread the Gospel to surrounding regions. He
therefore saw his twenty years on the continent as serving the cause of Christianity as much as black nationalism. For Delany, however, an African-
American settlement in Africa could base its claim of nationality only on the
surety of its sovereign power; the Liberian colony was funded and sponsored
by the white-organized American Colonization Society, which he saw at best
as a patronizing meddler in black affairs and, at worst, as an organization devoted to vitiating any attempt at black self-rule. Career choices are not always a
sure guide to political-moral ideologies, but we could sum up the difference
between the two leaders, one a minister and the other a physician, by saying
that if the former sought to nurture the African-American or African soul, the
latter sought to medicate the African-American geobody, to raise it from debilitation to power.[9] Delany is not, perhaps, a better gauge than Crummell or
other black leaders of the mood and political aspirations of nineteenth-century
African-Americans. It is, though, the singular intensity which he brought to
bear on the racial and national issues of his day, or more so, as Robert Levine
proposes, his unrelenting effort to make *himself* representative of a corporate
black identity, that makes him significant to the cultural historian; and in this
chapter I will accordingly give due weight to Delany's texts in their psychological as well as political dimensions—for, as we will see, the two fold together in complex ways which challenge any attempt to confirm that, if there is
an American way, there is also an African-American way. Delany is equally
unique and representative.

   Africa figures to varying degrees in nearly all of Delany's texts, yet he only
gradually toward the end of the 1850s came to deem it as the most viable locale
for the emergence of a black nation, having initially targeted the Caribbean or
Central America. I wish to begin, however, with how whites thought about
the continent and its peoples, for whatever Africa stood for in Delany's mind,
what it stood for in the majority culture's mind directly and indirectly informed his strategies for black racial uplift. Consider, first, the Bayard Taylor
poem that I cited in my introduction, "The Continents," typifying the genre of
the geographical allegory or masque, still popular in the antebellum era, in
which personified global regions sentiently bespeak their history, present
status, and future destiny. Taylor's stanzas on Africa describe it as a Niobe figure, grieving for her dispersed, enslaved children:

> Then from her seat, amid the palms embowered
>   That shade the Lion-land,
> Swart AFRICA in dusky aspect towered—
>   The fetters on her hand!
> Backward she saw, from out her drear eclipse,
>   The mighty Theban years,

And the deep anguish of her mournful lips
Interpreted her tears.

"Wo for my children, whom your gyves have bound
Through centuries of toil;
The bitter wailings of whose bondage sound
From many a stranger-soil!
Leave me but free, though the eternal sand
Be all my kingdom now—
Though the rude splendors of barbaric land
But mock my crownless brow!"[10]

Here, according to Taylor, Africa mournfully ruminates on the gulf between past Egyptian glories and present degradation. Africa, construed at once as the entirety of the continent and, more particularly, as the desert wasteland of Egypt, has not coalesced into a nation-state nor will it, it seems, in the future. And because the poet sees Africa as a political nonentity, he likewise cannot imagine that diaspora groups might desire to reaffiliate themselves with the ancestral homeland, finding empowerment by either recalling its ancient Egyptian and Ethiopian civilizations or by resettling there in the hopes of establishing a new black nation. Africa and African-Americans for Taylor can hold no positive, mutually beneficial relation, but only one of negativity. Slaves with their hopeless "bitter wailings" and the continent immobilized by grief: both, he implies, will remain inexorably "fetter[ed]" by their own political-historical inefficacy.

Taylor's poem brackets out alternative narratives that might complicate its hierarchical schemata. For other Americans, both white and black, the geographical/discursive sites of Haiti, Cuba, the Liberian colony, as well as ancient Egypt or Ethiopia loomed more importantly, and were key to debates over the relationship between Africa and U.S. slavery. Recent scholarship, such as that of Eric Sundquist and Wilson J. Moses, has insightfully charted the complex warp and woof of these non-U.S. contexts, which divulge the fabric of American history and culture to be poly-geographical, not a matter of only one dominant strand going, as it were, from New England across the Mississippi to the western frontier.[11] In the previous chapter, I addressed how, especially for Ephraim G. Squier, tropical America's hybrid races and history both vexed and intensified the quest toward some "pure" archaeological-historical space, and we could consider Delany's insertion of his fictional black hero, Blake, into the real scenes of mid-nineteenth-century Cuban politics (which I will speak of later) as being highly relevant as a minority counterstory to the white historical imaginary of tropical America represented by Squier.

The turmoil and bloodletting of the St. Domingo revolution appalled many U.S., and especially Southern, commentators, but white abolitionists often had more tempered responses. John Greenleaf Whittier, for example, wrote verses lauding Touissant L'Ouverture, the Haitian revolutionary, as a patriot of liberty undeservedly scorned because of his race:

> Dark Haytien! for the time shall come, yea,
> even now is nigh,
> When, everywhere, thy name shall be
> Redeemed from color's infamy.[12]

For the black author William Wells Brown, in his *St. Domingo: Its Revolutions and its Patriots* (1855), Touissant inspirationally obtained the stature (absent the flaws) of Napoleon and Washington. If the latter two embodied the motor-force of European or U.S. history at key moments, the black leader's liberty fight heralded nothing less than the angry resurgence of the total diasporic population: "The exasperated genius of Africa" will "rise from the depths of the ocean, and show its threatening form; and war against the tyrants would be the rallying cry."[13]

That was history in its recent or proleptic form. Moses shows that what Taylor cursorily sketches in "The Continents" only for contrast, the splendors of the black Egyptian or Ethiopian ancient *past*, was more amply filled in by a gamut of pre– and post–Civil War African-American authors, from Robert B. Lewis in his *Light and Truth: Collected from the Bible and Ancient Modern History, Containing the Universal History of the Colored and Indian Race* (1844) to Joseph E. Hayne in *The Ammonian or Hamitic Origin of the Ancient Greeks, Cretans, and All the Celtic Races* (1905).[14] More prominent African-American leaders, such as Crummell, Douglass, or, as we will see in the last section of this chapter, Delany himself, occasionally drew upon these Afro-centric stories of the past as modes of cultural ennoblement. They did not, though, lose sight of the need for current action, a virtue that Moses implicitly sees as missing in the cloudy musings of their less activist peers:

The misty days of lost civilizations and vaguely recorded histories were grist for the mills of black racial romantics who asserted the existence of a noble "Hamitic" race or a black "Pelasgian" empire that once dominated the ancient world. . . . The authors of this tradition envisioned a utopia of the past in which their ancestors, a race of superman, had erected civilizations from the banks of the Indus to the British Isles. According to various theories, the cultures of the Assyrians, the Babylonians, the Egyptians, the Carthaginians, the Cretans, the Pelasgians, and the Druids had all been black.

Racial enthusiasts asserted that the cultural relics of the primal civilizations were still to be detected among pristine African warrior tribes. The authors of this tradition explored various theories of decline to explain the descent of the African race from ancient glory into a state of barbarism. They were therefore concerned with interpreting the cycles of history, in order to understand those processes that might lead to a plan for African redemption based upon the virile barbarism and ancient dignity of warlike nations of the African interior.[15]

We should keep in mind, though, that the effort to resurrect a dignified racial-historical lineage took place in the context of white genealogies that granted Africans or African-Americans only the most debased roles in world history. The books of these Afro-"enthusiasts" are no more fanciful than *Types of Mankind*, the racist volume that Josiah C. Nott and George R. Gliddon published in 1854, which defamed the cultural past and legacy of all non-European peoples by its partisan, bigoted reading of cranial shapes and biblical and archaeological records.

Whether at the hands of romanticizing black historians or racist white ethnologists, depictions of Africa could be willfully shaped to serve each camp's agendas because, in part, knowledge about Africa and its peoples was only remotely informed by firsthand acquaintance (not until the 1860s and 1870s did the genre of white, masculinist-scientific exploration fully become popular, with the travel writings of Paul Belloni Du Chaillu and Henry Morton Stanley).[16] The U.S. naval squadron patrolled the eastern and western coastlines to hinder the traffic in slaves (with only checkered success), and Salem merchants maintained a sizable commercial trade in spices, hides, ivory, palm oil, gold dust, and dyewood in exchange for tools and household goods such as crockery, hatchets, and tin buckets.[17] The texts, including Horatio Bridge's *Journal of an African Cruiser* (1845) and Commander Andrew H. Foote's *Africa and the American Flag* (1854), reporting on U.S. relations with the coastal tribes of West and East Africa, repay study for their attempts to reconcile the bite of conscience (both are antislavery) and the militaristic thrill of taking punitive action against native raids on naval supplies.[18] But such reports were less influential in shaping the antebellum imaginary of Africa than the Classical and European tradition of mainly fabulistic travel and geographical writing, British exploratory-missionary texts such as Mungo Park's 1797 *Travels in the Interior Districts of Africa*, and, of course, the polemical depictions of Africa in pro- and antislavery literature.

Pre-Enlightenment travel and geographical texts—from the ancient accounts of Herodotus and Pliny the Elder to the fourteenth-century *Travels of Sir John Mandeville*—were based more on myth and fantasy than on direct contact, and typically populated Africa with odd beasts, exotic plants, and strange people. The portraits of Africa as a realm of aberration gradually diminished during the Renaissance: in part because of the availability of texts written by Muslim scholars living in Spain, Sicily, and the Middle East; and in part because the African landmass simply became clearer in outline after Vasco da Gama rounded the Cape of Good Hope in 1498. These Classical through Renaissance texts see Africans as exotic, often as grotesque, but also as wondrous and not necessarily inferior to Europeans.[19] Seventeenth-century rationalizations of the slave trade and then eighteenth-century Enlightenment theories of progressive history, however, combined to transform Africa from being the abode of odd bodies and species, of the heteroclite, to being the abject continent, the lowest on the hierarchy ascending from barbaric to pastoral, from pastoral to civilized. By the early decades of the nineteenth century, the discourses of history, ethnology, and geography collectively posited what hitherto could have been seen as merely differences of locale as being, rather, differences along a moralized, developmental continuum. And according to this new scheme, Africa was not just strange: it stood at the very nadir of social being.[20]

Such bias comported with the faith in the power of commerce, which typically was cast as enjoining more than the mere trade of commodities. Mercantile ideology, especially in the hands of Adam Smith, insisted upon sociability among nations as the instrument of an exchange of ideas. The notion became a commonplace in the nineteenth century and helped provide a racial-moral prop to commercialism. Horace Bushnell, one of the most famous U.S. theologians of the era, for example, in July of 1845 delivered a lecture on the "Moral Uses of Commerce and the Sea" while on board the packet-ship *Victoria*; it was later printed in *The Merchants' Magazine*:

> It is only in the great inland regions of the world, as in Central Africa and Asia, that bigotry and inveterate custom have their seat. In these vast regions that never saw the sea, regions remote from the visits of commerce and the moving world, men have lived from age to age without progress, or the idea of progress, crushed under their despotisms, held fast in the chains of indomitable superstition, rooted down like their trees, and motionless as their mountains.[21]

The imperatives of commercial sociability received metahistorical backing in the theories of G. W. F. Hegel, who in *The Philosophy of History* (1837) defined Africa as being a continent not just stagnated in the progress of time but also solipsistically self-enclosed. Hegel, reframing European ignorance of Africa and African peoples as African ignorance, offered his now notorious gloss on African isolation: "Africa . . . as far as History goes back, has remained—for all purposes of connection with the rest of the World—shut up; it is the Goldland compressed within itself—the land of childhood, which lying beyond the day of self-conscious history, is enveloped in the dark mantle of Night."[22]

Few midcentury scholars in the United States, much less the man or woman in the street, had read Hegel, but his and analogous ideas surfaced in a number of ways. Texts such as Samuel G. Morton's *Crania Aegyptiaca* (1841) or Josiah C. Nott and George R. Gliddon's ethnological treatise, *Types of Mankind*, drew upon European scholarship and the relatively new sciences of comparative anatomy to undercut African agency. A significant proportion of both are given over to showing that Caucasians ruled ancient Egypt, in the effort to eclipse Africans from a dignified role in the theater of world history. Morton, for instance, concluded that the "valley of the Nile, both in Egypt and in Nubia, was originally peopled by a branch of the Caucasian race. . . . Negroes were numerous in Egypt, but their social position in ancient times was the same that it now is, that of servants and slaves."[23] Frederick Douglass's appraisal of such ethnological bigotry—"scientific moonshine"—is apposite, but few whites except when briefly musing in poetry would credit ancient Egyptian civilization as being a black-ruled one.[24] The typical white response we may judge by hearing Bayard Taylor's nonpoetic evaluation in *A Journey to Central Africa* (1854): "Those friends of the African Race, who point to Egypt as a proof of what that race has accomplished, are wholly mistaken. The only negro features represented in Egyptian sculpture are those of slaves and captives taken in the Ethiopian wars of the Pharaohs."[25] The Hegelian theory of Africa's ignoble isolation was also confirmed, as we saw in Chapter 1, by Arnold Guyot's highly regarded 1849 geography textbook *The Earth and Man*. Guyot, we will recall, ranked all landmasses hierarchically; and, echoing Hegel, he explained how the African continent's topography inexorably determined its destiny: Africa "is far the most simple [of continents] in its forms. Its mass, nearly round or ellipsoidal, is concentrated upon itself. It projects into the ocean no important peninsula, nor any where lets into its bosom the waters of the ocean. It seems to close itself against every influence from without" (27). Such geographical discourse, in turn, shaped how U.S. missionaries and U.S. naval commanders perceived the continent. "[P]hysical geography has blighted Africa with the curse of barbarism," the Reverend Thomas J. Bowen stated in *Central Africa: Adventures and Missionary Labors in Several Countries in the Interior of Africa, from 1849 to 1856* (1857): the northern deserts "arose as an impassable barrier to that current of eastern civilization which has overflowed Europe and America," and the continent's immense "fertile interior has given unbounded scope to that barbarism which requires nothing but food and animal gratification."[26] Commander Foote of the U.S. naval squadron wrote, likewise, that the "sea does not deal kindly with Africa," for "it wastes or guards the shores with an almost unconquerable surf. . . . Hence ocean commerce was unknown to them." Paraphrasing Guyot's theory of geographical diffusion, Foote elaborates that in Africa "a declension of our nature took place from Egypt in two directions; one through the central plains down to the marshes of the Gaboon or the Congo river, where the aberrant peculiarities of the negro seem most developed; and the other along the mountains, by the Nile and the Zambeze, until the Ethiopian sank into the Hottentot."[27]

The image of Africa as a self-incarcerated body—lacking history, governmental forms, intellection—dominated both white pro- and antislavery polemics. In the proslavery novel *The Black Gauntlet: A Tale of Plantation Life in*

South Carolina (1852), penned by Mrs. Henry R. Schoolcraft (wife of the famed ethnologist, a direct quotation from Hegel serves in her conclusion to justify U.S. slavery as a stage of African liberation: "Hegel's Philosophy of History, an imperishable monument of human genius, says [that] 'slavery is itself a phase of advance from the merely isolated sensual existence, a phase of education, a mode of becoming participant in a higher morality and the culture connected with it.' "[28] For Schoolcraft, imposing fetters on the African-American is the solution to the African peoples' failure of self-liberation. Such denigrating depictions of Africa were a staple of proslavery literature, appearing for example in William J. Grayson's *The Hireling and the Slave* (1856):

> In this new home, whate'er the negro's fate—
> More blessed his life than in his native state!
> No mummeries dupe, no Fetich charms affright,
> No rites obscene diffuse their moral blight;
> Idolatries, more hateful than the grave,
> With human sacrifice, no more enslave;
> No savage rule its hecatomb supplies
> Of slaves fore slaughter when a master dies:
> In sloth and error sunk for countless years
> His race has lived, but light at last appears—
> Celestial light: religion undefiled
> Dawns in the heart of Congo's simple child.[29]

One did not need to embrace the peculiar institution to endorse the idea that U.S. slavery was a sort of geographical *felix culpa.* Virtually all white written documents on Africa and African colonization deem slavery, however deplorable, as part of a providential plot to redeem the continent. So spoke David Christy in *Ethiopia: Her Gloom and Glory, as Illustrated in the History of the Slave Trade and Slavery, the Rise of the Republic of Liberia, and the Progress of the African Missions* (1857), arguing that a new "passion for equal rights and privileges . . . [now] infused into their breasts" testifies to how the "captivity [of blacks] among us seems to have been but a preparatory step" toward the "powerful nation" of Liberia.[30] And so spoke the Reverend Bowen in *Central Africa,* as he witnessed "African colonization and African missions arising from this slavery, and flowing back as a river of light and life upon the African continent. . . . [We should] say with Jacob; 'Verily God is in this place, and I knew it not.' "[31]

The previously alluded to texts maintain a racist tautology: because of their association with a passive, stagnant Africa, U.S. blacks are to be denigrated; and so, too, is Africa because its denizens may potentially imbibe the lessons of civilization only when transported elsewhere. The crossover between abject body and benighted continent was complicated by a third element, usually skipped over in geographical writing, but emphasized in novels centered on blacks in Africa and America—that is, the black household. Harriet Beecher Stowe in her best-selling *Uncle Tom's Cabin* (1852) shows a high regard for the domestic virtues of the plantation slaves she portrays, yet the politics of domesticity do not quite translate for her into the politics of a black nation. Her slave characters are relegated to associative bonds only within the household or beyond the purview of the United States itself, in the nonspace in terms of what the novel represents of the Liberian colony, where George Harris after having heroically escaped slavery seeks refuge for himself and his family. Stowe was well informed about Liberia, and allows George to voice the "yearning" of his "soul . . . for an African *nationality*." Nowhere within the confines of the novel, however, does she permit the reader to situate himself or herself vicariously within a palpably realized black civic community. The African state that George desires, where his "people" shall "have a tangible, separate existence," does not fictionally materialize. Instead, the entirety of the African continent, in the main narrative, is metaphorically collapsed into the martyred, passive body of Uncle Tom, repeating, in essence, the trope of bondage that informs Bayard Taylor's poem "The Continents": "And this, oh Africa! latest called of nations,—called to the crown of thorns, the scourge, the bloody sweat, the cross of agony,—this is to be thy victory; by this shalt thou reign with Christ when his kingdom shall come on earth." Stowe's world-redemptive Ethiopianist language (based upon Psalms 68:31—"Princes shall come out of Egypt; Ethiopia shall soon stretch forth her hand unto God") was also adopted by some black nationalists, who linked African regeneration with Christian millennialism, and she might thereby be seen as confuting Hegel's or Guyot's premise of Africa's inactivity in world history. Stowe, to her credit, through multiple allusions enjoins her audience to heed the millennial story of African triumphalism; but such a story, cast forward upon a religious-utopic future horizon, necessarily cannot be concretely rendered in her narrative. The reader instead can dwell only on "Africa" physically subjugated, as Uncle Tom receives the lash whips that cause his death.[32]

Unlike Stowe, Sarah J. Hale in her *Liberia; or, Mr. Peyton's Experiments* (1853) takes her black characters back to Africa, yet she also has trouble conceptualizing black self-governance. Hale's novel traces the stymied efforts of a liberal-minded Virginia plantation owner, Mr. Peyton, to elevate the slaves that he has seen fit to free. The first half of the narrative portrays the liberated slaves as inept managers of their own economies, whether on land granted to them by Mr. Peyton or in urban Philadelphia, because of their ignorance and improvidence. In the second half, the hapless former slaves have been resettled in the colony of Liberia, and here they more competently manifest bourgeois values. Hale, notably, can like black self-governance only when it takes place outside of the nation, where, as Susan M. Ryan comments, credit mostly redounds to white Americans for teaching the colonists the lessons that they in turn impart to native Africans: "Liberian immigration is, for Hale, a civilizing process. In order for Africans to achieve status as 'real,' civilized men, they must have been colonized by white American society (through the institution of slavery), must have absorbed white values and, especially, white religion, and then must return to Africa to civilize and christianize their native 'cousins.'"[33]

To be sure, Africans were not uniformly disparaged. If seemingly barbaric, they still had sufficient humanity to justify missionary labor in the first place. The Reverend J. Leighton Wilson, for example, from his experience of eighteen years in Western Africa hazarded that the inhabitants there "show as much foresight as almost any other people, in providing for their future wants; have made very considerable proficiency in most of the mechanical arts, and, at the same time, they evince not only a decided taste, but an equal aptitude for commercial pursuits." The natives may lack "written literature," he adds, but their oral "fables, allegories, traditionary stories, and proverbial sayings" display "close observation, lively imagination, and extraordinary shrewdness of character."[34] Positive assessments tended, however, to be merited only when Africa did not seem like itself. The Reverend Bowen in *Central Africa*, for instance, spoke of Liberia via the chiaroscuro effect of a primitive Africa: "We were surrounded by black men in a new relation, the citizens of their own free republic, civilized, and standing forth in strong contrast with 'the naked negro,' in his primeval rudeness."[35] Bowen's text here reflects a confusion kindred to that I noted, in Chapter 1, arising in Goodrich's ambivalent passage on the Hottentots—an indeterminate basis for making ethnogeographical judgments. Bowen does not see the mutual exclusivity of his terms, that if "new relation[s]" can change the "naked negro" the latter cannot be deemed possessed of unalterable racial characteristics. Yet precisely this split between perceiving innate features or geographical-civic features as determinative served the purposes of racist ideology. The claim of intrinsic racial inferiority, of a predisposition toward nonintellection and so on, legitimated the physical servitude of African-Americans; whereas the seeming solipsism of Africa's physical geography implied the necessity of removing Africans to the United States, where they might, as Mrs. Schoolcraft put it in her quotation from Hegel, "advance from the merely isolated sensual existence."

These images of an Africa enslaved by its own barbarism affected Delany and his coemigrationists mainly because, in the eyes of the majority, racial and national identity were inseparable. It is anachronistic to apply the rubric of an hyphenated identity, but we might say that African-Americans did not seem to deserve citizenship because the "African" side of the hyphen would always undercut the perceived merits of the "American" half. Delany initially sought to champion his people's rights *as Americans,* and only gradually turned to insisting upon an African-based (that is, racially inheritable or constituted) nationality. In one of his most oft-quoted passages from *The Wretched of the Earth,* Frantz Fanon speaks of the postcolonial citizen's "secret hope of discovering beyond the misery of today, beyond self-contempt, resignation, and abjuration" a past "splendid era whose existence rehabilitates us both in regard to ourselves and in regard to others."[36] Although sympathetic, Fanon remains skeptical about this anguished nostalgia when it does not translate into tactical praxis. He addresses, of course, the dilemma of the indigenous rather than the diasporic subject, but his remarks should caution us in respect to Delany's separatism. He came to favor Africa as the proper locale for African-American renewal, yet he likewise could distinguish sentimental from politically useful Afrocentricism: when he traveled to the continent on an expedition intended to found a black state, he did not engulf himself in the mere emotionality of a return to the ancestral, racially linked homeland. Africa, instead, most attracted him as a geographical realm absent of white authority. Paul Gilroy rightly reminds us that his "primary concern was not with Africa as such but rather with the forms of citizenship and belonging that arose from . . . an autonomous, black nation state."[37] With this caveat in mind, let us now turn to Delany's first major text, in which he espouses both his faith and *loss* of faith in securing an "American" right to proud citizenship.

Abjection, Elevation, and the "Nation within a Nation"

Arnold Guyot, we will remember, merged European geographical thinking with homebred notions of U.S. exceptionalism. Uniquely in the history of nations, the United States had transcended geographical determinism. "We behold everywhere the free will of man overmastering nature, which has lost the power of stamping him with a local character," Guyot writes; in the republic the "great social country wins all interest" and "all affection" such that there no longer exist "distinct peoples" (301). Delany's first major salvo against black subordination, his 1852 *Condition,* illustrates why blacks had slight reason at midcentury to feel part of this affectional national compact. The social station of those in the North seemed little better than those below the Mason-Dixon line. "[We are] mere nonentities among the citizens," he sums up, little more than "excrescences on the body politic."[38] The latter trope, especially when we recall his medical training, carries however a less than straightforward meaning: for as much as he here impugns the nation for spurning the minority body that ought to be an organic part of it, he also seems to indict that body—

what he refers to as a "nation within a nation" (12)—for its own debilitation. The pariah status of the "nonentities" may be a matter of the white-ruled republic's having rejected them or the result of their own negligence or deficiency. The trope highlights the tension evident in *Condition*: should blacks through intensified self-generated efforts strive to improve their lot so that the majority culture will accept them into the national fold? Or, since the majority culture will likely ostracize them regardless of effort, should they not instead regroup themselves into a separate body politic on non-U.S. soil?[39]

The question of whether to emigrate was a vexed one for Northern black communities and other leaders besides Delany, and so requires attention before we look at the treatise itself.[40] A belief in emigration as a remedy for U.S. racial inequality or in the interlinked destinies of African and U.S. blacks was, of course, not new. Paul Cuffe, a black Quaker entrepreneur and merchant, helped fund the transportation of thirty-eight immigrants to Sierra Leone as early as 1816, mainly intending them to serve as evangelical carriers of Christian light to their less fortunate brethren. One of Delany's tutors in Pittsburgh, the minister Lewis Woodson, in the late 1830s saw black nationalism and emigration (although not necessarily to Africa) as interdependent. Yet black leaders who advocated resettlement—whether to Canada, Central America, the Caribbean, or to various locales in Africa—did not garner widescale support. Would not exodus mean leaving Southern slaves in the chains of bondage? The counterargument that a puissant black nation on non-U.S. soil would exert a reflex action, either by competing with the Southern cotton economy or by proving in the world's eyes the rights of blacks to self-governance, seemed more sophistical than plausible.

Distrust, ultimately though, had as much to do with the authorship as the content of an exodus scheme. Northern blacks also shied away from the emigrationists because their ideas did not seem to differ much from those held by the white-led American Colonization Society (ACS), founded in 1817 to transport free-born blacks and emancipated slaves to Africa, and the mainstay behind the growth of the Liberian colony, which began receiving freed slave immigrants in 1822. (Liberia gained its independence in 1847, or at least such was proclaimed by its leader, Joseph Jenkins Roberts; the young nation was not officially recognized by the United States until 1862, after the South seceded.)

Delany reviled the ACS, because he correctly recognized that its agenda, in effect, was to preserve Southern slavery by implementing a policy of global segregation, in which free-born or recently freed blacks would be deported via the ruse of voluntarism to the African settlement. No doubt many of its members were well intentioned, but the essence of its platform may be gauged by Henry Clay's speech (he was one of the ACS's first vice presidents) addressed to members in 1827. The ACS's goal, indeed, was to expunge Northern *free* blacks judged to constitute a disrupting effect: "Here . . . the African part of our population bears so large a proportion to the residue, of European origin, as to create the most lively apprehension. . . . Any project, therefore, by which, in a material degree, the dangerous element in the general mass, can be diminished . . . deserves deliberate consideration."[41] Many procolonization treatises, such as Jacob Dewees's tellingly titled *The Great Future of America and Africa; an Essay Showing Our Whole Duty to the Black Man, Consistent with Our Own Safety and Glory* (1854), embraced the idea of black enfranchisement, but only as long as it occurred on non-U.S. terrain. Dewees favored the Liberian settlement because he believed that white America would never countenance its black free population: that separate "races of men cannot inhabit the same country upon equal terms . . . [the] American experience distinctly proves."[42]

Frederick Douglass and his followers concluded that the end result of any emigrationist scheme would be to deplete the country of relatively prosperous, politically outspoken blacks and thereby lessen pressure on the South to abolish slavery. Cyril E. Griffith points out that the African-American community held a "well-nigh universal disdain" for what were deemed "treacherous" proposals that, by intent or not, buttressed the efforts of the white-led organization.[43] The rewards of departing were simply too doubtful; and, as Carla L. Peterson maintains, women especially had little interest in leaving their homes for an uncertain fate abroad.[44] Maria W. Stewart, a free-born black activist who addressed African-American audiences in Boston between 1831 and 1833, drew upon the rhetoric of a resurgent Ethiopia to elicit a sense of her community's cultural dignity, but she had little patience with geographical separatism: "[W]hite men . . . [might try to] drive us to a strange land," she avowed, "[but] before I go, the bayonet shall pierce me through."[45] The fight for liberty and equality was to be waged on American soil, not in a distant clime, far removed from hearth and kin. Perhaps more important, promoting a black settlement elsewhere in the belief that it might commercially compete with the South, and thus eventually eliminate slavery, seemed a too circuitous response to the latter's horrifying immediacy. What Douglass decreed in the *North Star* in 1849—"Here we are, and here we shall remain"—likely mirrored the opinion of the bulk of his readers.[46]

Were it not for the passage of the 1850 Fugitive Slave Law, Delany and other emigrationist adherents would probably have seen themselves increasingly marginalized within their own communities. But the law gave new life to the movement, for alleviating slavery by political agitation now itself seemed implausible; and indeed, hundreds of free blacks in New York, Boston, Philadelphia, and elsewhere fled to Canada in fear that they themselves might be legally kidnapped into slavery. Thus when in 1851 Delany met with fellow emigra-

tionist leaders, including Henry Highland Garnet and Henry Bibb, in Toronto
for the North American Convention of Emigrationists, their proclamation for
an exodus took on a more urgent cogency. They issued a resolute call to depart:
"[We] . . . earnestly entreat our brethren of the northern and southern states to
come out from under the jurisdiction of those wicked laws—from the power
of a Government whose tender mercies, towards the colored people, are
cruel."[47]

Under Delany's urging, the convention members had declared their position in no uncertain terms, and so it will seem odd that in *Condition*, published less than one year later, he himself waffles on the key issue. He delays
proposing an exodus until the last fourth of the text, devoting the previous
three-quarters to an analysis of how the status of Northern blacks may be
raised *within* the nation's borders through concerted emulation of white "pro-
ducers" (44). This backtracking to a more accommodating stance and *Condition*'s consequent seemingly confused message have puzzled virtually all Delany scholars. The haste and strain under which it was composed might explain away some of its perceived failings. The preceding years had been hectic
and disappointing. Delany's expulsion from Harvard had dimmed his medical
ambitions, and he had difficulty consolidating his role as a national black
spokesperson in a fashion that would distinguish him from the always more
stellar Douglass. Less generously, we can target his competition with his estranged colleague as the source of ambivalence in *Condition*. He was not quite
prepared to disavow the allegiance of the black community still committed to
staying within the United States; and yet he was also unwilling to compromise
a sense of autonomy, as he felt Douglass had, by aligning himself with white
abolitionists and their paternalism (as voiced, for instance, in Stowe's *Uncle
Tom's Cabin*, which Delany later scorned, it seems, mostly because Douglass
wrote favorably of it).[48]

No doubt, Delany's reluctance to abandon the United States as the land
most suited to fulfill his dream of personal glory partially accounts for *Condition*'s inconsistencies and its noticeable tension between affirming black rights
to egalitarian treatment within U.S. borders and asserting, more radically, the
need for an exodus to Central America or the Caribbean, with the goal of
founding a commercial empire. I wish, though, to proffer an alternative explanation of *Condition*'s seeming contradictions. The core issue that runs
throughout Delany's oeuvre is, as I initially suggested, a question of agency:
how might that concern, we should ask, affect the rhetorical strategies as much
as the content of the tract? Delany, I think, wants to lead his reader through the
psychopolitical *process* of national dis-affection, a dynamic strategy that the
work's digressions and repetitiveness, as much as its inconsistencies, have
unfortunately obscured. The text, rather than unfolding a single premise, so-

licits the audience affectively to participate in Delany's own emergent disillusionment with the country of his birth, the country that has "driv[en]" African-Americans "from her embraces" (203). Only after he has established the
invalidity of seeking communal power within America, can he then move his
audience to see the need to find it beyond America.

Let us follow the affective strategy, one I believe to be more canny than is
usually recognized. It begins with a dedication—"To the American People,
North and South" by "Their Most Devout, and Patriotic Fellow-Citizen"—
clearly at odds with the volume's separatist conclusion. Here, Delany enunci-
ates his title to citizenship within the national compact, and the bulk of the
first half of *Condition* accords with this expression of state fealty by showing
how blacks have wedded themselves to the national enterprise. "We are
Americans" (48), he declares, linked to the nation by virtue of the "loved en-
joyments of our domestic and fireside relations, and the sacred graves of our
departed fathers and mothers" (48). African-American labor both free and
slave—what he calls the "bone and sinews of the country"—has been the force,
moreover, that has transformed the republic into a vast pastoral land of "extensive verdant fields" (66). And, not least, African-Americans have loyally sacrificed their lives in the Revolutionary War, amply displaying "*Amor patria*, or
love of country" (67). Domestic attachment, bodily labor, battlefield sacrifices:
such have earned the nation's indebtedness and warrant full repayment in the
rights and privileges of citizenship.

African-Americans should also be brought fully into the nation's fold, Delany argues in a long middle-section, because of their exemplary professional,
civic, and artistic accomplishments. His lengthy tally of dozens of black success stories is intended, however, not just to impress a white audience. If *Condition* falls within the genre of the jeremiad, its import cuts two ways: against
white bigotry, but also against the present generation of blacks (especially
men) who need to emulate their forebears and pursue entrepreneurial initia-
tive in "all the various business enterprises, trades, professions, and sciences"
(44). Such self-directed efforts to climb into the ranks of the middle class, he
indicates, necessarily precede political and social change. (Delany, to be sure,
early on critiques systemic oppression, tracing, in particular, the historical
scandal by which dominant groups come to deploy racist distinctions to justify minority servitude. But he tends to emphasize less the social or political
roadblocks to black uplift in these sections than how individual responsibility,
in addition to its intrinsic merits, will earn the respect of the nation.) *Condition*'s argument thus far safely comports with the bourgeois belief that economic felicity mostly requires personal application, and Delany indeed adopts
at times an haughty tone toward the black masses who, he implies, have lacked
the wherewithal to climb out of their own meniality.[49]

That said, I believe that we should not be too quick to critique Delany's arrogance. For his more interesting point about minority servitude pertains to its psychological consequence: a loss of morale and a debilitated sense of personal agency. His slogan about indwelling willpower—"If we but determine it shall be so, it will be so" (46)—is less glib positive thinking than an urgent call to resist passivity and fatalism. He worries that a "system of regular submission and servitude, menialism and dependence" has been "handed down from father to son" until "it has become almost a physiological function of our system, an actual condition of our nature" (48). Discarding the jeremiadic lesson that sons must follow the precepts of the fathers, Delany here notes the crippling effect of an all-too-literal genealogical bequeathal. He comes close to proposing that subjection results from some essential flaw within his own community's psychophysiological economy rather than being the product of a racist majority. Yet the remark is qualified, and his basic intent is less to condemn than to foster a sense of individual autonomy and self-sovereignty. If I am reading the affective logic of the text correctly—a logic that will conclude with his call for emigration, not integration within the nation—Delany's insistence upon self-directed efforts at improvement will be seen, moreover, as shrewdly strategic. He wishes his black audience to feel their potential resourcefulness, for only when the members of the "nation within the nation" feel self-empowered and an internalized sense of solidarity can they summon the will to recombine as a nation *outside* of the United States.

We can now turn to the volte-face of *Condition*, occurring three-quarters of the way through the text. Delany has encouraged his black readers to exult in the spectacle of exemplary predecessors and thereby assume, perhaps, that the white audience would feel compelled to re-evaluate its own prejudices. Now, however, he pulls back and nullifies the hopes of remedying racial injustices within the country. Individual black effort, accretively or in combination, in fact will not sway an intransigently racist society. Further humiliation, not elevation, awaits those who take on the arduous task of self-improvement. Delany, in short, sentimentally invests his *black* reader in the ideology of upward mobility, only to show its futile application on U.S. soil. The last section obviates the purpose stated in the preface: that his tract would "make each [race] acquainted" with one another and "disabus[e] the public mind" (10) of prejudice and misperceptions about black culture and history. His audience, seemingly inclusive through the first three-quarters of *Condition*, now becomes explicitly only African-American as the national space of "America" becomes regarded as utterly resistant to minority appeals. Alluding to the Fugitive Slave Law as testimony of the white majority's intractability, Delany now refers to national subjects, "Americans," through the distance of irony: "[T]here are no people who ever lived, love their country and obey their laws as the Americans. . . . Their county is their Heaven—their Laws their Scriptures—and the decrees of their Magistrates obeyed as the fiat of God" (156). And, to further polarize his audience, he at this point inserts a piece of the oppressor's discourse—the congressional text of the Fugitive Slave Law—within his own as a sort of political roadblock.

Given this "political monstrosity" (157), blacks have no choice but to flee if they wish to better their lot. *Condition*'s affective logic moves its black audience through three stages in respect to the national covenant—desire, disillusionment, and realignment—with the last one focused on futurity. In the final section, Delany envisions a reconfigured black communal body, whose future palpability he renders in a bold appropriation of New World discourse. The sentiment of being an "American," voiced in the earlier sections, carries over for residual effect into the last one, but that patriotic emotion is now shorn of its attachment to U.S. soil per se. "America" now means American terrain exclusive of the United States. First, Delany turns to a precedent for exodus, comparing the plight of African-Americans both to that of the Jews fleeing Egypt and to the "ever memorable emigration of the Puritans . . . to the wilderness of the New World" (159). In an appendix to *Condition*, "A Project for an Expedition of Adventure to the Eastern Coast of Africa," he calls for a "Confidential Council" (210) to entertain the prospect of African repatriation, but in the main text he asserts that the best chance for a powerful black nation would be in Central America or the Caribbean (he precluded Canada because he felt that nation would eventually be absorbed into the United States). Central America appealed to Delany on two counts. He believed that a viable agricultural empire could be established that would compete with the U.S. cotton economy and thus bankrupt the plantation system. But he also, although alienated from the United States, wanted to endow his project with the glorious aura of New World rhetoric. "We must not leave this continent," he exhorts, because "America is our destination and our home" (171). The scheme, moreover, is sanctioned by a power no less than that of Providence itself: "Let us go on," he concludes, "and possess the land, and the God of Israel will be our God" (208). Most critics confess discomfort with this last section. Forsaking U.S. soil, Delany has not adequately forsaken the geopiety of U.S. exceptionalism. We can deem him as naïve in this regard; or we may deem him a rather skilled rhetorician. For here, he has adroitly decoupled the meaning of "America" from the specific U.S. geobody, reconceptualizing the non-U.S. New World as the future space for non-Caucasian, non-Anglo-Saxon enterprise.

Condition looks before and after, to the causes of U.S. racism and its dissolution in a nonspecified future. Disturbing, though, is how Delany would get himself and the black community to the middle ground, to a concrete temporal embodiment of a black nation. He turns out to seem like an imperialist himself, as when, entirely overlooking native ownership, he declares a right of inhabitancy by virtue of a dubious ancestry:

That the continent of America seems to have been designed by Providence as an asylum for all the various nations of the earth, is very apparent. From the earliest discovery, various nations sent a representation here, either as adventurers and speculators, or employed seamen and soldiers, hired to do the work of their employers. And among the earliest and most numerous class who found their way to the New World, were those of the African race. And it is now ascertained . . . that when the continent was discovered, there were found in Central America, a tribe of the black race, of fine looking people, having characteristics of color and hair, identifying them originally of the African race—no doubt being a remnant of the Africans who, with the Carthaginian expedition, were adventitiously cast upon this continent. (171–72)

Robert Levine, struck by the impracticality and overblown New Worldism of the Central American scheme, suggests that it carries mostly only rhetorical force. The plan could be vague and grandiose because its main intent was to secure its author an audience and to nullify the authority of Douglass, who adamantly opposed a wholesale exodus.[50] Yet if Levine seems right on the latter point, I also think that we should distinguish our moral response toward Delany's imperialism from our appraisal of his proposal's efficacy. *Condition*'s last pages may be operating only in the realm of a mystified, utopistic politics, in which real political-historical arrangements do not matter. The previous judgment, however, is premised on the accidents of history as much as a sense of Delany's illogic or self-deception. Of course, neither the United States nor Britain would have tolerated imperial black ventures in the region; but only historical hindsight, by which we can glean macropolitical outcomes, validates our sense of the implausibility of a New World black empire having arisen.

Africa and the Physiology of Nation Building

Condition is intriguing as a political document; it also reveals the allure for Delany of geographical spaces whose contours enclose a privileged racial lineage (the Carthaginian "tribe of the black race, of fine looking people"). That interest had been exercised in his participation in black Freemasonry societies in Pittsburgh, and *Condition* holds similarities to a lecture he published in 1853, *The Origins and Objects of Ancient Freemasonry*. The 1840s and 1850s witnessed a resurgence of white fraternal organizations that carved out social spaces at once egalitarian from the insider's perspective and exclusive from the outsider's perspective.[51] In *Condition*, Delany had borrowed from the white discourse of New World exceptionalism; in *Origins and Objects* he appropriates the equally mystifying lore of Freemasonry as he argues for the legitimacy, denied by white chapters, of black Freemason societies. For Delany, secretive black sects have genealogically secured Moses' esoteric wisdom. It is "an everlasting inheritance" passed down from generation to generation, deriving from "Africans" who "were the authors of this mysterious and beautiful Order." Later, in a theatrical flourish, he pauses at the threshold of Freemasonry arcana: "Must I hesitate to tell the world that, as applied to Masonry, the word—*Eureka*—was first exclaimed in Africa? But—there! I have revealed the Masonic *secret*, and *must stop!*"[52] *Origins and Objects*, in effect, answers white conspiracy with black conspiracies; and, like *Condition*, counters white depredations upon the black body politic with the mystique of black exceptionalism. We can designate the privileged spaces, a future black empire or the sites of black Freemason ritual, as utopic; but a more apt term, because it connotes oppositionality, can be taken from Michel Foucault. Foucault applies the term *heterotopia* to countersites in which "all the other real sites that can be found within" a culture are "simultaneously represented, contested, and inverted. Places of this kind are outside of all places, even though it may be possible to indicate their location in reality."[53] Foucault's term directs us to the strategic utility of such geosanctuaries, which in Delany's case comprised select black communities—from the self-help societies of his youth, to the "Confidential Council" of *Condition*, on to the secretive seclusions of *Blake*—that he hoped would thwart the forces of race bigotry.

Put more simply, such enclaves helped Delany to sustain his faith in the black body politic in the face of its patent spectrality. The early 1850s continued to be stressful for him, and the reception of *Condition* did little to boost his morale. Although the passage of the Fugitive Slave Law won the emigrationists black converts, Delany's manifesto was dismissed by the white press for denying, as Victor Ullman phrases it, the "doxology of abolitionism" that the "Israelites must remain in Egypt and attack the Pharaoh" rather than flee the house of bondage. But it also was largely ignored by the black press and, most irksomely, by Frederick Douglass, from whom Delany had hoped, as he wrote to him, something more than a "cold and deathly silence."[54] If anything, though, a sense of embattlement made Delany even more inflexible in his separatist stance; and by the time he met with other leaders—Reverend James T. Holly and James M. Whitfield—in the Cleveland Emigration Convention of 1854 he had begun to plan a reconnaissance trip to Western Africa. The convention's committee members, however, tabled all proposals that entertained Africa as a site for immigration. It was to take another four years before Delany, at the third National Emigration Convention of 1858, held in Chatham,

Canada West (where he had moved in 1856), was able to obtain official sanction for an expedition; and it took two more years for his plans to solidify sufficiently to mount the Niger Valley Exploring Party.[55]

The expedition, drastically underfunded, required near herculean labor to organize it and drum up support. Delany also had to humiliate himself and go begging at the doors of the American Colonization Society for resources. It is not surprising, then, that self-promotion—an assertion of *his* role—fused inseparably with the project itself. He apparently saw the Jamaican Robert Campbell less as a coexplorer than as a competitor in the field, and the document that he wrote upon his return from nine months in Africa, the 1861 *Official Report*, carries a sustained subtext exalting himself as the prototypical leader, indeed the governing intelligence, of a future corporate African-American body politic transplanted to African soil.

The preface entails some ground clearing, an opening up of space for him to enunciate his leadership role. Delany insists upon the autonomy of his decision to travel to Africa. He tells us that in the "winter of 1831–32, being then but a youth, I formed the design of going to Africa, the land of my ancestry."[56] The official policy of the 1854 Emigration Convention prohibited schemes with destinations outside of the Americas, but Delany—reflecting once again his obsession with elite enclaves—proudly refers to his sponsorship of the "Secret Sessions" that made "Africa, with its rich, inexhaustible productions, and great facilities for checking the abominable Slave Trade, its most important point of dependence" (33). Here, the allusion to a black inner council serves two interrelated functions: he foregrounds his own role as an informing intelligence and gives notice that white intervention did not compromise the convention's policies. The "Secret Sessions," Delany recollects, reflected not some discord between the rank-and-file and its leaders, but rather the need to confound the conspiracies and "mischievous interference" (44) of the American Colonization Society:

I owe it to posterity, the destiny of my race, the great adventure into which I am embarked and the position I sustain to it, to make this record with all Christian (or *African*, if you please) forgiveness, against [white attempts] to blast the negro's prospects in this his first effort in the Christian Era, to work out his own moral and political salvation, by the regeneration of his Fatherland, through the medium of a self-projected scheme. (45)

The concluding phrase ambiguously posits both communal and personal agency. It also implies a motif increasingly apparent in Delany's texts: the conflation of a longed-for liberatory space with the grandiosity of his own selfhood. Unintentionally, the passage betrays that the settlement plan was less valued in and of itself than for the prospect of imperially expanding its author's identity. Here, the promise of "destiny" applies to the personal as much as to the communal.

Charismatic leadership, founded on the leader's self-confidence, is needed to inspire mass bodies, and so the fusion of boast and boosterism should not be challenged as merely exhibiting egotism. Elsewhere, however, Delany's lordly designs are more open to critique. The preface begins to articulate the crux of the *Official Report*: the presumption that he or like-minded vanguard U.S. African-Americans are best suited to regenerate Africa and rule a black African state. In perhaps the volume's most famous lines, he fudges the issue of his own imperialism by eliding the distinction between Africans and African-Americans. Consanguinity of race, he argues, underwrites the right of black outsiders to lead an African body politic: "Our policy must be . . . *Africa for the African race, and black men to rule them*. By black men I mean, men of African descent who claim an identity with the race" (121). Such pan-African/diasporic identification can be, as Kwame Anthony Appiah warns, "an important force with real political benefits, but it doesn't work without its attendant mystifications."[57] In this case, Delany employs a racial genealogy mainly to secure a right to rule, a right that often seems more pressing than the founding of a black egalitarian nation-state per se. He nowhere foregrounds, as a problem, the questionable legitimacy of that right, but large portions of the text are given over to a strategic melding of Africa and his own nonindigenous presence. Besides the genealogical argument, he adopts a psychophysiological rhetoric to defend the propriety of an African state's being led by himself and a cadre of other elite African-Americans.

Delany landed in Monrovia, the capital of the Liberian settlement, in June 1860. Before proceeding upriver to the Yoruba villages of the Niger Valley, where he would conclude his travels by signing a treaty with the Egba tribal leaders for the future use of a large tract of their land, he reconnoitered the political scene. Liberia had been independent since 1847, and thus was no longer scorned merely as a stepchild of the white-led American Colonization Society. Black leaders once indifferent or opposed to the colony, such as Henry Highland Garnet, consequently began to see the logic of sending more emigrants there. And the colony could count on the testimony of a number of black luminaries, including the Anglo-American Alexander Crummell, whose first visit there in 1861 made him a convert: "[S]uch was the manliness I saw exhibited, so great was the capacity I saw developed, and so many were the signs of thrift, energy, and national life which showed themselves, that . . . aspirations after citizenship and nationality rose in my bosom, and I was impelled to go to a magistrate, take the oath of allegiance, and thus become a citizen of Liberia."[58] Delany was less impressed. In his earlier *Condition*, he had lampooned the Liberian "burlesque of a government" (169); and in an introduction to William Nesbit's *Four Months in Liberia: or African Colonization Exposed* (1855), he had remarked that the colony comprised little more than a "hovel of emancipated and superannuated slaves, and deceived colored freemen, controled by the intrigues of a conclave of upstart colored hirelings of the slave power in the United States."[59]

Even though Delany in fact managed a degree of rapprochement with the colony's leaders while in Monrovia, in the *Official Report* his animus was still strong. The capital of Liberia was hardly what Horatio Bridge reckoned as a "black man's paradise," nor was it, as President John Tyler had put it, quite "to Africa what Jamestown and Plymouth have been to America."[60] Monrovia indeed struck Delany as a hopelessly ill-regulated community. He notes, in particular, what he sees as a "great deficiency in public improvements" and "public spirit" (58–59): few harbor facilities, poor municipal roads, and no dignified-looking governmental buildings. He disapproves of the citizens of Liberia "degrading their Capital to a town" to save expenses, which he equates with "declaring that a court shall not have a judge—the nation a President or Executive, or [that] there shall be no head at all" (59). Delany caps his impressions by commenting that insufficient self-government and "national pride" (62) result from the absence of an effective ruling authority: they "must understand that nothing is greater than its head, and the people of a nation cannot rise above the level of the head of their nation any more than the body of the individual in its natural position can be raised above the head" (60).

In counterdistinction to this malfunctioning relation of ruling head to the body politic, Delany traces both the literal physiology and political physiology of how a "*new element*" (110) becomes integral to the country. In a deft maneuver similar to the one we saw in *Condition*, he leads the reader across the threshold from U.S. space to non-U.S. space as he describes the sensations attendant upon crossing boundaries. Poised liminally aboard ship off the coast of Africa, he recollects a pained sense of exile from having left his "*native country for a strange one.*" The nostalgia of exile, however, is a false emotion, a "*mere morbid affection of the mind*"; and upon recovery, after a psychonational reorientation, "the love of the [new] country" he assures us becomes "most ardent and abiding" (64). The description of his transit from the United States and his entry into Africa is brief, and its importance could be overemphasized, but it seems to me that Delany here records the dilemma of the diasporic subject: the desire to unite with a land that potentially rehabilitates psychologically as well as politically only when one, in an act of communal self-fashioning, constructs an imaginary ancestral memory or sense of belonging.[61] The motif of psychophysiological bonding picks up again when, later, he luxuriates in the pastoral virtues of Yoruba. Delany disliked the political Liberia; he also finds little satisfaction in its terrain—it is mostly "a dense, heavy-wooded, *primitive* forest, rank with the growth and putrified vegetation of a thousand ages" (87). The "whole face of the [Yoruba] country," by contrast, "is most beautifully diversified with plains, hills, dales, mountains, and valleys, interlined with numerous streams" (70). As for the health of the body politic of the Yorubas—they offer splendid evidence, Delany adds, of a "self-governing element and organized condition" (82).

Yet if Delany, formerly an "excrescence" when living in the United States, now becomes psychically re-membered as he traverses the Yoruba countryside, he does not thereby submerge himself in the scenery of the land or indigenous political affairs. The process of revitalization in fact goes both ways, as long as the proper role of head and body, between Delany and Africa, is maintained. His response to the landscape is not merely passive. A large section of the *Official Report* reviews various tropical diseases and problems of hygiene, and it concludes with Delany's boast that he has concocted prescriptions for fever and other ailments, which "are entirely new, originating with the writer" (92). Missionaries involved in the Liberian colony, such as James Washington Lugenbeel in his *Sketches of Liberia: Comprising a Brief Account of the Geography, Climate, Productions, and Diseases, of the Republic of Liberia* (1853), often included chapters on climate, ailments, and remedies. The text at this point holds the practical purpose of preparing future immigrants, but it also serves a more tactical role when Delany calls for a cadre of "scientific black men, her own sons" to "produce works upon the diseases, remedies, treatment and sanitary measures of Africa" (94). The national body politic and what might be called the natural body of Africa become conflated, with African-Americans—that is, Delany—functioning as the supreme intelligence ministering to the continent's physiopolitical health.

Delany spells out the metaphoric equation between the medicinally regulated body and the governed body politic in one of the *Official Report*'s most telling passages:

[T]he establishment of all those social relations and organizations, without which enlightened communities cannot exist . . . must be carried out by proper agencies, and these agencies must be a *new element* introduced into their midst, possessing all the attainments, socially and politically, morally and religiously, adequate to so important an end. This element must be *homogeneous* in all the *natural* characteristics, claims, sentiments, and sympathies—the *descendants of Africa* being the only element that can effect it. (110)

The trope of a sympathetic medical agency draws upon Delany's training as a physician, his wish to avoid a dictatorial stance, and the tactical logic that perhaps all political theoreticians must use when they regard their role in transforming a mass body, a constituency requiring the quickening agent of an elite outsider. The passage allows Delany to sidestep what he always felt was the intrusiveness of the American Colonization Society, for if benighted Africa here will come to consciousness via an outside force, that force turns out nonetheless to be native, or at least that of a diasporic native son. The argument, of course, is largely specious: the goal of "homogeneous" bonding applies to Delany, not to the Africans themselves, who did not invite him to their land nor decry their own social forms as "[un]enlightened." His thinking about national belonging, in fact, apparently precluded a sensitivity to the mores and customs of the African continent's own population. The indigenes would need to adopt bourgeois habits—learn, for example, to "eat with a knife and fork . . . instead of with their fingers" (105–6) and engage in "all the well-regulated pursuits of civilized life" (110).[62]

Ultimately, Delany does not come across as caring very much about the African groups he encountered. More crucial was Africa's suitability as the differential locale wherein he might reconstruct himself as a sovereign citizen and, as the new "son" of Africa, father future dignified generations.[63] As the "new element," operating to regenerate Africa and provide it with a "national character" (111), Delany at once incorporates himself within the African geopolitical body and becomes a fully self-sovereign subject. Having done so, he can now look back and declare his disallegiance from the country that at the outset of the *Official Report* he had mentioned feeling nostalgically exiled from: "I have outgrown, long since, the boundaries of North America, and with them have also outgrown the boundaries of their claims" (111). Having fully decathected himself from America, Delany now, in a marked contrast to the genealogy of abjection "handed down from father to son," which he had spoken of in *Condition*, forecasts a future genealogy of national subjecthood within Africa: "I have determined to leave to my children the inheritance of a country, the possession of territorial domain, the blessings of a national education, and the indisputable right of self-government; that they may not succeed to the servility and degradation bequeathed to us by our fathers" (111).

History, though, led elsewhere. On December 27, 1859, Delany and Campbell had signed a treaty with the *alake*, or king, of Abeokuta. But the Yoruba leader reneged on the treaty (because of internecine African war), and with the start of the Civil War all emigrationist schemes were suspended. From Lagos, Delany traveled to London, where he became something of a celebrity as he reported on his venture before the members of the African Christian Civilization Committee and the Royal Geographical Society. When he returned to the United States he continued to lecture on Africa for the next several years, and for good effect he drew upon the mystique of African black princes. A reporter for *The Liberator*, summarizing an 1863 lecture in Chicago, observed that the "dress which the Doctor wore on the platform was a long dark-colored robe, with curious scrolls upon the neck as a collar. He said it was the wedding dress of a Chief, and that the embroidery was insignia, and had a significance well understood in African high circles."[64] Although Delany at several later stages in his life made plans to revisit Africa and gave the name *Ethiopia* to his last-born daughter, he was not to touch African shores again.

Ritual, Spectacle, and Revolutionary Pedagogy

In the *Official Report* we have noted how Delany deploys tropes of the body politic to insert his own essentially foreign presence into the African landscape, anticipate a future African nation-state ruled by transplanted African-Americans, and thereby envision obtaining for himself a glorious lineage replacing the ignoble one of "servility and degradation." *Blake*, his only fictional work, manifests a similar desire to create a black nation-state and, like the former text, does so in part to furnish him with an emancipatory space for self-exaltation. In the *Official Report* Delany collapsed nation-making, nearly, into a personal genealogical project; in *Blake*, the perimeters of African-American nationality also collapse inward, extending not very far beyond the ken of Delany's charismatic surrogate hero, Henry Blake. Yet the text does not thereby become merely narcissistic. We should take our cue from the novel's title, which at once conflates and distinguishes the singular revolutionary and the oppressed black groups that he seeks to mobilize. That the novel consistently subordinates the agency of the black masses (the huts of America) to the agency of Blake, to his intense will-to-power, testifies to Delany's conceit—but also to his recognition that what the minority, revolutionary theoretician can imagine and what real historical conditions likely afford an oppressed people, en masse, to imagine are seldom quite in sync. In *Blake*, the black nation-state does not become corporealized. It remains spectral, although the task of the revolutionary theorist, arrogantly or not, is precisely to hold forth the promise of its future palpability.[65]

Delany probably started writing *Blake* as early as 1852, and did not complete it until he returned from Africa. It was partially serialized before his trip in *The Anglo-African Magazine* in 1859; and serialized perhaps in full (the last chapters, if written, have yet to be located) in *The Weekly Anglo-African* in 1861–62.[66] We may therefore consider the novel as drawing upon his thinking about black nationality roughly in the decade between the publication dates of *Condition* and the *Official Report*. But whereas in those texts he had alternated indecisively among possible specific sites for the founding of a black nation, one of the signal virtues of *Blake* is the poly-geographical basis of its narrative. Fiction gave him the opportunity to pull together the disparate strands of his previous emigrationist projects into a more global web. By showing how diversely located black groups might combine in a revolutionary struggle against white oppression, the text may be considered, as Paul Gilroy proposes, a key inaugural document in the history of diasporic ideology, anticipating subsequent pan-African or transnational liberational movements.[67]

Blake initiates his rebellion in order to reunite with Maggie, his mulatto wife, after she has been abruptly sold by Colonel Franks, a Natchez planter, to his Northern relatives because she has refused to consort sexually with him. Those kin, Judge Ballard and his wife, first take Maggie North and then to their Cuban estate, outside of Havana. Blake angrily confronts Franks and then escapes the plantation, but for much of the first half of the novel his struggle to regain Maggie is suspended for his clandestine tour throughout the South and Southwest, where he conducts secret "seclusion[s]" (41) to instruct the black populace in the art of rebellion. He makes the personal the political, and vows to "complete an organization in every slave state" (42), an underground revolutionary network encompassing a variety of groups—domestic slaves, field hands, artisans, free blacks in New Orleans, and the escapees in the Dismal Swamp. When he discovers that his wife has been taken to Cuba, he follows her there, purchases her freedom, and then continues to orchestrate insurrection by mobilizing Cuban plantation slaves, free Havana blacks and mulattos, including the famous Cuban revolutionary poet Placido, as well as a cargo of native Africans recently enslaved and transported to Cuba in the *Vulture*, a vessel outfitted by a group of disenchanted former U.S. naval officers who also are conspiring to overthrow the Spanish authorities in Cuba. In an extended and, at times, obscure subplot, Blake takes service aboard the slave ship with the goal of commandeering it and capturing its armaments. The mutiny does not take place, but the revolutionary plot goes forward, in the last fourth of the novel, as Blake marshals his Cuban forces and becomes accolated by them as the "Hero" and "Leader of the Army of Emancipation" (251). The novel ends, although it does not achieve closure (since the last chapters may be missing), with the portents of a future battle between the black-led conspirators and the oppressing Cuban authorities.

As Eric Sundquist has indicated, *Blake* transcends the more parochial vistas of typical pro- or antislavery novels. It draws sycretically upon multiple literary genres, surveys the conditions of black life in a wide gamut of settings, and reveals that the diaspora did not result in African cultural amnesia, the latter most interestingly toward the novel's end, when Delany describes the officially sanctioned, but in fact subversive, black Cuban carnivals that incorporated African folk rituals. It also weaves together different historical moments—Cuban slave uprisings and their repression in the early 1840s; the passage of the Compromise of 1850, with its Fugitive Slave Law; and the annexation and filibustering fever of the 1850s, hallmarked by the notorious Ostend Manifesto of

1854, which in effect designated Cuba as the legitimate future property of the United States.[68]

Blake's story line, as a consequence of its temporal and geographical reach, is often meandering, and some of its interwoven plot and thematic strands lack clarity and resolution. Although all the plot elements do not coalesce into a tidy whole, the novel's theory of black revolution and effort to conceive a necessarily nebulous transnational African-American/Cuban nation-state nonetheless make it a uniquely fascinating antebellum political text. Delany portrays a pure black hero without flaw, whose revolutionary authority depends upon his ability to foresee, amid all daunting obstacles, the future lineaments of liberty. That capacity, as Delany makes clear several times—for instance, when Blake recites a poem alluding to "where Moses stood,/ And view[ed] the landscape o'er" (69)—endows him with the visionary faculties of a millennial redeemer. He never suffers, however, from religious delusions or the self-absorption of the fanatic. He seeks his goals methodically, and exhibits throughout the narrative a near uncanny resourcefulness. We learn, for example, that he has managed to earn and sequester, without Franks's knowledge, more than two thousand dollars. But what most defines Blake's character is his virile and indomitable spirit, a sense of self-agency that suffices to overcome all impediments. "[He] again started with a manly will," Delany tells us, "as fixed and determined in his purpose as though no obstructions lay in his pathway" (83).

Blake's willpower and revolutionary insight separate him from the other black characters of the novel, virtually all of whom rely upon him for instruction in the means and manner of rebellion. Indeed, the plot for the most part tracks successive instances of his pedagogical prowess, in which other blacks of varying degrees of what one might call liberational competency accede to his superior wisdom. Blake's pedagogical elitism appears early on, in his patronizing attitude toward Maggie's mother, Mammy Judy, who invariably counsels Christian submission. Mrs. Franks mockingly refers to Judy as that "poor old black fat thing" who is "religious to a fault" (46), an assumption of docility belied by the fact that even as Mrs. Franks speaks, Judy and her husband are plotting to assist their son-in-law's escape from the Franks's plantation. Delany himself, though, betrays ambivalence about Judy's capacity to fathom fully his hero's revolutionary agenda. Her role seems less calculated to confirm that illiterate domestic slaves could hold revolutionary sentiments than to highlight, by contrast, the awe-striking and learned figure of her revolutionary mentor. In one scene, Delany offers us a sample of the chattering "gossip" (57) between Judy and the other "matronly old occupant[s]" of the slave huts, making their political ignorance the subject of humor—"Wy, dat ole ablish'neh, Miss Van Winteh! Ah wish da all dead, dese ole ablish'nehs, case da steal us an' sell us down souph to haud maustas, w'en we got good places" (56). He intends, of course, more than comedy here. *Blake* often functions as an exposé, unveiling in the huts of America an ethnography of oppression, and we are meant to see how ignorance buttresses the control of the masters. Yet those huts also are obliquely shown to be sites of resistance. Judy is not yet ready to join the revolutionary vanguard, but her gossip feeds into a vital, underground network of slave communication. Through her and the other elderly slave women, the word of Blake's covert visits back to the plantation gets spread, sustaining the house servants and field hands as they await the maturing of his plans.

Delany's uncertainty over how precisely to evaluate Judy and her matronly authority points to an uneasiness or competitiveness in respect to alternative modes of black subversion. We see this most distinctly when Blake visits a band of runaway slaves ensconced in the legendary Dismal Swamp. Blake has already encountered in his trek from plantation to plantation the debilitating "despondency [that] ensue[s] through fear and superstition" (103), and he now exposes the delusions of conjure as he describes its superannuated practitioners.

When approaching the region of the Dismal Swamp, a number of the old confederates of the noted Nat Turner were met with, who hailed the daring young runaway as the harbinger of better days. Many of these are still long-suffering, hard-laboring slaves on the plantations; and some bold, courageous, and fearless adventurers, denizens of the mystical, antiquated, and almost fabulous Dismal Swamp. . . . [The] names of Nat Turner, Denmark Veezie, and General Gabriel were held by them in sacred reverence; that of Gabriel as a talisman. With delight they recounted the many exploits of whom they conceived to be the greatest men who ever lived, the pretended deeds of whom were fabulous, some the narrators claiming to have been patriots in the American Revolution. (112–13)

Nostalgic rather than active, mystifying their leadership role instead of imparting useful lessons, the conjurers squander their potential power in the swamp's hidden depths. Delany allows Blake to be "anointed" a "priest of the order of High Conjurors," but such rituals he feels are more hokey than valuable. Indeed, one of the conjurers, Gamby Gholar, agrees to admit Blake within their ranks precisely because he heralds an alternative to the inefficacy of their former efforts. They have previously tried to incite the nearby plantation slaves to revolt, "go[ing] out among them with sufficient charms to accomplish all they desired"; nonetheless, we are told, they could "not induce the slaves to a general rising." Delany presents their covert counsels as a laughable version of Blake's. Their "official meeting[s]" take place either in the "forest, a gully, secluded hut, an underground room, or a cave" (114); and so like Blake they understand the need for secrecy. The upshot, however, of the "wishes, hopes, fears, pow-wows and promises of a never failing conjuration, and tears of the cloudy inhabitants of this great seclusion" (115) is their recognition, upon Blake's advent, of their own absurdity: "[H]aving so long, to no purpose, depended upon such persons and nonsense," they themselves "are sick at heart of them" (137). The episode, like others I will refer to momentarily, reveals Delany's self-consciousness about the role of ritual in political praxis: that it might solipsistically retard, rather than galvanize, revolutionary action. The danger here, though, is that the burlesque aspects of the episode, intended by contrast to legitimate Blake's insurrectionist campaign, almost end up underscoring the latter's own irrelevance.

That threat is in part countered by demonstrations of Blake's sheer pragmatism. He counsels his followers that, rather than passively relying on faith or superstitious ritual, they should seek out all useful tools, particularly money, to help them defeat their oppressors. And, in fact, Delany cleverly refashions what in the hands of Harriet Beecher Stowe in *Uncle Tom's Cabin* were melodramatic episodes typographically echoing Scripture (as when she compares a heroine fleeing over an ice-jammed river to the Israelites fleeing Egypt) into ones that argue the need for practical measures. In one episode, for instance, Blake pulls forth the coin of the realm, a "shining gold eagle" (135), to bribe a white river porter into granting him and a group of escaped slaves clear passage; and, in another instance, rather than mystifying the North Star as an emblem of freedom, he instructs a group of runaway slaves on how to use it to map their freedom trail. But the most important pedagogical lesson is that his cohorts must have sufficient willpower to overcome their oppression. In each of the seclusions he organizes, as he travels through the South, Blake engages other slaves in a ritualistic conversion to his revolutionary ethos. The reader-audience never is privy to what exactly transpires in these clandestine sessions, and so we do not learn the details of Blake's plans. What we do get, as typified by the dialogue below, is how Blake ushers his novitiates toward a sort of revolutionary epiphany:

Whilst yet upon their knees [praying], Henry imparted to them the secrets of his organization.

"O, dat's da thing!" exclaimed Andy.

"Capital, capital!" responded Charles. "What fools we was that we didn't know it long ago!"

"I is mad wid myse'f now!" said Andy.

"Well, well, well! Surely God must be in the work," continued Charles.

"E's heah; Heaven's nigh! Ah feels it! It's right heah!" responded Andy, placing his hand upon his chest, the tears trickling down his cheeks.

"Brethren," asked Henry, "do you understand it?"

"Understand it? Why, a child could understand, it's so easy!" replied Charles. (40)

Blake imparts his lessons: "a good general secret understanding among" (89) his oppressed brethren; but we never overhear the inspiring specifics. Here and subsequently, when Blake as a "messenger of light and destruction" (101) wins himself converts, Delany melodramatizes the occasions and places where revolutionary wisdom is acquired. In one example, he refers to the "most secret and romantic-looking rooms" where the representative "heads of . . . many plantations" (102) conspire to plot with Blake. Delany invites, perhaps, white paranoia about these subversive black councils, but he also illustrates how ritualized organization is the necessary proto-form of the black nation-state that Blake holds as the desired goal of the rebellion. In short, the seclusions function to unite disparate groups of slaves around Blake's own will-to-freedom, and the mere *act* of covertly joining together seems to have an efficacy over and above the specifics of Blake's otherwise undivulged plans.

The scenes in *Blake* in which mere solidarity becomes equated with revolutionary agency should be seen in light of Delany's lifelong leadership roles within black self-help organizations or the various emigrationist conventions in which he participated. Yet if Delany oftentimes makes a fetish of secrecy for secrecy's sake, we should also acknowledge that all political organizations, from the smallest enclave to the nation-state itself, rely upon ritualism in various guises to constitute themselves. One sign of his canny attitude toward ritualism's role is that he notes how it can work to negative as well as good effect, in the hands of the oppressors as well as their victims. As a sort of inverse mirror to all the initiatory dialogues between Blake and his fledgling band of revolutionaries, Delany presents us with the ritualized conversion of the Northerner, Judge Ballard, before a group of Southern conspirators. They grill him about his allegiance to their cause and require that he testify to his commitment to the peculiar institution: "How about the Compromise measures, Judge? Stand up to the thing all through, and no flinching" (61). Delany also carefully shows, as well, why an emphasis on organization and attendant rituals is necessary. In pointed contrast to Blake's methodical preparations for revolution is the case of the intemperate slave Tibb. Unable when drunk to contain his revolutionary fervor, he hastily runs from one of Blake's meetings shouting "Insurrection! Insurrection! Death to every white!" (106), with the result being his own death. Tibb's problem stems not just from his inability to control himself but also from his premature willingness to make a spectacle of his own revolutionary body. He has not grasped the virtues, apparently, of secrecy.

Blake's role as the spirit-of-revolution teaching various black individuals and groups about the proper revolutionary ethos becomes nearly allegorical as the novel proceeds. He achieves a miraculous mobility as he travels to enlighten those in Southern bondage:

Swiftly as the current of the fleeting Mississippi was time passing by, and many states lay in expanse before him, all of which, by admonishing impulses of the dearest relations, he was compelled to pass over as a messenger of light and destruction.

Light, of necessity, had to be imparted to the darkened region of the obscure intellects of the slaves, to arouse them from their benighted condition. (101)

The last sentence echoes the language we have heard in white authors who wanted to redeem Africa from moral and intellectual lethargy, and, in a sense, Blake here assumes the mantle of providence itself in respect to the downtrodden. Indeed, as the Messianic spirit of liberation, he becomes almost a detached body, and his progress through varied locales, within and outside of the United States, is rarely impeded as he pulls otherwise disparate black groups—those on Southern plantations, the escaped slaves of the Dismal Swamp, the mixed blacks in Cuba, and the kidnapped Africans aboard the *Vulture*—into his revolutionary campaign.[69] It also does not offend the Cubans that Blake, a foreigner, presumes to lead their forces, because he turns out actually to be Carolus Henrico Blacus, the freeborn son of a prosperous black Cuban merchant. He had been kidnapped when young, and brought as a slave to the Red River region of Louisiana. As Robert Levine indicates, by nominating Blake the "lost boy of Cuba" (193), Delany conveniently if rather tardily endows his hero with a genealogical lineage that legitimates his right to rule the Cuban black and mulatto insurrectionist forces.[70] By the narrative's end, with Blake having assumed a number of identities and having formed many allegiances, he belongs, as it were, to no specific geographical locale at all. Such mobility is necessary for the novel's transnational thematics, but it also threatens to transform the main character into an allegorical stick-figure who increasingly becomes detached from the specific contingencies of locale itself.[71]

Blake's ascension as the very spirit-of-revolution explains, I think, two of the more puzzling episodes of Part II, the Cuban half of the novel. Blake, upon learning that Maggie is in Cuba, assumes the role of a valet aboard a ship in transit from Baltimore to Cuba, whose passengers include the former U.S. naval officers plotting to overthrow the Spanish rule of Cuba. When Blake finally locates his wife on a plantation on the outskirts of Havana, inexplicably it seems, the two fail to recognize one another (Maggie is now going under the name of Lotty). Allegorically, however, the misrecognition between Blake and his wife makes sense. Maggie, when Blake meets her, displays an utterly dejected appearance—a "careworn expression of irreconcilable trouble, unhappiness and sorrow, sunken eyes, a full suit of crimpy hair, but carelessly worn, well mixed with grey, the scar of a deep cut wound on the right angle of the forehead" (179–80). Blake, seeking out fit subjects for conversion, cannot recognize his own spouse because her formerly independent demeanor (earlier, she had been accused of being haughty) has been broken by numbing abuse.

And Maggie, so abused, cannot recognize the spirit-of-liberty embodied by her husband as he stands before her.

The other perplexing passage involves Blake's peculiar detachment when, to further his revolutionary designs, he joins the slaver ship *Vulture* in the hope of liberating its cargo of kidnapped Africans and taking over the ship and its weaponry. The sequence of episodes tracing the ship as it takes port to pick up slaves, those episodes' critique of Africans' own complicity, and the later detailing of the horrors of the Middle Passage all appropriately broaden *Blake*'s geographical arena and add to its pan-African politics. But oddly, Blake, whom the white naval officers suspect of plotting revolt, does not finally lead a rebellion aboard ship. The hero of the book, rather than marshaling his virility for a daunting display of physical revolt, stays "strangely passive" (236). The simmering and menacing anger of the imprisoned Africans, especially that of the chieftain Mendi with his "great piercing eyes" (234), strikes terror among the ship's officers; but Delany does not let Blake, the tutelary spirit of rebellion, guide the suffering Africans below deck to their liberation.

It may have been that Delany felt that his white audience would likely have abhorred scenes of a slave mutiny, but it seems equally plausible that he cannot quite determine the precise role of the black African masses in his hero's revolutionary plot. This discomfort with the African body politic (as opposed to the African-American body politic, incarnated by Blake) appears especially in a key episode when, after the ship enters a bay in preparation to pick up its cargo of slaves, Blake leaves the ship and ventures "into the forest" (212) to spy on the barracoons, the "coffleshambles of suffering humanity" (212) at the "trading post of the great factor, a noted Portuguese, Ludo Draco, the friend of Geza, King of Dahomi" (211). While he is gone, the white officers nervously ponder why Blake has left his duties: some "suspect[ed] that he might have been the employed spy of the English; while Royer and Costello, the mates, believed that the tendency of the Negro being degeneracy, he having before been on the coast and in the country, must have seized the opportunity of returning to the usages of savage life" (218). The belief that Westernized blacks might succumb to the lure of African "savage life" was common enough for Horatio Bridge to remark in his *Journal of an African Cruiser* that many of the U.S. Liberian colonists "have mingled with [the natives] . . . and preferred their savage mode of life to the habits of civilisation."[72] Likewise, the Reverend J. Leighton Wilson, in *Western Africa: Its History, Condition, and Prospects* (1856), worried that Liberians "left wholly to their own resources" were typically "too weak to withstand the influences of barbarism and superstition with which they must be surrounded in their new homes."[73] Delany ironically emphasizes that what the officers misperceive as Blake's possible recidivism (when he returns one taunts him about "[r]eveling I suppose back in the bush among the heathen wenches" [220–21]), is in fact his guerrilla tactic of gathering information about which native groups may be relied upon to fight against the partnership of the Portuguese Draco, those running the slave ships, and the notorious King of Dahomi. We are, though, given only one sentence about Blake's "communicat[ing] with many of the natives opposed to the king" (219), with the bulk of the episode turning on Draco's change of heart. His mulatto daughter has fallen ill in appalled response to her discovery of her father's business, and when she pleads with him he promises "never again to traffic in human beings" (220). Blake, hidden within Draco's mansion, becomes the "unexpected auditor" of the "scene" (218) of the slave trader's conversion. Rather than evincing *his* agency in Africa, he simply watches.[74]

The subtextual pertinence of these latter episodes may be discerned if we return to the earlier one in which Blake misrecognizes his wife. He must quell an impulse to intervene when he sees Maggie being beaten (he does not yet know that she is his wife); he restrains himself and can only look on as a "serious spectator" (170). Here as elsewhere we are reminded that the hero, for all his whirlwind of activity in the novel, also spends a good deal of time merely in surveillance of the various sites of oppression. He obtains useful knowledge, requisite to the revolutionary plot, and in the scene just alluded to he naturally must balance prudence with his desire to assert himself manfully; but Delany also foregrounds the spectorial gaze of Blake per se. Why he should do so becomes clear when we recognize that his hero likely embodies both wishful thinking and anxiety about his own agency in transforming race relations. More particularly, we may speculate that what the novel puts in tension is Delany's longing to exert himself in revolutionary battle and his frustration of being only, ultimately, on the sidelines. He was well aware that physical rebellion had its time and place; fervid revolutionism need not enjoin, as in the case of Tibb, a fatal prematurity. Yet these passages about Blake's spectatorship also begin to seem like a self-directed critique. As much as secretive enclaves foster solidarity, they can also bracket one within a delusory, historically ineffectual and marginal space. The problem, we may more theoretically propose, is that the dyadic relation of inside/outside substitutes a visual, spatial dynamics for an active, intrasocial one. The nation refused to recognize him as a citizen. It saw him only as a black man; and, in response, he recoiled into heterodox, black spaces whose main function, other than bolstering revolutionary ardor, was to fend off the dominating gaze of whites. The visual dialectic of the black enclave in nearly all of his texts, accordingly, at once empowers and subjects those within to an almost paranoiac patrolling of its borders. When Delany's surrogate, Blake, moves outside of those borders, he seems to have no body, becoming instead only a "serious spectator." When he is within the enclave's borders—in revolutionary councils, and so on—he has a body, yet his main task is only to rule the enclave itself.

Delany's ambivalence in respect to the physical violence of his hero is indicated most strongly by the fact that the only real scene of bodily aggression on Blake's part occurs offstage. Earlier, in Part I, we are given a fantasy of retribution that makes violence per se hermetic. As Blake travels, intending to "scatter red ruin" (128) throughout the South, Delany tells us that he had "met with no obstruction except in one instance, when he left his assailant quietly upon the earth." Delany cannot resist, however, adding a line that by now should be regarded as especially pertinent: a "few days after an inquest was held upon the body of a deceased overseer—verdict of the Jury, 'By hands unknown'" (68). Here, the desire for physical vengeance is at once indulged and decorporealized in its enactment. Outside of the black enclave, in white territory, the black body must be invisible. The latter episode points to the larger challenge facing Delany as he composed his novel: the dilemma, in the final analysis, of conceiving a corporate black revolutionary body politic *in action*.

If Blake's agency is obscured in the scene of his killing an "assailant," the agency on a collective level, not surprisingly, becomes even more obscure. The plot murkiness of Part II seems a product of Delany's penchant for secrecy and his difficulty in seeing beyond his hero's lofty self-conception. A sea storm frustrates Blake's plan to liberate the Africans aboard the *Vulture*, and the rest of Part II dramatizes how Blake melds various black and mulatto Cuban constituencies together into an insurrectionist force. Yet the details of the rebellion remain vague, with Delany instead repeatedly depicting the ritualized pageants of the liberty fighters, which more often than not center upon the exaltation of Blake himself as their leader. Eric Sundquist has shown how the novel's second half complexly restages the conspiracies and counterconspiracies involved in antebellum U.S.-Cuban political and racial relations.[75] What most stands out, though, is the sheer reiteration of scenes in which Blake and his coconspirators will themselves, through near incantatory dialogue, into adopting their leader's revolutionary agenda:

> "I hope much from tomorrow," suggested Placido.
> "We must make much of tomorrow!" replied Blake.
> "We can if we will!" added Placido.
> "Then we will!" decisively concluded Blake. (241)
>
> .   .   .   .
>
> "Let us then," said Placido, "make ourselves respected."
> "So far as Cuba is concerned, we are here for that purpose," replied Blake.
> "And if we say it shall, it will be so!" added Madame Cordora.
> "Then it shall be so!" declared Blake. (263)
>
> .   .   .   .

"I'm sure God's word is His will," added the Madame.
"We would what God wills," responded Placido.
"Then let God's will be done," said Blake. (285)

Such ritualized exchanges, in essence tautological, do less to advance materially the insurrectionary plot than to confirm the will of the conspirators toward revolt. Delany reassures us that thus "organized, the oppressed became a dangerous element in the political ingredients of Cuba" (257); but we do not, by the novel's end, see the prospect of any political transformation. The threat to the racist status quo, indeed, seems mostly to exist inside Blake's, or Delany's, own mind; and the revolutionary mise en scène never, finally, extends very far beyond these grandiose dialogues and injunctions.[76] That we get only portents but no actual revolution itself might very well, as Sundquist proposes, work by intent or default to the novel's advantage, for conspiracies arguably are most powerful when nebulous, acting to solicit paranoia.[77] (As well, of course, Delany could not consummate Blake's insurrectionist designs because political-historical fictions can rearrange history only up to a certain point. To dramatize a specific revolt would go against the grain of history itself and transform the novel into the merely fabular.)

One more reason may be proffered for why vengeance against race crimes remains relatively abstract in *Blake*. Frantz Fanon comments that abruptly unleashed violence—those "lightning flashes of consciousness" in which "my blood calls for the blood of the other"—although legitimate cannot be sustained: "[T]he leader realizes, day in and day out, that hatred alone cannot draw up a [revolutionary] program." Such emotional militancy, Fanon elaborates, depends upon "fresh motives of hating," which the colonizing forces may, in fact, strategically avert by calculated interludes of appeasement. From this perspective, when Delany holds his hero's physical anger in check it may be because he realizes that such, if it expresses agency, also returns agency to one's antagonist, insofar as the latter is required as the goading impetus in the first place.[78] It sounds like a paradox, but seems to apply to Delany: his desire for sovereignty, for self-rule, was so strong that he did not want to give time, in a sense, to *battling* his oppressors.

I mentioned initially that perhaps what most allured Delany was the feeling of his own self-sovereignty when located within empowering interior spaces. One concluding sequence in the novel aptly revises this spatial dialectics of power. Lady Alcora, the wife of the governor of Cuba, has heard rumors of an impending black uprising. The uprising turns out later to consist of only one drunken "slave," shouting in a frenzy "Blood, blood, blood! Rise, Negroes, rise!" (303). He also is not of Blake's party; rather, he has been a pawn in the conspiracies of the group of proslavery, disaffected whites (the commanders of the *Vulture*), who, fearing that the Cuban authorities will proceed with a liberalizing slave policy, deploy him to elicit a reactionary movement and to shift attention away from themselves. In lieu of a concretely rendered revolt, though, Delany invokes a puissant black nation-state by placing it within the mind of the oppressor, the unnerved Lady Alcora:

"I dreamed," related the Countess, "of being in the interior of Africa surrounded entirely by Negroes, under the rule of a Negro prince, beset by the ambassadors of every enlightened nation, who brought him many presents of great value, whilst the envoy of Her Catholic Majesty sat quietly at the floor of the African Prince's throne. I cannot get this impression from my mind, it seems so indelibly fixed." (266)

The passage neatly trades on white, especially Southern, anxieties about black rule. It inverts, for example, the fantasy of power that Mrs. Schoolcraft indulged in her proslavery *Black Gauntlet*, in which she speculates that were she "an absolute Queen of these United States" her first item of state "would be to send to Africa, to bring its heathen as *slaves* to this Christian land, and keep them in bondage until *compulsory* labor had tamed their beastliness, and civilization and Christianity had prepared them to return as missionaries of progress to their benighted black brethren."[79] In the episode from *Blake*, Delany divests Lady Alcora—at least in her nightmares—of her own sense of white sovereignty. She dreams of being within a black kingdom, but that kingdom, we might say, is also within her. An early scene, even more so, draws upon white phobias against blackness. Judge Ballard, a Northerner, lights up a cigar, whereupon a cynical Southerner taunts him with this comment: "Did ever it occur to you that black fingers made that cigar, before it entered your white lips! . . . and very frequently in closing up the wrapper, they draw it through their lips to give it tenacity" (62–63).

Such episodes, regardless of whether we choose to amplify their sexual undertones, also invert the fantasies some white authors had of discovering whiteness within the interior of Africa. In William S. Mayo's popular *Kaloolah, or, Journeyings to the Djébel Kumri* (1849), the intrepid hero, Jonathan Romer, travels to the continent where he finds a magnificent white civilization ("Cities, palaces, aqueducts, bridges, monuments, stood forth. . . . I gazed as one entranced") and an exotically African, but white bride (her "features were not at all of the usual African stamp.")[80] The most famous example of phantasmagoric whiteness, however, is of course in Poe's *The Narrative of Arthur Gordon Pym*. Poe's text moves from dark enclosure to dark enclosure—the ship's hold that Pym first hides in, and then finally, toward the end, the obscure, hieroglyphically patterned chasm of the native group that the voyagers encounter in Southern latitudes. Pym does not go to Africa, but the indigenes are described in a fashion calculated to remind Poe's audience of supposed African barbarities. To the extent, as in most of Poe's fiction, that the itinerary is a psychological one, the threat is not of being engulfed in the dark other, but of discovering racial darkness within; or, rather, the text's agenda includes the positing of a phantasm of darkness within only so that it may be exorcised to produce, via the chiaroscuro of contrast, a sense of white purity: the travelers emerge from the land of cannibals to witness, by the tale's end, an approaching, looming white specter. In the case of Melville's "Benito Cereno," it is the specter of blackness itself that cannot be excised. Echoing Lady Alcora's anxiety over her "impression" of subordination, Cereno, the debilitated Spanish captain, cannot vanquish memories of the insurrectionary slave, Babo, who has humiliated him, exposing the precariousness of his rule. The brilliance of Melville's novel, whatever stance we may feel he held toward the events he portrays, is to show that black/white power relations typically involved unacknowledged internal dimensions of *white fear*: not just that white communities might be slaughtered in the event of black insurrection but also that whiteness itself—the psychological certitude of white self-sovereignty—might not survive the trauma. The last image we have of Cereno is his melancholic retreat to a monastery, which stands in the line of sight of his black antagonist's severed head, where "fixed on a pole" it "unabashed[ly]" confronts the "gaze of the whites."[81]

Blake lacks the subtly of either Poe's or Melville's novels, but it nonetheless in the passages cited above begins to investigate the psychological as opposed to strictly political aspects of potential white disempowerment. We may credit Delany with cannily relocating black insurgency within the oppressors' minds, or we may feel that attending to their shadowy fears is of little consequence. *Blake* may, as John Ernest aptly phrases it, have challenged its audience to conceive a "reconfigured government of mind" as the first step toward abolishing racial servitude.[82] Or, as in the instance of Lady Alcora's nightmare in which a white queen's envoy pays homage before an "African Prince's throne," we may judge Delany to be somewhat less concerned about engendering a corporate black body politic than fantasizing himself elevated to a position of stately grandeur.

African Blood and the Iconography of Black Nationality

Delany's main texts, as I have previously shown, fused his yearning for a separate, strong black nation-state with a less public-minded ambition to garner prestige. The more he became preoccupied with directing black enclaves the more those enclaves became mystified. One of the most revelatory scenes exhibiting his fascination with hermetic power, however, pertains to his desire to insert himself—his own black body—within the hallowed corridors of the *white* nation-state. In February of 1865, he traveled to Washington to petition

President Lincoln to sponsor greater black participation in the war effort. His early biographer, Frances E. Rollin Whipper, re-creates a dialogue between Delany and Henry Highland Garnet upon what the former had hoped to achieve:

He remarked to the reverend gentleman that "the mansion of every government has outer and inner doors, the outer defended by guards; the security of the inner is usually a secret, except to the inmates of the council-chamber. Across this inner lies a ponderous beam, of the finest quality, highly polished, designed only for the finest cabinet-work; it can neither be stepped over nor passed around, and none can enter except this is moved away; and he that enters is the only one to remove it at the time, which is the required passport for his admission. I can pass the outer door, through the guards, and I am persuaded that I can move this polished beam of cabinet-work, and I will do it."[83]

Once again, an interior sanctum of power draws Delany. That he should pursue access to such political spaces is by itself not remarkable. Striking, however, is the lingering, almost fetishizing manner in which he sees himself passing into the inward chamber, at once a sacrosanct space representing the very core of the democratical state and the privileged site, the "mansion," of executive authority. The motives of the egalitarianist and political egoist are, quite simply, inseparable.

Delany's rendering of inward and outward, hermetic and national, geopolitical spaces did not end after the Civil War. One of his most interesting, albeit most neglected, texts is the 1879 monograph *Principia of Ethnology: The Origin of Races and Color, with an Archeological Compendium of Ethiopian and Egyptian Civilization, from Years of Careful Examination and Enquiry.* I have cited in full the ponderous title to suggest the full range of its contents. But we should not let the volume's pretentiousness keep us from seeing its dual strategy of redeeming blackness on both micro and macro levels. *Principia* undertakes a refutation of the then still current theories of "Nott, Gliddon, and others" (9), the midcentury polygenesists who had advocated the idea of absolutely distinct races and claimed that ancient Egypt was white-ruled. In *Blake*, Delany slyly made Lady Alcora's nightmares the habitat of blackness. Here, he investigates white physiology. He proffers what he takes to be an astonishing fact of epidermal chemistry: the "color . . . of the negro . . . is no more nor less than *concentrated rouge*," and this pigment "gives also in turn, the most delicate rosy tint to the ruddy cheeks and ruby lips of the lily white skin of the proudest and most beautiful white lady of the Caucasian race" (32). Delany obviously intends to provoke and challenge anxieties, on the part of his white audience, about racial admixture or contamination. Yet the real purpose of this passage or the ones in *Blake* about a black invasion of white bodies or spaces has little to do with their shock value of racial threat. Delany was, to be sure, proud of his blackness, but ultimately he was more concerned about the politics of race than its supposed biology.

FIG. 13. Garden of the Hesperides iconography in Martin R. Delany's *Principia of Ethnology: The Origin of Races and Color* (1879; Baltimore: Black Classics Press, 1991), facing page 80. (Courtesy of the Black Classics Press.)

If *Principia* seeks to lend African-American blackness innate dignity on the micro or epidermal level, it seeks to do so as well on the macro level of state iconography. Delany in this last text also creates, to recall Foucault's term, an heterotopic archive. The bulk of the volume promotes a resolutely Afrocentric version of world history. He maintains that the rulers of Egypt were black rather than white, and that African wisdom has been genealogically transmitted through the ages: the "literature of the Israelites, both in the science of letters and government, also religion, was derived from the Africans" (55). Yet the text does not just look back nostalgically. *Principia* seeks to reclaim the glory of ancient Egypt and Ethiopa to invigorate his *contemporary* African-American community. Roman invaders, he laments, destroyed "emblems, paintings, statuary and designs, as well as other evidences of greatness of the African race" (74). Fortunately, though, a hermetic tradition has secured the forefathers' lore, expressed in the mythological iconography of the "Garden of the Hesperides" (Figure 13), which he refers to as an "allegorical disguisement of the wisdom of the Ethiopians and Egyptians, a philosophical depository of the mental and material possessions of those countries, presented in one view to themselves, while concealed from others" (79). The source of the Garden of the Hesperides symbolism is unknown; Delany may have fabricated it himself, although he insists that the arcane imagery derives from "most intimate intercourse with the native Africans of the highest intelligence in the interior" (72).

This African iconography of state, transported by Delany to the United States to inculcate his own community with racial-national pride, may well manifest what Timothy Brennan calls a national longing for form or, in a less positive fashion, what Terry Eagleton refers to as the "'subjunctive mood' . . . of premature utopianism."[84] That such national forms require inventing should not, however, discredit their merit. *Principia*'s iconographical mysticism precisely encapsulates Delany's desire, at once noble and arrogant, to yoke his inspiring intelligence (his "head," as we have seen) to variously conceived African-American nationalities. Delany's sense of selfhood, his pride in himself and his own sovereignty, never faltered; yet at the same time he sought all his life for the endowment of full citizenship. We can choose to emphasize when surveying his career, in for instance the hagiographic portrait in *The Weekly Anglo-African*, what may be called his autonomous intensity; or, we can reflect upon his equally profound need to conjoin selfhood to the dignities of statehood.

Delany's writings in this chapter may have come across as being too centered on personal ambition. He often speaks as if he were the only voice of truth in the wilderness of white American racism, and the stridency can at times become irksome. What he wanted, however, was nothing less than what the republic was founded to ensure: the self-sovereignty of its subjects. That self-sovereignty, for white citizens, had an added dimension: by reading nations comparatively, whether by means of geography textbooks or travel or archaeological-ethnographical volumes, the self in the form of white, racial identity could be linked to the ideal geobody that carried forth the ark of liberty into the future. The insular sovereignty of the nation took palpable shape not just through actual expansion westward, absorbing more and more to itself so it could become itself, a continent east-to-west, but through its capacity to gloss itself, contrastively, in relations to the non-European world.

Delany yearned with dignity—and by antebellum white standards, presumption—to yoke his noncitizen self to the nation. The pomp of state that he wished thereby to obtain always, I think, eluded him. Although the portrait of him as a Union soldier no doubt afforded him some satisfaction, the sweet sense of being held within the maternal bosom of the republic was never, even after the Civil War, to be his. He did not die until 1885, but my discussion— except for the latter portion on his monograph *Principia*—has only alluded in passing to his later career. The defamation of African-American identity, of being seen as "excrescences" as he had put it in his *Conditions*, hardly stopped being a problem for blacks in America after the Civil War. His tactics for strengthening African-American agency were sometimes contradictory, for he never reconciled in his own mind what came first: black communal self-respect, which he hoped would radiate outward to transform white racist perceptions; or a separate place, where the ostracized, otherwise abject black populace would discover their inward rights to full citizenship. To think, feel, and act like a citizen might compel the nation at large to respond in kind. Yet, conversely, he knew that a sense of citizenship required the geopolitical space of citizenship, of a nation that would not shun or put in servitude a portion of its members.

When after the Civil War he labored to further Reconstructionist aims, holding political appointments under the aegis of the Freedmen's Bureau, he largely abandoned his separatist stance. Had he lived into the next century, into the darker days of rampant Jim Crow law, we can well imagine that he would have shifted back into a more resistant posture of black nationalism. What oscillations Delany did exhibit during his long life, however, should not lead us to dismiss him as a confused tactician of black renewal. Instead, his politics of inward and outward geographies should be seen as polarizing those ambivalences of allegiance and hostility, of integrationist and more violently separatist attitudes, that have always been the burden of African-Americans to navigate. Frederick Douglass, Booker T. Washington, Marcus Garvey, Dr. Martin Luther King, Jr., Malcolm X: all illustrate, as I said earlier in respect to Delany's typicality as an African-American leader, that there is no singular African-American way. Some, such as Douglass and King, had a magisterial talent for sustaining an allegiance to "America" without compromising (Washington is often accused of the opposite) an invigorating anger against its failings. But both, no less than Delany, had to contend with the sad and scandalous noncoincidence, deriving from a history of forced servitude, between racial/group membership and national membership.

The World Archive and
the National Canon of Memory

> [The] subject—in the form of historical consciousness—will once
> again be able to appropriate, to bring back under his sway, all
> those things that are kept at a distance by difference, and find in
> them what might be called his abode.
>
> —Michel Foucault,
> *The Archaeology of Knowledge*

O NE FEATURE distinguishing European colonialism from the U.S.
advancement westward is that for the former, non-European realms
comprised, foremost, hordes of subaltern bodies to be mollified or coerced
according to designs of state radiating out from administrative, imperial centers. Native Americans, unlike the subdued populations of the British Empire,
always fell under the sign of extinction, and thus almost posed less a nagging
problem than an ideological benefit. Commiserating over the Indian's inexorable demise, and looking toward newly opened territories, reminded white
Americans that they were, after all, the race of the future. Enslaved blacks, to be
sure, formed an internally subjugated group that haunted the national body
politic, but as we have seen, one task of antebellum geographical writing was
to elide for national conscience the discomfiting facts of slavery. Even to those
who did not turn a blind eye, it could be thought of as a necessary evil, a precondition for Africa's elevation: for Guyot (speaking in his 1849 textbook, *The
Earth and Man*), the miseries of the shackled black in the South did not outweigh the "[u]nhapp[iness]" of the topographically shackled African who "refuse[d] to enter into those relations of intercourse with others which [would]
assure to him a superior life" (78).

That lesson would likely have been endorsed by Emerson, who in an 1844
journal entry offered this convoluted apology to himself for his political inac-
tion in behalf of abolitionism:

As the races advance & rise, order & rank appear, & the aurora of reason & of love. . . .
We do not wish a world of bugs or birds. Neither afterwards do we respect one of

Scythians, or Caraibs, or Feejees. As little interests us the crimes of the recent races, the grand style of nature & her periods is what they show us, but they are not for permanence, her foot will not rest. . . . When at last in a race a new principle appears an idea, that conserves it. Ideas only save races. If the black man is feeble & not important to the existing races, not a par with the best race, the black man must serve & be sold & exterminated. But if the black man carries in his bosum an indispensable element of a new & coming civilization . . . he will survive & play his part. So now it seems to be that the arrival of such men as Toussaint if he is pure blood, or of Douglass if he is pure blood, outweighs all the English & American humanity. The Antislavery of the whole world is but dust in the balance, a poor squeamishness & nervousness. The might & right is here. Here is the Anti-Slave. Here is Man; & if you have man, black or white is insignificant. . . . The intellect, that is miraculous, who has it has the talisman, his skin & bones are transparent, he is a statue of the living God.[1]

Humanity progresses upward toward ideality whereupon, Emerson asserts, "black or white" will become irrelevant. This ascension nonetheless also requires that racial categories ("order & rank") emerge out of nonhierarchical nature. He can thus willingly sacrifice specific black bodies (slaves) or tribal groups (the Caribs or Feejees) on the altar of futurity. The term "pure blood," rather than signifying racial type, stands for the mentally virile few animated by new "ideas." Emerson, though, does not quite see through race when he proposes that "skin & bones are transparent." For him, the exemplary black man such as Douglass or Toussaint "carries in his bosum" the seeds of destiny more typically engendered within the "best," that is, white race. As made clear by a later journal entry, from 1853, the transcendental alembic ("of reason & of love") was not cleansed of racism: the "Negro is imitative . . . in his successes," Emerson wrote, "there is no origination with him in mental & moral spheres."[2]

Not unlike Emerson's metaphysics of whiteness, gazing at non-European racial types or learning about their essentialized geographies (barbaric Africa, licentious Polynesia, hybridized Latin America, the torpid Levant) pulled one into a free-floating zone of sovereignty. Such is witnessed, for instance, by Bayard Taylor's poem that I cited in my introduction, in which Africa, Asia, and so on parade by in an allegorical pageant ushering in the ideal geobody that "from the Future, with a victor's hand / Claim[s] empire for the Free." There were, of course, naysayers. There were critics of national arrogance and widespread sentiment about the dangers of too presumptuously leaping into the future. The most famous instance of the latter, perhaps, appears in Thomas Cole's *Course of Empire* (1836), although we should note that his sequence of canvases envisions future catastrophe in the oblique guise of an allegory drawing upon phantasmal, distinctly non-U.S. imagery, as if national calamity could not be conceived in terms of the literal national body—its landscapes, urban scenes, or institutions. (It took, I might here add, the Civil War—in the form, for instance, of photographs of battle debris and carnage—to bring home, with shocking poignancy, the repressed body of the nation as it lay divided against itself; before that the viscera of the nation, the "dissevered members" of internecine conflict as Henry Clay put it during the Compromise of 1850, were simply unimaginable.³) Dissent about the American way or vocal activist support for a variety of causes—women's rights, abolitionism, prison reform, among others—sometimes drew upon revolutionary ferment abroad or upon socialist thinkers. More often, though, European revolution and bloodletting, and the disorder of the mob especially, betokened the sort of history that the nation seemed to be peculiarly isolated from: Margaret Fuller (one of the most cosmopolitan-minded thinkers of her age), even in the midst of excoriating her own country, could laud it as being "surely destined to elucidate a great moral law" and indeed the fit home of the "Goddess of Liberty" previously "impure" in Europe.⁴

The republic's utopian promise also came into relief by way of non-European regions and cultures. The relative lack of what might be called a thick, noncontinental colonizing agon meant that non-European places could function as symbolic markers of otherness, of different temporalities and delimiting geographies, that contrastingly testified to the nation's illimitable future. Specific regions might variously hold a purchase on particular national narratives: Africans requiring redemptive U.S. tutelage, for example, or the antiquities of Mesoamerica evoking a sense of New World temporal sublimity. To the populace at large, though, such regions mattered mostly only antithetically, as counterstories to what the United States was not.

The previous several paragraphs have formulated how thinking about foreign, including European, realms *overall* influenced U.S. ideology. I have, however, also ignored an important, but difficult to certify, factor. One of the liabilities of current cultural studies or culture theory is its overreliance on the issues and effects of power, its discounting of the possibility that the imaginary relations of one nation to other nations (in this book, confined to that between the United States and non-European ones) take shape through an affective dimension. Notwithstanding bigotry, the desire to dominate, or religious condescension, antebellum readers tended to regard the major global locales through the lens of primary emotions or cognitive sets. Polynesia equaled erotic pleasure or visceral repulsion (the threat of cannibalism); tropical America, the chance to exercise a masculinist or virile lust for gold and glory; Africa, the contrast to intellection and sociality; and the Holy Land, the sentimentality of weeping over a fallen land. Arnold Guyot, we will remember, wished to survey the entire globe as one huge, interconnected entity; and his readers found his text so compelling in part because they were already predisposed to witness the world, or rather to *feel* it, in terms of an ensemble of differentiated emotive-cognitive attributes within themselves. Stereotypes do not become effective just because they make lording it over the other, however the latter might be conceived, easier; they also always return us to ourselves, appear as a mode of national/self theater. To put it thusly, however, holds a danger no less than that of the too exclusive focus on power—for if the emotional life of the national citizen or the national body politic is deemed to be inhabited, or take form, by stereotypes, we come to the nearly useless maxim that elsewhere *is*, to some extent, always within, a formula that entails so severe a collapsing together of the national, the personal, and the other as to void purposeful, discrete claims or arguments.

One goal of contemporary geographical or ethnographic practice is to short-circuit the power of the stereotype by pulling, or attempting to pull, us into the density of the other's dispositions and ideologies such that we transcend our own. The writers that I have studied in the previous chapters did not, by and large, hold that honorable aim; yet they also did not in their works merely replicate the egregious desires of those, whether individuals or nations, who merely liked to dominate. The absence of strong colonial or imperial motives outside of the North American continent entailed, if not quite the full overcoming of stereotypes, at least a more multifaceted response to non-European realms.

Cultural studies theory typically deems subjectivity an effect, less a thing itself than a fold within the tapestry of culture and ideologies. The preceding case studies have for the most part balanced psychological and cultural exegesis, claiming that the idiosyncrasy of authorial identities is what in fact partially propels U.S. national narratives in respect to the non-European. If the citizen-subject is regarded as no more than a cipher, a vessel of national ideologies (however contradictory those might be), the foreign when encountered would need to be seen, in turn, as little else than a sort of vast parade ground for national ideologies to strut. The making of national narratives, to be sure, often involves an element of narcissistic U.S. self-display; but throughout this work I have wished to avoid simply conflating the propaganda of the nation with how national narratives per se get constructed. I have taken national narrative to mean ideology *as it is enacted*, which necessarily requires specific locales and specific individuals or discursive communities: even as my authors have worked through corporate national concerns and anxieties, their stories are to some extent sui generis. Paradoxically, however, that discreteness—the residue of the nonnational (the otherness within)—is exactly what compels U.S. ideologies and the factuality of the foreign to be pulled into conjunction; and it is out of that conjunction that national narratives, ones more than mere propaganda, emerge. (The "self," in this regard, is not desubjectified, becoming merely a hybrid space where ideologies and different affiliations or experiences collide; rather, it is the necessary precondition for ideologies to come into visibility. Ideologies may in a sense produce the "self"; but there is no ideology without an initial selfhood grounding it in the world.)

One of the signal virtues of looking at particular U.S. travelers is that they show the U.S. subject engaging non-European places and peoples not from the abstract vantage point of the geographical gaze but in more material confrontations, and those encounters, while not free of ethically dubious motives or actions, produced we have seen a plurality of narratives not entirely circumscribed by first-world/third-world power structures. Tommo's befuddlement over the historicity of Polynesian taboos and monuments, Squier's fears about tropical American declension or racial admixture, and Stephens's or Lynch's attempt to align the actual Levantine landscape with Scriptural temporality: in each case the authors or narrators could not rely, as did Emerson and Taylor, upon a sense of free-floating, atemporal citizenship. For the traveler, the resonant aspects of a non-European realm—its monuments, landscapes, or inhabitants' bodies—do not become detached signs (in a semiotic manner) to be manipulated, willy-nilly, for either self-fashioning or national theatrics.

Consider the following inventory of some of the most heavily charged scenes or motifs in the travel texts that I have examined: Tommo's description of Kory-Kory behind the prison-bars of his own culture, or his brutal stabbing of Mow-Mow with a boat-hook; Lynch's meditations on the Ottoman Sultan's melancholy; Meredith's gaze, in Cummins's Holy Land novel, at Oriental, arabesque designs as he falls asleep; Melville's approaches toward and detours away from the Dead Sea; or Squier's opposition of loathly and alluring native prophetesses. These examples, among many others, may be regarded as a form of geographical dreamwork, with themes or "objects" getting reassembled for symbolic (personal or national) purposes in the form of the travel stories told; yet their materiality also keeps them from becoming mere stage props for self-fashioning or for the nation's imaginary of itself. The resistant materiality of these "props"—brought into focus by the scopic gaze, but not fully decipherable or made manageable by it—is what propels the gaze in the first place, or rather sustains it beyond those mere fleeting glances that are requisite, otherwise, for the confirmations of only stereotypic looking. Delany's minority status inverted this pattern. He sought to escape the curtailing boundaries of the United States itself and to carve out in Africa and elsewhere a utopic, future space of nonabjection, emblematized in the disguised Garden of the Hesperides engraving of his late work, *Principia*. The engraving's scopic excitement for the African-American separatist stems from its resistance to white decoding; it attracts Delany just to the extent that he believes it will mystify his white audience.

In each text studied, Delany's included, the locale of the non-European *as depicted* rarely becomes inhabited by complexly rendered non-Europeans themselves. Partially this is a reflection of travelistic writing itself, in which human subjects (other than the narrator, that is) typically fold into the scenery rather than becoming dramatic actors in their own right. And partially the diminished subjectivity of non-Europeans derives from the fact that all my authors had an agenda, political or personal or a combination of both, that tended to grant the Polynesian, African, Indian, or Oriental a reality only in terms of U.S. national topoi. This does not mean, however, that their texts are solipsistic: for the agendas themselves come into clarity or reveal ideological impasses, respectively for example, in Squier's effort to escape hybridized history in *Waikna* or in Melville's discovery of the law's vexed historicity in *Typee*, by virtue of the U.S. subject crossing over, albeit temporarily, into a non-European locale.

The preceding examples of Delany, Squier, or Melville highlight that geographical thinking invariably involves notions of history, and it would not be too much to say that during the antebellum era geographical and linked protoanthropological writing was really history by, as it were, *other* means. The United States—it is one reason why the collective populace so willingly embraces utopic tropes—has always lacked, relatively speaking, the European density of accumulated pasts that define present identities. Combine with that what Philip Fisher among other scholars has noted as the peculiar homogeneity of U.S. space, of the solvent ethos of democracy, and we should not be surprised that comparative geography satisfied longings for distinction. Manifest Destiny offered the promise of boundlessness; and geographical metaphor, the hierarchical taxonomy of nations, gave that otherwise abstract, always emergent national entity a sense of superior form, of being *embodied*.[5]

The taxonomies of Arnold Guyot and his peers mapped nations on a progressive timeline. U.S. geographical discourse whether in geography textbooks per se, travel writing, or related archaeological works conjoined the scopic and the temporal. Non-European bodies, artifacts, and terrains typically solicited musings on archaic, congealed historicity, a product it would seem of debilitated faculties—the incapacity to comprehend or usher in the future, to have "new" ideas as Emerson had written. I would like now to turn more explicitly to the intersection between U.S. temporality and the non-European. The following discussion I present as a sort of opposite bookend to my first chapter on the abstractions of geographical textbooks, but I also wish to open up the lens beyond the focus on how non-Europeans were represented. Ultimately, how U.S. citizens regarded third-world terrains and peoples should not be separated from more embracing considerations of what I call the world archive and the national canon of memory.

William H. Prescott, Francis Parkman, George Bancroft: these are names that still have currency in the interpretation of nineteenth-century U.S. historical thinking. It is doubtful, however, whether their volumes shaped attitudes toward the past, the nation, and other countries more so than textbooks of what was referred to as universal history or the spaces of (and accompanying guidebooks to) the nation's privately owned and state-run museums. Universal history textbooks and antebellum museums were the discursive and institutional spaces where U.S. nationhood and temporal concerns most expressly or palpably came into conjunction. In both, the national canon of memory—at once iconographic, artifactual, and textual—takes measure of the world archive, absorbing it to its own purposes.

Universal history traced the past of all nations, and covered a time span reaching from the Mosaic account, through antiquity, up to the moment of the particular textbook itself. Its practitioners' goal was to show how world culture was advancing forward toward an endpoint of true liberty. Proto-anthropological science, as it emerged in both the United States and Europe around the middle decades of the nineteenth century, ran as a parallel discourse, basing itself on the teleologies of evolutionism. Universal history in its American guise, however, was a religiously conservative rather than secular social science, designed to teach the body politic to discern the providential hand behind history. Its intent, much like Arnold Guyot's in *The Earth and Man*, was to pull the reader above the contingencies of history, and in effect to cast the U.S. citizen into the future tense logos of Divinity. The engraving opposite the title page to Samuel Goodrich's *History of all Nations, from the Earliest Periods to the Present Time; or, Universal History* (first published in 1850), for example, presents the bourgeois (presumably Protestant, U.S.) unit at once as the culmination of universal history and its *only* spectator. The family members, as they survey the parade of figures representing different historical epochs and nations, stand both within and without the stream of time (Figure 14). The family enjoys the privileged "sovereignty of consciousness," which Michel Foucault designates as the goal of nineteenth-century historicism.[6] In the words of Emma Willard, author of the popular *Universal History in Perspective* (first published in 1835, it went through twelve editions by 1852), the aim was to see panoramically, to comprehend history "at a single glance."[7] The desired object of such sovereignty, though, is perhaps best illustrated in *Universal History; Arranged to Illustrate Bem's Charts of Chronology* (1859), written by Elizabeth Palmer Peabody (Nathaniel Hawthorne's sister-in-law). Bem was a Polish educator, and Peabody adapted his methods to the needs of "this

FIG. 14. Frontispiece for Samuel Goodrich's *History of all Nations*... (Auburn: Derby and Miller, 1853). (In the Nietz Textbook Collection, courtesy of the Special Collections Department, University of Pittsburgh Library System.)

great democracy [that] is waking to self-consciousness" and which must be taught "how to dispose the elements of a *new* world into a truly Christian order."⁸ Unlike Emerson, who at most pays lip service to the notion that the *volk* rather than the strong male leader is the motor behind history, Willard and Peabody believed in the potential virtue of what the latter called the "mass of the people" (ii), although that citizenry needs to grasp the larger patterns of history so that it will not revert to those types of flawed "institutions, that, with their death-in-life, cumber Asia and Africa, and even Europe," nor "act to-day principles which have rendered desert, and strewed with ruins, regions the most favored on the globe" (ii). According to Peabody, such a lofty agenda can best be realized by properly internalizing history. The eradication of tyranny, the spread of democracy, the harmony of nations: these require not external political suasion, but rather that the juvenile citizen-to-be introject history's totality, recognize God's agenda, and act accordingly.

Peabody's key device to install universal history into her pupils' minds was an elaborate polychromatic mnemonic chart. A grid of one hundred squares denotes each century, with each square inscribed by iconographic marks that stand for classes of events (wars, revolutions, treaties, and so forth). Separate colors distinguish national landscapes or racial pigmentations—"India, golden yellow (chrome 3); . . . China, pale yellow; . . . Ethiopia, burnt umber" (ix–x). In turn, depending upon the historical episode or countries involved, squares or subdivisions of the squares are to be filled in with appropriate icons or patterns ("sometimes diagonals are drawn in whole squares or in subdivisions, because two or more nations concur in an event; and then the colors denoting the two nations must slant to each other" [viii]). The end product, "a symmetrical picture, brilliant with colors," enables the "outlines and general views" of history that "were so inappreciable by the memory when they were hidden in words, [to be] daguerotyped on it" (viii). The goal, though, is not merely to remember. The charts permit the student to survey the "intervals in which human individualities have had time to expend themselves" and ultimately to supply from "his own mind and conscience, that which only the prophet-historian gives; namely, the light of God's truth" (v).

If one examines a chart actually colored in, the efficacy of this mode of historical inquiry might seem doubtful at best (Figure 15). The quaintness of what turns out to look like a modern abstract painting should not, however, lead us to dismiss Peabody's high seriousness. For her, understanding history as God does will conduct us to the Millennium when human-ordered time is no more. Peabody chronicles history comprehensively, marking both epochs absent of republican principles and her own country's lapses from those principles. Her text in effect takes the form of a jeremiad indicting the entire span of history, and it draws, in a manner that I think most present-day readers

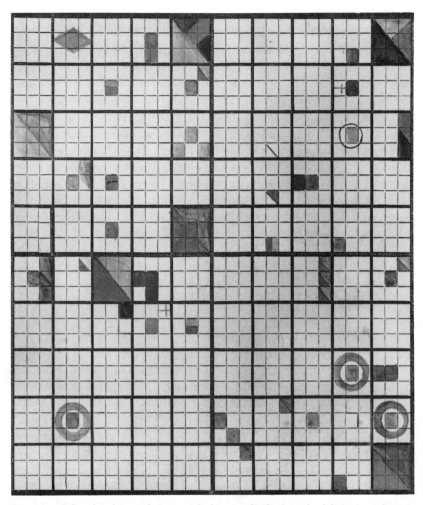

FIG. 15. Colored-in history lesson work chart in Elizabeth Peabody's *Universal History; Arranged to Illustrate Bem's Charts of Chronology* (New York: Sheldon and Co., 1859). (Courtesy of the Annenberg Rare Book and Manuscript Library, University of Pennsylvania.)

must admire, upon the key Enlightenment directive to maximize the forces of liberty and to transcend partisan, nationalist perspectives. Nina Baym, one of the few literary scholars to have noticed Peabody, suggests that she challenged male-authored history, both in terms of events (wars and conquests) and the writing about those events: "Peabody's republican millennialism does not dictate—indeed, it precludes—that the United States should engage in such imperialist enterprises as the Mexican War, expanding its territory to the Pacific Ocean, exterminating or removing the American Indians, or dispatching missionaries around the world. God's plan of free spiritual development could not be furthered by imposing Christianity on a resisting people."[9] Although Peabody's text does not decouple its audience from the geospatially concrete body of the United States, for her that nation, its promise and its *essential* reality, exists on history's far side. Attachment to the material entity of the nation should not foster a low-level patriotism, but rather a commitment to the mission of leading the republic to a time and global order transcendent of national affiliations.

To be sure, thinking of the nation-as-telos can easily become a ruse. From John Winthrop's trope of the City on the Hill to the symbolic icon of the Statute of Liberty, an aura of destiny surcharges national space, as opposed to that space being regarded as secondary to providential intent. Universal history was not just "theory"; it informed politics, for instance that of the filibuster William Walker who, in *The War in Nicaragua* (1860), put it to ends that would have shocked Peabody:

If we look at Africa in the light of universal history, we see her for more than five thousand years a mere waif on the waters of the world. . . . But America was discovered, and the European found the African a useful auxiliary in subduing the new continent to the uses and purposes of civilization. . . . Then only do the wisdom and excellence of the divine economy in the creation of the black race begin to appear with their full lustre. . . . A strong, haughty race, bred to liberty in its northern island home, is sent forth with a mission to place America under the rule of free laws; but . . . [how] are they, when transplanted from their rugged native climate where freedom thrives to retain their precious birthright in the soft, tropical air which woos to luxury and repose? Is it not for this that the African was reserved? And is it not thus that one race secures for itself liberty with order, while it bestows on the other comfort and Christianity.[10]

Delany likely was familiar with Walker's volume, for he himself in the early 1850s had focused on Central America as a site for a potential black nation.[11] And it was from his sense of the white majority's scandalous use of terms such as "liberty" that he, from early to late in his life, distrusted the U.S.'s claim of having a special destiny in respect to world history. He knew the costs and enchantments of geopiety perhaps more intensely than any of the other authors appearing in this study, and was not seduced by the national fantasy of ascension. If universal history could be co-opted to ignoble aims as Walker does in the above passage, Delany cannily understood how to read history antithetically. In the Garden of the Hesperides engraving, he replaces the majoritarian, Protestant interpretation of America's role in universal history with an Afrocentric, hermetic one, especially designed to be decoded by a black minority audience, trained in the lore of their ancestral home. Delany's black or African mysticism was not the product of romantic delusions. It was a response to the hollowness he detected, even after the Civil War, in the nation's promise that all of its members would be fully enfranchised.

Universal history, in Peabody's or Willard's hands, taught the student to gloss the nation as being more instructive in its principles of republicanism and Protestantism than in local temporal facts, the offspring of "human individualities." Peabody herself is not duped by vulgar geopiety, but because universal history abstracts the viewer-reader out of temporal discreteness, actual conflicts with the non-European world or within the ranks of European nations do not become subjected to lingering scrutiny. Her volume in fact rigorously works to make national or transnational conflict unproblematic, because all of history up to the millennial transformation carries little real weight, seeming hardly more than a motley display of ignorant struggle. Eschatology informs her strong moral vision; it also, though, reduces the visceral bite of studying the bloody outcomes of power contests. The student who used Peabody's color charts mastered non-European (and European) difference, but at such a level of abstraction that history itself became utterly impalpable, aesthetic rather than messy.[12]

Not surprisingly, the national canon of memory became more vexatious and less shapely when it entailed surveying, in museum collections, physical relics of the nation's past in conjunction with nonnational ones. In the antebellum museum the detritus of cultures, not abstraction, dominates. Fully proving the latter would require gathering together a host of guidebooks and other documents as evidence. Yet I believe its truth can be suggested by looking briefly at what should be judged to be the first national museum in the United States.

The first collection that had the pretense of being national, rather than provincial (or, as in Charles Willson Peale's earlier Philadelphia Museum, naturalist in orientation), was the National Institute in Washington.[13] It became, in fact, the initial home of the artifacts—some forty tons' worth—brought back from the 1838–42 Wilkes Expedition, the ambitious naval venture to secure thorough naturalist, oceanographic, and commercial knowledge of the Southern Hemisphere. The collection became subject to debates over the rights of ownership, and it along with the National Institute was eventually absorbed into the Smithsonian in the late 1850s after years of bickering among the parties concerned. Still, even in its somewhat inchoate form the National Institute's museum, when we turn to the texts written about it, can be said to articulate the nation to itself in terms of the world beyond its borders. It did so; but the sheer materiality of the non-European artifacts displayed also rendered the national script or national temporality a matter of some ambivalence.[14]

In 1841, Joel Poinsett published a pamphlet sponsoring the National Institute as a nucleus for distributing across the land art works. These works, he argued, by portraying the lives of the forefathers would preserve the citizenry from moral decline. What was needed, he insisted, was a sort of internal imperialism, a diffusion of the national state throughout the states. The republic should be saturated with tokens sanctifying the Founding Fathers: their "heroic deeds" should be commemorated by copies of "pictures, statues, and medals, [and they] should be spread far and wide over the land, that they may penetrate into every hamlet, and inspire the people universally with gratitude and emulation."[15] The threat of national amnesia might well be countered by such culture campaigns, by what Frantz Fanon discerns as the effort to "make the totality of the nation a reality to each citizen."[16] The space of the museum collection itself, however, disrupted as much as it furthered such nationalist aims, because it housed not only national memorabilia (along with naturalist exhibits) but also an array of Native American and non-European artifacts. This miscellaneous array implied the vanity, and indeed impiety, of collecting together what in effect constituted a national reliquary.

The best evidence of these insecurities is an 1855 guidebook, *A Popular Catalogue of the Extraordinary Curiosities in the National Institute, Arranged in the Building Belonging to the Patent Office.* The bulk of the pamphlet inventories items or briefly describes their origins, but we can also see it as disclosing a narrative logic in respect to national temporality. The museum included three groups of curiosities: a large assortment of Indian artifacts (representing the nation's prehistory); "Revolutionary Relics of extraordinary interest" (representing the nation's founding); and a multitude of non-U.S. artifacts—Egyptian mummies, artwork, and pieces of monuments, as well as the hoard of objects collected by the Wilkes Expedition "at a cost to Government of several millions of dollars" (representing the world beyond the nation).[17] The first group, the Indian relics, evokes the archaic: the race which, being extirpated from national soil, confirms expansionist prowess and glory. The trophy of a "Seminole war-plume, picked up on Dade's battle-ground by Col. Alexander Thompson," for example, recalls an heroic exploit: the "gallant Dade and his comparatively small force [were] massacred—one alone escaping to relate the destruction of his comrades. The loss of the enemy was enormous—and it is to this day a subject of wailing and anguish at their councils"

(23). The second group, the filiopietistic relics, functions to bolster national memory. Among the objects likely to be viewed with the "utmost satisfaction," the pamphlet directs us, are Benjamin Franklin's cane, the coat Washington wore when he resigned his commission at Annapolis, and the "ORIGINAL DECLARATION OF INDEPENDENCE" (31–34).

The binary set of relics (the memorabilia of the Founding Fathers; the ritual objects of conquered Indian tribes) thus far stages a coherent narrative of national inception, conquest, and expansion. The museum's artifacts up to this point may be regarded as being marshaled so as not to disrupt the national canon of memory. Oddly, however, if the catalogue celebrates the acquisition of war trophies, it also moralizes upon the weapons of slaughter: "Observe our fierce spirit of contest—our arsenals stored with destruction, as yet silent and unscattered; but ready for their grim interpreters and disseminators; the war ship, the mine and red artillery. We invoke battles and invite famine—its gaunt handmaiden—to our realms. May not the Being whose intelligence levels all earthly superiority, consider our wrath and acts of bloodshed to be . . . inexcusable and preposterous" (19). This jeremiadic detour enjoins the spectator to con lessons kindred to those in the universal histories: to abjure patriotic hubris and elevate oneself to a humbling godly perspective.

A less confident sense of national mission and destiny also emerges when non-European relics are pondered as evidence of cultural impermanence. We can detect this most notably in the guidebook's preface, written by Alfred Hunter, one of the museum's officers. With the national citizen now embodied—in the personal voice of the preface—the monolithic time of national progress begins to fracture. Initially, Hunter extols the Wilkes Expedition because it had left "scarcely a shore, however remote, or the interior of a continent, however barbarous or difficult of access" yet to be "surveyed and described" (iv). The museum housed the cultural spoils brought back by the Wilkes global cruise—Polynesian war clubs, masks, ornaments, and so on— but, interestingly, Hunter begins to suggest that such items invite, to his mind at least, dialogic possibilities. Although existing "under laws foreign to our firesides," they mentally conduct the spectator to the "shores [from] where they came" such that one becomes those regions' "spiritual and self-transported denizen" (v).[18] Yet such musings, what Hunter calls a "liberal curiosity" (iv), also hold a threat. The manifest instability of other, foreign nations indicated by the detritus of their cultures (unlike the Indian trophies) blurs into how he regards the republic, disclosing his insecurity about *its* memorabilia and permanence.

Toward the end of his preface, Hunter segues into the significance of the Washington Monument, whose initial construction got underway in 1848 (the monument was not to be completed until 1884) and whose semifinished interiors apparently contained some Egyptian architectural bric-a-brac. The use of architectural motifs from one of ancient history's more despotic and hieratic cultures in the buildings of a democratic state constitutes a subject of inquiry in and of itself. The fad for things Egyptian in the 1840s and 1850s—the absorption of the non-European within the nation—suggests, among other possibilities, a desire for archaic (that is, nondemocratic) modes of being and expression, for aristocratic forms (artistic, governmental, religious) strictly prohibited by national conscience.

Egyptian architecture itself, though, had the distinct virtue of its imposing but plain designs, so abstract that it did not seem Orientalized. Hunter makes the point himself. The Washington Monument's obelisk profile, being relatively austere, could be deemed to memorialize republican virtue rather than encouraging national vainglory. It is, Hunter insists, an "authentic and accepted emblem of a people . . . betoken[ing] the grandeur of a virtuous, uncontaminated nation, unrotted with luxury or the purple porticoes of Belteshazzar" (ix). He cannot, however, quite push aside the troubling thought of national vanity. He cannot decide whether the edifice stands in for Washington or the nation en masse; whether its iconography is patriotic or idolatrous; or whether, finally, it forestalls national amnesia or solicits thoughts about history's vagaries, the inexorable cyclic rise and fall of *all* nations:

[T]his edifice, so chaste, so fair and stately, is filled with fragments of [Egyptian] edifices more magnificent and indestructible than itself. Nay, with those relics are commingled the [mummified] remains of their architects, once as intelligent, as curious, and as animated as ourselves to-day. . . . It is true that the Almighty being has in no instance directed either a people or its patriarchs to erect a monument to one of their number, or to any of their deeds,—still, he has not forbidden it as idolatrous, but furthered such pious designs and perpetuated their evidences. Excepting only those who are enfibred with the religious faith of our species or riveted to it with supernatural awe,—whose names are sacred to their followers; no mere MAN, of human pretension only, possesses so much the commendation of the whole world,—nor to any clime, nor to any race, was Sage or Hero sent, whom it loved, honored, and reverenced as the American heart loves, honors, reverences, and would EXALT the memory of GEORGE WASHINGTON. . . . We, living among the contemporaries of the Father of our country, have the great privilege of first evincing our piety, and impressing his greatness and excellence on future generations, by dedicating to his fame the loftiest monumental shaft ever yet attempted by our species. . . . When the fullness of its time shall have ripened, and it, too, is overthrown, the DIVINE HISTORIAN may deign to prolong the annuals of another favored race, and decree the memory of our *illustrious dead* to be coextensive with all habitable space, and co-eternal with the mind of man. (ix–x)

The amorphous syntax almost seems intention: as if Hunter wants it both ways, recognizing that national memory needs to be anchored in the body of its hero (his monument) yet also keenly aware that such embodiments come close to idolatry. To adopt the Lacanian terminology of identity formation to nation formation, the haunting sense of the "*corps morcelé* [body in bits and pieces]"—that is, the non-European, Egyptian relics—must be countered by a solidified, totalized national-body image, the fetishized memory of Washington and his iconographical body, the Washington Monument.[19] The memory of the founding "Hero," thus amplified, will withstand the nation's and the monument's own destruction. If Peabody's and Willard's universal history textbooks taught the lesson that "individualities" must be seen through to God's time, Hunter proposes that although the republic may not survive time's passage, its ghostly "Father" will.

Whether these anxieties about a fragmentary national body, in everyday life, disturbed the national collective antebellum mentality, however, is open to question. Hunter, an official of the museum, speaks officially. When we turn to the most popular museum at mid-century, P. T. Barnum's American Museum, we see the danger of making too much of such pageants of crisis in national consciousness.[20] Having, by the 1850s, absorbed the collections of Peale's defunct naturalist Philadelphia museum and a number of other regional or private ones, Barnum's was by far the largest museum of its day in the United States. An amalgamation of natural history museum, zoo, freak show, theater, and art gallery, the American Museum (located on Broadway Street of New York City) put on view curiosities of all sorts: life-size wax figures of Chinese families; assorted Indian, Asian, African, Central and South American, and Polynesian artifacts; Egyptian mummies; and, of course, the human anomalies—the Fat Girl, the Aztec Children, the Giant Baby, the Swiss Bearded Lady, the Androgynous Singer, and, if not always Tom Thumb in person, at least the court apparel he wore when he was presented to Queen Victoria.[21]

Patrons could visit taxonomically ordered cabinets of shells, birds, or minerals, which were especially praised by contemporary naturalists, in several rooms; but for the most part the human, the natural, and the historical were randomized and maximally disordered. A typical example of such disorder is witnessed in Case number 794, described in a guidebook for 1864:

Ball of Hair found in the Stomach of a Sow; Indian Collar, composed of grizzly bear claws; Sword of a Swordfish penetrating through the side of a ship; Algerine Cartouche Box; Algerine boarding pike; African pocket-book; Chinese pillow; Horse's foot, injected; a petrified piece of Pork, which was recovered from the water after being immersed 60 years; Fragment of the first canal-boat which reached New York through the Canals; African Sandals; Turkish Shoes; Sultan Slippers; Turkish Slippers; Ancient Iron Breast-plate, found in Wall Street, 1816; Arabian Bridle; wrought metal Mexican Stirrup; Turkish Ladies' Boots.[22]

There is no classificatory scheme that can make sense of this profligacy: the ordering, in part, might be sharpness (bear claws, swordfish sword, boarding pike); exotic footwear (African sandals, Turkish shoes); or, once-submerged objects (the ball of hair, the piece of pork, fragment of the canal-boat). From the heterogeneous dispersal along incompatible axis—geographic, historical, natural, manufactured, recovered, sharp—within this cabinet, no edifying lesson or cohesive narrative may be drawn. David Lowenthal, in *The Past is a Foreign Country*, speculates that the "existential concreteness" or sensuous immediacy of relics "explains their evocative appeal."[23] The pleasure of juxtapositions such as those in Barnum's American Museum, however, has more to do, I think, with the power of the aleatory, of objects escaping rational classification. There is, on the one hand, the thrill of illicit scopic excitation; there is also, on the other, the satisfaction of a certain religious urge, the tantalization of a different, suprarational order that comes from staring at jumbled objects shorn from their explanatory contexts: odd curiosities emit, we might say, an holy aura.

My latter remark may seem too fanciful, but Barnum's museum continued the tradition of *wunderkammern*, or cabinets of curiosities, that from the Renaissance period and on held the allure of secretive knowledge, the promise of peeping into the arcana of God. Barnum's exhibitions represent the debased, popularizing tail end of that tradition, mere amusement for the masses, as Barnum well knew. The structure of revelation—the excitation of wonder via a movement from outside the museum and its promotions to inside, and then inside again to particular chambers—remained the same, although what was revealed invariably turned out to ring loudly of the hoax. Barnum's machinery of curiosity did not replace or displace the structure of religious emotion (the seeking of some hallowed core), but I would suggest that it, museums proper, texts about racial typologies, narratives of archaeological digging in foreign lands, and indeed universal history and geography textbooks themselves all variously drew upon a desire with overlapped religious, sexual, and racist inflections to make the invisible visible, to get at the *within* of history. The challenge for the culture analyst is to tease out the relays without becoming reductive. To look panoptically may or may not involve an element of aggressivity, depending upon the instance in question, and I think some circumspection is warranted when we want to conclude that all, especially scientific, modalities of looking are baleful. The flip side—which makes critiques of nineteenth-century science necessary—is that blunt racism (as sampled in Josiah C. Nott and George R. Gliddon's 1854 treatise *Types of Mankind*) could blur over into what might be taken as a disinterested, not racistly motivated inquiry into human origins or what makes history tick. Arnold Guyot's explanations of humankind's history and destiny are plausible up to a certain point: coastal contours and so on doubtless did, and do, have large historical effects. When his geographical science overlays geographical feature with racial types, however, we are right to maintain that the discipline as he practiced it was not even initially free of racist thinking.

No less than antebellum archaeology or geography, Barnum's museum drew upon the hazy border between curiosity as a noble and ignoble motivation, but it also flattened its meanings into the structure of a joke, which rubs it components together to produce nothing at all, but itself, or the polar reverse of religious enthusiasm, that is, laughter. Ultimately, history in Barnum's museum just does not count. When one toured the American Museum one got the thrill, it seems, of *not thinking* about the nation. Consider, for instance, how national memorabilia bumped up against unfamiliar foreign artifacts or relics. The 1864 guidebook and an earlier 1850 one show national symbols or icons to be randomly mixed within the welter of other curiosities. One cabinet displays a "Fragment of a Door of the House in which Christopher Columbus was born," a "Chinese Curiosity Ball," and an icon of the "Virgin Mary . . . carved complete out of one elephant's tusk, at Rome" together with a "Stone from Washington's Tomb at Mount Vernon" and an "Autograph of Washington." Elsewhere, a replica of the Declaration of Independence appears next to a case containing "a large number of curious old copper coins, together with the severed handcuffs of a man named George Wilson, who robbed this case many years ago." And, in another room, we pass from "an American flag, torn and discolored by age" to "a Brain Stone from Turk's Island," then on to a swordfish, a seal, several Roman Urns, to end, finally, with the withered arm of a "notorious pirate named Tom Trouble."[24]

In these cabinets, the items taken from the national canon of memory such as the flag or memorabilia of Washington still elicit reverence, but only solipsistically so. They are no longer part of a narrative of national time unfolding. The vacuation of *national* history from the relic-as-curiosity seems to be the point of Herman Melville's satire of the American Museum. Attributed to him is a brief sketch in *Yankee Doodle* (July 1847), which was accompanied by a cartoon displaying "SANTA ANNAS WOODEN LEG ONE THOUSAND TINES BIGER THAN ANY OTHER MANS LEG," surrounded by other Barnumesque oddities. The cartoon mocks the exaggerated claims Barnum made about his exhibits; but it and the prose sketch also emphasize how the American Museum quite effectively converted geopolitical, historical conflict into a joke. "We give an interior view of the Barnum Property," Melville writes, "embracing a life-sized exhibition of the great Santa-Anna Boot, which has been brought on—by the loops of two able-bodied young negroes—direct from the seat of war."[25] Melville reads the American Museum as turning history into tawdry spectacle, and we can confidently say that Barnum heralded a culture of consumeristic looking (the guidebook for 1850, for example, after listing the assorted curiosities, ends with a list of the fixtures of the museum—the drapery of the lecture room, its chandelier, the iron-work on staircases—and then appends ten pages of advertisements of the diverse products for sale in the streets surrounding the museum).[26]

The delights Barnum's museum afforded seemed to have infantilized the spectator into mindless gaping. Another possibility, though, should be acknowledged. We can dislike the hoaxiness and crude exploitation. We can dislike Barnum himself, when, for instance, he glibly requested that a U.S. traveler abroad "buy a beautiful Circassian woman for $200"; or when he displayed a microcephalic African-American named William Henry Johnson as "Zip," and advertised him as being a "CONNECTING LINK BETWEEN THE WILD NATIVE AFRICAN AND THE BRUTE CREATION."[27] Yet if we might be tempted to assert that the voyeurism that Barnum so shrewdly elicited shut down thought, as Melville's cartoon and sketch would suggest, his museum also came close to approximating the utopic wish of many recent multicultural and transnational theorists. Acts of othering require a normative center, a panoptical position, against which the nonnormative may be construed as heteroclite. In Barnum's American Museum, however, otherness was not strategically controlled, at least not along ethnographic, geographic, or nationalist lines, but rather allowed to proliferate to the extent that the term itself becomes voided of any critical significance. When everything is different, nothing is different. The world archive, rather than being reproduced in a progressive, hierarchical constellation, is reduced to aleatory chaos—to nonconsciousness, to the seductive quiddity of objects that precede being mapped, temporally or geographically, by post-Enlightenment nationalist, ethnographic, or naturalist regimes of meaning.

Robert W. Rydell in his study of later nineteenth-century American world fairs shows how anthropological hierarchies, demonstrating evolutionary advancement up the scale of humanity, came to dominate midway exhibitions.[28] Tony Bennett, drawing upon Rydell, suggests that such disciplinary, quasi-anthropological displays in effect "coloniz[ed] the space of earlier freak and monstrosity shows."[29] Barnum had no trouble, as several cultural historians have argued, opportunistically aligning his American Museum in its later post–Civil War incarnations with the discourses of U.S. imperialism and ethnocentric ethnology.[30] But here, in its antebellum guise, the American Museum without intent satisfies the longing of those who would ask us to open ourselves to polynational, polysemous possibilities. One virtue of Barnum's extravaganza of oddity is that no Westernizing master story places the curiosities within a hierarchy.[31] And, from that standpoint, the relics are not unlike how Melville presents Tommo's native friend, Kory-Kory, in *Typee*. There, we will recall, Tommo equated the lavishly tattooed Polynesian with Oliver Goldsmith's illustrated, textual collection of the world's flora and fauna. Yet the ultimate point to be made about the "Portrait of Kory-Kory" is how reticent Melville is about what can be known about him. If the passage seems to make Kory-Kory a sort of specimen in a museum of natural history via the prison-bar trope, the bars that Tommo no less than Kory-Kory cannot pass through, the image nonetheless preserves the Polynesian's—even if semifictional—inviolable selfhood.

My final reading of Tommo's prison-window trope draws upon my sense of Melville's ethnographic skepticism; or his equivocation, for it is not clear whether he wishes to condemn Tommo for the latter's *failure* to pass through the prison-bars and see Kory-Kory and his culture, or condemn him for the presumption of the effort in the first place. Obversely, Melville can be regarded as absolving Tommo of culpability on both counts: he implicitly judges the desire to fathom Kory-Kory as being not ignoble (he respects the attempt), even though he also shows us that cross-cultural barriers may be insurmountable. And perhaps we should follow Melville's lead, or at least let him caution us about our desire to indict all forms of othering. If contemporary ethnographers have come to an impasse, often more preoccupied with the protocols of self-reflexivity than positive knowledge, I think we should accord Melville a certain acuity in his recognition, via the "Portrait of Kory-Kory," of pure otherness as such: to not understand may, paradoxically, be the highest form of empathy, that is, if we take seriously the injunction that all ethnographical or geographical practices inherently cannot look beyond their own discursive optics.

I do not believe that we should forsake our efforts, whatever our national or ethnic allegiances or identities might be, to comprehend those that are foreign to us, nor should we abandon critical discussion of practices that inhibit or further that aim. Proximal knowledge, a willingness to think that we are entering into the interstitial space between ourselves and the other, need not be judged as compromised by the fact that we probably do not ever cross over into the space of difference per se or really very far into the interstitial space, rhetorical or material, itself. Calls for various methods in geographical, travel, and ethnographical writing to be attentive to hybridity are all to the good, as long as we also recognize that metaphors of hybridity are exactly that: they do not likely designate real political or psychological locales we might readily inhabit.

Theory tells us that cultures do not exist in and of themselves. They are, as I remarked in my introduction, always comparative. To what extent, however,

is the cultural analyst therefore obliged to trace down all the comparative fila-
ments? Following the logic of culture being differentially defined, of always
within the realm of hybridity, leads us to plotting endless lines of interconnectedness, to locating positions that can have no position because they exist
only in the eerie, contentless dimension of positionality.[32] These are grave co-
nundrums for those of us who wish to conduct Americanist studies on a more
global scale, to transcend the allure of the nation's grandiosity. I have tried to
skirt them by using a case-study method, and by presenting a delimited set of
cultural, national topoi as they resonated with particular geographical regions:
the law for Melville in Polynesia; the fear of racial admixture and desire for heroic archaeology in the case of Squier and Stephens in Central America; the
wish, for Lynch and other Holy Land travelers, to coordinate Scriptural temporality with the actual Levantine landscape; and, finally, the goal for Delany
and his coemigrationists, of constructing a strong national African-American
identity and state in Africa. Theoretically, and more so when I ramble the
stacks in my home institution's library, I know that I have missed much. My
chapters have assembled only partial stories, excluding a vast network of
voices and interconnections germane to analyzing how U.S. subjects regarded
themselves and their nation vis-à-vis the non-European world.

But methodologically, always a tradeoff between pragmatics and theory, I
think that I am on the right track. By looking at specific authors engaging the
non-European world we do not end up with the chaos of hybridity, but with
very particular narratives about aspects of U.S. national ideology. Those aspects encompass a spectrum from ones widely endorsed at the level of the average, majoritarian citizen; to those more peculiar to select communities or
minority individuals, of whom Delany is an example. If the United States is to
be situated within a more global perspective, the chapter paths taken in this
study—which have triangulated the national, non-European regions or peoples (however mediated), and discrete discursive communities—will need to
be supplemented, amended, or perhaps radically corrected by new and other
ensembles of relationships. Ultimately, my own and those other ensembles
will not produce a unified national narrative, but a proliferation of narratives
about, if I may return to my title, an American geographics, with emphasis
weighted equally on both words, on affiliations deriving from national self-
consciousness or being a national U.S. subject as well as those deriving from
encounters with the plurality of the far-flung world.

Reference Matter

Notes

Introduction

1. Taylor, *At Home and Abroad*, 1. An excellent overview of Taylor's career is Wermuth, *Bayard Taylor*.

2. See Pratt, *Imperial Eyes*, especially chapter 9, for travelers' panoptical self-positioning.

3. Taylor, *At Home and Abroad*, 354–59. I use the term *scopic* or variations on it frequently in this study. The term originates in Freud's sundry discussions of scopophilia (the sexual pleasure derived from visual impressions), was picked up by his epigones, and now has become part of the standard vocabulary in critiques of colonial mimesis and fantasy, especially when the latter (such as Homi K. Bhabha's essays in *The Location of Culture*) draw upon Jacques Lacan's psychoanalytical/semiotic theories of identity formation vis-à-vis the other. In this study, the term will occasionally, but not necessarily, be loaded with the psychoanalytical valences it has for Bhabha, Lacan, or kindred scholars. I use it to designate a drive—with multiple inflections: erotic, political, scientific—that exceeds the motive of looking just for the sake of looking. Moments of encounter, in which the scopic drive or gaze holds a surcharged power and intent, depend for their resonance on widely different discursive contexts (religion, the law, archaeology, geography, and so on). I have not, therefore, been inclined to develop a unified theory about the "scopic" or the "gaze," which would sacrifice the precision of specific cases and circumstances for the allure of reductive—and too complacent—grand claims.

4. Melville, "Traveling: Its Pleasures, Pains, and Profits," in Hayford, MacDougall, and Tanselle, eds., *The Piazza Tales*, 423.

5. Taylor, *A Visit to India, China, and Japan*, 285. All subsequent references will be cited parenthetically.

6. Hawks, *Narrative of the Expedition of an American Squadron*, 187. The best account of Perry is Wiley, *Yankees in the Lands of the Gods*.

7. Hawks, *Narrative of the Expedition of an American Squadron*, 188.

8. Some of the most forceful calls for a less insular approach to American studies include, among others, Desmond and Domínguez, "Resituating American Studies in a Critical Internationalism"; Erkkila, "Ethnicity, Literary Theory, and the Grounds of Resistance"; Kolodyn, "Letting Go Our Grand Obsessions"; Carolyn Porter, "What We Know that We Don't Know"; Saldívar, *The Dialectics of Our America*; and Spillers, "Introduction: Who Cuts the Border? Some Readings on 'America,'" in Spillers, ed.,

Comparative American Identities. Other scholars have advocated that internal, domestic, or gendered discourses and imperial discourses should not be separated. See, for instance, Amy Kaplan, "Romancing the Empire"; and Sánchez-Eppler, "Raising Empires like Children." One of the richest remappings of American studies pertains to cisatlantic affiliations: see, especially, Buell, "American Literary Emergence as a Post-colonial Phenomenon"; Gilroy, *The Black Atlantic*; Shields's groundbreaking *Oracles of Empire*; and Spengemann, "Early American Literature and the Project of Literary History." Postmodernists, suspicious of grand narratives in general, have also come to critique nationalism as a governing aegis for cultural studies. Ella Shohat, for instance, argues for a "relational" analysis of cultural identities that would focus "at once within, between, and beyond the nation-state framework" (quoted in Caren Kaplan, *Questions of Travel*, 186).

9. The theoretical prolegomena (see note 8 above) arguing for revision in the field of American studies has only recently led to specific work on non-European representations in the antebellum period: see, in particular, Obenzinger, *American Palestine*; Schueller, *U.S. Orientalisms*; and Wertheimer, *Imagined Empires*. An invaluable bibliographical survey of the literary culture of U.S. expansionism that also encompasses works describing peoples and nations beyond the present continental United States is Sundquist, "The Literature of Expansion and Race," in Bercovitch, ed., *The Cambridge History of American Literature*, vol. 2. Bibliographical and biographical information on a number of U.S. travelers to all regions of the world may be found in Schramer and Ross, eds., *Dictionary of Literary Biography*, vol. 183.

10. Alcott, *Journals*, excerpted in Davis, ed., *Antebellum American Culture*, 456.

11. Taylor, "The Continents," in *Rhymes of Travel, Ballads and Poems*, 132–36.

12. Amy Kaplan, "Left Alone with America," in Kaplan and Pease, eds., *Cultures of United States Imperialism*, 4.

13. For a useful set of diplomatic documents relevant to expansionism, see Chester, *The Scope and Variety of U.S. Diplomatic History*, vol. 1 (*The Creation of a Republican Empire, 1776–1865*). Two excellent volumes on literary-cultural texts involving imperialistic thematics are Rowe, *Literary Culture and U.S. Imperialism*; and Kaplan and Pease, *Cultures of United States Imperialism* (this collection of essays is, however, skewed mostly toward post–Civil War literature). Vintage studies of expansionism per se include Merk, *Manifest Destiny and Mission*; Tuveson, *Redeemer Nation*; Van Alstyne, *The Rising American Empire*; and Weinberg, *Manifest Destiny*. See also Drinnon, *Facing West*; Hietala, *Manifest Destiny*; Horsman, *Race and Manifest Destiny*; and Hunt, *Ideology and U.S. Foreign Policy*. For notable discussions of the literary representation of nationalist space or the frontier, see Kolodny, *The Lay of the Land*; Marx, *The Machine in the Garden*; Slotkin, *Regeneration through Violence* and *The Fatal Environment*; and Henry Nash Smith, *Virgin Land*. For a brilliant analysis of how U.S. literary works colonize non-European voices, see Cheyfitz, *The Poetics of Imperialism*. Throughout this study, I have also found useful a number of more specialized, geographically oriented works: Lawson-Peebles, *Landscape and Written Expression*; McKinsey, *Niagara Falls*; David C. Miller, *Dark Eden*; and Stigloe, *Common Landscape of America*. For the relations between painting and Manifest Destiny ideology, see, especially, Boime, *The Magisterial Gaze*; Manthorne, *Tropical Renaissance*; and Angela Miller, *The Empire of the Eye*.

14. For a compilation of travel titles, many pertaining to non-European realms, see Harold Smith, *American Travellers Abroad*.

15. Charles A. Goodrich, ed., *The Universal Traveller*, 10–12. In particular, Goodrich indicates that his volume will induce reflection on the true sphere of womanhood: "You

will be able to judge of the value of the Bible and Christian institutions, especially as in their influence on *woman*—how they raise her to her proper rank in the domestic state— expand her mind and refine her character. The false religions and superstitions of the earth, will be seen in all their polluting, degrading, and distressing influence on the sex" (12).

16. Emerson, "Wealth," from *The Conduct of Life* (1860) in Joel Porte, ed., *Emerson: Essays and Lectures*, 995.

17. Emerson, "Power," ibid., 979–80.

18. Emerson, "Wealth," ibid., 994.

19. Henry Howe, ed., *The Travels and Adventures of Celebrated Travellers*, iv, iii.

20. Taylor, ed., *Cyclopaedia of Modern Travel*, viii.

21. For an overview of the relation between exploration and U.S. commercial competition (especially with Great Britain), see Goetzmann, *New Lands, New Men*, 331–62.

22. Herndon's South American expedition, for example, was intended to "put [the government] in possession of certain information" in respect to the navigability of the Amazon and the surrounding valley's "capacities for cultivation, and to the character and extent of its undeveloped commercial resources, whether of field, the forest, the river, or the mine" (Herndon, *Exploration of the Valley of the Amazon*, 20). The Brazilian government restricted foreign navigation of the Amazon and its tributaries; Herndon devotes much of his volume's preface to arguing why the Amazon should be considered an international waterway. An invaluable assortment of reports and narratives written by U.S. naval commanders are reprinted in the series, Hollon, intro., *The New American State Papers: Explorations and Surveys*. For discussions of the artistic, ethnographical, and other aspects of the Wilkes Expedition, see Viola and Margolis, eds., *Magnificent Voyagers*.

23. Wilkes, *Voyage Round the World*, iii.

24. MacCannell, *The Tourist*, xiv–xv.

25. For the imperialistic strategies of appropriation in British and European nineteenth-century travelogues, see Pratt, *Imperial Eyes*. For the relations between Victorian literature and Victorian colonialism, see Brantlinger, *Rule of Darkness*. The field of postcolonial studies, following on the wake of Edward Said's seminal *Orientalism*, is everexpanding: two comprehensive introductions are Ashcroft, Griffiths, and Tiffin, *The Empire Writes Back*; and Moore-Gilbert, *Postcolonial Theory*. See also the anthologies Ashcroft, Griffiths, and Tiffin, eds., *The Post-Colonial Studies Reader*; and Williams and Chrisman, eds., *Colonial Discourse and Post-Colonial Theory*. Other wide-ranging works examining aspects of imperialism, travel-writing, and anthropological discourse include Clifford, *The Predicament of Culture*; Nicholas Thomas, *Colonialism's Culture*; and Torgovnick, *Gone Primitive*.

26. "Political Clap-Trap," *National Intelligencer* (January 15, 1848), in Graebner, ed., *Manifest Destiny*, 239–41.

27. Van Alstyne, in *The Rising American Empire*, explains that with "the appearance of protest and criticism against the island conquests of 1898 and against the alleged 'big stick' policies of Theodore Roosevelt, 'imperialism' became an epithet applied indiscriminately to various nations but to the United States only for the years 1898 to 1912. This period is torn out of context and given a unique frame of reference, leading to the profound historical fallacy that the United States under the influence of Roosevelt suffered an unfortunate temporary 'aberration' from its hallowed traditions, from which it subsequently recovered as from a sickness. From this arose the curious belief that only na-

tions with island possessions are empires" (6). Van Alstyne's point is well taken; but he obscures, I think, the important distinction between colonialism and continental expansionism. For a more speculative approach to the origins of U.S. imperialism (rich in theoretical perspective, although side-stepping historical chronology per se), see Spanos, *America's Shadow*. Spanos summarizes that the "triumphant 'American' way of thinking is not exceptionalist, as it has always been claimed by Americans, especially since de Tocqueville's announcement of the advent of democracy in America, but European, which means metaphysical: an imperial thinking, whose provenance resides in Roman antiquity, that *sees* the being into which it inquires as a totalized spatial image, a 'field' or 'region' or 'domain' to be comprehended, mastered, and exploited" (191).

    28. Calhoun, quoted in Merk, *Manifest Destiny*, 162.

    29. Clayton, quoted in Franchot, *Roads to Rome*, 53.

    30. Perkins, *The Cambridge History of American Foreign Relations*, 1:173.

    31. Taylor, quoted in Beatty, *Bayard Taylor*, 153.

    32. Perry, quoted in Goetzmann, *New Lands, New Men*, 345.

    33. Walker, *The War in Nicaragua*, 280.

    34. Stern, *The Fine Hammered Steel of Herman Melville*, 65.

    35. Breitwieser, "False Sympathy in Melville's *Typee*," 398. Breitwieser himself in several instances cites corrective twentieth-century ethnohistorical assessments of Polynesian culture.

    36. The watershed volumes on the vexing issue of what constitutes authentic ethnographic representation are Clifford, *The Predicament of Culture*; and Clifford and Marcus, eds., *Writing Culture*.

    37. Cheyfitz reminds us of the danger of interpreting Native Americans in Cooper's Leatherstocking novels for "their rhetorical deployment," as if "Indians do not matter, except as they are used to organize desired affect in the European reader" ("Savage Law," in Kaplan and Pease, *Cultures of United States Imperialism*, 121).

    38. For a fascinating account of the constructedness of ethnic genealogy, see Sollors, *Beyond Ethnicity*. An important recent study on monumental (white) history that works to elide or contain counternarratives is Castronovo, *Fathering the Nation*.

    39. Boon, *Other Tribes, Other Scribes*, ix.

    40. Young, *White Mythologies*, 149.

    41. Said claims in *Orientalism* that "if it is true that no production of knowledge in the human sciences can ever ignore or disclaim its author's involvement as a human subject in his own circumstances, then it must also be true that for a European or American studying the Orient there can be no disclaiming the main circumstances of *his* actuality: that he comes up against the Orient as a European or an American first, as an individual second" (11). The assumption that Western subjects invariably or monolithically other the Orient has been impugned by a number of scholars: see, especially Clifford, *The Predicament of Culture*, chapter 11. Moore-Gilbert cautions us that we should avoid positing a "vast synchronic structure whose own unvarying vision detects, in any given Western text on the Orient, an invariant will to power—no matter what its historical context or setting, its specific discursive mode (whether ethnology, law or literature), the culture from which it originates or the culture it represents" (*Postcolonial Theory*, 56).

    42. See, for instance, Blunt and Rose, eds., *Writing Women and Space*. The editors, in their introduction, insist that colonial maps "today should be deconstructed to destabilize" their "power and authority" (9). Deconstruction, apparently, becomes the political tool that will usher in an utopian agenda: "It is central to the efforts of many feminists to

rethink the hegemonic maps of representation in order to move toward the postcolonial moment" (14).

43. I am referring to Kolodyn's clarion call to revise the field of American studies in "Letting Go Our Grand Obsessions": "American literary scholars must begin to create their own new frontiers, openly declaring their agenda as radically comparativist, demandingly interdisciplinary, and exuberantly multilingual" (15).

44. Delany, *Condition*, 14.

45. Fuller, *American Romantic: A Selection from Her Writings and Correspondence*, ed. Perry Miller, 214.

46. For recent feminist efforts to transform phallocentric geographical discourse, see Blunt and Rose, *Writing Women and Space*; and Rose, *Feminism and Geography*. Two of the most important feminist-oriented studies of European travel literature and related texts are (in addition to Pratt's *Imperial Eyes*) McClintock, *Imperial Leather*; and Mills, *Discourses of Difference*.

47. An invaluable collection of U.S. women's travel writing, including a few accounts of travels to non-European lands before the Civil War, is Schriber, ed., *Telling Travels*. See also Schriber's study, *Writing Home*. The scholarship on antebellum Americans' travels to, or representations of, the Old World is extensive. See, especially, Kasson, *Artistic Voyagers*; and Stowe, *Going Abroad*. For fascinating takes on a variety of modern and contemporary U.S. travelers, see Caesar, *Forgiving the Boundaries*.

48. Standard introductions to the history of post–Civil War U.S. imperialism include LaFeber, *The New Empire*; May, *Imperial Democracy*; and Plesur, *America's Outward Thrust*.

Chapter 1

1. For Hannah Adams dispute with Morse, see the entry on Adams in *The Dictionary of American Biography*, 1:60–61.

2. For a psychocultural account of Morse's agoraphobic apprehensions, see Lawson-Peebles, *Landscape and Written Expression*, 64–73. Additional biographical background and information about Morse's geographical career may be found in Ralph H. Brown, "The American Geographies of Jedidiah Morse." Brown also supplies a bibliography listing Morse's various geographies and their multiple editions. For a discussion of Morse in the context of cartographic thematics in Cotton Mather, Benjamin Franklin, and other early American writers, see Boelhower, "Stories of Foundation, Scenes of Origin."

3. Morse to Ebeling, May 27, 1794, quoted in Lawson-Peebles, *Landscape and Written Expression*, 66.

4. Parish to Morse, October 27, 1800, quoted in Ralph H. Brown, "The American Geographies of Jedidiah Morse," 194.

5. Such fears as Morse's over the inadequacy of geographic representation, although intensified because of the Enlightenment drive toward encyclopedic knowledge, are perhaps endemic to geography. See Gregory, "Geography and Cartographic Anxiety," chapter 2 of *Geographical Imaginations*.

6. Ebeling to Morse, August 16, 1794, quoted in Ralph H. Brown, "The American Geographies of Jedidiah Morse," 180–81.

7. See Ralph H. Brown, ibid., 171–83.

8. Bentley, quoted in Ralph H. Brown, ibid., 200.

9. Rigal, in *An American Manufactory*, offers an illuminating analysis of Early Nationalist concerns over knowledge-as-production.

10. Morse to Ebeling, May 27, 1794, quoted in Ralph H. Brown, "The American Geographies of Jedidah Morse," 211.

11. Morse, quoted in Ralph H. Brown, ibid., 186.

12. Morse, *Elements of Geography*, 158. For a discussion of sixteenth- and seventeenth-century New England "geopiety," see Wright, "Notes on Early American Geography," in Wright, *Human Nature in Geography*, 250–85.

13. For Morse's overreliance upon British models of geographical description, I have drawn upon Lawson-Peebles, *Landscape and Written Expression*. He concludes that Morse, prone to anxieties about conspiracy and subversion in the wake of the French Revolution, shrank "further and further from the American terrain, transforming his books into self-referential microcosms which bore little relation to the 'ever changing state of the world' that he had once again lamented in the Preface to his 1812 *Geography*" (71).

14. Ebeling to Morse, September 1, 1811, quoted in Ralph H. Brown, "The American Geographies of Jedidiah Morse," 204–5.

15. Washington, "Farewell Address," in Richard Hofstadter, ed., *Great Issues in American History*, 219.

16. Brückner, "Lessons in Geography," 326, 328.

17. Washington, quoted in Ralph H. Brown, "The American Geographies of Jedidiah Morse," 176.

18. Hamilton, "Method of Geographical Observation," 78. Hamilton was president of the London Royal Geographical Society.

19. "S. E. Morse's Geography," 181.

20. Malte-Brun's geography was first published in America in 1826 as *Universal Geography, or a Description of All Parts of the World, on a New Plan, According to the Great Natural Divisions of the Globe.*

21. For a brief review of the contents, demographics of use, and successive editions of antebellum geographies, see Belok, *Forming the American Minds*; Carpenter, *History of American Schoolbooks*; and Nietz, *The Evolution of American Secondary School Textbooks* and *Old Textbooks*. For the nativist bias in geography textbooks, see Fell, *The Foundations of Nativism in American Textbooks*. The best treatment of the role that American textbooks played in supporting orthodox (New England) values is Elson, *Guardians of Tradition*; she concludes that the "world created in nineteenth-century schoolbooks is essentially a world of fantasy—a fantasy made by adults as a guide for their children, but inhabited by no one outside the pages of the schoolbooks" (337). See also Avery, *Behold the Child*. A partial bibliography of nineteenth-century American geographies (some of which are not listed in the bibliographies of the previously cited volumes) may be found in Svobodny, ed., *Early American Textbooks*.

22. Warntz, *Geography Now and Then*, 26–27. The decline of geography as a formal, academic science in the early decades of the nineteenth century occurred in Britain and Europe as well. Capel, in "Institutionalization of Geography and Strategies of Change," in Stoddart, ed., *Geography, Ideology, and Social Concern*, summarizes the findings of a number of geographical historians and concludes that in the first half of the nineteenth century "geography frequently appears as a science on the point of disappearance, lacking academic interest—except for historians—forgotten or impugned by many scientists and appreciated solely by the general public because of the descriptions of exotic coun-

tries that it contained" (46). He also notes, however, that the "necessity to train geography teachers for primary and middle schools," starting from the beginning of the 1850s, "was the essential factor which led to the [re]institutionalization of geography in the university and the appearance of the scientific community of geographers" (38). For an overview of the emergence of geography as a modern science, see Dickinson, *The Makers of Modern Geography*; and Stoddart, *On Geography and Its History*. No antebellum geographers are discussed in either study, because geography remained in the United States until after the Civil War a pedagogical, rather than scientific, discipline. Three excellent critiques of the history of Eurocentric geographical practices are Blaut, *The Colonizer's Model of the World*; Dathorne, *Imagining the World*; and Martin W. Lewis and Wigen, *The Myth of Continents*. For valuable critiques of (and efforts to replace) totalizing geographic schemes, see Duncan and Ley, eds., *Place/Culture/Representation*; and Lutz and Collins, *Reading National Geographic*. A useful introduction to the academic zeitgeist in respect to spatial studies and related discourses is Blair, "Cultural Geography and the Place of the Literary."

23. Woodbridge, *A System of Universal Geography*, vii–viii. The phrase "durability of impression" comes from the preface to Emma Willard's *Rudiments of Geography* (1821), which Woodbridge excerpts at length in his own preface.

24. Savage, *The World: Geographical, Historical, and Statistical*, 4.

25. Samuel Goodrich, *A Pictorial Geography of the World*, 1:9.

26. Mitchell, *Mitchell's Geographical Reader*, 4.

27. Savage, *The World: Geographical, Historical, and Statistical*, 3.

28. Samuel Goodrich, *The World and Its Inhabitants*, vol. 20 (the concluding one) of *Parley's Cabinet Library*, 314, 318, 323.

29. Smith, quoted in Nietz, *Old Textbooks*, 196.

30. Willard, from *Rudiments of Geography*, quoted in Woodbridge, *A System of Universal Geography*, x.

31. Mitchell, *Geographical Reader*, iii.

32. For Adam Ferguson's influence on the American conceptualization of history and, more particularly, historical romances, see Dekker, *The American Historical Romance*, 74–80.

33. Samuel Goodrich, *Peter Parley's Method of Telling about Geography to Children*, 108–10.

34. The best concise account of the polygenesis debate, which emerged in the 1840s, remains Stanton, *The Leopard's Spots*. See also Young, "Egypt in America, the Confederacy in London," chapter 5 of his *Colonial Desire*.

35. William Warren, *A Systematic View of Geography*, 122.

36. Guyot, quoted in Elson, *Guardians of Tradition*, 67.

37. Foucault, *The Order of Things*, 55. Fabian, in *Time and the Other*, similarly observes that "by allowing Time to be reabsorbed by the tabular space of classification, nineteenth-century anthropology sanctioned an ideological process by which relations between West and its Other, between anthropology and its object, were conceived not only as difference, but as distance in space *and* Time" (147). See also note 46 below.

38. Fitch and Colton, *Colton and Fitch's Introductory School Geography*, 16–17.

39. Mitchell, *Mitchell's Primary Geography*, iv.

40. For a discussion of how nineteenth-century geographies, histories, and other textbooks treat the issue of American slavery, see Elson, *Guardians of Tradition*, 88–94. Not surprisingly, one of the major exceptions to the general pattern of mollification was

Harriet Beecher Stowe's *First Geography for Children*, published in 1855: "[In] slave states the land is divided into plantations, and the owners force men to work for them whether they wish to or not; and if they do not do as much as is required, they are whipped by the overseers.... Those people in the Southern States who are too poor to own slaves, seeing labor is disgraceful, become shiftless and indolent. And those who have slaves are tempted to be cruel and unjust; so that, though many are kind to their slaves, many others become unjust, severe, and cruel" (72–74).

41. Colton and Fitch, *Introductory School Geography*, 49, 89.

42. Mitchell, *A General View of the World*, iv.

43. "Stowe's *Primer Geography*," 550.

44. Stowe, *First Geography for Children*, 12.

45. Samuel Goodrich, *Manners and Customs of the Principal Nations of the Globe*, in *Parley's Cabinet Library*, 19:8–11.

46. Blaut in *The Colonizer's Model of the World* refers to such geographical-moral polarities as "spatial elitism" (12), the result of a long-standing belief in "diffusionism" or the axiomatic notion that core values of civilization and enlightenment emerge from one particular geographical (always Western) locale. Livingstone, "Climate's Moral Economy: Science, Race and Place in Post-Darwinian British and American Geography," in Godlewska and Smith, eds., *Geography and Empire*, remarks that geographical discourse emphasizing "climatic matters throughout the nineteenth, and well into the twentieth century, were profoundly implicated in the imperial drama and were frequently cast in the diagnostic language of ethnic judgment" (137).

47. The only biography of Goodrich is Roselle, *Samuel Griswold Goodrich*. It offers a complete listing of the Parley titles.

48. Hart, *The Popular Book*, 153.

49. Samuel Goodrich, *Peter Parley's Method of Telling about Geography to Children*, 20–25.

50. Samuel Goodrich, *The Tales of Peter Parley about Asia*, 1.

51. Samuel Goodrich, *Peter Parley's Tales about the Islands in the Pacific Ocean*, 80–81.

52. Ibid., 103.

53. Samuel Goodrich, *The Tales of Peter Parley about Africa*, 42.

54. Samuel Goodrich, *The Tales of Peter Parley about Asia*, 39.

55. Samuel Goodrich, *Peter Parley's Tales about the Islands in the Pacific Ocean*, 111–12.

56. Samuel Goodrich, *Peter Parley's Method of Telling about Geography to Children*, 97.

57. Samuel Goodrich, *Peter Parley's Tales about the Islands in the Pacific Ocean*, 100–101.

58. The *Typee* redaction appeared under the title "Typee" and refers to Melville directly as the narrator/experiencer of the adventures. For a superb analysis of Child's entire oeuvre, including her tales for juveniles, see Karcher, *The First Woman in the Republic*.

59. Samuel Goodrich, *The Tales of Peter Parley about Africa*, 121.

60. JanMohamed, "The Economy of Manichean Allegory," in Ashcroft, Griffiths, and Tiffin, eds., *The Post-Colonial Studies Reader*, 19.

61. Charles A. Goodrich, *The Universal Traveller*, 503–4.

62. Samuel Goodrich, *A Pictorial Geography of the World*, 2:855–56.

63. For a discussion of Cuvier's description of the so-called Hottentot Venus and the European tradition of maligning the Hottentot (now referred to as the San or !Kung)

tribes for their physiognomy, see Gilman, "Black Bodies, White Bodies," in Gates, ed., *"Race," Writing, and Difference*, 223–61.

64. Boelhower aptly remarks that "no encyclopedia can pretend to control ethnic sign production" (*Through a Glass Darkly*, 32).

65. The title of the Dakota edition is *Maka-oyakapi: Guyot's Elementary Geography in the Dakota Language;* it was published in 1876.

66. James D. Dana, "Memoir of Arnold Guyot, 1807–1884," in *National Academy of Sciences: Biographical Memoirs*, 2:335. Professor William Libbey, a student of Guyot's who succeeded him in 1902 at Princeton, wrote that "his influence did not terminate in the classroom or study. His books reached the teachers of the land, and his methods adopted with much interest and zeal, served to reform geographical teaching on this continent" (quoted in Warntz, *Geography Now and Then*, 87). Besides Dana's memoir, for biographical information on Guyot, I have drawn upon the Guyot entry in Larkin and Peters, *Biographical Dictionary of Geography*, 101–7.

67. For these and other encomiums, see the "Advertisement" section preceding the text proper of Guyot, *The Earth and Man*. All subsequent page references to Guyot's text will be cited parenthetically.

68. "Guyot's *The Earth and Man*," 435.

69. For the connections between Guyot and his mentors Ritter and Humboldt, I have relied upon Wright, *Geography in the Making*, 44–46.

70. For a discussion of Humboldt's *Cosmos* as it contributed to nineteenth-century geographical practice, and for eighteenth- and nineteenth-century European geographical science in general, see Dickinson, *The Makers of Modern Geography*, 10–48.

71. Brooks Adams, *The New Empire*, vii.

72. In March 1852, Guyot delivered in New York City a public course of lectures, which appeared in print in the *Evening Post;* they were published, after three decades of being reworked in 1884, as *Creation or the Biblical Cosmogony in the Light of Modern Science*. For a comprehensive study of the complex rhetoric that fused science and religion in nineteenth-century America, see Bozeman, *Protestants in an Age of Science*.

73. Tocqueville, *Democracy in America*, 2:106.

74. See Lutz and Collins, *Reading National Geographic*, for a thorough analysis of the photos of the journal as crucial to its U.S./Euro-centric dynamics.

Chapter 2

1. See, for instance, Sanborn, *The Sign of the Cannibal*, which programmatically positions Melville as a postcolonial writer whose texts put on *stage* imperial discourses rather than merely embodying or debunking them. See note 6 below for a review of other critics that highlight the ethnographic self-consciousness of *Typee*.

2. Stowe, *First Geography for Children*, 164.

3. Melville, *Typee*, 83. All subsequent page references will be cited parenthetically.

4. JanMohamed, "The Economy of Manichean Allegory," in Ashcroft, Griffiths, and Tiffin, eds., *The Post-Colonial Studies Reader*, 19.

5. Berthold, in "Portentous Somethings," discusses the ethnocentrism of the prison metaphor as it foregrounds the "pitfalls inherent in the telling of a captivity tale" (567), that is, of an outsider attempting to convey an insider's view of the other.

6. Breitwieser in "False Sympathy" and Samson in *White Lies*, for instance, both forcefully argue that Tommo's ambivalent response to native culture is shaped more by

the conflicted mid-Victorian American values he brings with him than by his compre-
hension of what the *real* Typees may have been like. Both challenge, and in essence condemn, Tommo for the poverty or inconsistencies of his ethnographic method. Samson
claims that Melville primarily intends to subvert Tommo's (and his culture's) myths of
primitivism and progress. Breitwieser believes that we must not conflate the mature, self-
reflective artist with the naive, resentful Tommo, who exploits the Typees because he is
"only interested in them as a negation of what he detests rather than as a culture that is
comprehensively alien to *all* aspects of his own" ("False Sympathy," 398). Their argument
that Melville critiques Tommo for self-aggrandizing representations serves, in part, to
insulate the former from blame. The author escapes the problem of depicting the Typees
in some more authentic, less instrumental fashion because he does not depict them at
all—only Tommo does. If, however, we do not believe that Melville fully achieves the de-
familiarization effect of the aesthetic, if we do not accept the absolute noncoincidence between Tommo's and Melville's perspectives, *Typee* must be seen as a text complicit with
rather than exposing Tommo's tendentious portrayal. In a usefully nontraditional
reading, "*Typee*: Melville's Critique of Community," Dimock observes that, thematically, "Typee stands not as the polar opposite of America, but as its analogy" (27); she believes that Melville's statements about Typeean conformity—for example, that the natives "all thought and acted alike" (*Typee*, 203)—should register as his complaint against
antebellum America's obsession with realizing a "perfect community" (35). Dimock's
approach relieves her from the need to question the ethnographical soundness of how the
Typees are represented, because whatever "particular[ity]" the Typees may have had for
Melville, that particularity becomes subsumed in the author's "generic" (37) critique of
community. This interpretive strategy has the advantage of allowing Dimock to skirt the
perplexing issue of how and when we are to distinguish the authorial Melville from
Tommo, as he appears in either the guise of retrospective narrator or embodied character. But it also has a disadvantage: if Typee is deemed only analogous to the United States,
the specific historical-political conditions of Polynesia in the early 1840s may be overly
slighted. In the symbolic and allegorical works that Melville next wrote, *Omoo* (1847) and
Mardi (1849), factual U.S. relations to Polynesia may be largely irrelevant to interpretation. In the case of *Typee*, however, those relations simply cannot be ignored. For more
recent essays examining Melville's vexed imperial dynamics, see Rowe, "Melville's *Typee*:
U.S. Imperialism at Home and Abroad," in Pease, ed., *National Identities and Post-
Americanist Narratives*; and Schueller, "Indians, Polynesians, and Empire Making," in
Quinby, ed., *Genealogy and Literature,* who argues that the "Melvillean narrator, although critical of colonialism, nonetheless situates himself within the discourse as colo-
nist in order to maintain the separation between himself and the natives, a separation on
which his racial and cultural identity depends" (49). For two opposed perspectives on
whether Melville transcends colonial racist thinking or is, at least partially, embedded
within it, see Otter, "'Race' in *Typee* and *White-Jacket*," in Levine, ed., *The Cambridge
Companion to Herman Melville*; and Sanborn, *The Sign of the Cannibal*. Sanborn proposes that *Typee* should be regarded as a postcolonial text that exposes the constructedness of the cannibalism topos: Melville "attempts to redirect our attention from the symbolic meaning *of* cannibalism to the antisymbolic implications of the discourse *on* cannibalism. Using nothing but explanations of cannibalism that are already in circulation, he
takes us down a path of reflection that ends at the moment when the perception of cannibalism as a romantic act of vengeance gives way to the perception of cannibalism as a kind
of stage effect, the function of certain exterior signs that are activated in the name of ter-

ror" (77–78). Otter, in his reading of *Typee*'s bodily thematics (especially that of race), less willingly elevates Melville above his era's discourses: "Melville is an immanent, not a transcendent, manipulator of antebellum ideas about race, subject to all the dangers of entanglement and complicity such a position implies" (14). For an insightful analysis of *Typee* in relation to the general ethnographical problem of conveying an insider's view of cultural difference, see Calder, "The Thrice Mysterious Taboo"; for a broad discussion of the liabilities of expecting travel writers to be good ethnographers, see Caesar, *Forgiving the Boundaries*, 116–28.

7. Dennis Porter in *Desire and Transgression in European Travel Writing*, chapter 3, provides an excellent reading of Bougainville and the debate over Polynesian cultural virtues. For a far-ranging study of the cultural uses of primitivism, see Torgovnick, *Gone Primitive*.

8. My analysis of *Typee* overlaps with a number of previous interpretations that warrant review here (besides those mentioned in note 6 above). Stern, *The Fine Hammered Steel of Herman Melville*, established a critical tradition that maps the narrative's thematics along a binary divide (body/mind, mythological time/chronological time, sensual pleasure/bourgeois restraint, oral culture/written culture, and so on) and that analyzes Tommo's discomfort in terms of what he would have to forsake if he continued to dwell with the Typees. His landmark analysis of the novel suggests that Tommo finally finds himself discontent in the valley of the Typees because he dreads succumbing to mental torpor, to a day-to-day complacency, that, however pleasurable when compared with the toils and brutalities of shipboard life, cannot satisfy the questing, essentially modern Western hero. Rogin (in *Subversive Genealogy*, 42–49) and Ziff (in *Literary Democracy*, 1–12), although defining the antebellum milieu that Tommo initially rejects when he seeks refuge with the Typees, do not attend to specific U.S.-Polynesian relations.

9. Charles Anderson in *Melville in the South Seas* charts the interplay among biographical fact, borrowings, and fiction in Melville's sea novels. For a discussion of *Typee* triangulated with the reports of Porter and Stewart, see T. Walker Herbert, Jr., *Marquesan Encounters*. For an overview of additional eighteenth- and nineteenth-century European travel texts about the South Seas, see Rennie, *Far-Fetched Facts*.

10. For an intriguing account of how American and European trade in sandalwood affected the internal politics and economics of Hawaii, see Sahlins, "Cosmologies of Capitalism," in Dirks, Eley, and Ortner, eds., *Culture/Power/History*. My discussion of American-Polynesian relations in general draws upon Bradley, *The American Frontier in Hawaii*; Dodge, *New England and the South Seas*; Joesting, *Hawaii*; Strauss, *Americans in Polynesia*; and Van Alstyne, *The Rising American Empire*, 124–46. For a history of the Protestant missionary movement, see Gunson, *Messengers of Grace*. An excellent account of Hawaii's drawn-out emergence as a U.S. state is Roger Bell, *Last among Equals*. The most comprehensive study of European representations of the South Seas remains Bernard Smith's *European Vision and the South Pacific*. See also, Edmond, *Representing the South Pacific*.

11. Richard Henry Dana, Jr., "Cleveland's *Voyages*," 193, 192, 195–96. In his *Two Years Before the Mast: A Personal Narrative of Life at Sea* (1840), Dana claimed that "diseases" spread by traders "are now sweeping off the native population of the Sandwich Islands, at the rate of one fortieth of the entire population annually. They seem to be a doomed people" (322).

12. Jarves, "Laws of the Sandwich Islands," 311. In the main the laws established, for both the masses and the Hawaiian chiefs, the rights of property. Jarves achieved modest

fame later as the author of several travel guides (on Paris and Rome) and as an interpreter of Oriental art and artifacts. He also wrote *Kiana: A Tradition of Hawaii* (1857), a romantic, pseudohistorical novel about a shipwrecked sixteenth-century Spanish priest and woman who, through intermarriage, become linked with Hawaiian nobility. For a discussion of *Kiana*, and other nineteenth-century texts about Polynesia, in the context of indigenous traditions and knowledge, see Sumida, *And the View from the Shore.*

    13. Alexander, quoted in Bradley, *American Frontier*, 324.

    14. Dana, quoted in Rufus Anderson, *The Hawaiian Islands*, 105.

    15. Cheever, *Life in the Sandwich Islands*, 3. All subsequent page references will be cited parenthetically.

    16. Bingham, *A Residence of Twenty-One Years in the Sandwich Islands*, 93–94. All subsequent page references will be cited parenthetically.

    17. Cheever, *The Island World of the Pacific*, 20.

    18. Jarves, *History of the Hawaiian or Sandwich Islands*, 377. All subsequent page references will be cited parenthetically.

    19. When Jarves emphasizes the spread of Anglo-Saxon law, he illustrates Reginald Horsman's comment that by the middle decades of the nineteenth century "American expansionism [was] viewed in the United States less as a victory for the principles of free democratic republicanism than as evidence of the innate superiority of the American Anglo-Saxon branch of the Caucasian race" (*Race and Manifest Destiny*, 1). The missionaries, who up to the 1840s held a monopoly on printing, were instrumental in importing a canon of British and American cultural texts beyond the Bible. Lessons in English were provided; but initially the missionaries, after having reduced the Hawaiian oral language to writing, translated texts into Hawaiian, and they maintained (at least the pretense) that the speech of the Hawaiians should be preserved. See Bradley, *American Frontier*, 130–55. In his South Seas lecture of 1858, Melville particularly objected to linguistic imperialism: "But now Americans and other foreigners are there, and lately a suggestion has been reported to abolish the Hawaiian language in their schools and exclude those children who speak it. I threw down the paper on reading this, exclaiming, 'Are they to give up all that binds them together as a nation or race—their language? Then are they indeed blotted out as a people'" ("The South Seas," 420). For a suggestive study of Melville's preoccupation with markings as a sign of authorial labor, in the sense of revisions and other sources of writerly anxiety, see Renker, "Melville's Spell in *Typee*."

    20. Some of the missionaries acquired land and became wealthy. "Gradually the missionary inclined to change first into a governmental official, and thence into a landowner and speculator. Thus the Reverend Richard Armstrong exchanged a meager mission pittance for $3000 a year from the king, which he proceeded to use toward the purchase of land. By 1849 Armstrong held 600 acres, [and] tripled his holdings during the next year. ... By 1852 ten missionaries had acquired land, averaging 400 acres apiece" (Van Alstyne, *Rising American Empire*, 129).

    21. John Sullivan Dwight, quoted in Branch, ed., *Melville: The Critical Heritage*, 113, 75–76.

    22. Bourdieu, *Outline of a Theory of Practice*, 21.

    23. Tommo says that the "civil institutions of the Marquesas Islands appear to be ... directly the reverse of those of the Tahitian and Hawiian groups, where the original power of the king and chiefs was far more despotic than that of any tyrant in civilized countries" (186). Spate in *Paradise Found and Lost* states that "Hawaii is *sui generis* in the Polynesian world; not so much in material culture as in the degree of centralised political

organization. . . . The final form of the Hawaiian State was certainly affected by direct European influences, but both traditional and archaeological evidences suggest that the trend to formal quasi-monarchical rule, initially over a single island, set in some centuries earlier" (17). Tommo's—or Melville's—attitude toward the differing polities of the South Seas also reflects racist categories; see note 50 below.

24. Charles S. Stewart, *A Visit to the South Seas*, 1:265.

25. The editors of the Northwestern-Newberry edition of *Typee* note that, for an 1892 reissue by Arthur Griffin Stedman, Mrs. Melville requested the following change: "In Chap 3d . . . substitute 'Desolate' (Island) for 'Buggerry' (Island)" (cited in "Note on the Text," *Typee*, 312).

26. My abbreviated reading of the homoerotic/cannibalism link in *Typee* derives, in part, from Crain, "Lovers of Human Flesh":

[By] the time Melville sat down to write *Typee* . . . he was aware that the savages of the Marquesas were famous for two secret practices outrageous to Victorian civilization. The public already associated the South Seas with cannibalism and a peculiar voluptuousness. Melville was free to play with these associations. Among his innovations was to associate this cannibalism and voluptuousness with each other.

Cannibalism and homosexuality shared the trope of preterition and the topos of the South Seas in the culture at large. A third similarity—panic at discovery—is perhaps more Melville's innovation than it is common intellectual property. The discovery of cannibalism in Melville resembles the discovery of homosexuality in Gothic novels. (32)

For other insightful discussions of the thematics of cannibalism in *Typee* and Melville's later novels, see Lyons, "From Man-Eaters to Spam-Eaters"; and Sanborn, *The Sign of the Cannibal*.

27. An absorbing study of seventeenth- and eighteenth-century efforts to square biblical history to the emerging disciplines that chronicle time and how those efforts involved theories of writing and the law may be found in Rossi, *The Dark Abyss of Time*.

28. Breitwieser feels that Tommo's "uneasy imitation" of the language of the Declaration of Independence in this episode "betrays rather than disguises the moral dubiousness of the desertion" ("False Sympathy," 401). Berthold argues that although Tommo's rationale is not entirely "unpersuasive," "it lacks specificity" and therefore seems more a product of "a powerful but uncertain urge to flee" ("Portentous Somethings," 551). Revolt often legitimates itself through reference to higher law or the invocation of precursor declarations; but there is no reason to assume, at least in this case, that Tommo is not the victim he portrays himself to be.

29. Locke, *Two Treatises of Government*, 448.

30. Turner, *Drama, Fields, Metaphors*, 37.

31. According to Rogin, the "swollen leg signifies the stimulation of Tommo's desire, and prevents him from satisfying it. . . . To get pleasure, Tommo gives up power" (*Subversive Genealogy*, 44). For Ziff, the wound is "symbolic of the psychic wound visited upon him by civilization and of the wholeness that can be reclaimed by submission to the natural—specifically, it symbolizes the malfunctioning of the sexual organ inhibited by arbitrary social codes and its restoration in a sexual environment that knows no guilt" (*Literary Democracy*, 9).

32. Even Rogin, otherwise finely attuned to the interplay between psychological dynamics and historical context in Melville's novels, reads *Typee* primarily in terms of ahis-

torical psychoanalytical oppositions (a desire to subvert paternal authority; a longing for—but also fear of engulfment by—the maternal). See *Subversive Genealogy*, 42–49.

33. Ledyard, *A Journal of Captain Cook's Last Voyage*, 75–76.

34. Bartram, *Travels of William Bartram*, 388; Jefferson, *Notes on the State of Virginia*, in Peterson, ed., *The Portable Thomas Jefferson*, 133–34.

35. Jarves emphasized, as well, that non-Protestant history meant declension from Scriptural truth: "[K]nowledge of the true God was lost among many families soon after the world was peopled; else was buried amid a mass of superstitions and heathen ceremonies, which each generation increased" (*History of the Hawaiian or Sandwich Islands*, 41). Notions of theological degeneracy go back at least as far as Johann Boemus's *Omnium Gentium Mores* (1520; English title, *Fardle of facions* [1555]), which, as James Boon writes, "syncretized the Bible and ethnological information from travelers, missionaries, and traders" in order to explain diversity as declension-from-divinity, when there can be no theological transmission, as Boemus puts it, between "minde to minde without letters" (*Affinities and Extremes*, 40). Here, David Spurr's comment on how the typical imperialist perceives native social behavior is apposite: "They live . . . in their bodies and in natural space, but not in a body politic worthy of the name" (*The Rhetoric of Empire*, 22).

36. Dening, in *Islands and Beaches*, explains that late eighteenth- and nineteenth-century visitors to the Polynesian islands found the taboo system puzzling because while it clearly prescribed behavior, its structuration eluded their perceptions: taboos seemed "bewilderingly irrational. Some *tapu* were thought to be intelligible as means by which women were kept in a degraded state; others were intelligible as symbols and instruments of social class. Most were seen to be without purpose or function and were taken as haphazard superstitions, sacraments of savagery that signaled benighted minds and would keep them as such perpetually. They were seen as burdensome and capricious, morally disgusting, socially oppressive. . . . [Visitors] found it difficult to recognize a political and social reality which did not display in sign and ritual the sorts of authority they thought natural" (52). For a fascinating account of how early anthropological studies influenced British Victorian notions of social control, see Christopher Herbert, *Culture and Anomie*. For a wide-ranging discussion of the interplay between travel writing, anthropological discourse, and the history of European-Polynesian colonial relations, see Nicholas Thomas, *In Oceania*.

37. The genealogy of British common law, the history of its transmission to the colonies, and its subsequent modification to fit into the post-Revolutionary era is extraordinarily complex and involves issues particular to the changing functions of the judiciary and aspects of antebellum society at large. The best overviews may be found in Friedman, *A History of American Law*; Horwitz, *The Transformation of American Law*; and William E. Nelson, *Americanization of the Common Law*. For a less technical survey, see Perry Miller, *The Life of the Mind in America from the Revolution to the Civil War*, 99–265, which superbly covers the connections among antebellum legal rhetoric, practice, and theory and broader intellectual and cultural patterns; and Perry Miller's prefaces to the legal documents collected in *The Legal Mind in America*. An excellent discussion of temporality and British common law, especially in respect to Edmund Burke, may be found in Pocock, *Politics, Language and Time*, 202–32.

38. Root, "The Origin of Government and Laws in Connecticut, 1798," quoted in Perry Miller, *Legal Mind in America*, 35. Kent, quoted in Perry Miller, *The Life of the Mind in America*, 132. Frelinghuysen, quoted in Schlesinger, *The Age of Jackson*, 330.

39. Melville's understanding that the Typees' cohesive social-political structure is

founded on the efficiency of unwritten law is also emphasized by Scorza, "Tragedy in the State of Nature."

40. Sampson, *An Anniversary Discourse*, 5, 11. Alexis de Tocqueville summed up what legal reformists thought of the common law, when he wrote that because he relies upon common law, "the English or American lawyer resembles the hierophants of Egypt, for like them he is the sole interpreter of an occult science" (*Democracy in America*, 1:287). Obfuscation occurred in the main because actual legal practice did not correspond to legal rhetoric. Friedman explains that "in theory, the common law was not man-made in the ordinary sense; the judges uncovered the law (or 'found' it); they did not make it, or tamper with it as it was found" (*A History of American Law*, 19). In practice, however, judges in effect made new laws to fit new contingencies; this elastic and progressive concept of the law, as Friedman shows, was difficult to square with the convention of law being discovered, and it led to even more convoluted writing in decisions being handed down from the bench.

41. Shaw, quoted in Chase, *Lemuel Shaw*, 233.

42. Story, *A Discourse*, 6.

43. Ziff, *Literary Democracy*, 9, 10.

44. Skepticism about native oral historiography is a topos of nineteenth-century archaeological and travel writing; modern-day anthropologists as well often posit the native in a "timeless" realm and themselves in a chronologically progressive time. See Fabian's now-standard *Time and the Other*.

45. This supererogatory legal rhetoric was likely also part of the "entertainment" that Melville had promised his future father-in-law, Judge Shaw, in a letter written directly before the novel's publication (quoted in Rogin, *Subversive Genealogy*, 43). Another instance is when Tommo describes a native chief's use of a razor presented as a gift: he concludes that "as the chief expressed the liveliest satisfaction at the result, I was too wise to dissent from his opinion" (122).

46. Nietzsche, *On the Genealogy of Morals*, 61.

47. Bhabha, in *The Location of Culture*, analyses colonizers' stereotyping as crucially structured by ambivalence, by an oscillating transition from scopic certainty/objectification to a certain contagion of identities between the colonizer and colonized during the moment of the stereotypic gaze:

> An important feature of colonial discourse is its dependence on the concept of 'fixity' in the ideological construction of otherness. Fixity, as the sign of cultural/historical/racial difference in the discourse of colonialism, is a paradoxical mode of representation: it connotes rigidity and an unchanging order as well as disorder, degeneracy and daemonic repetition. Likewise the stereotype, which is its major discursive strategy, is a form of knowledge and identification that vacillates between what is always 'in place', already known, and something that must be anxiously repeated ... as if the essential duplicity of the Asiatic or the bestial sexual license of the African that needs no proof, can never really, in discourse, be proved. ... [The] play between metaphoric/narcissistic and metonymic/aggressive moments in colonial discourse ... crucially recognizes the prefiguring of desire as a potentially conflictual, disturbing force. ... In the objectification of the scopic drive there is always the threatened return of the look; in the identification of the Imaginary relation there is always the alienating other (or mirror) which crucially returns its image to the subject; and in that form of substitution and fixation that is fetishism there is always the trace of loss, absence. (66, 81)

Throughout my study, however, I have resisted the allure of Bhabha's perspective, which to my mind so emphasizes ambivalence and oscillating rhetorical movements, is so driven by a rhetorical drive to inhabit a critical posture of interstitiality, that discrete claims about what colonizers or imperialists *thought* becomes entirely obscured.

48. Giltrow, "Speaking Out," 19.

49. Very few interpretations of *Typee* engage the crucial appendix. In the essays collected in Stern's *Critical Essays on Herman Melville's "Typee,"* for instance, there are by my count only three passing references to Paulet and the appendix.

50. Charles Anderson offers one explanation of why Melville's attitude in the appendix is so hostile toward the Hawaiians. Whereas Melville delighted in the Marquesans because they had not yet been tainted by intercourse with Europeans, the Hawaiian natives "he evidently considered already polluted beyond redemption; it was of little moment, then, that the English or any nation should usurp control of their mock civilization which was already in the hands of a foreign rabble" (*Melville in the South Seas*, 336). Melville (or Tommo), we should note, distinguishes the Marquesans not only along lines of political organization, but also along racial lines. For example, the ruler of Hawaii, King Kamehameha III, is referred to as a "fat, lazy, negro-looking blockhead" (189); and Typee women are observed to have complexions "almost as white as any Saxon damsel's" (182). Schueller points out that in "terms of the racial politics of antebellum United States, the Typees, we could say, could almost 'pass' for white and therefore, it is implied, their being called 'savages' is a gross injustice" ("Indians, Polynesians, and Empire Making" [59]).

51. For Melville's misremembering and other details of his stay in Honolulu during these months, see Howard, *Herman Melville*, 68–70.

52. Paulet's imperial intent is a matter of historical record. In his report to England's secretary of the admiralty, he observed that this second cession of Hawaii had occurred precisely forty-nine years after Captain George Vancouver received the islands for England from the hands of Kamehameha I. Evaluating Paulet's rule is difficult because contemporary reports are clouded by nationalist sentiment and the interests of the various, competing power-brokers (missionaries, Hawaiian royalty, and representatives of American and British mercantilism). Bradley feels that Paulet was a "virtual dictator" (*American Frontier*, 436) of the subordinated Hawaiian government, and the missionaries despised him (which is why, in part, Melville takes his side). Joesting summarizes: "He was lionized by the English community, and even some of the Americans thought he ruled the Islands well. Women found the handsome, outgoing captain to be a very attractive man, and Paulet did what he could to encourage their interest. . . . The Hawaiian government [however] was bruised by Paulet's actions and desperately needed a champion. Admiral Thomas proved to be that hero. He quickly made it known that the official feeling of the British government was that the Islands should be returned to the Hawaiian monarchy" (*Hawaii*, 134). The effect of the usurpation on Kamehameha III was considerable: "[It] was a time of heartbreak. The situation drove him to the edge of madness" (*Hawaii*, 131). For a firsthand, partisan account of how the resident American missionaries regarded Paulet, see Laura Fish Judd's *Honolulu*, 174–82.

53. Bradley, *American Frontier*, 2.

54. Judd, *Honolulu*, 174.

55. Rousseau, *The Social Contract*, in Bair, trans., *The Essential Rousseau*, 37–38.

56. The appendix's assertion of a unified, authorial self can usefully be seen in light of McClintock's brief comments on cannibalism and imperial fantasies of control in *Impe-*

rial Leather: "This anxious vision marks one aspect . . . of a recurrent doubling in male imperial discourse. This may be seen as the simultaneous dread of catastrophic boundary *loss* (implosion), associated with fears of impotence and infantilization and attended by an *excess* of boundary order and fantasies of unlimited power" (26).

57. Rogin believes the dedication to be satiric, since Typee society represents "an alternative to the family exclusiveness of the Melvills and Gansevoorts, and the propertied legalism of Judge Shaw. On Typee the judge was superfluous" (*Subversive Genealogy*, 44). Although not implausible, Rogin's interpretation discounts Melville's counterinvestment in, or longing for, benign authority. For Melville's engagement in his post-*Typee* fiction with the legal thinking and decisions of Shaw, see Brooks Thomas, *Cross-examinations of Law and Literature.*

58. For a book that "looks at the savage life with a captivated eye," William Bourne wrote in the *Christian Parlor Magazine*, it comes as a "matter of surprise . . . that [it] could have obtained the name of LEMUEL SHAW" (in Branch, *Melville: The Critical Heritage*, 88).

59. Boon, *Affinities and Extremes*, 195.

60. Melville, "The South Seas," 419–20.

61. Mark Twain, *Roughing It*, 345.

Chapter 3

1. For a brilliant analysis of how Melville's travel fictions and *Clarel* complexly bring into conjunction the non-European other and the otherness of, for Melville particularly, the unknowable deity of Protestantism, see Franchot, "Melville's Traveling God," in Levine, *The Cambridge Companion to Herman Melville*, 157–85. She writes, in summary, that "Melville's authorial project involves the translation or forced travel of his religious inheritance into fiction, a translation which abases *and* reanimates the sacred by bringing it down into the horizontal trajectory of fictional narrative. Beginning with his early Polynesian fictions, Melville's lifelong narrative and poetic investigation into the nature and limits of religious belief is entangled with the dynamics of cultural encounter. His writings braid the incomprehensibilities of cultural and religious otherness to those of the Judeo-Christian God and indeed draw their characteristic style and energy from this awkward, passionately allegorical union. A way to expel the inner voice of Protestant deity into the spaces of Western expansion, this braiding splices 'Jehovah' to native 'other' in an ironic version of missionary outreach; Melville does not aim to convert cultural others but to author an urgent narrative of Western searching through and against them" (160–61).

2. Schueller in *U.S. Orientalisms* provides an insightful reading of the formation of U.S. national identity in terms of the Barbary War conflict and its associated texts (see chapter 2, "Algerian Slavery and the Liberty Vision: Royall Tyler, James Ellison, Susanna Rowson, Washington Irving, Peter Markoe").

3. For background on Americans in the Holy land, I have drawn upon Moshe Davis, ed., *With Eyes toward Zion*; John Davis, *The Landscape of Belief*; Field, *America and the Mediterranean World*; Finnie, *Pioneers East*; Greenberg, *The Holy Land in American Religious Thought*; Le Beau and Mor, eds., *Pilgrims and Travelers to the Holy Land*; and Vogel, *To See a Promised Land.* Vogel's volume, in particular, carries a thorough bibliography of U.S. traveler, missionary, and archaeological accounts of the Holy Land. For European, as well as U.S., experiences in the Holy Land, see also Ben-Arieh, *The Rediscov-*

ery of the Holy Land. For a survey of Orientalist allusions, myths, religion, and philosophy in mainly nineteenth-century U.S. authors, see Yu, *The Great Circle*. Information about U.S. literary Orientalism may also be found in Finkelstein, *Melville's Orienda*; Luedtke, *Nathaniel Hawthorne and the Romance of the Orient*; and Schueller, *U.S. Orientalisms*.

4. Curtis, *The Howadji in Syria*, 12. All subsequent page references will be cited parenthetically.

5. Browne, *Yusef*, 142, 145.

6. Twain, *The Innocents Abroad*, 318.

7. The story of Clorinda Minor's career may be found in Kreiger, *Divine Expectations*, chapter 1. For an excellent discussion of U.S. settlers in Palestine and their connection with the political motifs in Melville's and Twain's Holy Land texts, see Obenzinger, *American Palestine*.

8. The best comprehensive study of Protestant anxieties about the Catholic other within the country during the antebellum period is Franchot, *Roads to Rome*.

9. For details about Robinson's career, I have relied upon Hovenkamp, *Science and Religion in America*, 150–57; and Vogel, *To See a Promised Land*, 190–91.

10. Robinson, *Biblical Researches*, 1:373–75.

11. Hovenkamp, *Science and Religion in America*, 150. One long quotation will suffice to give a sense of Robinson's typical procedure, as he queries where the Red Sea's waters parted to allow Moses and the Israelites safe passage:

> The question here has respect to the part of the sea where the passage took place. . . .
> The discussion of this question has often been embarrassed, by not sufficiently attending to the circumstances narrated by the sacred historian. . . . In this narration
> there are two main points, on which the whole question may be said to turn. The first
> is, *the means* or instruments with which the miracle was wrought. The Lord, it is said,
> caused the sea to go (or flow out) *by a strong east wind*. The miracle therefore is represented as mediate; not a direct suspension of, or interference with the laws of nature,
> but a miraculous adaptation of those laws to produce a required result. It was
> wrought by natural means supernaturally applied. For this reason we are here entitled to look only for the natural effects arising from the operation of such a cause. In
> the somewhat indefinite phraseology of the Hebrew, an east wind means any wind
> from the eastern quarter; and would include the N.E. wind, which often prevails in
> this region. Now it will be obvious from the inspection of any good map of the Gulf,
> that a strong N.E. wind acting here upon the ebb tide, would necessarily have the effect to drive out the waters from the small arm of the sea which runs up by Suez, and
> also from the end of the Gulf itself, leaving the shallower portions dry. . . . On this
> ground, then, the hypothesis of a passage through the sea opposite to Wady Tawârik,
> would be untenable. (*Biblical Researches*, 1:81–83)

12. "Dead Sea, Sodom, and Gomorrah," 187.

13. According to Vogel (*To See a Promised Land*, 105), only the Bible and Harriet Beecher Stowe's *Uncle Tom's Cabin* eclipsed Thomson's book in terms of nineteenth-century sales.

14. Thomson, *The Land and the Book*, 2:355, 1. All these texts were in competition for each other. James Turner Barclay, for instance, in his *The City of the Great King*, debunks his competitors for inaccurately describing Jerusalem, manufacturing in effect "magnificent paper castles of Jerusalem" (xviii).

15. Melville, *Redburn*, 46. The editor of this volume, Harold Beaver, in his note 46 (415), confidently surmises Melville is alluding to Stephens.

16. For information on European predecessors in the Holy Land, I have drawn upon Hovenkamp, *Science and Religion*, 151. All biographical information about Stephens comes from Von Hagen's *Maya Explorer* and his introduction to his edition of Stephens's *Incidents of Travel in Egypt, Arabia Petræa, and the Holy Land*.

17. Cited in Von Hagen's introduction to Stephens, *Incidents of Travel in Egypt, Arabia Petræa, and the Holy Land*, xiv.

18. Stephens, ibid., 70, 89. All subsequent page references will be cited parenthetically.

19. Harrison, ed., *The Complete Works of Edgar Allan Poe*, 10:1. Poe's review of Stephens's *Incidents* appeared in the *New York Review*, October 1837.

20. In a discussion of Chateaubriand's *Itinéraire de Paris à Jérusalem* (1810–11), Edward Said notes a similar desire: Chateaubriand sees himself becoming a "visionary seer more or less contemporary with God; if the Judean desert has been silent since God spoke there, it is Chateaubriand who can hear the silence, understand its meaning, and—to his reader—make the desert speak again" (*Orientalism*, 173).

21. De Forest, *Oriental Acquaintance*, 81; Barclay, *City of the Great King*, xx.

22. For details about John Banvard's Holy Land Panorama, I have relied upon John Davis, *The Landscape of Belief*, 65–70.

23. For biographical information on Lynch, I have drawn upon Kreiger, *The Dead Sea*, 58–59; Field, *America and the Mediterranean World*, 277–79, 282–85; and Rook, *The 150th Anniversary of the United States' Expedition*.

24. Lynch promoted his ideas about commercial development of the Levant in *Commerce and the Holy Land*, published in 1860.

25. Finnie, *Pioneers East*, 269–70

26. Montague, *Narrative of the Late Expedition to the Dead Sea*, 13.

27. For Robinson's discussion of the Dead Sea, see *Biblical Researches*, 2:205–30, 669–74.

28. Maundrell, quoted in Kreiger, *The Dead Sea*, 23. For my overview of Dead Sea exploration, I have drawn upon Kreiger, 3–28, 31–32.

29. Lynch, *Narrative of the United States' Expedition*, 410. All subsequent page references will be cited parenthetically.

30. For Troye's Holy Land paintings, see Mackay-Smith, *The Race Horses of America*, 188–202; and John Davis, chapter 6, "Edward Troye's Hold Land Series: The Flow of Sacred Waters," in *Landscape of Belief*, 127–48. Davis refers to Troye's Dead Sea canvas as an "astonishingly empty painting," depicting a "prostrate landscape" in which "there is nothing aspiring to the vertical" (143).

31. W. J. T. Mitchell in his provocative and wide-ranging analysis of landscapes that have a more-than-secular resonance, "Holy Landscape," observes that "ignorance, a certain kind of willful unknowing, is central to the concept of landscape" (197), insofar as attention to aesthetic framing precludes or represses the intrusion of history and historical agents. His comments on Timothy O'Sullivan's photographs of Nevada's Great Salt Lake (taken during the Clarence King U.S. Geological Survey of 1867–74) are particularly applicable to how antebellum citizens regarded the Dead Sea: "This is the landscape of monotheism . . . the land of the abstract, invisible god who speaks and writes, but does not show his face, who leaves his catastrophic footprints on the earthquake-riven terrain and retreats into the invisible distance. . . . This emptying and abstracting tendency is en-

demic to the very concept of landscape. . . . This is the landscape whose purification makes it innocent of all possible idolatry" (209).

32. Taylor, *The Lands of the Saracens*, 353. All subsequent page references will be cited parenthetically.

33. For a discussion of Willis's "exaggerated ennui" (782) throughout his writing, including his main Orientalist text first published in 1835, *Pencillings by the Way*, see Tomc, "An Idle Industry."

34. See Douglas, *The Feminization of American Culture*.

35. Cummins, *El Fureidîs*, 18. All subsequent page references will be cited parenthetically.

36. An excellent brief note on the novel's theme of self-sacrifice may be found in Baym's introduction to her edition of *The Lamplighter*, ix–xxxi. Baym sees Havilah's independence in *El Fureidîs* as reflecting a countertradition, in which female heroines "claim a right to pleasure and happiness without paying for them in advance by a long apprenticeship of suffering" (xxix).

37. For a different reading of this scene, which emphasizes its (and the novel's) disruption of "heteronormative gender identity," see Schueller, *U.S. Orientalisms*, 99. Schueller's fine study examines *El Fureidîs* in the context of other mid-nineteenth-century novels (and related texts) of the Middle East.

38. Melville, *Redburn*, 46.

39. Ibid., 310, 315.

40. See Martin, *Hero, Captain, and Stranger*; and Martin, "Melville and Sexuality," in Levine, *The Cambridge Companion to Herman Melville*.

41. See Sedgwick, *Between Men*. Sedgwick traces, from the sixteenth century and on, the ways in which male bonding as represented in English literary texts manifest the "potential unbrokenness of a continuum between homosocial[ity] and homosexual[ity]" (1), a continuum fraught with both desire and anxiety because the two forms of affection merge into each other. Sedgwick applies her theory to an extremely cogent reading of Melville's *Billy Budd* in "*Billy Budd*: After the Homosexual," in Myra Jehlen, ed., *Herman Melville: A Collection of Critical Essays*.

42. A useful collection of essays on Egyptology in America is Nancy Thomas, ed., *The American Discovery of Ancient Egypt*. For a discussion of Gliddon and other early Egyptologists in America, see John A. Wilson, *Signs and Wonders upon Pharaoah*. See also Irwin, *American Hieroglyphics*.

43. Melville, "I and My Chimney," in Hayford, Parker, and Tanselle, eds., *The Piazza Tales and Other Prose Pieces*. All subsequent page references will be cited parenthetically. For a useful discussion of the gender dynamics of "I and My Chimney," see Bertolini, "Fireside Chastity."

44. Eliade, *The Sacred and the Profane*, 37.

45. Melville, *Journals*, 87–88. All subsequent page references will be cited parenthetically. For a fine overview of Melville's journal and related writings, see Milder, "An Arch between Two Lives."

46. Franchot, *Roads to Rome*, summarizes that in "the cautious turn toward the redemptive powers of the material dimension, issues of the body, of church architecture, of art, and of food converged to form a distinctive Protestant gaze on Rome, a gaze that acknowledged its spiritual desire, celebrated Catholicism as spectacle, and fantasied the consumption of this foreign substance rather than conversion to it. This Protestant gaze was forged from the terms of anti-Catholic discourse in its preoccupation with Roman-

ism's bodily excesses, ranging from decomposition to nakedness, mortification, and frankly displayed crucifixion" (234).

47. See Tolchin, *Mourning, Gender, and Creativity.*

48. Goux, *Symbolic Economies,* 147.

49. For a discussion of Melville's homoerotic thematics through much of his oeuvre, albeit with only a few references to *Clarel,* see Martin, *Hero, Captain, and Stranger.* The two longest studies of *Clarel*—Goldman, *Melville's Protest Theism*; and Shurr, *The Mystery of Iniquity*—are virtually silent about the homosexual dynamics of the poem. Goldman dismissively remarks that those who would "persist in seeing Clarel's attempt at making a human connection as a sign of the failure of heterosexual love and the hope for homosexual love ignore the poem's theme of spiritual sympathy" (37). For a brilliant discussion of Melville's genealogical obsessions in *Pierre* (and related texts), see Sundquist, *Home as Found,* chapter 4, "'At home in his words': Parody and Parricide in Melville's *Pierre.*"

50. For discussion of Orientalist imagery in Melville's writing, and his extensive reading of Orientalist texts (both U.S. and European) that informs those texts, see Finkelstein, *Melville's Orienda.* See also the copious notes and other editorial apparatus in the Northwestern-Newberry editions of Melville's *Journals* and *Clarel.* Other valuable interpretations of *Clarel* include, besides those cited in note 49 above, Arvin, *Herman Melville,* 269–78; Kelley's discussion of its urban thematics in *Melville's City,* 252–63; and Schueller, *U.S. Orientalisms,* 128–39.

51. For a thorough analysis of *Clarel*'s political dimensions in relation to Mark Twain's *Innocents Abroad* and other nineteenth-century Holy Land texts, see Obenzinger, *American Palestine.*

52. Melville, *Clarel,* 1.1.3–5. All subsequent references will be cited parenthetically.

53. See Baym's brilliant "The Erotic Motif in Melville's *Clarel.*" My interpretation concurs with Baym's, except that I view the Dead Sea and the homosocial or homoerotic elements of the poem as being more intimately interlinked and thematically central.

54. The story of Lot and his wife is one that clearly haunted Melville. In *White-Jacket* (1850), for example, he writes, "Those who are solely governed by the Past stand like Lot's wife, crystallized in the act of looking backward, and forever incapable of looking before" (152).

55. Eliade writes in *The Sacred and Profane* that what "is found in the profane world is a radical secularization of death. . . . [T]here remains [however] vague memories of abolished religious practices and even a nostalgia for them" (186).

56. Vine, as many critics have pointed out, likely recasts Melville's frustrated longing for strong brotherly attachment to Hawthorne. See the review of scholarship on the Vine-Hawthorne connection in the editorial apparatus of the Northwestern-Newberry edition of *Clarel,* 593–604.

57. Schueller supplies an alternative reading of this scene, proposing that "Clarel's attraction to Vine is a displacement of his desire to overcome the otherness of the Near East through a hermeneutical understanding that denies the separation between self and other. Melville's embodiment of Clarel thus resists the imperial paradigms of Near Eastern Orientalism that operate through a need to exclude the Other. Although distantiated, Clarel's desire for Vine questions the separations and demarcations between the New World and the Near East on which the construction of the imperial body rests" (*U.S. Orientalisms,* 134).

58. For an extremely suggestive take on the significance of carceral imagery in this

canto and in *White-Jacket*, see Casarino, "Gomorrahs of the Deep," and (for *Clarel* more generally) his note 36.

59. See Goodwin, "Destruction of Sodom"; and Hall, "Destruction of Sodom."

60. Davidson, *Poetical Remains*, 146–47.

61. Warner, "New English Sodom," 20.

62. Burton, quoted in Phillips, "Writing Travel and Mapping Sexuality," in Duncan and Gregory, eds., *Writes of Passage*, 73. Burton views about the "Sotadic Zone" appear in his *Plain and Literal Translation of the Arabian Nights' Entertainments or The Book of a Thousand Nights and a Night* (1885–86).

63. For evidence of Taylor's homoerotics or homosocial panic, see Martin, "Bayard Taylor's Valley of Bliss"; and Wermuth, "My Full, Unreserved Self." Serviceable biographies of Taylor are Beatty, *Bayard Taylor*; and Wermuth, *Bayard Taylor*.

64. Such symptoms of homosexual longing and panic are more typically and intensely conveyed in scenes of the Oriental bath. For a fascinating discussion of mainly twentieth-century European literary travelers to the Near East and the dynamics of projecting onto the region homosexual desire and anxiety, see Boone, "Vacation Cruises." He remarks that in "accounts of orientalism that assume the heterosexuality of the erotic adventurer . . . the confrontation with the specter of homosexuality that lurks in Western fantasies of Eastern decadence destabilizes the assumed authority of the tourist as a distant, uncontaminated spectator. . . . [The] story of many Western men's encounters with the Near East, whatever these tourists' putative sexual orientation, has also been the story of a crisis in male subjectivity—the crisis that by definition is occidental masculinity itself" (104).

65. Branch, *Melville: The Critical Heritage*, 400.

66. Twain, *The Innocents Abroad*, 381–82.

67. The best analysis of the theme of Adamic hope and its frustration in antebellum literature and culture is R. W. B. Lewis's classic study, *The American Adam*.

68. Franchot, "Melville's Traveling God," 183.

69. Kyle, *Explorations at Sodom*, 11.

70. Ibid., 52.

Chapter 4

1. Twain, *The Innocents Abroad*, 441.

2. Ibid., 332.

3. Cox, from *Congressional Globe* (35th Cong., 2nd Sess., 1859), in Graebner, ed., *Manifest Destiny*, 325–26.

4. For a discussion of Neagle's painting in the context of other antebellum artistic representations of Latin America, see Manthorne, *Tropical Renaissance*, 34–35.

5. Charles S. Stewart, *A Visit to the South Seas*, 1:99–100.

6. The legislative request is quoted from Charles H. Brown, *Agents of Manifest Destiny*, 122–23.

7. Sundquist incisively discusses this complex geopolitics in his analysis of Herman Melville's "Benito Cereno" and Martin R. Delany's *Blake* in *To Wake the Nations*, chapter 2, "Melville, Delany, and New World Slavery."

8. John Esaias Warren, "The Romance of the Tropics," 504.

9. Willis, *Health Trip to the Tropics*, 261.

10. Julia Ward Howe, *A Trip to Cuba*, 26.

11. Mitchell, "Imperial Landscape," chapter 1 of Mitchell, ed., *Landscape and Power*, 10.

12. Taylor, *Eldorado*, 2:188–89.

13. Winthrop, *A Companion*, 10.

14. For a discussion of *The Heart of the Andes* and its exhibition history, see Kelly, "A Passion for Landscape: The Paintings of Frederic Edwin Church," in Kelly, ed., *Frederic Edwin Church*, 55–58.

15. For an analysis of Church's tropical American paintings in relation to nine-teenth-century, in particular Humboldtian, geological/naturalist thought, see Novac, *Nature and Culture*, 68–77; for an analysis of Humboldt's aesthetic ideas by a professional geographer, see Bunkse, "Humboldt and an Aesthetic Tradition in Geography."

16. Winthrop, *A Companion*, 3.

17. Manthorne, *Tropical Renaissance*, 3. The most recent work addressing how ante-bellum literary and historical authors defined the United States against the other Americas is Wertheimer, *Imagined Empires*.

18. For William Walker's story see his own *War in Nicaragua* and Charles H. Brown's superlative *Agents of Manifest Destiny*, 174–93, 291–408.

19. The most comprehensive study to date of antebellum literary-cultural responses to Catholicism is Franchot, *Roads to Rome*.

20. Barlow, *The Vision of Columbus*, Book 1:115–16.

21. Prescott, quoted in Squier, *Peru*, 2. All subsequent page references will be cited parenthetically. Unless otherwise cited, for factual information pertaining to Squier's life and political career, I have drawn upon Alleger's introduction to his edition of Squier's *Waikna*; Olien; "E.G. Squier and the Miskito"; and Meltzer's superlative introduction to a reprint of Squier and Edwin H. Davis's *Ancient Monuments of the Mississippi Valley*. Alleger's introduction I should add, however, uncritically lauds Squier's representations ("his descriptions of places, peoples, and customs rings with authenticity" [xii–xiii]), and he adopts the stance of what could be called imperial-colonialist nostalgia ("Best of all, the area he describes, still primitive and challenging, offers any would-be adventurer suf-ficient thrills to fill a long life with enchanted memories" [xii]; it "is always with a degree of nostalgia that I read of Bard's first glimpse in the dim distance of the Bay of Honduras. . . . It is at this point, according to legend, that Columbus first landed on the mainland of the Americas [xxxii]"). Olien's article highlights the political motive behind *Waikna*, and offers an ethnohistorical account of the Mosquito (or Miskito) tribes to discredit Squier's distorting caricatures.

22. The inquiry report is quoted in Olien, "E. G. Squier and the Miskito," 130, note 2.

23. For biographical background on Stephens, see Von Hagen, *Maya Explorer*. For an overview of American and European exploration of ancient Mayan sites, see Adam-son, *The Ruins of Time*. For more particular analyses of Stephens's Yucatán volumes, see, besides Von Hagen's *Maya Explorer*, Adamson, *The Ruins of Time*, 139–60; Brunhouse, *In Search of the Maya*, 84–112; Gunn, *American and British Writers in Mexico*, 21–27; John-son, "Writing in the Dark"; and Preston, "America's Egypt."

24. See Bloom, *The Anxiety of Influence*. For a fascinating discussion of Humboldt's New World texts and their influence, see Pratt, *Imperial Eyes*, chapter 6, "Alexander von Humboldt and the Reinvention of America."

25. Poinsett, quoted in Gunn, *American and British Writers in Mexico*, 15.

26. Taylor, *At Home and Abroad*, 354–59.

27. Stephens, *Incidents of Travel in Central America, Chiapas, and Yucatan*, 1:96–99. All subsequent page references will be cited parenthetically.

28. Even before Stephens's volumes appeared, some citizens were wondering why the government refused to sponsor exploratory expeditions: "[Considering] the very relics which so justly astonish us, and which, if rightly investigated, might roll back the darkness of ages, and let in from the remote past a flood of light, is it a matter of less astonishment to every enlightened American, that but few efforts have yet been made to investigate a subject so important to the civilized world? Why, we would ask—and we believe the question is on the lips of every patriotic citizen—why does not our general government take this matter into consideration? . . . Paltry indeed would be the requisite cost, compared with that incurred for infinitely less valuable purposes; and yet not a solitary effort has been made to call it forth" ("American Antiquities," 129).

29. *Incidents of Travel in Yucatan*, 1:167–68. All subsequent page references will be cited parenthetically. William Prescott, although concurring that the ruins evidenced "in its essential features" a "peculiar and indigenous civilization" was a bit more circumspect about precluding influences from Eastern Asia: "Whichever way we turn, the subject is full of embarrassment" (Prescott, in the appendix, "The Origin of Mexican Civilization," to *History of the Conquest of Mexico*, 713–15).

30. Pratt writes that the "European imagination produces archaeological subjects by splitting contemporary non-European peoples off from their precolonial, and even their colonial, pasts. To revive indigenous history and culture as archaeology is to revive them as dead" (*Imperial Eyes*, 134).

31. Jones, from *An Original History of Ancient America*, quoted in Von Hagen, *Maya Explorer*, 202. Although Stephens's narrative was very popular, the comment of one reviewer is apposite: "The merit of philosophical analysis of, and deductions from, the facts, the work certainly has not; and it must be owned, that it were to be wished the writer had approached his task with better preparation of whatever there is, that may properly called learning, bearing upon it" ("Stephens's *Travels in Central America*," 503). The reviewer's vagueness about what preparatory "learning" might comprise underscores that archaeology, as a discipline, had not yet fully emerged from a diffused field that included antiquarianism, protoanthropology, and Scriptural ethnology. See note 34 below.

32. Johnson in "Writing in the Dark" situates this and kindred passages within a thematics of writing: "[In] Stephens, wonder facilitates the rhetorical movement from subjective loss before the alterity of the New World to subjective recovery in the reconstruction of the New World in the language of the Old" (16); the "mere existence [of the hieroglyphs], illegible to the Anglo-American travel-writer, does not add up to history [and does not] shed light on the other, pre-Columbian Americas" (18). He concludes that the "history of encounter in the Americas has been the institutionalization of indigenous ignorance, of the obscurity of Amerindian self-knowledge in order to publish . . . Amerindian civilizations as darkness and as the property of . . . European-North American travelers-writers" (21).

33. Prescott to Stephens, April 1843, quoted in Von Hagen, *Maya Explorer*, 257.

34. The most authoritative overview of Squier's first work may be found in Meltzer's long introductory essay for its recent Smithsonian Institution reprint. For the role *Ancient Monuments* played in the dispute over the emerging theory of polygenesis, I have re-

lied upon Stanton, *The Leopard's Spots*, 82–89. Dana D. Nelson suggests in an analysis of antebellum male fraternity, "The Haunting of White Manhood: Poe, Fraternal Ritual, and Polygenesis," that the intimate circle of Morton and his colleagues defined itself as a privileged male space, which was a "pure world protected from abrasive encounters with 'otherness'—from . . . women who were challenging the rights, spaces, and habits of manhood, [and] from the frictions, the woundings professional men experienced among other white men in scholarly and marketplace competitions" (528). Nelson elaborates upon her theory of racist white male professional fraternalism (centered by her analysis of Poe's 1845 short story "Some Words with a Mummy") in *National Manhood*. The formation of anthropology from earlier ethnology is briefly reviewed in Bieder and Tax, "From Ethnologists to Anthropologists," in Murra, ed., *American Anthropology*, 11–22. By the middle years of the nineteenth century, archaeology, antiquarianism, and ethnology had begun to separate into distinct disciplines, with, to some extent, turf wars between them (the American Ethnological Society, founded in 1849, was at pains to distinguish its global preoccupations from the merely local concerns of the American Antiquarian Society). Anthropology was not to be distinguished from ethnology until the early 1870s (Squier helped to formulate the distinction). In modern usage, ethnography is considered a branch of anthropology, dealing with the scientific description of individual cultures; ethnology deals with the historical development of cultures and their similarities and differences—in the antebellum context, with the origin, history, and distribution of the "races" of humankind. The terms overlap; but Squier may be considered primarily an archaeologist (and secondarily, an ethnographist) and Nott, Gliddon, and Morton ethnologists. See also Willey and Sabloff, *A History of American Archaeology*. An anthology of early archaeological documents relating to the Americas is Deuel, *Conquistadors without Swords*.

35. Nott to Squier, August 19, 1848, quoted in Stanton, *The Leopard's Spots*, 87.

36. Quoted in ibid., 85.

37. For a discussion of the conflict between the new historical sciences (especially geology) and religion, see Bozeman, *Protestants in an Age of Science*.

38. Squier to his parents, June 29, 1846, quoted in Stanton, *The Leopard's Spots*, 82–83.

39. Squier, "American Ethnology," 385, 386, 395, 398.

40. Clark, quoted in Manthorne, *Tropical Renaissance*, 100.

41. Prescott, *History of the Conquest of Mexico*, 729–30.

42. For a fine discussion of the thematics of blindness, historical insight, and difficulty of interpreting the Aztec's hieroglyphic writing, see Wertheimer, "Noctography."

43. Parkman to Squier, May 13, 1849, in Jacobs, ed., *Letters of Francis Parkman*, 1:63.

44. For the following account of Squier's diplomacy and the crisis between the United States and Britain that arose over the Nicaraguan/Mosquito dispute, I have relied upon Connell-Smith, *The United States and Latin America*, 82–87; Squier's own accounts in *Nicaragua*, 672–91, and in his "Historical Sketch of the Mosquito Shore," appended to *Waikna*, 335–53; and Charles H. Brown, *Agents of Manifest Destiny*, 221–37.

45. Squier, *Nicaragua*, 685–88.

46. Squier, "Our Foreign Relations: Central America—The Crampton and Webster Project." The essay appeared in *Democratic Review* 31 (1852), and the quotation comes from Olien, "E. G. Squier and the Miskito," 118.

47. Squier, "Historical Sketch of the Mosquito Shore," *Waikna*, 350. All subsequent page references will be cited parenthetically.

48. Hopkins, "Memoir of the Geography, History, Productions, and Trade of Paraguay," 40–41.

49. Cox, in Graebner, *Manifest Destiny*, 323.

50. Squier, *Nicaragua* (1852 edition), quoted in Van Alstyne, *The Rising American Empire*, 169.

51. Squier, "San Juan de Nicaragua," 50.

52. For an intriguing discussion of imperialism, masculinist issues, and canal building, see Bill Brown, "Science Fiction, the World's Fair, and the Prosthetics of Empire," in Kaplan and Pease, *Cultures of United States Imperialism*, 129–63.

53. Squier, *The States of Central America*. This volume was an expansion of *Notes on Central America*, published in 1855.

54. Ibid., 63.

55. For brief discussion of Squier's *Serpent Symbol* in the context of Squier's other researches into North American Indians, see Bieder, *Science Encounters the Indian*, chapter 4, "Ephraim George Squier and the Archaeology of Mental Progress."

56. See Squier, *Nicaragua*, 174. For Oriental motifs in American paintings of tropical America, see Manthorne, *Tropical Renaissance*, 8, 175–76.

57. Parkman to Squier, April 2, 1850, in *Letters of Francis Parkman*, 1:68.

58. For the history of the Mosquitos, I have drawn upon Charles H. Brown, *Agents of Manifest Destiny*, 227–29.

59. For a fascinating analysis of a twentieth-century colonialist text holding the same fantasy of discovering uncontaminated indigenes—R. O. Marsh's 1934 *White Indians of Darién*—see Taussig, *Mimesis and Alterity*, 151–66. Marsh, who had served as the U.S. chargé d'affaires in Panama in 1910, led a successful Cuna rebellion against the Panamanian state in 1925; he was obsessed with locating a lost tribe of white Indians in the interior.

60. "Squier's *Waikna*," 320.

61. Manthorne speculates that Squier modeled Sam Bard on the New York artist Wilhelm Heine, who accompanied him on his second expedition to Nicaragua in 1851 (*Tropical Renaissance*, 99).

62. Nott and Gliddon, *Types of Mankind*, 373. For a brilliant analysis of the American and British ethnological debate on hybridity, see Young, *Colonial Desire*.

63. Rose, *Feminism and Geography*, 106. For a excellent study of the thematics of the swamp, see David C. Miller, *Dark Eden*. Miller argues that swamp images often represent "at the deepest level, the simultaneous attraction to and flight from death that typified Victorian culture in America" (32) and that the "swamp defies the pervasive logical distinctions at the basis of culture: the demarcation between life and death and polarities such as good and evil, light and dark, male and female" (78). Squier's hysteria over the low, swampy habitats of the Mosquitos (versus the high, pure regions of the Poyer Indians) may profitably be seen in light of the larger nineteenth-century bourgeois habit of mapping bodily discourses onto urban and natural topographies. See chapter 3, "The City: The Sewer, the Gaze and the Contaminating Touch," in Stallybrass and White, *The Politics and Poetics of Transgression*.

64. For a brief accounts of the Maya rebellion, see Bolland, "The Maya and the Colonization of Belize in the Nineteenth Century"; and Dumond, "Independent Maya of the Late Nineteenth Century," in Jones, ed., *Anthropology and History in Yucatán*.

65. McClintock, *Imperial Leather*, 361.

66. Squier's sampling in *Waikna* of Mosquito words derives from his treatise, "Observations on the Archaeology and Ethnology of Nicaragua," published in 1853 in the American Ethnological Society's series *Transactions*, 3:83–158. Squier's text included a lexicon of several Nicaraguan tribes' languages, but he acknowledges that the Mosquito portion came from the work of a colleague, Alexander J. Cotheal's "A Grammatical Sketch of the Language Spoken by the Indians of the Mosquito Shore," published the preceding year in *Transactions*, 2:235–64. For a reprint of Squier's text, see Comparato, ed., *Observations on the Archaeology and Ethnology of Nicaragua*. In this text, Squier's politics and ethnology work at cross purposes no less than in *Waikna*—he includes the Mosquito lexicon yet also disparages the tribe itself as the "wretched . . . Mosquitos, who—by a brazen fraud—are attempted to be passed off upon the world as a sovereign nation" (5).

67. Kroeber, "American Indian Persistence and Resurgence," *Boundary 2*, 12, 14.

68. Squier, "Nicaragua: An Exploration from Ocean to Ocean," 577.

69. Franchot's larger argument is that Prescott imposes upon New World history his anxieties about the clash between his Protestant ethos and the ethos of the Catholic other (figured, respectively, by the energetic Cortés and the effete Montezuma): "In a New World empty of architectural enclosures to investigate, the mind of the 'superstitious' savage served as the Catholicized interior for anti-Catholic readers to tour without risk of contamination. Empowered by the interpretive guidelines of reformed Christianity, American tourist-readers of Prescott's *Mexico* could peer into the mind of Montezuma, whose effeminate 'Catholic' distresses reduced the threatening complexities of New World racial differences to the familiarities of Old World religious difference" (*Roads to Rome*, 61).

Chapter 5

1. Delany, *Principia of Ethnology*, 61. All subsequent page references will be cited parenthetically.

2. Wallace, "Are We Men?" 413.

3. For biographical information on Delany, here and subsequently unless otherwise cited, I have drawn upon Sterling, *The Making of an Afro-American*; and Painter, "Martin R. Delany," in Litwack and Meier, eds., *Black Leaders of the Nineteenth Century*, 149–72.

4. For a discussion of whether such terms as *African-American* would have held for Delany and other U.S. blacks a more than geographical or political resonance (that is, would have spoken to specific cultural attributes), see Stuckey, *Slave Culture*, chapter 4, "Identity and Ideology: The Names Controversy." He reminds us that "Delany never spoke at length on the significance of an appropriate name for his people. . . . Perhaps he would have alienated his fellow leaders had he insisted that most blacks of his day were largely African in culture and for that reason should be called African" (230).

5. Cited in Sterling, *Making of an Afro-American*, 55.

6. Cited in Griffith, *The African Dream*, 6.

7. Douglass, quoted in Sterling, *Making of an Afro-American*, 227.

8. For a superbly nuanced comparison of Douglass's and Delany's careers (and certainly the best study to date on Delany, to which I am much indebted in this chapter), see Levine, *Martin Delany*. Reid-Pharr's psychoanalytical reading of *Blake*—"Violent Ambiguity," in Blount and Cunningham, eds., *Representing Black Men*—although highly speculative, is one of the few analyses that accords the novel a complexity extending beyond the strictly political. Peterson, in *Doers of the Word*, offers a brilliant, feminist-

oriented discussion of Delany's elitism (see, especially, 113–16 and 169–71). For additional critiques of Delany's bourgeois elitism, see note 49 below.

9. For discussions of Alexander Crummell's career, see the volumes on African-U.S. relations listed in note 40 below.

10. Taylor, "The Continents," in *Rhymes of Travel, Ballads and Poems*, 132–36.

11. See Moses, *Afrotopia;* and Sundquist, *To Wake the Nations.*

12. Whittier, quoted in Dash, *Haiti and the United States*, 6. Dash argues that abolitionist sentimentality could also go too far, especially when downplaying the violence of the Haitian revolutionaries or when recasting Touissant as a passive, innocent martyr, rather than as a prime instigator of insurrection: such sentimentalizing or idealizing is "simply another example not of an objective truth but of the pervasiveness of one rhetorical strategy designed to keep Haiti at a distance. In its own way, it is no less pernicious than the Southern distrust of the barbaric unpredictability of the black mentality" (10).

13. William Wells Brown, *St. Domingo*, 38.

14. These and other titles are cited in Moses, *Afrotopia*, 95.

15. Ibid., 97.

16. For brief but intriguing remarks on Du Chaillu, see Pratt, *Imperial Eyes*, 208–10.

17. For an overview of early trade between New England merchants and the coastal regions of Africa, see Duignan and Gann, *The United States and Africa.*

18. See note 60 below for Nathaniel Hawthorne's involvement, when he edited Bridge's text for publication, in these questions of conscience in respect to U.S. naval interventions in Africa.

19. An overview of these pre-Enlightenment accounts may be found in McCarthy, *Dark Continent*, 3–17.

20. See Gregory, *Geographical Imaginations*, 27. A valuable discussion of the interlink between the emphasis on progress and "diffusionism" ideology—by which non-Western regions became perceived as heteroclite—may be found in Blaut, *The Colonizer's Model of the World*. See also Fabian, *Time and the Other.*

21. Bushnell, "Moral Uses of Commerce and the Sea," 62.

22. Hegel, quoted in Gates, *Figures in Black*, 19.

23. Morton, quoted in Schueller, *U.S. Orientalisms*, 37.

24. Douglass, "The Claims of the Negro Ethnologically Considered," in Foner, ed., *The Life and Writings of Frederick Douglass*, Vol. 1 (*Early Years, 1817–1849*): 291. For an intriguing discussion of David F. Dorr's *Colored Man Round the World, by a Quadroon* (1858), in which Dorr celebrates Egypt as a black nation, see Schueller, *U.S. Orientalisms*, 105–8. See, for a review of the American and British ethnological debate on the white or black origins of Egypt, Young, *Colonial Desire*, chapter 5, "Egypt in America, the Confederacy in London."

25. Taylor, *A Journey to Central Africa*, 158.

26. Bowen, *Central Africa*, 63.

27. Foote, *Africa and the American Flag*, 50–51. Few nineteenth-century American or European commentators on Africa cite that one reason the interior of Africa was largely unknown was that Africans resisted incursions. Duignan and Gann write that a "major obstacle to investigations of the African interior was the determination of many of the coastal peoples that no European should pass through their territories. The Africans of the seacoast were middlemen between the white traders and the people of the interior; they effectively controlled the highly lucrative traffic in slaves, ivory, gold dust, and other products that came from deep in the continent. The coastal tribes feared that if Europe-

ans succeeded in getting to the interior, their own positions would be lost and their monopoly destroyed" (*The United States and Africa*, 107).

28. Schoolcraft, *The Black Gauntlet*, 405.

29. Quoted in Sundquist, "The Literature of Expansion and Race," in Bercovitch, *The Cambridge History of American Literature*, 2:247.

30. Christy, *Ethiopia*, 90. Christy was best known for his support of slavery through the economic argument of cotton's necessity to the total economy of the nation in *Cotton is King* (1855).

31. Bowen, *Central Africa*, 60.

32. Stowe, *Uncle Tom's Cabin*, 608, 562. For an excellent discussion of Stowe's racial attitudes, see Gossett, *Uncle Tom's Cabin and American Culture*, chapter 5, "Stowe's Ideas of Race." For a brief overview of "ethiopianist" thought in the nineteenth century, see Fredrickson, *Black Liberation*, 31–44.

33. Ryan, "Errand into Africa," 575. For a discussion of Hale's novel in the context of her other political texts, see Baym, *Feminism and American Literary History*, chapter 11, "Sarah Hale, Political Writer."

34. J. Leighton Wilson, *Western Africa*, 32.

35. Bowen, *Central Africa*, 28.

36. Fanon, *The Wretched of the Earth*, 210.

37. Gilroy, *The Black Atlantic*, 23.

38. Delany, *Condition*, 14. All subsequent page references will be cited parenthetically.

39. For an excellent interpretation of *Condition*, see Levine, *Martin Delany*, 63–71. See also note 40 below for discussions of Delany's *Condition* and his other political treatises in the context of the emigrationist movement.

40. For a thorough discussion of U.S. policy toward Africa, see Skinner, *African Americans and U.S. Policy toward Africa*. For brief discussion of Paul Cuffe and other later emigrationist leaders, including Edward Wilmot Blyden and Alexander Crummell, see Carlisle, *The Roots of Black Nationalism*. For discussions of black nationalism, emigrationism, Pan-Africanism, and debates with integrationists, see Fredrickson, *Black Liberation*; Floyd J. Miller, *The Search for a Black Nationality*; and Moses, *The Golden Age of Black Nationalism*.

41. Clay, "Secretary of State Henry Clay's Speech to the American Colonization Society," in Chester, *The Scope and Variety of U.S. Diplomatic History*, 1:58.

42. See Dewees, *The Great Future of America and Africa*, 47.

43. Griffith, *The African Dream*, 29.

44. See Peterson, *Doers of the Word*, 113–18.

45. Stewart, quoted in Romero, *Home Fronts*, 57.

46. Douglass, *The North Star*, January 26, 1849, in Foner, ed., *The Life and Writings of Frederick Douglass*, Vol. 1 (*Early Years, 1817–1849*): 351.

47. Cited in Griffith, *The African Dream*, 16–17.

48. Levine, *Martin Delany*, chapter 2, provides a thorough analysis of the triangulated Delany-Douglass-Stowe debate.

49. Painter critiques Delany for mirroring "the Jacksonian ideal of the self-made man" and his "elitism" which made him dismissive of blacks who had failed to elevate themselves ("Martin R. Delany," 152). Fredrickson comments upon Delany's and other black leaders' "thoroughly middle-class outlook" and their condescending attitude toward lower-class blacks who "were objects of improvement and uplift more than com-

rades in struggle" (*Black Liberation*, 25). Peterson, in particular, critiques Delany's elitism and a patriarchal assumption of masculine capitalism in *Doers of the Word*, 113–16 and 169–71. See also Reid-Pharr, who strongly claims that Delany "actively sought to recreate African Americans in the image of the bourgeois subjects who were arguable responsible for the construction and maintenance of the system of slavery he found so onerous" ("Violent Ambiguity," 74). Levine, taking a different approach, sees Delany's egotism as a function of how he legitimated leadership: "Delany emphasized his black skin and blood as signifiers of a 'natural' aristocracy that authorized his leadership role as the embodiment of Africa in America" (*Martin Delany*, 13).

50. Levine comments that Delany's elision of the question of whether Central American peoples would wish to be ruled "suggests that at this point in his career his emigrationism remains strictly utopian . . . allow[ing] him to be simultaneously ideally inside and practically outside 'America' " (*Martin Delany*, 66).

51. For a valuable assessment of Douglass and the black freemasonry tradition, see Wallace, "Are We Men?"

52. Delany, *The Origin and Objects of Ancient Freemasonry*, 12, 18, 40.

53. Foucault, "Of Other Spaces," 24.

54. Ullman, *Martin R. Delany*, 145. Delany, letter to Douglass, July 10, 1852, quoted in Ullman, 145.

55. Griffith supplies a comprehensive account of the development of Delany's African project in the context of the emigrationist debate (see *The African Dream*, 30–57).

56. Delany, *Official Report*, in Howard Bell, ed., *Search For a Place*, 32. Bell's volume also includes the report of Robert Campbell, *A Pilgrimage to My Motherland*. All subsequent page references will be cited parenthetically.

57. Appiah, *In My Father's House*, 175.

58. Crummell's laudatory remarks come from his "The Progress and Prospects of the Republic of Liberia" (a speech delivered at the annual meeting of the New York State Colonization Society, May 9, 1861), in Moses, ed., *Destiny and Race: Selected Writings*, 165–66.

59. Nesbit, *Four Months in Liberia*, 5. A facsimile reprint of Nesbit's track, along with Samuel Williams's *Four Years in Liberia: A Sketch of the Life of the Rev. Samuel Williams* (1857), is available in Redkey, ed., *Two Black View of Liberia*.

60. Bridge, *Journal of an African Cruiser*, 164. Bridge was a close friend of Nathaniel Hawthorne, and the latter edited his journal for publication. For a discussion of Hawthorne's editorial role, see Brancaccio, "The Black Man's Paradise." Liberia, as a hybrid nation, presented a "convoluted picture" (Bridge, *Journal*, 61) for those who would assess it. Bridge, however, also saw Monrovia and Freetown, what he called "promiscuously" designed cities, as evidence of a lack of "civilizing" (137) energy. Tyler (who was also the president of the Virginia Colonization Society) is quoted in Katherine Harris, *African and American Values*, 61.

61. Gilroy, who also highlights this scene, suggests that the "ambivalence over exile and homecoming . . . has a history that is probably as long as the presence of African slaves in the west." He adds that "it is necessary to appreciate that any discomfort at the prospect of fissures and fault lines in the topography of affiliation that made pan-Africanism such a powerful discourse was not eased by references to some African essence that could magically connect all blacks together" (*Black Atlantic*, 24).

62. This occlusion of an African present recurs in later African-American texts: see

Kenneth W. Warren, "Appeals for (Mis)recognition," in Kaplan and Pease, *Cultures of United States Imperialism*, 392–406.

63. For a suggestive discussion of how the concept of the body politic traditionally privileges a masculinist politics and depends upon phallocentric tropes, see Gatens, "Corporeal Representation in/ and the Body Politic," in Diprose and Ferrell, eds., *Cartographies*.

64. *The Liberator*, May 1, 1863, quoted in Ullman, *Martin R. Delany*, 257.

65. Useful interpretations of *Blake* may be found (besides in the more comprehensive studies of Delany already mentioned) in Herzog, *Women, Ethnics, and Exotics*, chapter 5; and Yellin, *The Intricate Knot*, chapter 9. For a concordant, but more celebrative, approach to the thematics of liminality and secrecy in Delany, especially *Blake*, see Ernest's superb *Resistance and Reformation in Nineteenth-Century African-American Literature*, chapter 4.

66. For the publishing history of *Blake*, see Floyd J. Miller's introduction (especially, xi and xix–xx) to his edition. All citations to this edition will be cited parenthetically.

67. Gilroy states that the "version of black solidarity *Blake* advances is explicitly anti-ethnic and opposes narrow African-American exceptionalism in the name of a truly pan-African, diaspora sensibility. This makes blackness a matter of politics rather than a common cultural condition" (*Black Atlantic*, 27).

68. See Sundquist, *To Wake the Nations*, 182–221, for a superb analysis of the multiple historical-political contexts of *Blake*.

69. In *The Wretched of the Earth*, Fanon remarks on fantasies of empowerment are appropriate to Blake's geographical machismo: "The first thing which the native learns is to stay in his place, and not to go beyond certain limits. That is why the dreams of the native are always of muscular prowess; his dreams are of action and of aggression. I dream I am jumping, swimming, running, climbing; I dream that I burst out laughing, that I span a river in one stride, or that I am followed by a flood of motorcars which never catch up with me" (52).

70. Levine comments that Delany "attempts to resolve the problem of imperialism inherent in Blake's building of a black nation by connecting the revolutionary hero to the region through his personal history and black body" (*Martin Delany*, 203). Blake's genealogical revelation suggests a sort of Freudian family romance, a longing for aristocratic affiliation.

71. Peterson critiques Delany for portraying Blake as a "single hero—a picaro—who sets himself above the rest of his community. While he seeks to create a community by linking the 'huts of America' to one another in a revolutionary organization, he always remains apart from their inhabitants" (*Doers of the Word*, 170). For a suggestive, if hyperbolic, reading of the dynamics of masculine and domination in Delany's *Blake*, see Reid-Pharr, "Violent Ambiguities." He proposes, in particular, that a scene in which a young black slave is brutally whipped functions as ritualized sacrifice reinforcing Blake's own nonabjection: the "boy stands in for all that is, on the one hand, weak, innocent, and feminine and, on the other, dirty, promiscuous, and undisciplined. . . . With the death of the young boy, Blake achieves his untarnished manhood and is able, thereby, to bring discipline—and definition—to African America" (85–86). Wiegman, in *American Anatomies*, provides an extensive discussion of black masculinity/femininity as a vexed, but necessary, response to racism: "[T]he reduction of human being to chattel effects a reification of 'personhood' that necessitates a rhetorical counterclaim to a distinctly

gendered social and political subjectivity. For the African(-American) in the late eighteenth and nineteenth centuries, in other words, the ability to be gendered marked the entrance to the human, public community, providing both civic roles (such as the reproduction of mothering) while simultaneously fragmenting citizenship according to a deeply exclusive masculine universalism" (68).

72. Bridge, *Journal of an African Cruiser*, 59.

73. J. Leighton Wilson, *Western Africa*, 408.

74. Levine remarks that Blake here "assumes a spectatorial role appropriate more to an evaluator of talent than a fellow revolutionary.... Portraying Blake as watching more than doing, Delany may be giving expression to his own fears, similar to Douglass's, that uncontrolled revolutionism could erupt as a form of intemperance" (*Martin Delany*, 208).

75. See Sundquist, *To Wake the Nations*, 210–21.

76. In a different reading of these rituals of revolution, Crane, in "The Lexicon of Rights, Power, and Community in *Blake*," argues that, in opposition to a political-juridical tradition that based community on past customs, Delany's hero develops "an African American alternative—creating a pluralistic community and determining individual rights through a *present* dialogue that discovers and establishes a civic consensus" (540).

77. Sundquist writes that "perhaps ... [Delany] saw that such a surprising eclipse of the novel's revolutionary import augmented its threat" (*To Wake the Nations*, 220).

78. Fanon, *The Wretched of the Earth*, 139.

79. Schoolcraft, *The Black Gauntlet*, vii.

80. Mayo, *Kaloolah*, 425, 149.

81. Melville, "Benito Cereno," in Hayford, Parker, and Tanselle, *The Piazza Tales and Other Prose Pieces*, 116.

82. Ernest, *Resistance and Reformation*, 114. For a recent discussion of the cultural dynamics of envisioning heroic black resistance, see Sale, *The Slumbering Volcano*.

83. Rollin, *Life and Public Services of Martin R. Delany*, 163.

84. See Brennan, "The National Longing for Form," in Bhabha, ed., *Nation and Narration*; and Eagleton, "Nationalism: Irony and Commitment," in Eagleton, Jameson, and Said, *Nationalism, Colonialism, and Literature*, 25.

Conclusion

1. Emerson, *Selected Writings of Ralph Waldo Emerson*, ed. William H. Gilman, 122.

2. Ibid., 159.

3. Clay, February 5–6, 1850, in Hofstadter, ed., *Great Issues in American History*, 348.

4. Fuller, *Woman in the Nineteenth Century*, 25, 24.

5. Fisher notes the flattening effect of democratic space in his wide-ranging essay "Democratic Social Space: Whitman, Melville, and the Promise of American Transparency," in Fisher, ed., *The New American Studies: Essays from "Representations"*: "Democratic society grounds itself in what we might call a Cartesian social space, one that is identical from point to point and potentially unlimited in extent. In this it differs from the Greek *polis*, which both Plato and Aristotle limited in population to a few thousand—to a number that could gather and speak together, see one another in one place, and act in common.... Democratic social space would, ideally, be a universal and everywhere similar medium in which rights and opportunities are identical" (74).

6. Foucault, *The Archaeology of Knowledge*, 12.

7. Willard, *Universal History in Perspective*, iii.

8. Peabody, *Universal History*, viii. All subsequent page references will be cited parenthetically. This was first published in 1849 as *The Polish-American System of Chronology, Reproduced, with Some Modifications, from General Bem's Franco-Polish Method.*

9. Baym, *Feminism and American Literary History*, 146.

10. Walker, *The War in Nicaragua*, 271–72.

11. A curious footnote to Delany's career is that he himself assumed the colonialist role, albeit in absentia, in Nicaragua. A friend of Delany's, David J. Peck, played a part in an election in Greytown that ousted the white rulers and put in their place local black ones. In 1852, while living in New York, Delany heard that he had been "duly chosen and elected mayor of Greytown, civil governor of the Mosquito reservation, and commander-in-chief of the military forces of the province!" Delany did not travel south to assume his post, and Levine, who traces this Nicaraguan connection, speculates upon— whatever truth lay behind the episode—its element of wish-fulfillment. The quotation comes from Delany's biographer, Frances Rollin, and is cited in Levine's analysis of Delany's Central American emigration schemes (see *Martin Delany*, 62–63).

12. McClintock, in *Imperial Leather*, discusses a kindred pictorializing of world history and evolutionary theory in late British Victorian culture. She refers to "panoptical time," which "became a geography of social power, a map from which to read a global allegory of 'natural' social difference. Most importantly, history took on the character of a spectacle [and was] consumed—at a glance—in a single spectacle from a point of privileged invisibility" (37).

13. The most comprehensive studies of Charles Willson Peale and his Philadelphia Museum are Sellers's *Mr. Peale's Museum* and *Charles Willson Peale and His World.*

14. For detailed histories of the debate between scientists, curators, government officials, and the expedition members about what was to be done with the artifacts and specimens brought back from the expedition, see Evelyn, "The National Gallery at the Patent Office," and Reingold and Rothenberg, "The Exploring Expedition and the Smithsonian Institution," both in Viola and Margolis, eds., *Magnificent Voyagers*, 227–42 and 243–54; Stanton, *The Great United States Exploring Expedition*, 290–316; and Tyler, *The Wilkes Expedition*, 386–98.

15. Poinsett, *Discourse on the Objects*, 42–43, 45–46.

16. Fanon, *The Wretched of the Earth*, 200.

17. Hunter, *A Popular Catalogue of the Extraordinary Curiosities*, title-page. All subsequent page references will be cited parenthetically.

18. Hinsely emphasizes that the curators of the National Institute, rather than being interested in developing the collection in a scientific manner and as an aid to science, "showed primary concern for national greatness as exhibited in collections of exotic objects—a kind of scientific and cultural boosterism—but little sympathy for patient, loving understanding of the specimens themselves" (*Savages and Scientists*, 19).

19. For a discussion of Jacques Lacan's notion of the body in bits and pieces, see Gallop, *Reading Lacan*, 79–80. For a brilliant analysis of the Washington Monument and Bunker Hill Monument in terms of the white monumentalizing of the Revolutionary generation, see Castronovo, *Fathering the Nation*, 122–41.

20. Kammen observes that, apparently, the average antebellum citizen was apathetic about the preservation of the nation's past or the memories of its founders: the "small number of people who did care about the past were perceived, at best, as being quaint"

and the "widespread indifference to historic sites . . . often resulted in neglect or damage. Philadelphians permitted Benjamin Franklin's home to be destroyed in 1812, and George Washington's presidential mansion in 1832. John Trumbull visited Independence Hall in 1819, three years after the original ornamentation had been stripped from the room where the Constitutional Convention met. 'The spirit of innovation laid unhallowed hands upon it,' he mourned, 'and violated its venerable walls by modern improvement, as it is called' " (*Mystic Chords of Memory*, 52–53).

21. For discussion of early curiosity collections, or *wunderkammern*, see Impey and MacGregor, eds., *The Origins of Museums*. For the relation between collecting and mercantilism, see Bunn, "The Aesthetics of British Mercantilism." The best semiotic analysis of museum collections and associated cultural phenomena remains Susan Stewart's *On Longing*. For recent developments in museology, see Pearce, ed., *Museum Studies in Material Culture*; and Vergo, ed., *The New Museology*. For museum-collecting as an aspect of anthropology, see Clifford, *The Predicament of Culture*, chapters 9 and 10; Lumley, ed., *The Museum Time-Machine*; and Stocking, ed., *Objects and Others*. For serviceable histories of American museums, see Coleman, *The Museum in America*; Herbert Katz and Marjorie Katz, *Museums, U.S.A*; and the essays in Whitehall, intro., *A Cabinet of Curiosities*.

22. *An Illustrated Catalogue and Guide Book to Barnum's American Museum*, 93.

23. Lowenthal, *The Past Is a Foreign Country*, 245.

24. *An Illustrated Catalogue and Guide Book to Barnum's American Museum*, 95, 60; *Barnum's American Museum, Illustrated*, 21.

25. Melville, "A View of the Barnum Property," 447–48.

26. For Barnum's "operational aesthetic," see Neil Harris, *Humbug*, 61–89. The best biography of Barnum is Saxon, *P. T. Barnum*. See also Fitzsimons, *Barnum in London*; and Rourke, *Trumpets of Jubilee*. For additional cultural interpretations of the American Museum from a variety of perspectives, see Betts, "P.T. Barnum and the Popularization of Natural History"; Bogdan, *Freak Show*, 32–35; Dizikes, "P. T. Barnum: Games and Hoaxing"; Green, "Show-Man"; and Philip B. Kunhardt, Jr., Philip B. Kunhardt III, and Peter W. Kunhardt, *P.T. Barnum*. For Barnum and consumeristic spectacle, see Wicke, *Advertising Fictions*, 55–72.

27. Barnum to John Greenwood, Jr., May 14, 1864, in Saxon, ed., *Selected Letters of P. T. Barnum*, 125. The advertisement for "Zip" is cited in Saxon, *P. T. Barnum*, 99.

28. See Rydell, *All the World's a Fair*, 160–83.

29. Bennett, "The Exhibitionary Complex," in Dirks, Eley, and Ortner, eds., *Culture/Power/History*, 148.

30. See, for instance, Bluford Adams, *E Pluribus Barnum*, which links Barnumesque spectacle to a wide range of popular, especially post–Civil War, discourses and cultural concerns in respect to ethnography, imperialism, and consumerism.

31. In a fascinating discussion of curiosity, relic, and protoenthnographical collections in the eighteenth century, *In Oceania*, Nicholas Thomas indicates that cabinets of aberrant curiosities potentially "parodically exposed the license and ambivalence internal to proper forms of [official Enlightenment] inquiry" (116–17).

32. In a colloquy with James Clifford, in the latter's *Routes*, Stuart Hall worries about the critical stance of embracing the endless coils of hybridity, of the too-easily adopted "fashionable postmodernist notion of nomadology—the breakdown of everything into everything" (44).

Works Cited

Adams, Bluford. *E Pluribus Barnum: The Great Showman and the Making of U.S. Popular Culture*. Minneapolis: University of Minnesota Press, 1997.

Adams, Brooks. *The New Empire*. 1902. Cleveland: Frontier Press, 1967.

Adamson, David Grant. *The Ruins of Time: Four and a Half Centuries of Conquest and Discovery among the Maya*. New York: Praeger, 1975.

Alcott, Bronson. *Journals of Bronson Alcott*. Ed. Odell Shepard. Boston: Little, Brown and Co., 1938. Excerpted in David Brion Davis, ed., *Antebellum American Culture: An Interpretive Anthology*, 456. Lexington, Mass.: D. C. Heath and Co., 1979.

"American Antiquities." *Knickerbocker* 11 (1838): 128–37.

Anderson, Charles. *Melville in the South Seas*. 1939. Rev. ed. New York: Dover Publications, 1966.

Anderson, Rufus. *The Hawaiian Islands: Their Progress and Condition under Missionary Labors*. 2d ed. Boston: Gould and Lincoln, 1864.

Appiah, Kwame Anthony. *In My Father's House: Africa in the Philosophy of Culture*. New York: Oxford University Press, 1992.

Arvin, Newton. *Herman Melville: A Critical Biography*. New York: Viking Press, 1957.

Ashcroft, Bill, Gareth Griffiths, and Helen Tiffin. *The Empire Writes Back: Theory and Practice in Post-Colonial Literatures*. New York: Routledge, 1989.

———, eds. *The Post-Colonial Studies Reader*. New York: Routledge, 1995.

Avery, Gillian. *Behold the Child: American Children and Their Books, 1621–1922*. Baltimore: Johns Hopkins University Press, 1994.

Barclay, James Turner. *The City of the Great King; or, Jerusalem as It was, as It is, and as It is to be*. 1858. Facsimile rpt. New York: Arno Press, 1977.

Barlow, Joel. *The Vision of Columbus*. 1787. Excerpted in Myra Jehlen and Michael Warner, eds., *The English Literatures of America, 1500–1800*, 1094–98. New York: Routledge, 1997.

Barnum's American Museum, Illustrated, a Pictorial Guide to that Far-Famed Establishment; Containing Much Interesting Matter, and Highly Useful to Visitors. New York: J. S. Redfield, 1850.

Barnum, P. T. *Selected Letters of P. T. Barnum*. Ed. A. H. Saxon. New York: Columbia University Press, 1983.

Bartram, William. *Travels of William Bartram.* Ed. Mark Van Doren. 1928. Rpt. New York: Dover Publications, 1955.

Bataille, George. *Literature and Evil.* Trans. Alastair Hamilton. 1957. Rpt. New York: Urizen Books, 1973.

Baym, Nina. "The Erotic Motif in Melville's *Clarel.*" *Texas Studies in Literature and Language* 16 (1974): 315–28.

———. *Feminism and American Literary History: Essays.* New Brunswick: Rutgers University Press, 1992.

Beatty, Richmond Croom. *Bayard Taylor: Laureate of the Gilded Age.* Norman: University of Oklahoma Press, 1936.

Bell, Howard, ed. *Search for a Place: Black Separatism and Africa, 1860.* Ann Arbor: University of Michigan, 1969.

Bell, Roger. *Last among Equals: Hawaiian Statehood and American Politics.* Honolulu: University of Hawaii Press, 1984.

Belok, Michael V. *Forming the American Mind: Early School-Books and Their Compilers, 1783–1837.* Moti Katra, Agra-U.P, India: Satish Book Enterprise, 1973.

Ben-Arieh, Yehoshua. *The Rediscovery of the Holy Land in the Nineteenth Century.* Detroit: Wayne State University Press, 1979.

Bennet, Tony. "The Exhibitionary Complex." In Nicholas B. Dirks, Geoff Eley, and Sherry B. Ortner, eds., *Culture/Power/History: A Reader in Contemporary Social Theory,* 123–54. Princeton: Princeton University Press, 1994.

Berthold, Michael C. "'Portentous Somethings': Melville's *Typee* and the Language of Captivity." *New England Quarterly* 60 (1987): 549–67.

Bertolini, Vincent J. "Fireside Chastity: The Erotics of Sentimental Bachelorhood in the 1850s." *American Literature* 68 (1996): 707–37.

Betts, John Rickards. "P. T. Barnum and the Popularization of Natural History." *Journal of the History of Ideas* 20 (1959): 353–68.

Bhabha, Homi K. *The Location of Culture.* New York: Routledge, 1994.

Bieder, Robert E. *Science Encounters the Indian, 1820–1880: The Early Years of American Ethnology.* Norman: University of Oklahoma Press, 1986.

Bieder, Robert E., and Thomas G. Tax. "From Ethnologists to Anthropologists: A Brief History of the American Ethnological Society." In John V. Murra, ed., *American Anthropology: The Early Years,* 11–22. New York: West Publishing Co., 1976.

Bingham, Hiram. *A Residence of Twenty-One Years in the Sandwich Islands; or the Civil, Religious, and Political History of those Islands.* Hartford: Hezekiah Huntington, 1847.

Blair, Sara. "Cultural Geography and the Place of the Literary." *American Literary History* 10 (1998): 544–67.

Blaut, J. M. *The Colonizer's Model of the World: Geographical Diffusionism and Eurocentric History.* New York: Guilford Press, 1993.

Bloom, Harold. *The Anxiety of Influence: A Theory of Poetry.* New York: Oxford University Press, 1973.

Blunt, Alison, and Gillian Rose, eds. *Writing Women and Space: Colonial and Postcolonial Geographies.* New York: Guilford Press, 1994.

Boelhower, William. "Stories of Foundation, Scenes of Origin." *American Literary History* 5 (1993): 391–428.

———. *Through a Glass Darkly: Ethnic Semiosis in American Literature.* New York: Oxford University Press, 1987.

Bogdan, Robert. *Freak Show: Presenting Human Oddities for Amusement and Profit.* Chicago: University of Chicago Press, 1988.

Boime, Albert. *The Magisterial Gaze: Manifest Destiny and American Landscape Painting c. 1830–1865.* Washington, D.C.: Smithsonian Institution Press, 1991.

Bolland, O. Nigel. "The Maya and the Colonization of Belize in the Nineteenth Century." In Grant D. Jones, ed., *Anthropology and History in Yucatán,* 69–99. Austin: University of Texas Press, 1977.

Boon, James A. *Affinities and Extremes: Crisscrossing the Bittersweet Ethnology of East Indies History, Hindu-Balinese Culture, and Indo-European Allure.* Chicago: University of Chicago Press, 1990.

———. *Other Tribes, Other Scribes: Symbolic Anthropology in the Comparative Study of Cultures, Histories, Religions, and Texts.* New York: Cambridge University Press, 1982.

Boone, Joseph A. "Vacation Cruises; or, The Homoerotics of Orientalism." *PMLA* 110 (1995): 89–107.

Bourdieu, Pierre. *Outline of a Theory of Practice.* Trans. Richard Nice. New York: Cambridge University Press, 1977.

Bowen, Thomas J. *Central Africa: Adventures and Missionary Labors in Several Countries in the Interior of Africa, from 1849 to 1856.* 1857. Facsimile rpt. New York: Negro Universities Press, 1969.

Bozeman, Theodore Dwight. *Protestants in an Age of Science: The Baconian Ideal and Antebellum Religious Thought.* Chapel Hill: University of North Carolina Press, 1977.

Bradley, Harold Whitman. *The American Frontier in Hawaii: The Pioneers, 1789–1843.* Stanford: Stanford University Press, 1942.

Brancaccio, Patrick. "'The Black Man's Paradise'": Hawthorne's Editing of the *Journal of an African Cruiser.*" *New England Quarterly* 53 (1980): 23–41.

Branch, Watson G., ed. *Melville: The Critical Heritage.* Boston: Routledge and Kegan Paul, 1974.

Brantlinger, Patrick. *Rule of Darkness: British Literature and Imperialism, 1830–1914.* Ithaca: Cornell University Press, 1988.

Breitwieser, Mitchell. "False Sympathy in Melville's *Typee.*" *American Quarterly* 34 (1982): 396–417.

Brennan, Timothy. "The National Longing for Form." In Homi K. Bhabha, ed., *Nation and Narration,* 44–70. New York: Routledge, 1990.

Bridge, Horatio. *Journal of an African Cruiser.* London: 1845. Rpt. London: Dawsons of Pall Mall, 1968.

Brown, Bill. "Science Fiction, the World's Fair, and the Prosthetics of Empire, 1910–1915." In Amy Kaplan and Donald E. Pease, eds., *Cultures of United States Imperialism,* 129–63. Durham: Duke University Press, 1993.

Brown, Charles H. *Agents of Manifest Destiny: The Lives and Times of the Filibusters.* Chapel Hill: University of North Carolina Press, 1980.

Brown, Ralph H. "The American Geographies of Jedidiah Morse." *Annals of the Association of American Geographers* 31 (1941): 145–217.

Brown, William Wells. *St. Domingo: Its Revolutions and Its Patriots.* Boston: Bela Marsh, 1855.

Browne, John Ross. *Yusef; or the Journey of the Frangi: A Crusade in the East.* 1853. Facsimile rpt. New York: Arno Press, 1977.

Brückner, Martin. "Lessons in Geography: Maps, Spellers, and Other Grammars of Nationalism in the Early Republic." *American Quarterly* 51 (1999): 311–43.

Brunhouse, Robert L. *In Search of the Maya: The First Archaeologists.* Albuquerque: University of New Mexico Press, 1973.

Buell, Lawrence. "American Literary Emergence as a Post-colonial Phenomenon." *American Literary History* 4 (1992): 411–42.

Bunkse, Edmund V. "Humboldt and an Aesthetic Tradition in Geography." *Geographical Review* 71 (1981): 127–46.

Bunn, James H. "The Aesthetics of British Mercantilism," *New Literary History* 11 (1980): 303–21.

Bushnell, Horace. "Moral Uses of Commerce and the Sea." *Merchants' Magazine, and Commercial Review* 14 (1846): 60–63.

Caesar, Terry. *Forgiving the Boundaries: Home as Abroad in American Travel Writing.* Athens: University of Georgia Press, 1995.

Calder, Alex. "'The Thrice Mysterious Taboo': Melville's *Typee* and the Perception of Culture." *Representations* 67 (1999): 27–43.

Capel, Horacio. "Institutionalization of Geography and Strategies of Change." In D. R. Stoddart, ed., *Geography, Ideology, and Social Concern,* 37–89. Oxford: Basil Blackwell, 1981.

Carlisle, Rodney. *The Roots of Black Nationalism.* Port Washington, N.Y.: Kennikat Press, 1975.

Carpenter, Charles. *History of American Schoolbooks.* Philadelphia: University of Pennsylvania Press, 1963.

Casarino, Cesare. "Gomorrahs of the Deep or, Melville, Foucault, and the Question of Heterotopia." *Arizona Quarterly* 51 (1995): 1–25.

Castronovo, Russ. *Fathering the Nation: American Genealogies of Slavery and Freedom.* Berkeley: University of California Press, 1995.

Chase, Frederic. *Lemuel Shaw: Chief Justice of the Supreme Judicial Court of Massachusetts, 1830–1860.* Boston and New York: Houghton Mifflin, 1918.

Cheever, Henry T. *The Island World of the Pacific.* Glasgow: William Collins, n.d.

———. *Life in the Sandwich Islands; or, the Heart of the Pacific, as It Was and Is.* New York: A. S. Barnes and Co., 1851.

Cheyfitz, Eric. *The Poetics of Imperialism: Translation and Colonization from "The Tempest" to "Tarzan."* New York: Oxford University Press, 1991.

———. "Savage Law: The Plot against American Indians in *Johnson and Graham's Lessee v. M'Intosh* and *The Pioneers.*" In Amy Kaplan and Donald Pease, eds., *Cultures of United States Imperialism,* 109–28. Durham: Duke University Press, 1993.

Christy, David. *Ethiopia: Her Gloom and Glory, as Illustrated in the History of the Slave Trade and Slavery, the Rise of the Republic of Liberia, and the Progress of the African Missions.* 1857. Rpt. New York: Negro Universities Press, 1969.

Clay, Henry. "Secretary of State Henry Clay's Speech to the American Colonization Society." Excerpted in Edward W. Chester, ed., *The Scope and Variety of U.S. Diplomatic History.* Vol. 1, *Readings to 1913,* 57–58. Englewood Cliffs, N.J.: Prentice Hall, 1990.

———. Senatorial Speech of February 5–6, 1850. Excerpted in Richard Hofstadter, ed., *Great Issues in American History: From the Revolution to the Civil War, 1765–1865,* 346–49. New York: Random House, 1958.

Clifford, James. *The Predicament of Culture: Twentieth-Century Ethnography, Literature, and Art.* Cambridge, Mass.: Harvard University Press, 1988.

———. *Routes: Travel and Translation in the Late Twentieth Century.* Cambridge, Mass.: Harvard University Press, 1997.

Clifford, James, and George E. Marcus, eds. *Writing Culture: The Poetics and Politics of Ethnography*. Berkeley: University of California Press, 1986.

Coleman, Laurence Vail. *The Museum in America*. 3 vols. Washington, D.C.: American Association of Museums, 1939.

Connell-Smith, Gordon. *The United States and Latin America: An Historical Analysis of Inter-American Relations*. New York: John Wiley and Sons, 1974.

Crain, Caleb. "Lovers of Human Flesh: Homosexuality and Cannibalism in Melville's Novels." *American Literature* 61 (1994): 25–53.

Crane, Gregg D. "The Lexicon of Rights, Power, and Community in *Blake*: Martin R. Delany's Dissent from *Dred Scott*." *American Literature* 68 (1996): 527–53.

Crummell, Alexander. *Destiny and Race: Selected Writings, 1840–1898*. Ed. Wilson Jeremiah Moses. Amherst: University of Massachusetts Press, 1992.

Cummins, Maria Susanna. *El Fureidîs*. 1860. Cambridge, Mass.: University Press, n.d.

———. *The Lamplighter*. 1854. Ed. and intro. Nina Baym. New Brunswick: Rutgers University Press, 1988.

Curtis, George William. *The Howadji in Syria*. New York: Harper and Brothers, 1852.

Dana, James D. "Memoir of Arnold Guyot, 1807–1884." In *National Academy of Sciences: Biographical Memoirs*. Vol. 2. Washington, D.C.: National Academy, 1886.

Dana, Richard Henry, Jr. "Cleveland's *Voyages*." *North American Review* 55 (1842): 144–200.

———. *Two Years Before the Mast: A Personal Narrative of Life at Sea*. 1840. Ed. and intro. Thomas Philbrick. Rpt. New York: Viking Penguin, 1987.

Dash, J. Michael. *Haiti and the United States: National Stereotypes and the Literary Imagination*. 1988. 2d ed. New York: St. Martin's Press, 1997.

Dathorne, O. R. *Imagining the World: Mythical Belief versus Reality in Global Encounters*. Westport, Conn.: Bergin and Garvey, 1994.

Davidson, Lucretia Maria. *Poetical Remains of the Late Lucretia Maria Davidson, Collected and Arranged by her Mother: with a Biography by Miss Sedwick*. Philadelphia: Lea and Blanchard, 1843.

Davis, John. *The Landscape of Belief: Encountering the Holy Land in Nineteenth-Century American Art and Culture*. Princeton: Princeton University Press, 1996.

Davis, Moshe, ed. *With Eyes toward Zion: Scholars Colloquium on America-Holy Land Studies*. New York: Arno Press, 1977.

"Dead Sea, Sodom, and Gomorrah." *Harper's New Monthly Magazine* 10 (1855): 187–93.

De Forest, John W. *Oriental Acquaintance; or, Letters from Syria*. New York: Dix, Edwards, and Co., 1856.

Dekker, George. *The American Historical Romance*. New York: Cambridge University Press, 1987.

Delany, Martin R. *Blake; or the Huts of America: A Tale of the Mississippi Valley, the Southern United States, and Cuba*. 1859–62. Ed. Floyd J. Miller. Boston: Beacon Press, 1970.

———. *The Condition, Elevation, Emigration, and Destiny of the Colored People of the United States*. 1852. Facsimile rpt. New York: Arno Press, 1968.

———. *Official Report of the Niger Valley Exploring Party*. 1860. Rpt. with Robert Campbell, *A Pilgrimage to My Motherland: An Account of a Journey Among the Egbas and Yorubas of Central Africa, in 1859–60*, in Howard H. Bell, ed., *Search for a Place: Black Separatism and Africa, 1860*. Ann Arbor: University of Michigan, 1969.

———. *The Origin and Objects of Ancient Freemasonry: Its Introduction into the United States, and Legitimacy Among Colored Men*. Pittsburgh: W. S. Haven, 1853.

————. *Principia of Ethnology: The Origin of Races and Color, with an Archeological Compendium of Ethiopian and Egyptian Civilization, from Years of Careful Examination and Enquiry.* 1879. Rpt. Baltimore: Black Classics Press, 1991.

Dening, Greg. *Islands and Beaches: Discourse on a Silent Land, Marquesas, 1774–1880.* Honolulu: University Press of Hawaii, 1980.

Desmond, Jane C., and Virginia R. Domínguez. "Resituating American Studies in a Critical Internationalism." *American Quarterly* 48 (1996): 475–90.

Deuel, Leo. *Conquistadors without Swords: Archaeologists in the Americas.* 1967. Rpt. New York: Schocken Books, 1974.

Dewees, Jacob. *The Great Future of America and Africa; an Essay Showing Our Whole Duty to the Black Man, Consistent with Our Own Safety and Glory.* 1854. Facsimile rpt. Freeport, New York: Books for Libraries Press, 1971.

Dickinson, Robert E. *The Makers of Modern Geography.* New York: Frederick A. Praeger, 1969.

Dictionary of American Biography. Ed. Allen Johnson and Dumas Malone. 20 vols. New York: Charles Scribner, 1931.

Dimock, Wai-chee. "*Typee*: Melville's Critique of Community." *ESQ* 30 (1984): 27–39.

Dizikes, John. "P. T. Barnum: Games and Hoaxing." *Yale Review* 67 (1978): 338–56.

Dodge, Ernest S. *New England and the South Seas.* Cambridge, Mass.: Harvard University Press, 1965.

Douglas, Ann. *The Feminization of American Culture.* New York: Anchor Press, 1977.

Douglass, Frederick. *The Life and Writings of Frederick Douglass.* Vol. 1, *Early Years, 1817–1849.* Ed. Philip S. Foner. New York: International Publishers, 1950.

Drinnon, Richard. *Facing West: The Metaphysics of Indian-Hating and Empire-Building.* 1980. New York: Schocken Books, 1990.

Duignan, Peter, and L. H. Gann. *The United States and Africa: A History.* New York: Cambridge University Press, 1984.

Dumond, D. E. "Independent Maya of the Late Nineteenth Century: Chiefdoms and Power Politics." In Grant D. Jones, ed., *Anthropology and History in Yucatán,* 104–38. Austin: University of Texas Press, 1977.

Duncan, James, and David Ley, eds. *Place /Culture/Representation.* New York: Routledge, 1993.

Eagleton, Terry. "Nationalism: Irony and Commitment." In Terry Eagleton, Frederic Jameson, and Edward Said, *Nationalism, Colonialism, and Literature.* Minneapolis: University of Minnesota Press, 1990.

Edmond, Rod. *Representing the South Pacific: Colonial Discourse from Cook to Gauguin.* New York: Cambridge University Press, 1997.

Eliade, Mircea. *The Sacred and the Profane: The Nature of Religion.* Trans. Willard R. Trask. New York: Harcourt Brace Jovanovich, 1959.

Elson, Ruth Miller. *Guardians of Tradition: American Schoolbooks of the Nineteenth Century.* Lincoln: University of Nebraska Press, 1964.

Emerson, Ralph Waldo. *Emerson: Essays and Lectures.* Ed. Joel Porte. New York: Viking Press, 1983.

————. *Selected Writings of Ralph Waldo Emerson.* Ed. William H. Gilman. New York: New American Library, 1965.

Erkkila, Betsy. "Ethnicity, Literary Theory, and the Grounds of Resistance." *American Quarterly* 47 (1995): 563–94.

Ernest, John. *Resistance and Reformation in Nineteenth-Century African-American Literature: Brown, Wilson, Jacobs, Delany, Douglass, and Harper.* Jackson: University Press of Mississippi, 1995.

Evelyn, Douglas E. "The National Gallery at the Patent Office." In Herman J. Viola and Carolyn Margolis, eds., *Magnificent Voyagers: The U.S. Exploring Expedition, 1838–1842*, 227–42. Washington, D.C.: Smithsonian Institution Press, 1985.

Fabian, Johannes. *Time and the Other: How Anthropology Makes Its Objects.* New York: Columbia University Press, 1983.

Fanon, Frantz. *The Wretched of the Earth.* Trans. Constance Farrington and intro. Jean-Paul Sartre. 1961. New York: Grove Press, 1963.

Fell, Marie Léonore. *The Foundations of Nativism in American Textbooks, 1783–1860.* Washington, D.C.: Catholic University of America Press, 1941.

Field, James A., Jr. *America and the Mediterranean World, 1776–1882.* Princeton: Princeton University Press, 1969.

Finkelstein, Dorothee Metlitsky. *Melville's Orienda.* New York: Octagon Books, 1971.

Finnie, David H. *Pioneers East: The Early American Experience in the Middle East.* Cambridge, Mass.: Harvard University Press, 1967.

Fisher, Philip. "Democratic Social Space: Whitman, Melville, and the Promise of American Transparency." In Philip Fisher, ed., *The New American Studies: Essays from "Representations,"* 70–111. Berkeley: University of California Press, 1991.

Fitch, George W., and G. Woolworth Colton. *Colton and Fitch's Introductory School Geography.* New York: J. H. Colton and Co., 1856.

Fitzsimons, Raymund. *Barnum in London.* New York: St. Martin's Press, 1970.

Foote, Andrew H. *Africa and the American Flag.* 1854. Facsimile rpt. New York: Negro Universities Press, 1969.

Foucault, Michel. *The Archaeology of Knowledge and the Discourse on Knowledge.* Trans. A. M. Sheridan Smith. New York: Pantheon Books, 1972.

———. "Of Other Spaces." *Diacritics* 16 (1986): 22–27.

———. *The Order of Things: An Archaeology of the Human Sciences.* New York: Random House, 1970.

Franchot, Jenny. "Melville's Traveling God." In Robert S. Levine, ed., *The Cambridge Companion to Herman Melville*, 157–85. New York: Cambridge University Press, 1998.

———. *Roads to Rome: The Antebellum Protestant Encounter with Catholicism.* Berkeley: University of California Press, 1994.

Fredrickson, George M. *Black Liberation: A Comparative History of Black Ideologies in the United States and South Africa.* New York: Oxford University Press, 1995.

Friedman, Lawrence M. *A History of American Law.* New York: Simon and Schuster, 1973.

Fuller, Margaret. *American Romantic: A Selection from Her Writings and Correspondence.* Ed. Perry Miller. Garden City, N.Y.: Doubleday and Company, 1963.

———. *Woman in the Nineteenth Century.* Ed. Bernard Rosenthal. New York: W. W. Norton and Company, 1971.

Gallop, Jane. *Reading Lacan.* Ithaca: Cornell University Press, 1985.

Gatens, Moira. "Corporeal Representation in/and the Body Politic." In Rosalyn Diprose and Robyn Ferrell, eds., *Cartographies: Post-Structuralism and the Mapping of Bodies and Spaces*, 79–97. North Sydney, Australia: Allen and Unwin, 1991.

Gates, Henry Louis, Jr. *Figures in Black: Words, Signs, and the "Racial" Self.* New York: Oxford University Press, 1989.

Gilman, Sander L. "Black Bodies, White Bodies: Toward an Iconography of Female

Sexuality in Late Nineteenth-Century Art, Medicine, and Literature." In Henry Louis
Gates, Jr., ed., *"Race," Writing, and Difference*, 223–61. Chicago: University of Chicago Press, 1985.

Gilroy, Paul. *The Black Atlantic: Modernity and Double Consciousness.* Cambridge, Mass.: Harvard University Press, 1993.

Giltrow, Janet. "Speaking Out: Travel and Structure in Herman Melville's Early Narratives." *American Literature* 52 (1980): 18–32.

Goetzmann, William H. *New Lands, New Men: America and the Second Great Age of Discovery.* New York: Viking Penguin, 1986.

Goldman, Stan. *Melville's Protest Theism: The Hidden and Silent God in "Clarel."* DeKalb: Northern Illinois University Press, 1993.

Goodrich, Charles A., ed. *The Universal Traveller: Designed to Introduce Readers at Home to an Acquaintance with the Arts, Customs, and Manners, of the Principal Modern Nations of the Globe.* Hartford: Canfield and Robins, 1838.

Goodrich, Samuel. *A History of all Nations, from the Earliest Periods to the Present Time; or, Universal History. . . .* Auburn and Buffalo: Derby and Miller, 1853.

———. *Parley's Cabinet Library.* 20 vols. Boston: Bradbury, Soden and Co., 1845.

———. *Peter Parley's Method of Telling about Geography to Children.* 1830. Philadelphia: Thomas Cowperthwait and Co., 1839.

———. *Peter Parley's Tales about the Islands in the Pacific Ocean.* 1831. Philadelphia: Thomas, Cowperthwait and Co., 1846.

———. *A Pictorial Geography of the World.* 2 vols. Boston: C. D. Strong, 1840.

———. *The Tales of Peter Parley about Africa.* 1830. Boston: Carter, Hender and Co., 1835.

———. *The Tales of Peter Parley about Asia.* Boston: Gray and Bowen, 1830.

Goodwin, Harley. "Destruction of Sodom." *Ladies' Repository* 5 (1845): 272–73.

Gossett, Thomas F. *Uncle Tom's Cabin and American Culture.* Dallas, Tex.: Southern Methodist University Press, 1985.

Goux, Jean-Joseph. *Symbolic Economies: After Marx and Freud.* Trans. Jennifer Curtiss Gage. Ithaca: Cornell University Press, 1990.

Graebner, Norman A., ed. *Manifest Destiny.* Indianapolis, Ind.: Bobbs-Merrill, 1968.

Green, Gregory. "Show-Man." *Journal of Popular Culture* 14 (1980): 385–93.

Greenberg, Gershon. *The Holy Land in American Religious Thought, 1620–1948: The Symbiosis of American Religious Approaches to Scripture's Sacred Territory.* New York: University Press of America, 1994.

Gregory, Derek. *Geographical Imaginations.* Cambridge: Blackwell, 1994.

Griffith, Cyril E. *The African Dream: Martin R. Delany and the Emergence of Pan-African Thought.* University Park: Pennsylvania State University Press, 1975.

Gunn, Drewey Wayne. *American and British Writers in Mexico, 1556–1973.* Austin: University of Texas Press, 1969.

Gunson, Niel. *Messengers of Grace: Evangelical Missionaries in the South Seas, 1797–1860.* New York: Oxford University Press, 1978.

Guyot, Arnold. *Creation or the Biblical Cosmogony in the Light of Modern Science.* New York: Charles Scribner's Sons, 1884.

———. *The Earth and Man: Lectures on Comparative Physical Geography, in its Relation to the History of Mankind.* Boston: Gould, Kendall, and Lincoln, 1849.

"Guyot's *The Earth and Man.*" *Putnam's Monthly* 6 (1855): 435.

Hale, Sarah J. *Liberia; or, Mr. Peyton's Experiments*. 1853. Rpt. Upper Saddle River, N.J.: Gregg Press, 1968.

Hall, C. "Destruction of Sodom." *Ladies' Repository* 1 (1841): 202–3.

Hamilton, W. J. "Method of Geographical Observation." *Bulletin of the American Geographical and Statistical Society* 1 (1852): 77–79.

Harris, Katherine. *African and American Values: Liberia and West Africa*. New York: University Press of America, 1985.

Harris, Neil. *Humbug: The Art of P. T. Barnum*. Chicago: University of Chicago Press, 1973.

Hart, James D. *The Popular Book: A History of America's Literary Taste*. Berkeley: University of California Press, 1961.

Hawks, Francis L. *Narrative of the Expedition of an American Squadron to the China Seas and Japan, Performed in the Years 1852, 1853, and 1854*. 1856. Facsimile rpt. New York: Arno Press, 1967.

Herbert, Christopher. *Culture and Anomie: Ethnographic Imagination in the Nineteenth Century*. Chicago: University of Chicago Press, 1991.

Herbert, T. Walter, Jr. *Marquesan Encounters: Melville and the Meaning of Civilization*. Cambridge, Mass.: Harvard University Press, 1980.

Herndon, William Lewis. *Exploration of the Valley of the Amazon, Made under the Direction of the Navy Department*. Washington, D.C.: Robert Armstrong, 1854.

Herzog, Kristin. *Women, Ethnics, and Exotics: Images of Power in Mid-Nineteenth-Century American Fiction*. Knoxville: University of Tennessee Press, 1983.

Hietala, Thomas R. *Manifest Destiny: Anxious Aggrandizement in Late Jacksonian America*. Ithaca: Cornell University Press, 1985.

Hinsely, Curtis M., Jr. *Savages and Scientists: The Smithsonian Institution and the Development of American Anthropology, 1846–1910*. Washington, D.C.: Smithsonian Institution Press, 1981.

Hollon, W. Eugene, intro. *The New American State Papers: Explorations and Surveys*. 15 vols. Wilmington, Del.: Scholarly Resources, 1972.

Hopkins, Edward A. "Memoir of the Geography, History, Productions, and Trade of Paraguay." *Bulletin of the American Geographical and Statistical Society* 1 (1852): 14–42.

Horsman, Reginald. *Race and Manifest Destiny: The Origins of American Racial Anglo-Saxonism*. Cambridge, Mass.: Harvard University Press, 1981.

Horwitz, Morton J. *The Transformation of American Law, 1780–1860*. Cambridge, Mass.: Harvard University Press, 1977.

Hovenkamp, Herbert. *Science and Religion in America, 1800–1860*. Philadelphia: University of Pennsylvania Press, 1978.

Howard, Leon. *Herman Melville: A Biography*. Berkeley: University of California Press, 1951.

Howe, Henry, ed. *The Travels and Adventures of Celebrated Travellers in the Principal Countries of the Globe*. Cincinnati, Ohio: C. A. Morgan and Co., 1855.

Howe, Julia Ward. *A Trip to Cuba*. 1860. Rpt. New York: Frederick A. Praeger, 1969.

Hunt, Michael H. *Ideology and U.S. Foreign Policy*. New Haven: Yale University Press, 1987.

Hunter, Alfred. *A Popular Catalogue of the Extraordinary Curiosities in the National Institute, Arranged in the Building Belonging to the Patent Office*. Washington, D.C.: Alfred Hunter, 1855.

Illustrated Catalogue and Guide Book to Barnum's American Museum. New York: Wynkoop, Hallenbeck, and Thomas, 1864.

Impey, Oliver, and Arthur MacGregor, eds. *The Origins of Museums: The Cabinet of Curiosities in Sixteenth- and Seventeenth-Century Europe.* Oxford: Clarendon Press, 1985.

Irwin, John T. *American Hieroglyphics: The Symbol of the Egyptian Hieroglyphics in the American Renaissance.* Baltimore: Johns Hopkins University Press, 1983.

JanMohamed, Abdul R. "The Economy of Manichean Allegory." In Bill Ashcroft, Gareth Griffiths, and Helen Tiffin, eds., *The Post-Colonial Studies Reader,* 18–23. New York: Routledge, 1995.

Jarves, James Jackson. *History of the Hawaiian or Sandwich Islands.* Boston: Tappan and Dennet, 1843.

———. *Kiana: A Tradition of Hawaii.* Boston: James Munroe and Company, 1857.

———. "Laws of the Sandwich Islands." *American Jurist and Law Magazine* 25 (1841): 310–17.

Jefferson, Thomas. *The Portable Thomas Jefferson.* Ed. Merrill D. Peterson. New York: Viking Press, 1975.

Joesting, Edward. *Hawaii: An Uncommon History.* New York: W. W. Norton, 1972.

Johnson, David E. "'Writing in the Dark': The Political Fictions of American Travel Writing." *American Literary History* 7 (1995): 1–27.

Judd, Laura Fish. *Honolulu: Sketches of Life in the Hawaiian Islands from 1828 to 1861.* Ed. Dale L. Morgan. Chicago: R. R. Donnelley, 1966.

Kammen, Michael. *Mystic Chords of Memory: The Transformation of Tradition in American Culture.* New York: Random House, 1993.

Kaplan, Amy. "'Left Alone with America': The Absence of Empire in the Study of American Culture." In Amy Kaplan and Donald E. Pease, eds., *Cultures of United States Imperialism,* 3–21. Durham: Duke University Press, 1993.

———. "Romancing the Empire: The Embodiment of American Masculinity in the Popular Historical Novel of the 1890s." *American Literary History* 2 (1990): 659–90.

Kaplan, Amy, and Donald Pease, eds. *Cultures of United States Imperialism.* Durham: Duke University Press, 1993.

Kaplan, Caren. *Questions of Travel: Postmodern Discourses of Displacement.* Durham: Duke University Press, 1996.

Karcher, Carolyn L. *The First Woman in the Republic: A Cultural Biography of Lydia Maria Child.* Durham: Duke University Press, 1994.

Kasson, Joy. *Artistic Voyagers: Europe and the American Imagination in the Works of Irving, Allston, Cole, Cooper, and Hawthorne.* Westport, Conn.: Greenwood Press, 1982.

Katz, Herbert, and Marjorie Katz. *Museums, U.S.A.: A History and Guide.* Garden City, N.Y.: Doubleday and Company, 1965.

Kelley, Wyn. *Melville's City: Literary and Urban Form in Nineteenth-Century New York.* New York: Cambridge University Press, 1996.

Kelly, Franklin. "A Passion for Landscape: The Paintings of Frederic Edwin Church." In Franklin Kelly, ed., *Frederic Edwin Church,* 32–75. Washington, D.C.: National Gallery of Art, 1989.

Kolodny, Annette. *The Lay of the Land: Metaphor as Experience and History in American Life and Letters.* Chapel Hill: University of North Carolina Press, 1975.

———. "Letting Go Our Grand Obsessions: Notes Towards a New Literary History of the American Frontiers." *American Literature* 61 (1992): 1–18.

Kreiger, Barbara. *The Dead Sea: Myth, History, and Politics.* Hanover, N.H.: Brandeis University Press, 1997.

———. *Divine Expectations: An American Woman in 19th-Century Palestine.* Athens: Ohio University Press, 1999.

Kroeber, Karl. "American Indian Persistence and Resurgence." *Boundary 2,* no. 19 (1992): 1–25.

Kunhardt, Philip B., Jr., Philip B. Kunhardt III, and Peter W. Kunhardt. *P.T. Barnum: America's Greatest Showman: An Illustrated Biography.* New York: Alfred A. Knopf, 1995.

Kyle, Melvin Grove. *Explorations at Sodom: The Story of Ancient Sodom in the Light of Modern Research.* 1928. Facsimile rpt. New York: Arno Press, 1977.

LaFeber, Walter. *The New Empire: An Interpretation of American Expansion, 1860–1898.* Ithaca: Cornell University Press, 1963.

Larkin, Robert P., and Gary L. Peters. *Biographical Dictionary of Geography.* Westport, Conn.: Greenwood Press, 1993.

Lawson-Peebles, Robert. *Landscape and Written Expression in Revolutionary America: The World Turned Upside Down.* New York: Cambridge University Press, 1988.

Le Beau, Bryan F., and Menachem Mor, eds. *Pilgrims and Travelers to the Holy Land.* Bronx, N.Y.: Fordham University Press, 1996.

Ledyard, John. *A Journal of Captain Cook's Last Voyage.* 1783. Chicago: Quadrangle Books, 1963.

Levine, Robert S. *Martin Delany, Frederick Douglass, and the Politics of Representative Identity.* Chapel Hill: University of North Carolina Press, 1997.

Lewis, Martin W., and Kären E. Wigen. *The Myth of Continents: A Critique of Metageography.* Berkeley: University of California Press, 1997.

Lewis, R. W. B. *The American Adam: Innocence, Tragedy, and Tradition in the Nineteenth Century.* Chicago: University of Chicago, 1955).

Livingstone, David N. "Climate's Moral Economy: Science, Race and Place in Post-Darwinian British and American Geography." In Anne Godlewska and Neil Smith, eds., *Geography and Empire,* 132–54. Cambridge, Mass.: Blackwell, 1994.

Locke, John. *Two Treatises of Government.* Ed. Peter Laslett. 1960. Rpt. New York: New American Library, 1965.

Lowenthal, David. *The Past Is a Foreign Country.* New York: Cambridge University Press, 1985.

Luedtke, Luther S. *Nathaniel Hawthorne and the Romance of the Orient.* Bloomington: Indiana University Press, 1989.

Lugenbeel, James Washington. *Sketches of Liberia: Comprising a Brief Account of the Geography, Climate, Productions, and Diseases, of the Republic of Liberia.* Washington, D.C.: C. Alexander, 1853.

Lumley, Robert, ed. *The Museum Time-Machine: Putting Cultures on Display.* New York: Routledge, 1988.

Lutz, Catherine A., and Jane L. Collins. *Reading National Geographic.* Chicago: University of Chicago Press, 1993.

Lynch, William F. *Commerce and the Holy Land.* Philadelphia: King and Baird Printers, 1860.

———. *Narrative of the United States' Expedition to the River Jordan and the Dead Sea.* 1849. Facsimile rpt. New York: Arno Press, 1977.

Lyons, Paul. "From Man-Eaters to Spam-Eaters: Literary Tourism and the Discourse of Cannibalism from Herman Melville to Paul Theroux." *Arizona Quarterly* 51 (1995): 33–62.

MacCannell, Dean. *The Tourist: A New Theory of the Leisure Class.* 1976. New York: Schocken Books, 1989.

Mackay-Smith, Alexander. *The Race Horses of America, 1832–1872: Portraits and Other Paintings by Edward Troye.* Saratoga Springs, N.Y.: National Museum of Racing, 1981.

Manthorne, Katherine Emma. *Tropical Renaissance: North American Artists Exploring Latin America, 1839–1879.* Washington, D.C.: Smithsonian Institution Press, 1989.

Martin, Robert K. "Bayard Taylor's Valley of Bliss: The Pastoral and the Search for Form." *Markham Review* 9 (1979): 13–17.

———. *Hero, Captain, and Stranger: Male Friendship, Social Critique, and Literary Form in the Sea Novels of Herman Melville.* Chapel Hill: University of North Carolina Press, 1986.

———. "Melville and Sexuality." In Robert S. Levine, ed., *The Cambridge Companion to Herman Melville,* 186–201. New York: Cambridge University Press, 1998.

Marx, Leo. *The Machine in the Garden: Technology and the Pastoral Ideal in America.* New York: Oxford University Press, 1964.

May, Ernest R. *Imperial Democracy: The Emergence of America as a Great Power.* 1961. Rpt. New York: Harper and Row, 1973.

Mayo, William S. *Kaloolah, or, Journeyings to the Djébel Kumri, an Autobiography of Jonathan Romer.* 1849. 3d ed. 1850. Rpt. Freeport, N.Y.: Books for Libraries Press, 1972.

McCarthy, Michael. *Dark Continent: Africa as Seen by Americans.* Westport, Conn.: Greenwood Press, 1983.

McClintock, Anne. *Imperial Leather: Race, Gender and Sexuality in the Colonial Contest.* New York: Routledge, 1995.

McKinsey, Elizabeth. *Niagara Falls: Icon of the American Sublime.* New York: Cambridge University Press, 1985.

Melville, Herman. *Clarel: A Poem and Pilgrimage in the Holy Land.* Ed. Harrison Hayford, Alma A. MacDougall, Hershel Parker, and G. Thomas Tanselle, with Walter Bezanson. Evanston, Ill., and Chicago: Northwestern University Press and the Newberry Library, 1991.

———. *Journals.* Ed. Howard C. Horsford, with Lynn Horth. Evanston, Ill., and Chicago: Northwestern University Press and the Newberry Library, 1989.

———. *The Piazza Tales and Other Prose Pieces, 1839–1860.* Ed. Harrison Hayford, Alma A. MacDougall, and G. Thomas Tanselle. Evanston, Ill., and Chicago: Northwestern University Press and the Newberry Library, 1987.

———. *Redburn, His First Voyage.* 1849. Ed. and intro. Harold Beaver. New York: Penguin, 1984.

———. *Typee: A Peep at Polynesian Life.* 1846. Ed. Harrison Hayford, Hershel Parker, and G. Thomas Tanselle. Evanston, Ill., and Chicago: Northwestern University Press and the Newberry Library, 1968.

———. *White-Jacket; or, the World in a Man-of-War.* 1850. New York: New American Library, 1979.

Merk, Frederick. *Manifest Destiny and Mission in American History.* New York: Random House, 1963.

Milder, Robert. "An Arch between Two Lives: Melville and the Mediterranean, 1856–57." *Arizona Quarterly* 55 (1999): 21–47.

Miller, Angela. *The Empire of the Eye: Landscape Representation and American Cultural Politics, 1825–1875*. Ithaca: Cornell University Press, 1993.

Miller, David C. *Dark Eden: The Swamp in Nineteenth-Century American Culture*. New York: Cambridge University Press, 1989.

Miller, Floyd J. *The Search for a Black Nationality: Black Emigration and Colonization, 1787–1863*. Urbana: University of Illinois Press, 1975.

Miller, Perry. *The Legal Mind in America: From Independence to the Civil War*. 1962. Rpt. Ithaca: Cornell University Press, 1969.

———. *The Life of the Mind in America from the Revolution to the Civil War*. New York: Harcourt, Brace and World, 1965.

Mills, Sara. *Discourses of Difference: An Analysis of Women's Travel Writing and Colonialism*. New York: Routledge, 1991.

Mitchell, S. Augustus. *A General View of the World, Comprising a Physical, Political, and Statistical Account of its Grand Divisions, America, Europe, Asia, Africa, and Oceanica*. 1845. Philadelphia: H. Cowperthwait and Co., 1859.

———. *Mitchell's Geographical Reader: A System of Modern Geography, Comprising a Description of the World, with its Grand Divisions, America, Europe, Asia, Africa, and Oceanica; Designed for Instruction in Schools and Families*. Philadelphia: Thomas, Cowperthwait and Co., 1840.

———. *Mitchell's Primary Geography: An Easy Introduction to the Study of Geography, Designed for the Instruction of Children in Schools and Families*. Rev. ed. Philadelphia: Thomas, Cowperthwait and Co., 1848.

Mitchell, W. J. T. "Holy Landscape: Israel, Palestine, and the American Wilderness." *Critical Inquiry* 26 (2000): 193–223.

———, ed. *Landscape and Power*. Chicago: University of Chicago Press, 1994.

Montague, Edward P. *Narrative of the Late Expedition to the Dead Sea, from a Diary by one of the Party*. Philadelphia: Carey and Hart, 1849.

Moore-Gilbert, Bart. *Postcolonial Theory: Contexts, Practices, Politics*. New York: Verso, 1997.

Morse, Jedidiah. *Elements of Geography, Exhibited Historically, from the Creation to the End of the World on a New Plan, Adapted to Children in Schools and Private Families*. 6th ed. New Haven: H. Howe, 1825.

Moses, Wilson Jeremiah. *Afrotopia: The Roots of African American Popular History*. New York: Cambridge University Press, 1998.

———. *The Golden Age of Black Nationalism, 1850–1925*. Hamden, Conn.: Archon Books, 1978.

Nelson, Dana D. "The Haunting of White Manhood: Poe, Fraternal Ritual, and Polygenesis." *American Literature* 69 (1997): 515–46.

———. *National Manhood: Capitalist Citizenship and the Imagined Fraternity of White Men*. Durham: Duke University Press, 1998.

Nelson, William E. *Americanization of the Common Law: The Impact of Legal Change on Massachusetts Society, 1760–1830*. Cambridge, Mass.: Harvard University Press, 1975.

Nesbit, William. *Four Months in Liberia: or African Colonization Exposed*. 1855. Facsimile rpt. In Edwin S. Redkey, ed., *Two Black Views of Liberia*. New York: Arno Press, 1969.

Nietz, John A. *The Evolution of American Secondary School Textbooks*. Rutland, Vt.: Charles E. Tuttle Company, 1966.

————. *Old Textbooks.* Pittsburgh, Pa.: University of Pittsburgh Press, 1961.

Nietzsche, Friedrich. *On the Genealogy of Morals, Ecce Homo.* Trans. and ed. Walter Kaufmann. New York: Vintage Books, 1969.

Nott, Josiah C., and George R. Gliddon. *Types of Mankind: or, Ethnological Researches.* 1854. Facsimile rpt. Miami: Mnemosyne Publishing Co., 1969.

Novac, Barbara. *Nature and Culture: American Landscape and Painting, 1825–1875.* New York: Oxford University Press, 1980.

Obenzinger, Hilton. *American Palestine: Melville, Twain, and the Holy Land Mania.* Princeton: Princeton University Press, 1999.

Olien, Michael D. "E. G. Squier and the Miskito: Anthropological Scholarship and Political Propaganda." *Ethnohistory* 32 (1985): 111–33.

Otter, Samuel. "'Race' in *Typee* and *White-Jacket*." In Robert S. Levine, ed., *The Cambridge Companion to Herman Melville,* 12–36. New York: Cambridge University Press, 1998.

Painter, Nell Irvin. "Martin R. Delany: Elitism and Black Nationalism." In Leon Litwack and August Meier, eds., *Black Leaders of the Nineteenth Century,* 149–72. Urbana: University of Illinois Press, 1988.

Parkman, Francis. *Letters of Francis Parkman.* 2 vols. Ed. Wilbur R. Jacobs. Norman: University of Oklahoma Press, 1960.

Payne, A. R. M. *Rambles in Brazil; or, A Peep at the Aztecs, by One Who Has Seen Them.* 2d ed. New York: Charles B. Norton, 1854.

Peabody, Elizabeth. *Universal History; Arranged to Illustrate Bem's Charts of Chronology.* New York: Sheldon and Co., 1859.

Pearce, Susan, ed. *Museum Studies in Material Culture.* London: Leicester University Press, 1989.

Perkins, Bradford. *The Cambridge History of American Foreign Relations.* Vol. 1, *The Creation of a Republican Empire, 1776–1865.* New York: Cambridge University Press, 1993.

Peterson, Carla L. *"Doers of the Word": African-American Women Speakers and Writers in the North (1830–1880).* New York: Oxford University Press, 1995.

Phillips, Richard. "Writing Travel and Mapping Sexuality: Richard Burton's Sotadic Zone." In James Duncan and Derek Gregory, eds., *Writes of Passage: Reading Travel Writing,* 70–91. New York: Routledge, 1999.

Plesur, Milton. *America's Outward Thrust: Approaches to Foreign Affairs, 1865–1890.* DeKalb: Northern Illinois University Press, 1971.

Pocock, J. G. A. *Politics, Language and Time: Essays on Political Thought and History.* New York: Atheneum, 1971.

Poe, Edgar Allan. *The Complete Works of Edgar Allan Poe.* 17 vols. Ed. James A. Harrison. 1902. New York: AMS Press, 1965.

Poinsett, Joel R. *Discourse on the Objects and Importance of the National Institute for the Promotion of Science, Established at Washington, 1840, Delivered at the First Anniversary.* Washington, D.C.: P. Force, 1841.

"Political Clap-Trap." *National Intelligencer* (January 15, 1848). Excerpted in Norman A. Graebner, ed., *Manifest Destiny,* 239–41. New York: Bobbs-Merrill, 1968.

Porter, Carolyn. "What We Know that We Don't Know: Remapping American Literary Studies." *American Literary History* 6 (1994): 467–526.

Porter, Dennis. *Desire and Transgression in European Travel Writing.* Princeton: Princeton University Press, 1991.

Pratt, Mary Louise. *Imperial Eyes: Travel Writing and Transculturation.* New York: Routledge, 1992.

Prescott, William. *History of the Conquest of Mexico.* 1843. New York: Random House, 1936.

Preston, Richard. "America's Egypt: John Lloyd Stephens and the Discovery of the Maya." *Princeton University Library Chronicle* 53 (1992): 243–63.

Reid-Pharr, Robert. "Violent Ambiguity: Martin Delany, Bourgeois Sadomasochism, and the Production of a Black National Masculinity." In Marcellus Blount and George P. Cunningham, eds., *Representing Black Men*, 73–94. New York: Routledge, 1996.

Reingold, Nathan. "The Exploring Expedition and the Smithsonian Institution." In Herman J. Viola and Carolyn Margolis, eds., *Magnificent Voyagers: The U.S. Exploring Expedition, 1838–1842*, 243–54. Washington, D.C.: Smithsonian Institution Press, 1985.

Renker, Elizabeth. "Melville's Spell in *Typee.*" *Arizona Quarterly* 52 (1995): 1–31.

Rennie, Neil. *Far-Fetched Facts: The Literature of Travel and the Idea of the South Seas.* Oxford: Clarendon Press, 1995.

Rigal, Laura. *An American Manufactory: Art, Labor, and the World of Things in the Early Republic.* Princeton: Princeton University Press, 1998.

Robinson, Edward. *Biblical Researches in Palestine, Mount Sinai and Arabia Petræa.* 3 vols. 1841. Facsimile rpt. New York: Arno Press, 1977.

Rogin, Michael Paul. *Subversive Genealogy: The Politics and Art of Herman Melville.* 1979. Berkeley: University of California Press, 1985.

Rollin, Frank A. [Mrs. Frances E. Rollin Whipper]. *Life and Public Services of Martin R. Delany.* 1868. Facsimile rpt. of 1883 edition, with an intro. by Howard H. Bell. New York: Arno Press, 1969.

Romero, Lora. *Home Fronts: Domesticity and Its Critics in the Antebellum United States.* Durham: Duke University Press, 1997.

Rook, Robert E. *The 150th Anniversary of the United States' Expedition to Explore the Dead Sea and the River Jordan.* Amman, Jordan: American Center of Oriental Research, 1998.

Rose, Gillian. *Feminism and Geography: The Limits of Geographical Knowledge.* Minneapolis: University of Minnesota Press, 1993.

Roselle, Daniel. *Samuel Griswold Goodrich, Creator of Peter Parley: A Study of His Life and Work.* Albany: State University of New York Press, 1968.

Rossi, Paolo. *The Dark Abyss of Time: The History of the Earth and the History of Nations from Hooke to Vico.* Trans. Lydia G. Cochrane. Chicago: University of Chicago Press, 1984.

Rourke, Constance. *Trumpets of Jubilee: Henry Ward Beecher, Harriet Beecher Stowe, Lyman Beecher, Horace Greeley, P. T. Barnum.* New York: Harcourt, Brace, 1927.

Rousseau, Jean-Jacques. *The Essential Rousseau.* Trans. Lowell Bair. New York: New American Library, 1974.

Rowe, John Carlos. *Literary Culture and U.S. Imperialism: From the Revolution to World War II.* New York: Oxford University Press, 2000.

———. "Melville's *Typee*: U.S. Imperialism at Home and Abroad." In Donald E. Pease, ed., *National Identities and Post-Americanist Narratives*, 255–78. Durham: Duke University Press, 1994.

Ryan, Susan M. "Errand into Africa: Colonization and Nation Building in Sarah J. Hale's *Liberia.*" *New England Quarterly* 68 (1995): 558–83.

Rydell, Robert W. *All the World's a Fair: Visions of Empire at American International Expositions, 1876–1916.* Chicago: University of Chicago Press, 1984.

Sahlins, Marshall. "Cosmologies of Capitalism: The Trans-Pacific Sector of 'The World System.' " In Nicholas B. Dirks, Geoff Eley, and Sherry B. Ortner, eds., *Culture/Power/History: A Reader in Contemporary Social Theory,* 412–55. Princeton: Princeton University Press, 1994.

Said, Edward W. *Orientalism.* New York: Random House, 1978.

Saldívar, José David. *The Dialectics of Our America: Genealogy, Cultural Critique, and Literary History.* Durham: Duke University Press, 1991.

Sale, Maggie Montesinos. *The Slumbering Volcano: American Slave Ship Revolts and the Production of Rebellious Masculinity.* Durham: Duke University Press, 1997.

Sampson, William. *An Anniversary Discourse, Delivered before the Historical Society of New York, on Saturday, December 6, 1823; Showing the Origin, Progress, Antiquities, Curiosities, and Nature of the Common Law.* New York: E. Bliss and E. White, 1824.

Samson, John. *White Lies: Melville's Narrative of Facts.* Ithaca: Cornell University Press, 1989.

Sanborn, Geoffrey. *The Sign of the Cannibal: Melville and the Making of a Postcolonial Reader.* Durham: Duke University Press, 1998.

Sánchez-Eppler, Karen. "Raising Empires like Children: Race, Nation, and Religious Education." *American Literary History* 8 (1996): 399–425.

Savage, Charles C. *The World: Geographical, Historical, and Statistical; Containing a Description of the Several Continents, Empires, Republics, Kingdoms, and Islands on the Globe.* 1853. New York: Ensign, Bridgman, and Fanning, 1861.

Saxon, A. H. *P. T. Barnum: The Legend and the Man.* New York: Columbia University Press, 1989.

Schlesinger, Arthur M., Jr. *The Age of Jackson.* Boston: Little, Brown and Co., 1945.

Schoolcraft, Mrs. Henry Rowe [Mary Howard]. *The Black Gauntlet: A Tale of Plantation Life in South Carolina.* 1852. Rpt. in *Plantation Life: The Narratives of Mrs. Henry Rowe Schoolcraft.* New York: Negro Universities Press, 1969.

Schramer, James, and Donald Ross, eds. *Dictionary of Literary Biography.* Vol. 183, *American Travel Writers, 1776–1864.* Washington, D.C.: Bruccoli Clark Layman, 1997.

Schriber, Mary Suzanne. *Writing Home: American Women Abroad, 1830–1920.* Charlottesville: University Press of Virginia, 1997.

———, ed. *Telling Travels: Selected Writings by Nineteenth-Century American Women Abroad.* DeKalb: Northern Illinois University Press, 1995.

Schueller, Malini Johar. "Indians, Polynesians, and Empire Making: The Case of Herman Melville." In Lee Quinby, ed., *Genealogy and Literature,* 48–67. Minneapolis: University of Minnesota Press, 1995.

———. *U.S. Orientalisms: Race, Nation, and Gender in Literature, 1790–1890.* Ann Arbor: University of Michigan Press, 1998.

Scorza, Thomas J. "Tragedy in the State of Nature: Melville's *Typee.*" *Interpretation: Journal of Political Philosophy* 8 (1979): 103–20.

Sedgwick, Eve Kosofsky. *Between Men: English Literature and Male Homosocial Desire.* New York: Columbia University Press, 1985.

———. "*Billy Budd*: After the Homosexual." In Myra Jehlen, ed., *Herman Melville: A Collection of Critical Essays,* 217–34. Englewood Cliffs, N.J.: Prentice Hall, 1994.

Sellers, Charles Coleman. *Charles Willson Peale and His World*. New York: H. N. Abrams, 1983.

———. *Mr. Peale's Museum: Charles Willson Peale and the First Popular Museum of Natural Science and Art*. New York: W. W. Norton and Co., 1980.

"S. E. Morse's Geography." *North American Review* 16 (1823): 176–81.

Shields, David S. *Oracles of Empire: Poetry, Politics, and Commerce in British America, 1690–1750*. Chicago: University of Chicago Press, 1990.

Shurr, William H. *The Mystery of Iniquity: Melville as Poet, 1857–1891*. Lexington: University Press of Kentucky, 1972.

Skinner, Elliott P. *African Americans and U.S. Policy toward Africa, 1850–1924: In Defense of Black Nationality*. Washington, D.C.: Howard University Press, 1992.

Slotkin, Richard. *The Fatal Environment: The Myth of the Frontier in the Age of Industrialization, 1800–1890*. Middletown, Conn.: Wesleyan University Press, 1985.

———. *Regeneration through Violence: The Mythology of the American Frontier, 1600–1860*. Middletown, Conn.: Wesleyan University Press, 1973.

Smith, Bernard. *European Vision and the South Pacific, 1768–1850*. 2d ed. New Haven: Yale University Press, 1985.

Smith, Harold. *American Travellers Abroad: A Bibliography of Accounts Published before 1900*. Carbondale: Southern Illinois University Press, 1969.

Smith, Henry Nash. *Virgin Land: The American West as Symbol and Myth*. Cambridge, Mass.: Harvard University Press, 1950.

Sollors, Werner. *Beyond Ethnicity: Consent and Descent in American Culture*. New York: Oxford University Press, 1986.

Spanos, William V. *America's Shadow: An Anatomy of Empire*. Minneapolis: University of Minnesota Press, 2000.

Spate, O. H. K. *Paradise Found and Lost*. Minneapolis: University of Minnesota Press, 1988.

Spengemann, William C. "Early American Literature and the Project of Literary History." *American Literary History* 5 (1993): 512–41.

Spillers, Hortense J. "Introduction: Who Cuts the Border? Some Readings on 'America.'" In Hortense J. Spillers, ed., *Comparative American Identities: Race, Sex, and Nationality in the Modern Text*, 1–25. New York: Routledge, 1991.

Spurr, David. *The Rhetoric of Empire: Colonial Discourse in Journalism, Travel Writing, and Imperial Administration*. Durham: Duke University Press, 1993.

Squier, Ephraim G. "American Ethnology: Being a Summary of Some of the Results which have Followed the Investigation of this Subject." *American Whig Review* 9 (1849): 385–99.

———. "Nicaragua: An Exploration from Ocean to Ocean," *Harper's New Monthly Magazine* 11 (1855): 577–90.

———. *Nicaragua; its People, Scenery, Monuments, Resources, Condition, and Proposed Canal*. 1852. Rev. ed. New York: Harper and Brothers, 1860.

———. *Observations on the Archaeology and Ethnology of Nicaragua*. Ed. Frank E. Comparato. Culver City, Calif.: Labyrinthos, 1990.

———. *Peru: Incidents of Travel and Exploration in the Land of the Incas*. 1877. New York: AMS Press, 1973.

———. "San Juan de Nicaragua." *Harper's New Monthly Magazine* 10 (1854): 50–61.

———. *The Serpent Symbol, and the Worship of the Reciprocal Principles of Nature in America*. New York: George P. Putnam, 1851.

————. *The States of Central America; their Geography, Topography, Climate, Population, Resources, Productions, Commerce, Political Organization, Aborigines, etc., etc.* New York: Harper and Brothers, 1858.

————[Samuel A. Bard, pseud.] *Waikna; or, Adventures on the Mosquito Shore.* 1855. Facsimile rpt. with intro. Daniel E. Alleger. Gainesville: University of Florida Press, 1965.

Squier, Ephraim G., and Edwin H. Davis. *Ancient Monuments of the Mississippi Valley.* 1848. Ed. and intro. David J. Meltzer. Washington, D.C.: Smithsonian Institution Press, 1998.

"Squier's *Waikna*," *Putnam's Monthly* 6 (1855): 320.

Stallybrass, Peter, and Allon White. *The Politics and Poetics of Transgression.* Ithaca: Cornell University Press, 1986.

Stanton, William. *The Great United States Exploring Expedition of 1838–1842.* Berkeley: University of California Press, 1975.

————. *The Leopard's Spots: Scientific Attitudes toward Race in America, 1815–59.* Chicago: University of Chicago Press, 1960.

Stephens, John Lloyd. *Incidents of Travel in Central America, Chiapas, and Yucatan.* 2 vols. 1841. Dover Publications, 1969.

————. *Incidents of Travel in Egypt, Arabia Petræa, and the Holy Land.* 1837. San Francisco: Chronicle Books, 1991.

————. *Incidents of Travel in Yucatan.* 2 vols. 1843. Dover Publications, 1963.

"Stephens's *Travels in Central America.*" *North American Review* 53 (1841): 479–506.

Sterling, Dorothy. *The Making of an Afro-American: Martin Robison Delany, 1812–1885.* 1971. Rpt. New York: Da Capo Press, 1996.

Stern, Milton R. *The Fine Hammered Steel of Herman Melville.* Urbana: University of Illinois Press, 1957.

Stewart, Charles S. *A Visit to the South Seas, in the U.S. Ship Vincennes, During the Years 1829 and 1830.* 2 vols. 1831. New York: Praeger Publishers, 1970.

Stewart, Susan. *On Longing: Narratives of the Miniature, the Gigantic, the Souvenir, the Collection.* Baltimore: Johns Hopkins University Press, 1984.

Stigloe, John R. *Common Landscape of America, 1580 to 1845.* New Haven: Yale University Press, 1982.

Stocking, George W., Jr., ed. *Objects and Others: Essays on Museums and Material Culture.* Madison: University of Wisconsin Press, 1985.

Stoddart, D. R. *On Geography and Its History.* New York: Basil Blackwell, 1986.

Story, Joseph. *A Discourse Pronounced upon the Inauguration of the Author, as Dane Professor of Law in Harvard University.* Boston: Hilliard, Gray, Little, and Wilkins, 1829.

Stowe, Harriet Beecher. *First Geography for Children.* Boston: Phillips, Sampson and Co., 1855.

————. *Uncle Tom's Cabin; or, Life Among the Lowly.* 1852. New York: Penguin, 1981.

"Stowe's *Primer Geography.*" *Putnam's Monthly* 5 (1855): 550.

Stowe, William W. *Going Abroad: European Travel in Nineteenth-Century American Culture.* Princeton: Princeton University Press, 1994.

Strauss, W. Patrick. *Americans in Polynesia, 1783–1842.* East Lansing: Michigan State University Press, 1963.

Stuckey, Sterling. *Slave Culture: Nationalist Theory and the Foundations of Black America.* New York: Oxford University Press, 1987.

Sumida, Stephen H. *And the View from the Shore: Literary Traditions of Hawai'i.* Seattle: University of Washington Press, 1991.

Sundquist, Eric J. *Home as Found: Authority and Genealogy in Nineteenth-Century American Literature.* Baltimore: Johns Hopkins University Press, 1979.

———. "The Literature of Expansion and Race." In Sacvan Bercovitch, ed., *The Cambridge History of American Literature.* Vol. 2, *Prose Writing, 1820–1865*, 125–328. New York: Cambridge University Press, 1995.

———. *To Wake the Nations: Race in the Making of American Literature.* Cambridge, Mass.: Harvard University Press, 1993.

Svobodny, Dolly, ed. *Early American Textbooks, 1775–1900: A Catalog of the Titles Held by the Educational Research Library.* Washington, D.C.: U.S. Department of Education, 1985.

Taussig, Michael. *Mimesis and Alterity: A Particular History of the Senses.* New York: Routledge, 1993.

Taylor, Bayard. *At Home and Abroad: A Sketch-Book of Life, Scenery, and Men.* 1859. New York: G. P. Putnam's Sons, 1889.

———. *Eldorado, or, Adventures in the Path of Empire.* 2 vols. New York: George P. Putnam, 1850.

———. *A Journey to Central Africa; or, Life and Landscapes from Egypt to the Negro Kingdoms of the White Nile.* 1854. 11th ed. New York: G. P. Putnam, 1862.

———. *The Lands of the Saracens; or, Pictures of Palestine, Asia Minor, Sicily, and Spain.* 1854. New York: G. P. Putnam's Sons, 1880.

———. *Rhymes of Travel, Ballads and Poems.* 2d ed. New York: George P. Putnam, 1849.

———. *A Visit to India, China, and Japan, in the Year 1853.* 1855. New York: G. P. Putnam, 1862.

———, ed. *Cyclopaedia of Modern Travel: A Record of Adventure, Exploration and Discovery, for the Past Fifty Years: Comprising Narratives of the Most Distinguished Travelers since the Beginning of this Century.* Cincinnati, Ohio: Moore, Wilstach, Keys and Co., 1856.

Thomas, Brooks. *Cross-examinations of Law and Literature: Cooper, Hawthorne, Stowe, and Melville.* New York: Cambridge University Press, 1987.

Thomas, Nancy, ed. *The American Discovery of Ancient Egypt.* Los Angeles: Los Angeles County Museum of Art, 1995.

Thomas, Nicholas. *Colonialism's Culture: Anthropology, Travel and Government.* Princeton: Princeton University Press, 1994.

———. *In Oceania: Visions, Artifacts, Histories.* Durham: Duke University Press, 1997.

Thomson, William M. *The Land and the Book; or, Biblical Illustrations Drawn from the Manners and Customs, the Scenes and the Scenery of the Holy Land.* 1858. 2 vols. New York: Harper and Brothers, 1873.

Tocqueville, Alexis de. *Democracy in America.* Ed. Phillips Bradley and trans. Francis Bowen. 2 vols. New York: Random House, 1945.

Tolchin, Neal L. *Mourning, Gender, and Creativity in the Art of Herman Melville.* New Haven: Yale University Press, 1988.

Tomc, Sandra. "An Idle Industry: Nathaniel Parker Willis and the Workings of Literary Leisure." *American Quarterly* 49 (1997): 780–805.

Torgovnick, Marianna. *Gone Primitive: Savage Intellects, Modern Lives.* Chicago: University of Chicago Press, 1990.

Turner, Victor. *Drama, Fields, Metaphors: Symbolic Action in Human Society*. Ithaca: Cornell University Press, 1974.

Tuveson, Ernest Lee. *Redeemer Nation: The Idea of America's Millennial Role*. Chicago: University of Chicago, 1968.

Twain, Mark. *The Innocents Abroad or the New Pilgrims Progress*. 1869. New York: Penguin, 1980.

————. *Roughing It*. 1872. New York: Penguin, 1980.

Tyler, David B. *The Wilkes Expedition: The First United States Exploring Expedition (1838–1842)*. Philadelphia: American Philosophical Society, 1968.

"Typee." *Robert Merry's Museum*. Ed. Samuel Goodrich. Vol. 14 (1847): 109–14, 135–39, 173–78.

Ullman, Victor. *Martin R. Delany: The Beginnings of Black Nationalism*. Boston: Beacon Press, 1971.

Van Alstyne, R. W. *The Rising American Empire*. New York: Oxford University Press, 1960.

Vergo, Peter, ed. *The New Museology*. London: Reaktion Books, 1989.

Viola, Herman J., and Carolyn Margolis, eds. *Magnificent Voyagers: The U.S. Exploring Expedition, 1838–1842*. Washington, D.C.: Smithsonian Institution Press, 1985.

Vogel, Lester I. *To See a Promised Land: Americans and the Holy Land in the Nineteenth Century*. University Park: Pennsylvania State University Press, 1993.

Von Hagen, Victor Wolfgang. *Maya Explorer: John Lloyd Stephens and the Lost Cities of Central America and Yucatán*. 1947. Rpt. San Francisco: Chronicle Books, 1990.

Walker, William. *The War in Nicaragua*. 1860. Facsimile rpt. with intro. Robert Houston. Tucson: University of Arizona Press, 1985.

Wallace, Maurice. "'Are We Men?': Prince Hall, Martin Delany, and the Masculine Ideal in Black Freemasonry, 1775–1865." *American Literary History* 9 (1997): 396–424.

Warner, Michael. "New English Sodom." *American Literature* 64 (1992): 19–47.

Warntz, William. *Geography Now and Then: Some Notes on the History of Academic Geography in the United States*. New York: American Geographic Society, 1964.

Warren, John Esaias. "The Romance of the Tropics." *Knickerbocker* 33 (1849): 496–504.

Warren, Kenneth W. "Appeals for (Mis)recognition: Theorizing the Diaspora." In Amy Kaplan and Donald Pease, eds., *Cultures of United States Imperialism*, 392–406. Durham: Duke University Press, 1993.

Warren, William. *A Systematic View of Geography, with Special Reference to Conciseness, Arrangement, Classifications, Association, and Reviews*. Bangor, Maine: E. F. Duren, 1842.

Weinberg, Albert K. *Manifest Destiny: A Study of Nationalist Expansionism in American History*. Baltimore: Johns Hopkins University Press, 1935.

Wermuth, Paul C. *Bayard Taylor*. New York: Twayne Publishers, 1973.

————. "'My Full, Unreserved Self': Bayard Taylor's Letters to Charles Melancthon Jones." *Resources for American Literary Study* 17 (1991): 220–38.

Wertheimer, Eric. *Imagined Empires: Incas, Aztecs, and the New World of American Literature, 1771–1876*. New York: Cambridge University Press, 1999.

————. "Noctography: Representing Race in William Prescott's *History of the Conquest of Mexico*." *American Literature* 67 (1995): 303–27.

Whitehall, Walter Muir, ed. *A Cabinet of Curiosities: Five Episodes in the Evolution of American Museums*. Charlottesville: University Press of Virginia, 1967.

Wicke, Jennifer. *Advertising Fictions: Literature, Advertisement, and Social Reading*. New York: Columbia University Press, 1988.

Wiegman, Robyn. *American Anatomies: Theorizing Race and Gender*. Durham: Duke University Press, 1995.

Wiley, Peter Booth. *Yankees in the Lands of the Gods: Commodore Perry and the Opening of Japan*. New York: Viking, 1990.

Wilkes, Charles. *Voyage Round the World, Embracing the Principal Events of the Narrative of the United States Exploring Expedition in One Volume*. Philadelphia: Geo. W. Gorton, 1849.

Willard, Emma. *Universal History in Perspective*. 12th ed. New York: A. S. Barnes and Co., 1852.

Willey, Gordon R., and Jeremy A. Sabloff. *A History of American Archaeology*. 2d ed. San Francisco: W. H. Freeman and Company, 1980.

Williams, Patrick, and Laura Chrisman, eds. *Colonial Discourse and Post-Colonial Theory: A Reader*. New York: Columbia University Press, 1994.

Willis, Nathaniel Parker. *Health Trip to the Tropics*. New York: Charles Scribner, 1853.

Wilson, John A. *Signs and Wonders upon Pharaoah: A History of American Egyptology*. Chicago: University of Chicago Press, 1964.

Wilson, J. Leighton. *Western Africa: Its History, Condition, and Prospects*. New York: Harper and Brothers, 1856.

Winthrop, Theodore. *A Companion to the "Heart of the Andes."* 1859. Facsimile rpt. New York: Olana Gallery, 1977.

Woodbridge, William Channing. *A System of Universal Geography, on the Principles of Comparison and Classification*. Hartford: Oliver D. Cooke and Sons, 1824.

Wright, John Kirtland. *Geography in the Making: The American Geographical Society, 1851–1951*. New York: American Geographical Society of New York, 1952.

———. "Notes on Early American Geography." In Wright, *Human Nature in Geography: Fourteen Papers, 1925–1965*, 250–85. Cambridge, Mass.: Harvard University Press, 1966.

Yellin, Jean Fagan. *The Intricate Knot: Black Figures in American Literature, 1776–1863*. New York: New York University Press, 1972.

Young, Robert J. C. *Colonial Desire: Hybridity in Theory, Culture and Race*. New York: Routledge, 1995.

———. *White Mythologies: Writing History and the West*. New York: Routledge, 1990.

Yu, Beongcheon. *The Great Circle: American Writers and the Orient*. Detroit, Mich.: Wayne State University Press, 1983.

Ziff, Larzer. *Literary Democracy: The Declaration of Cultural Independence in America*. New York: Viking Press, 1981.

Index

In this index an "f" after a number indicates a separate reference on the next page, and an "ff" indicates separate references on the next two pages. A continuous discussion over two or more pages is indicated by a span of page numbers, e.g., "57–59." *Passim* is used for a cluster of references in close but not consecutive sequence.

Baym, Nina, 135, 253, 286n36
Belzoni, Giovanni Battista, 129
"Benito Cereno," 153, 237
Bennett, Tony, 261
Bentley, William, 30
Bhabha, Homi K., 18, 267n3, 281n47
Bibb, Henry, 214
Biblical geography, 102, 104, 108, 122, 284n11. *See also* Holy Land
Biblical Researches in Palestine, Mount Sinai and Arabia Petræa, 103, 115
Bigotry, *see* Protestant beliefs
Bingham, Hiram, 9, 69ff, 73, 80, 83
The Black Gauntlet: a Tale of Plantation Life in South Carolina, 207f, 236
Blacks, *see* African-Americans; Racial attitudes; Slavery
Blake; or, the Huts of America, 23f, 200–237 *passim*, 297n65, 297n67, 297n71
Bloom, Harold, 162
Boas, Franz, 190
Book of Nature, 38
Boon, James A., 17, 94
Bourdieu, Pierre, 72
Bowen, Thomas J., 207f, 210
Breitwieser, Mitchell, 15
Brennan, Timothy, 240
Bridge, Horatio, 205, 222, 232, 296n60
Brown, William Wells, 204
Browne, John Ross, 101
Brückner, Martin, 32
Bulwer, Sir Henry, 177f
Burckhardt, Johannes, 105, 108
Burton, Richard, 142
Bushnell, Horace, 206

Cabot, Samuel, 161, 168
Calhoun, John, 13, 101
Campbell, Robert, 200, 220, 224
Cannibalism, 9f, 66, 68, 74, 80, 85–89, 94, 97f, 195, 245, 276n6, 279n26
Catherwood, Frederick, 161–69 *passim*, 180, 188, 195
Central Africa: Adventures and Missionary Labors in Several Countries in the Interior of Africa, from 1849 to 1856, 207f, 210
Central America, 3, 8, 14f, 22f, 61, 79, 151–

57 *passim*, 162f, 175, 217f, 245, 247, 263. *See also* Mosquito natives; Squier, Ephraim G.; Stephens, John Lloyd
Chateaubriand, François, 105
Cheever, Henry T., 69ff
Child, Lydia Maria, 48
Christianity, *see* Protestant beliefs
Christy, David, 208
Church, Frederic, 155f
Church of the Holy Sepulcher, 102, 112f, 131f, 134, 145, 148. *See also* Holy Land
The Circassian Slave: or, the Sultan's Favorite, 101
The City of the Great King; or, Jerusalem as It was, as It is, and as It is to be, 112
Clarel: A Poem and Pilgrimage in the Holy Land, 2, 26, 74, 98, 104, 122–48 *passim*, 283n1, 287n49–287n50
Clark, M. Lewis, 174
Clay, Henry, 212, 245
Clayton, John, 13
Clayton-Bulwer Treaty, 177f
Clemens, Samuel L., *see* Twain, Mark
Cleveland Emigration Convention, 219f
Cole, Thomas, 244
Colton, George W., 41ff
Commercial interests of explorers, 11f, 14, 46, 68, 92, 206, 277n10, 282n52
The Condition, Elevation, Emigration, and Destiny of the Colored People of the United States, 23, 200, 211–25 *passim*, 241
The Conduct of Life, 9f
The Confidence-Man, 141
The Conquest of Peru, 176
Conquistadors, 119, 151, 165, 169, 171, 189, 191f
"The Continents," 7, 202ff, 209
Cook, Captain James, 8f, 67, 78, 95
Cooper, James Fenimore, 16, 24, 67, 95f, 137, 162
Cosmos, 53
The Course of Empire, 244
Cox, Samuel S., 151
Crania Aegyptiaca, 174, 206
Crania Americana, 173f
The Crater, 95
Cresson, Warder, 101